D1219563

THE NEW CREATIVE COOKBOOK

Edited by Charlotte Turgeon

WEATHERVANE BOOKS

New York

Created and manufactured by arrangement with
Ottenheimer Publishers, Inc.
© MCMLXXXVI by Ottenheimer Publishers, Inc.
All Rights Reserved

This 1986 edition published by Weathervane Books,
distributed by Crown Publishers, Inc.,
225 Park Avenue South, New York, New York 10003

Printed in Hong Kong

Library of Congress Cataloging-in-Publication Data

The New creative cookbook.

    Includes index.
    1. Cookery. I. Turgeon, Charlotte Snyder, 1912-
TX715.N5155 1987   641.5   86-23437

ISBN 0-517-62730-2 (Crown)
h g f e d c b a

Contents

Appetizers

Pineapple, Cucumbers, and Melon with Spicy Peanut Dressing

Yield: 4 servings

dressing
1 tablespoon peanut oil
½ teaspoon hot pepper flakes (or more)
¼ cup peanut butter, creamy or chunky
2 tablespoons hot water
2 tablespoons soy sauce
2 tablespoons red wine vinegar
1 tablespoon sesame oil

salad
1 small fresh pineapple
2 medium cucumbers
1 medium cantaloupe
1 large or 2 small ripe bananas
¼ pound fresh spinach leaves
1 small bunch scallions, thinly sliced (including green)

In a small pan, heat the peanut oil and pepper flakes, swirling the pan over the fire until the pepper flakes turn dark. This takes only a few seconds on a hot fire. Strain into a small bowl and whisk in the peanut butter and hot water. Add soy sauce, vinegar and sesame oil and whisk again. This amount of pepper has a nice sting to it, but for really hot dressing increase to ¾ teaspoon or add Chinese chili oil to taste.

Keep all the ingredients in separate bowls. Peel and core the pineapple, slice, then cut the slices into wedges. You should have about 3 cups. Remove a few narrow strips of green peel from the cucumbers with a vegetable peeler, split cucumbers lengthwise and seed and then cut in lengthwise halves again. Cut crosswise in ½-inch slices.

Clam Pie

Peel melon. Cut in half lengthwise and seed. Cut into ½-inch slices. Do all this ahead if necessary and arrange the plate just before you plan to serve.

To serve, cover a round chilled serving dish with the spinach leaves, and arrange the fruit in circles around the circumference starting with the pineapple, next a circle of cucumber within, then a ring of melon. Finally, peel the banana, cut it lengthwise in quarters and crosswise in ½-inch slices. Mount it in the center of the dish and sprinkle the entire dish with scallions. Drizzle on the dressing and serve. This dish looks best if you don't toss it with the dressing, but serve a little of each ingredient onto cold salad plates at the table.

Peanut Butter Dip

Yield: 1 cup

½ cup peanut butter
½ cut carrot, finely shredded
¼ cup orange juice

In small bowl, stir together peanut butter, carrot, and orange juice until well mixed. Serve as dip for fresh fruits and vegetables.

Apple-Nut Horseradish Dip

Yield: 1 cup

2 apples, peeled, cored
1 tablespoon lemon juice
¼ cup yogurt
1 tablespoon prepared horseradish
2 tablespoons walnuts, minced or ground

Grate apples; immediately combine with lemon juice to prevent discoloration. Blend in remaining ingredients.

Serve dip at once with chips, crackers, or vegetable dippers.

Sweet-Potato Fingers

Yield: 10 servings

4 to 6 cooked sweet potatoes
¼ cup flour
Fat for deep frying
½ cup brown sugar
1 teaspoon salt
½ teaspoon nutmeg

Cut sweet potatoes into strips or fingers. Score lightly with fork. Dip each finger into flour until well coated.

Heat fat in medium skillet. Fry potato fingers until golden brown. Drain on paper towels. Sprinkle with mixture of brown sugar, salt, and nutmeg. Makes about 40 fingers.

Toasted Pecans

Yield: 24 servings

12 cups pecans
¼ pound butter
Salt

Place pecans in rectangular oven dish. Toast in 250°F oven 30 minutes. Add butter over all by slicing or dotting it over nuts. Stir once or twice, until pecans and butter have mixed well. Nuts will be greasy at this point.

Sprinkle generously with salt. Toast pecans 1 hour; salt again several times. Stir as you go. When done, butter will be completely absorbed and nuts crisp. Yield 12 cups.

Fish Pâté

Yield: 4 to 6 servings

½ pound pike or other firm white fish
1 egg
1 cup cream
Salt
Pepper
¼ cup pistachio nuts, chopped
8 thin slices fresh salmon
8 fillets of sole

Finely grind up the pike meat in a meat-grinder or mix it in a food processor so that it becomes a smooth mousse. Carefully mix in the egg and the cream. Stir well with a wooden spoon. Season with salt and pepper, and fold in the nuts. Refrigerate.

Grease a round cake pan or a ring mold. Salt and pepper the salmon and sole slices lightly and place them overlapping in the pan with a piece of each slice hanging out over the round edge of the pan. Fill with the fish mousse; then fold the part of the fish that hangs over the sides over the mousse. Smooth the surface. Cover with aluminum foil and bake in a pan of water in a 350°F oven for about 35 to 40 minutes. Allow the pâté to cool before turning it upside down, out of the pan. Serve with dill hollandaise sauce and rice.

Chicken Liver Pâté

Yield: 6 to 8 servings

1 package bacon or 3 large, thin slices lard
⅔ pound chicken liver
1 egg plus 2 egg whites, or 2 whole eggs
¾ cup heavy cream
1 tablespoon butter
2 tablespoons flour
½ to 1 teaspoon salt
¼ teaspoon ground black pepper
½ bunch chives
2 large leaves sage, or ¼ teaspoon dried sage
1 sprig thyme
2-3 leaves marjoram, or ¼ teaspoon dried marjoram
¼ cup hazel nuts

Boil the bacon slices in water for about 5 minutes so that most of the smoked taste disappears. Let the slices cool.

Cover a 1-quart oven dish with the bacon slices (or the lard slices) so that most of the inside edges of the dish are covered. It is easiest to place several of the bacon slices across the dish and to let several of the shorter pieces just hang over the edges.

Mix the rest of the ingredients together in an electric mixer or food processor until everything is finely blended. Pour the mixture into the bacon-covered dish. Place in a water bath in a preheated 400°F oven for about 60 minutes. Let it cool before turning out of the dish.

Calico Relish Dip

Yield: 4 servings

½ cup sour cream
¼ cup salad dressing
1 teaspoon sugar
½ teaspoon salt
2 tablespoons scallions, minced
2 tablespoons radishes, minced
2 tablespoons cucumber, minced
2 tablespoons green pepper, minced
½ clove garlic, minced
Raw vegetables

Combine sour cream with salad dressing, sugar, salt, scallions, radishes, cucumber, green pepper, and garlic. Refrigerate.

Serve in a small bowl surrounded by raw vegetables such as cauliflower, carrots, celery, and cucumbers.

Fish Pâté

Lamb Pâté

Yield: 14 to 16 servings

1 pound good-quality ground lamb
⅔ pound not-too-lean ground pork
1½ teaspoons salt
About ½ teaspoon pepper
A little more than ½ teaspoon thyme
1 to 2 cloves garlic, crushed
3 eggs
2 tablespoons flour
¾ cup cream

Mix the ground meats with the spices. Add the eggs, one at a time, then the flour; moisten with the cream. Fry a small amount and test for taste.

Pour the mixture into a greased, 6-cup bread pan. Cover with aluminum foil and bake in a water bath at 350° to 400°F for about 1 hour, or until the meat juice is clear when tested with a toothpick. Let the pâté cool in the pan.

Serve with currant sauce (see below).

Black Currant Sauce

Yield: About 6 servings

¾ cup black currant jelly
¼ cup lemon juice
¼ teaspoon coarsely ground black pepper

Melt the jelly over low heat. Add lemon juice and pepper. Let the sauce cool. Serve over lamb pâté.

Fried Cheese

Yield: 4 to 6 servings

8 ounces Swiss or Muenster cheese cut into
    1-inch cubes
3 egg whites, slightly beaten
1 cup cornflake crumbs
1 quart (about) corn oil

Dip cheese cubes into egg whites, then in crumbs. Let dry a few minutes, then repeat coating.

Pour corn oil into heavy, sturdy, flat-bottomed, 3-quart saucepan or fondue pot, filling utensil no more than ⅓ full. Heat over medium heat to 375°F.

Fry cheese, a few pieces at a time, 1 minute or until golden brown. Drain on absorbent paper. Serve with jam, if desired. Makes 24.

Cheddar-Cheese Puffs

Yield: 8 servings

2 cups Cheddar cheese, grated
½ cup butter or margarine, softened
1 cup flour, sifted
½ teaspoon salt
½ teaspoon paprika
48 small green olives, stuffed with pimientos

Blend cheese with butter. Add flour, salt, and paprika; mix well. Mold 1 teaspoon of dough around each olive to cover. At this point, you can refrigerate or freeze puffs for up to 10 days.

Bake puffs at 400°F for 15 minutes. Serve hot.

Cheese Straws

Yield: 6 servings

1 stick butter
2 cups flour, sifted
½ teaspoon cayenne pepper
1 teaspoon salt
1 pound Cheddar cheese, shredded

Cream butter well. Sift dry ingredients together and add to butter. Add the cheese. Press through cookie press onto greased tin and bake at 400°F for 10 minutes.

The dough also can be rolled thin on a floured board and cut into strips for cheese straws or into round wafers. Makes 36.

Stuffed Bread Dip

Yield: About 12 servings

1⅓ cups sour cream
1⅓ cups mayonnaise
2 tablespoons parsley
2 tablespoons onion
2 tablespoons seasoned salt
5-6 small olives, dried
½ teaspoon garlic
¼ cup Parmesan cheese
¼ cup Cheddar cheese, shredded
1 round rye bread or Italian bread

Mix all ingredients very well. Let mixture sit overnight or for several hours before serving. Slice a piece of bread off top to act as a lid. Scoop the bread out of the middle and break into pieces.

Put a bowl into hole of bread. Fill bowl with dip just before serving. Place broken bits of bread around the bread bowl.

Cheddar Walnut Spread

Yield: About 12 servings

2 cups sharp Cheddar cheese, grated
1 cup walnuts, finely chopped
⅓ cup green onions (white only), finely chopped
2 tablespoons dry white wine
1 teaspoon caraway seeds
½ cup butter or margarine, softened

Combine cheese, nuts, onions, wine, and caraway seeds and mix well. Stir in butter to make a spreadable mixture. Chill, covered, and bring to room temperature before serving.

Cheese Mousse

Yield: About 10 servings

¾ cup milk
2 medium eggs, separated
5 ounces Parmesan cheese, finely grated
⅓ cup cottage cheese
Grated rind and juice of 1 medium-sized lemon
½ cup whipping cream, stiffly beaten
1 envelope unflavored gelatin
⅓ cup water
¼ teaspoon salt
⅛ teaspoon white pepper
Generous dash of nutmeg
Dash paprika
2 drops hot sauce

Heat milk to lukewarm. Blend egg yolks slightly in mixing bowl with electric mixer. Pour milk gradually into yolks, beating at low speed until blended. Stir in parmesan and cottage cheeses, blending well. Stir in lemon juice and rind.

Fold whipped cream into egg yolk mixture. Soften gelatin in water, dissolve over low heat. Pour into cream mixture gradually, stirring until blended. Beat egg whites until stiff, then fold into gelatin mixture. Add seasonings. Turn into oiled, 1-quart ring mold. Chill until set. Unmold on platter. Serve with crackers or pretzels.

Potted Herb Cheese

Yield: About 12 servings

3 cups Cheddar cheese, grated
1 tablespoon whipping cream
2 tablespoons sherry
6 tablespoons butter
1 teaspoon chopped chives
1 teaspoon tarragon leaves
1 teaspoon sage
1 teaspoon thyme
1 teaspoon parsley flakes
Clarified butter

Place all the ingredients except clarified butter in the top of a double boiler over hot water. Stir over medium heat until the cheese and butter melt and the mixture is thoroughly blended. Pour into pint jar; chill until cold.

Cover with a ¼-inch deep layer of clarified butter. Cover and store in refrigerator. Let come to room temperature and serve with fingers of hot buttered toast or tiny, hot biscuits.

Calzones

Yield: About 15 servings

1 envelope instant onion soup mix
⅔ cup mozzarella cheese, shredded
½ cup ricotta or creamed cottage cheese
¼ cup salami, pepperoni, or cooked Italian sausage, chopped
2 tablespoons cooked green pepper, finely chopped (optional)
½ teaspoon oregano
3 8-ounce packages refrigerated buttermilk biscuits
Oil for deep-fat frying

In small bowl, combine onion soup mix, cheeses, salami, green pepper, and oregano.

Flatten each biscuit into a 1-inch circle. Place ½ teaspoon of mixture on each biscuit; fold over to form semi-circle and seal edges tightly with fork. Fry in hot oil (360°F) until golden brown, drain. Makes 30 calzones.

Note: To reheat, bake at 400°F on rack in baking pan for 10 minutes.

Chicken Liver Pâté

Party Cheese Ball

Yield: 8 servings

3 ounces cream cheese
1 tablespoon onion, finely chopped
4 ounces cold pack smoked cheese
1 teaspoon Worcestershire sauce
1 teaspoon stuffed green olives, chopped
2 ounces blue cheese, crumbled
Chopped nuts

Soften cheese. Mix with all the ingredients, except the nuts. Place in refrigerator until firm. Form a ball. Roll in chopped nuts.

Cheese Yule Log

Yield: About 16 servings

2 3-ounce cream cheese, softened
1 cup blue cheese, crumbled
3 tablespoons chili sauce
2 tablespoons onion, grated
1 tablespoon Dijon-style prepared mustard
1 teaspoon Worcestershire sauce
3 cups sharp Cheddar cheese, shredded

¼ cup green pepper, chopped
Coarsely crushed pretzels
Garnish, if desired
Assorted crackers

Beat the first 6 ingredients in large mixing bowl until almost smooth. Stir in Cheddar cheese and green pepper. Shape mixture into log. Wrap in plastic wrap and chill several hours to allow flavors to blend. Just before serving, roll in crushed pretzels. Garnish and serve with assorted crackers.

Cheese Snacks

Yield: 6 servings

4 ounces Cheddar cheese, grated
1 stick margarine
⅔ cup flour
½ teaspoon celery seed

Beat cheese and margarine together until well blended. Gradually add flour and celery seed. Form into balls and place on ungreased cookie sheet. Flatten each with a fork. Refrigerate overnight or for 6 hours. Remove and bake in 425°F oven for 10 minutes. Makes 24 balls.

Marinated Clams

Yield: 8 to 10 servings

2 pounds clam meats
2 onions, minced
2 cloves garlic, crushed
⅓ cup oil, preferably olive oil
About ⅓ cup parsley, chopped
2 tablespoons lemon juice
½ teaspoon salt
1 teaspoon pepper

garnish
2 to 3 hard-cooked eggs
1 small head of lettuce
2 to 3 tomatoes
Sprigs of dill

Drain the clam meats well and place in a bowl. Mix the onion, garlic, oil, parsley, lemon juice, salt, and pepper and pour over the clams. Refrigerate for 2 to 3 hours.

Rinse the lettuce. Tear the larger leaves in half and place on a large plate. Place the marinated clams with most of the marinade on the lettuce. Place wedges of egg and tomatoes around the clams. Decorate with sprigs of dill.

Lamb Pâté

Clam Balls

Yield: 6 to 8 servings

3 5-ounce cans minced clams
3 stalks celery, minced
1 onion, ground
Salt and freshly ground pepper to taste
6 hard-boiled eggs, diced
½ pound moist bread crumbs

Drain the clams, reserving 2 cups of broth. Add water to make 2 cups of broth if needed. Combine the celery, onion, and 1½ cups of clam broth in a saucepan, then simmer until the vegetables are tender.

Add the clams, salt, and pepper to the vegetable mixture, then simmer for about 10 minutes. Add the eggs, remaining broth, and bread crumbs, mixing well. Shape the clam mixture into small balls and chill thoroughly. Fry in deep fat at 350°F until browned. Serve immediately with wooden picks.

Clam Puffs

Yield: 4 to 6 servings

½ pound minced clams, drained and chopped
¼ cup imported Swiss cheese, freshly grated
1 clove garlic, mashed or put through garlic press
About 1 tablespoon mayonnaise
Salt
White pepper
Cayenne pepper

Mix all ingredients, adding enough mayonnaise to bind. Add salt and white pepper to taste and a light dash of cayenne. All this may be mixed together ahead of time.

Preheat the broiler. Spread the mixture, forming a crown, on toasted rounds of white bread. Broil for 3 to 4 minutes, watching carefully so they don't burn. Remove when golden and serve hot. Makes 16 to 18.

Fried Crab Canapes

Yield: 10 to 15 servings

½ pound crabmeat
4 water chestnuts, finely chopped
1½ tablespoons cornstarch
1 egg, lightly beaten
2 teaspoons Worcestershire sauce
¾ teaspoon salt
Dash Tabasco sauce
8 slices day-old, firm white bread
Oil for frying

Combine all ingredients except bread and oil; mix well. Trim crusts from bread. Cut each slice into 4 triangles. Spread triangles with crabmeat mixture.

Preheat deep fat to 375°F. Add triangles, crab side down. Fry for 1 minute on each side. Drain on paper towels. Serve immediately. Makes 32 hors d'oeuvres.

Spinach and Crab Supreme

Yield: 12 servings

1 bunch green onions and tops, minced
1 clove garlic, crushed
¼ pound butter
1 tablespoon Parmesan cheese
Salt, pepper, and Tabasco to taste
1 pound crabmeat, flaked
2 packages frozen chopped spinach, cooked as directed, drained

Sauté onions and garlic in butter in small skillet. Add this and the remaining ingredients to cooked spinach, stirring gently to mix well. Add extra seasonings if needed. Put this into chafing dish to warm.

Hot Crabmeat Appetizer

Yield: 15 servings

1 pound backfin crabmeat
2 8-ounce packages soft whipped cream cheese
1 cup milk
2 tablespoons onion, minced

Mix together softened cream cheese, milk, and minced onion; fold in crabmeat. Place mixture in greased casserole. Heat, covered, for 30 minutes at 350°F. Serve hot on crackers or cocktail bread.

Party Crabmeat

Yield: 50 servings

1 cup butter
1½ cups flour
2 quarts milk
3 pounds crabmeat, picked over
1 pound mushrooms, sliced and sautéed
1 cup dry sherry
Hearty dash lemon juice
Hearty dash Worcestershire sauce
Dash nutmeg
Parsley

In a large pan, melt butter, stir in flour, and then add milk. Stir constantly until white sauce is thick.

Add all remaining ingredients and heat until mixture is hot. (Be careful mixture does not scorch). Serve from chafing dish with toast rounds or favorite crackers.

Crab and Cheese Appetizer

Yield: 4 servings

16 ounces cream cheese
12 ounces crabmeat
4 tablespoons mayonnaise
4 tablespoons milk
4 tablespoons onion, chopped
1 teaspoon horseradish
½ teaspoon salt
Paprika

Combine all ingredients and blend well. Spoon into ovenproof dish and sprinkle with paprika. Bake at 375°F for 18 minutes. Serve with party rye or crackers. Makes 8-12 appetizers.

Clam Pie

Yield: 6 servings

2 tablespoons shallot, minced
3¼ tablespoons butter
4 ounces clam meats
Salt
Pepper
2 tablespoons Madeira or dry white vermouth
3 eggs
⅔ cup cream
2 tablespoons tomato paste

pie dough
1⅓ cups flour, sifted
½ teaspoon salt
9 tablespoons butter
4 tablespoons water
¼ cup grated cheese

Sauté the shallot in the butter for a few minutes over low heat so that it becomes soft without becoming brown. Add the clams and stir carefully for 2 minutes. Season with salt and pepper. Pour in the wine, increase the heat, and allow to boil for a few seconds. Let cool.

Beat the eggs together with the cream, tomato paste, and salt and pepper. Add the clams a few at a time and adjust the seasoning.

Make the pie dough and refrigerate it for at least an hour. Roll out the dough and place it in a pie form that has a detachable edge. Pre-bake the pie crust in a 400°F oven for about 10 minutes.

Pour the mixture into the pie crust and sprinkle cheese over it. Bake for 25 to 30 minutes at 400°F until the pie has risen and become golden brown.

Mushroom Oysters on the Shell

Yield: 4 servings

2½ dozen oysters shucked onto the half shell
1½ cups thick white sauce, seasoned
2 tablespoons mayonnaise
½ cup grated cheese
2 tablespoons melted butter
½ cup shallots, chopped
½ cup ham, chopped
1½ cups mushrooms, chopped
2 tablespoons parsley, chopped
Salt and pepper
Tabasco sauce
Extra grated cheese to garnish

Poach the shucked oysters in their own juice for five minutes in a hot oven. Set aside.

Heat the white sauce over low heat and add the mayonnaise and cheese.

Heat the butter until foaming and add the shallots, ham, and mushrooms. Cook, stirring frequently, for five minutes. Add the parsley and the seasonings to taste. Simmer for five more minutes.

Lift the oysters from the half shells and discard the juice. Then spoon 1 or 2 teaspoons of the mushroom mixture into the shells. Place an oyster on top and spoon the cheese-flavored sauce over each. Sprinkle a little extra grated cheese over the sauce.

Arrange on a shallow pan and bake in a moderate oven, 375°F, until the sauce is bubbling and lightly browned. Serve immediately, while hot.

Marinated Clams

Mousse with Smoked Herring

Yield: 4 servings

1 envelope gelatin
3 medium smoked herrings
1 egg
¼ cup onion, minced
¼ cup dill, snipped
⅛ teaspoon thyme
¼ teaspoon salt
1 teaspoon lemon juice
¾ cup crème fraîche or sour cream
Lettuce, shredded
Lemon and dill for garnish

Place the gelatin in ¼ cup cold water.

Clean the fish and finely mash up the meat, or run it through a food processor using the metal knife attachment. Mix in the egg by hand or use a food processor. Add the onion and dill to the fish together with the thyme, salt, and lemon juice.

Dissolve the gelatin over low heat and add the fish mixture. Finally fold in the crème fraîche or sour cream.

Pour into a mold or bowl and refrigerate so that the mousse becomes firm, about 2 hours. Spoon the mousse out onto lettuce leaves and garnish with lemon and dill.

Spiced Herring

Yield: 8 servings

20 medium, fresh herring (about 4½ pounds)
⅛ cup white vinegar
4 cups water
2 cups sugar
⅓ cup coarse salt
⅓ cup fine salt
2 tablespoons allspice, coarsely ground
2 tablespoons black pepper, coarsely ground
3 tablespoons oregano
3 bay leaves, crumbled

Clean the herrings, removing the heads but keeping the backbones. Quickly rinse the fish and let drain.

Mix the vinegar and water, measuring the ingredients carefully. Place the herrings in a bowl, and pour the liquid over them. The pickling juice should completely cover the fish. If it does not, make more of the mixture, so that you are sure the fish lies in the juice. Place the bowl in the refrigerator for 24 hours.

After 24 hours, the meat of the fish should be completely white, all the way down to the bone. Make a cut in the back to check. If the meat is not white, let the fish stand in the juice for another 6

Spiced Herring

hours. Make sure that it is completely covered with the liquid.

Combine the sugar, 2 kinds of salt, allspice, black pepper, oregano, and bay leaves. Remove the herring from the pickling juice and let it drain before alternating it in an earthenware pot with the spice mixture. Place something heavy over the herring so that it sinks down into the juices that are made. Let it sit for 4 to 7 days before eating it.

Angels on Horseback

Yield: 4 servings

12 oysters, shucked
4 to 6 slices bacon

Cut the slices of bacon into lengths just long enough to wrap once around each oyster. Secure with wooden toothpick.

Bake in preheated 450°F oven about 10 minutes on each side, or until bacon is brown and crisp. Watch carefully. Drain and serve hot. Makes 12.

Note: You can also use shucked cherrystone or littleneck clams.

Oysters Botany Bay

Yield: 6 servings

4 dozen fresh oysters, opened and left in the shell
4 tablespoons dry sherry
3 ounces butter
1 large clove garlic, crushed
1⅓ cups fresh white bread crumbs
1½ tablespoons fresh parsley, chopped
2 teaspoons lemon rind, grated
Salt and freshly ground black pepper

Arrange the oysters on plates and drizzle the sherry over them. In a heavy frying pan, heat the butter and sauté the garlic in it. Stir in all the remaining ingredients and cook, stirring, until the bread crumbs are golden. Spoon the mixture over the oysters and place in a 425°F oven for 5 minutes or until heated through. Serve at once, garnished with a lemon half.

Oysters Colette

Yield: 12 servings

2 ounces anchovies
3 ounces pimientos
3 ounces Parmesan cheese, grated
2 ounces white wine
2 tablespoons parsley, chopped
1 pound butter, creamed
8 dozen oysters in the shell
6 ounces Swiss cheese, grated

Blend anchovies, pimiento, Parmesan cheese and wine. Mix with creamed butter in a bowl. Add chopped parsley, folding it into the mixture gently. Be careful not to blend it in too vigorously as this will give the mixture a green color.

Shuck the oysters, leaving the oysters on the half shell. Place on baking sheets. Put ½ teaspoon of the butter paste on each oyster. Sprinkle Swiss cheese on top of the butter paste.

Bake in a 350°F oven until the butter is melted.

Be careful not to overcook the oysters; they will become gummy.

Mousse with Smoked Herring

Salmon Ball

Yield: About 8 servings

1 8-ounce package cream cheese
1 large can pink salmon
1 small onion, chopped
1 teaspoon parsley
1 tablespoon lemon juice
1 teaspoon horseradish

Soften cream cheese and set aside. Drain salmon. Mix drained salmon, chopped onion, parsley, lemon juice, and horseradish together. Add cream cheese to salmon mixture. Form a ball and roll in chopped nuts. Great on celery and crackers.

Shrimp Dip

Yield: About 12 servings

1 8-ounce package cream cheese, softened
3 tablespoons milk
2 tablespoons fresh onion, grated
1/2 teaspoon Worcestershire sauce
1 cup boiled shrimp, finely chopped

Combine the cream cheese and milk in a small mixer bowl and beat with an electric mixer until smooth. Add the onion and Worcestershire sauce and beat until fluffy. Stir in the shrimp. Serve with dipping chips or crackers.

New Orleans Shrimp

Yield: 6 servings

4 cups water
4 green onions, finely chopped
1 small clove garlic, pressed
Salt and freshly ground pepper to taste
1 small bay leaf
4 celery heart stalks, finely chopped
1 pound medium-sized shelled, deveined shrimp
2 tablespoons olive oil
1/4 cup lemon or lime juice
1/4 cup chili sauce
1/4 cup catsup
1 tablespoon freshly grated horseradish
1 tablespoon prepared mustard
1 teaspoon paprika
Dash cayenne pepper

Pour the water into a medium-sized saucepan and bring to a boil. Add 1/2 of the green onions, the garlic, salt, pepper, bay leaf, and celery and cover. Simmer 5 minutes longer. Drain the shrimp mixture and remove the bay leaf.

Place the shrimp mixture in a medium-sized bowl and cool. Place the remaining green onions, olive oil, lemon juice, chili sauce, catsup, salt, horseradish, mustard, paprika, and cayenne pepper in a small bowl and mix well. Pour over the shrimp mixture and mix until well blended. Cover and place in the refrigerator to marinate in the sauce overnight.

Serve the shrimp and sauce in a glass bowl placed in a bowl of cracked ice. Serve with cocktail picks.

Shrimp Ball

Yield: 8 to 10 servings

1/2 pound small shrimp
2 tablespoons onion, minced
1/4 teaspoon salt
8-ounce package cream cheese
1 tablespoon lemon juice
1 tablespoon horseradish

Mix all ingredients. Form into 2 balls. Roll in either nuts or parsley. Serve on crackers. This freezes well.

Shrimp Mold

Yield: 12 to 16 servings

1/4 cup water
1 envelope gelatin
1 can tomato soup
8 ounces cream cheese
1/2 cup onion, chopped
1 cup celery, chopped
1 cup mayonnaise
1 pound cooked shrimp, chopped

Soften gelatin in water. Warm soup and add gelatin and cream cheese. Mix well. Add other ingredients.

Pour into an oiled 6-cup mold. Refrigerate until firm. Unmold to serve. Serve with light and dark cocktail rye.

Fried Shrimp Balls

Yield: 10 servings

1 medium onion, grated
1 medium raw potato, grated
1 1/2 pounds raw shrimp, shelled, deveined, grated chopped
1 egg
Salt and pepper to taste
Fat for deep frying

Mix the onion, potato, and shrimp in a large bowl. Stir in egg, salt, and pepper. Potato is the thickening; batter will be thick.

Heat fat to 375°F; drop batter in by spoonfuls. Fry until golden brown; remove with slotted spoon. Drain on paper towels. Serve hot. Makes 36 to 48 balls.

Luxury Toast

Yield: 4 servings

4 slices white bread
1 9-ounce can asparagus
Butter
About 1 pound shrimp, preferably frozen
2 egg whites
2 tablespoons chili sauce
4 tablespoons mayonnaise
Lettuce leaves
Sprigs of dill

Fry the slices of white bread in lightly browned butter until they are crisp and golden brown on both sides. Allow them to cool. Pour off the asparagus juice: Make sure the asparagus are well drained. Divide up the asparagus between the slices of bread, placing 2 rows of double asparagus on each slice. Shell the shrimp and divide them between the bread slices so that they seem to "ride" on top of the asparagus.

Beat the egg whites into unusually stiff peaks. Blend the chili sauce with the mayonnaise before carefully folding this mixture into the egg whites. Spread the egg mixture over the shrimp and the asparagus so that they are totally covered. Immediately bake the sandwiches at 400°F until the mayonnaise soufflé has risen and become golden brown.

Serve immediately, garnished with lettuce and dill sprigs.

Marinated Beef Appetizer

Yield: 10 to 12 servings

2½ pounds round steak, London broil, or flank steak, cubed
½ cup soy sauce
½ cup brown sugar
½ teaspoon cinnamon
1 garlic clove, crushed
1 can pineapple chunks (medium)
¼ pound mushrooms

Mix all ingredients except pineapple and mushrooms. Marinate at least three hours or as much as 24 hours. Remove meat from marinade and broil until medium done.

In the meantime, add pineapple and mushrooms to marinade and heat until bubbly. Return cooked meat to liquid and serve in a chafing dish.

Hot Tamales

Yield: 15 to 20 servings

1½ pounds beef stew meat
2½ pounds chicken pieces
Water
Salt
1 clove garlic, crushed
1 small onion, sliced
¼ cup vinegar
1 cup minus 2 tablespoons catsup
1 teaspoon sugar
2 tablespoons chili seasoning mix
6 tablespoons chili powder
3 cups cornmeal
Cornhusks, soaked until soft, drained and dried, or 7-by-5-inch sheets of parchment.

Place beef and chicken in separate saucepans. Cover each with water and season to taste with salt. Add crushed garlic clove to beef and sliced onion to chicken. Bring to a boil; cover and cook until tender.

Drain beef and chicken, reserving broths. Shred chicken. Chop beef. Place beef in saucepan with vinegar, catsup, sugar, 1 teaspoon salt, chili seasoning mix, and 4½ tablespoons chili powder. Add enough broth to moisten slightly.

Measure 6 cups combined chicken and beef broth. Strain, place in large saucepan, and add salt to taste and remaining chili powder. Bring to a boil and stir in cornmeal. Cook slowly for 15 minutes, until very thick, and remove from heat.

For each tamale, place 2 to 3 tablespoons mush mixture in center of cornhusk or parchment square. Press until thin. Add a heaping tablespoon of beef mixture and one or more chicken slivers in center. Roll husks or fold parchment and tie. Steam over boiling water for 1 hour. When thoroughly cooked, store in refrigerator. Reheat by steaming or put in top of double boiler. Makes about 40 small tamales.

Meatball Appetizers

Yield: 4 servings

1 pound ground beef
⅓ cup dry bread crumbs
1 egg
⅓ cup plus 2 tablespoons steak sauce
2 tablespoons oil
2 tablespoons light brown sugar
2 tablespoons butter

Combine beef, bread crumbs, egg, and 2 tablespoons steak sauce. Mix and shape into 1-inch meatballs. Brown in oil in skillet. Drain fat from skillet.

Add ⅓ cup steak sauce, brown sugar, and butter to meatballs in skillet. Simmer, covered, for 15 minutes until done. Makes 2 dozen meatballs.

Brandied Meatballs

Yield: 6 to 8 servings

meatballs
2 pounds ground beef
¾ cup milk
½ cup bread crumbs
1 tablespoon Worcestershire sauce

brandied peach sauce
1 jar peach preserves
¾ cup light brown sugar, firmly packed
½ cup brandy
¼ teaspoon nutmeg

Combine all meatball ingredients and roll into balls; set aside.

Combine sauce ingredients. Add a small amount of meat drippings and simmer for 10 minutes. Add meatballs to sauce and coat thoroughly. Cover and simmer for 45 minutes to 1 hour. Makes 40 small meatballs.

Chafing Dish Meatballs

Yield: 10 to 12 servings

2 pounds ground meatloaf mixture or beef
1 egg, slightly beaten
1 large onion, grated
Salt to taste
1 12-ounce bottle chili sauce
1 10-ounce jar grape jelly
Juice of 1 lemon

Combine ground meat, egg, onion, and salt. Mix and shape into small balls. Mix chili sauce, grape jelly, and lemon juice. Drop meatballs into sauce and simmer until brown. Refrigerate or freeze.

To serve, bring to room temperature. Reheat in chafing dish and serve with cocktail picks. Makes 50 to 60 meatballs.

Party Croissant

Yield: 8 servings

1 ounce yeast
5 tablespoons butter or margarine
⅔ cup lukewarm water
Salt
½ teaspoon sugar
2 eggs
1 tablespoon sesame seeds, without skins, plus more to sprinkle over croissant
2 cups flour

Filling:
5 ounces garlic cheese
¼ pound smoked ham, in thin slices
18-20 olives, pimiento filled

Crumble the yeast in a large bowl. Melt the butter in a pot and add the water. Pour a little of the warm liquid over the yeast and stir. Pour in the rest of the liquid. Add salt, sugar, 1 egg, and the sesame seeds. Add nearly all of the flour and work until the dough becomes smooth and shiny. Let rise under a cloth for about 30 minutes.

Place the dough onto a lightly floured baking board and knead it until it stops sticking to the board. Roll out the dough into a triangle. Lay the filling in an even strip across the widest part of the triangle. Roll together toward the point. Form into a croissant.

Place the croissant on a prepared baking sheet and let it rise for approximately 20 minutes. Brush with the second egg and sprinkle some sesame seeds over the croissant. Bake at 400°F on the lowest rack in the oven for about 20 minutes. Test with a toothpick.

Luxury Toast

Sausage Pies

Yield: 10 to 12 servings

Pie crust mix (1 pie)
¾ pound sausage meat
20 to 24 cherry tomatoes, halved

Prepare pie crust; set aside.

Break up sausage in heavy skillet; cook until all pink has disappeared, about 10 minutes. Drain off fat on paper towels. Cool completely.

Roll out pie-crust dough; cut into 4-inch squares. Moisten corner of each square with a little cold water. Place squares on lightly greased baking sheet. Spoon drained sausage, about 1 spoonful per square, into center of each square. Pinch corners to seal, but don't close completely. Bake at 450°F 12 to 15 minutes. Then place half of cherry tomato, cut-side-down, on top of sausage—this is why you didn't seal the pie crust. Bake 10 minutes more or until pie crust is golden brown. Serve at once. Makes 20 to 24 pies.

Sausage Biscuits

Yield: 12 servings

8 ounces sharp Cheddar cheese, grated
1 pound hot pork sausage
2 cups biscuit mix

Mix everything together in bowl, working in sausage and cheese well. Drop onto ungreased cookie sheets; shape slightly with your fingers if you wish. Bake at 400°F about 15 minutes or until nicely browned.

Serve biscuits piping hot. Makes about 3 dozen biscuits.

Sausage and Apple Snack

Yield: 6 servings

1 pound sausage meat
2 tablespoons parsley, chopped
½ teaspoon curry powder
½ teaspoon mixed herbs
2 tablespoons flour
Butter
2 dessert apples
6 thin slices bacon
A few sprigs of parsley
Toast

Combine sausage meat, parsley, curry powder, herbs, and seasoning, and shape into 6 patties. Coat lightly with flour and fry in butter about 5 minutes on each side. Remove from the pan and keep hot.

Core but do not peel the apples; cut each into three slices and fry for about 2 minutes on each side.

Roll up the bacon; put it on a skewer and fry or broil.

Put the sausage patties on a serving dish with an apple ring on top. Arrange the bacon rolls in the center and garnish with parsley. Serve with hot toast.

Savory Appetizer Franks

Yield: About 10 servings

1 cup catsup
¼ cup steak sauce
¼ cup brown sugar, packed
2 tablespoons vinegar
1 pound hot dogs, cut in 1-inch pieces

In medium saucepan, combine all ingredients except the hot dogs; simmer ten minutes. Add hot dogs; simmer fifteen minutes longer. To serve, keep warm in chafing dish or fondue pot. Makes about 50 appetizers.

Sweet and Sour Hot Dogs

Yield: 10 to 20 servings

¾ cup prepared mustard
1 cup currant jelly
2 pounds hot dogs

Heat mustard and jelly in top of double boiler. Slice hot dogs diagonally ½ inch thick. Add to sauce and cook for five minutes. Refrigerate or freeze.

When ready to serve, place in chafing dish and heat. Serve with toothpicks. Makes 60 to 80 pieces.

Pigs in Bacon

Yield: 4 to 6 servings

12 frankfurters
2 teaspoons prepared mustard or catsup
½ cup cheese
12 slices bacon

Cut a slit the length of the frankfurter, but not quite through to the bottom. Spread with mustard (or catsup) and fill the slits with thin strips of cheese.

Roll a slice of bacon in a spiral around each frankfurter, and fasten with toothpicks. Cook until the bacon is crisp, turning frequently. Makes 12.

Ham and Melon Balls

Yield: 6 to 8 servings

6 to 8 ounces ham, very thinly sliced
Honeydew melon, cantaloupe, or Spanish melon

Slice ham into pieces 1 inch wide by 4 inches long. These will wrap comfortably around melon balls.

Cut melon into balls; place on paper towels to

drain excess water. Wrap each melon ball with ham; secure with toothpick. Refrigerate until ready to serve. Makes 24 to 36 balls.

Avocado Cream with Sherry

Yield: 8 servings

1 can consommé
1¼ cups cold water
5 ripe avocados
¼ cup leek, minced
Juice from ½ lemon
1 teaspoon herb salt
1 teaspoon Italian salad spice
¾ cup heavy cream
2 tablespoons sherry
Caviar or shrimp for garnish

Mix the consommé with the cold water and chill.

Divide the avocados in half, remove the pits, and peel off the skins. Mash the fruit in a blender or food processor together with the leek, lemon, and the spices, so that it becomes a smooth purée. Dilute with the consommé and mix in the cream and the sherry.

Place on individual dishes. Garnish with caviar or shrimp, and a little dill and lemon. Refrigerate.

Deviled Ham Twists

Yield: About 12 servings

3 4½-ounce cans deviled ham
3 tablespoons walnuts, chopped
3 tablespoons onion, minced
¼ cup pimiento-stuffed olives, minced
½ teaspoon ground red pepper
6 saltines, finely crushed
¾ cup milk
2 ¾ cups all-purpose buttermilk biscuit mix
Paprika

Stir ham, walnuts, onion, olives, red pepper, and saltines together until well blended.

Make a soft dough by combining milk and biscuit mix. Beat until stiff. Divide dough in half and roll into 2 12-inch squares; spread 1 cup ham mixture on half of each square. Fold uncovered half over ham mixture to form a 12 × 6-inch rectangle. With a sharp knife, cut pastry into 36 rectangles. Twist each gently to form a bow and dust with paprika. Place on a greased baking sheet and bake 15 minutes at 400°F or until lightly browned.

Avocado Cream with Sherry

Warm Avocado

4 small eggs
4 cups water
2 teaspoons salt
1 teaspoon vinegar
1 egg yolk
1 teaspoon lemon juice
1 tablespoon cream
3½ tablespoons butter
Pinch salt
Tarragon, finely crushed
Snipped parsley
2 large, ripe avocados
Juice from ½ lemon

Start by poaching the eggs. Break each egg into its own cup. Combine the water, salt, and vinegar and bring to a boil. Lift from the heat and let 1 egg slide out of the cup into the water. Fold the egg white that spreads out into the water back to the egg with a spoon. Cook the egg carefully for about 4 to 5 minutes, so that the egg white becomes firm. Do only 1 egg at a time. Remove the egg from the water, using a large spoon with holes in it. Trim the egg with a pair of scissors so that it has an even edge and looks attractive. It should not be larger than the hole from the seed in the avocado half. Keep the eggs warm by placing over 98.6°F water next to the stove.

Mix the egg yolk, lemon juice, and cream in a small saucepan (it should not be an aluminum pan). Carefully warm over low direct heat while stirring constantly. Lift the pan every now and then from the burner so that it doesn't become too warm. As soon as the mixture starts to foam or thicken, add the butter in small dabs while continuing to beat constantly. Beat until the sauce is thick and light and all the butter has been added. Remove from the heat and season with salt, finely crushed tarragon, and a little snipped parsley. Keep warm by placing it in 98.6°F water next to the stove.

Divide the avocados in half, remove the seeds, and dig out a slightly larger hole using a spoon. Place the avocado halves in a skillet. Pour in warm water so that it just covers the avocados and add the lemon juice. Bring slowly to a boil without covering the pan. Remove the avocados with a spoon that has holes in it so that the water drains off; place each of the 4 halves on a warm plate.

Pour a little of the sauce into each hole. Also place a poached egg into each of the holes, then cover the eggs with the rest of the sauce.

Warm Avocado

Vegetable Antipasto

1 small head cauliflower, sliced
2 medium carrots, cut into 2-inch strips
2 celery ribs, cut into 1-inch pieces
1 green pepper, cut into 2-inch strips
2 whole pimientos, drained and cut into strips
1 2½-ounce jar pitted green olives, drained
½ cup salad oil
¼ cup water
3 tablespoons Worcestershire sauce
3 tablespoons white vinegar
2 tablespoons sugar
1 teaspoon salt
⅛ teaspoon Tabasco

In a large saucepan, combine all ingredients. Bring to boiling point. Cover, reduce heat, and simmer 10 minutes, stirring occasionally. Cool; refrigerate at least 24 hours. Drain well.

Toasted Asparagus Rolls

Yield: 12 servings

24 thin slices white bread
1 cup Swiss or Cheddar cheese, grated
24 cooked whole asparagus
¼ cup margarine or butter, melted

Trim crusts from bread and arrange slices between two damp towels. Gently roll bread thin. Sprinkle each slice with grated cheese. Place asparagus at one corner and roll up like a jelly roll. Fasten with toothpicks.

Arrange rolls on a greased cookie sheet and brush each with melted butter or margarine. Bake at 400°F for 10 minutes or until delicately browned. Serve hot. Makes 24 rolls.

Leeks with Mustard Greens and Cress

Yield: 4 servings

1 pound small leeks
Water
Salt
Mustard greens and cress

dressing
1 tablespoon vinegar
½ teaspoon salt
½ teaspoon tarragon
1 tablespoon water
1 teaspoon mustard
3 to 4 tablespoons oil

Wash the leeks well and trim the root ends and most of the green. In a wide, shallow pan, bring the water to a boil, adding 2 teaspoons salt per quart of water. Divide leeks into 2 or 3 pieces, if they are very long. Cook for about 2 minutes, depending on thickness. Do not overcook.

Blend the ingredients for the dressing and beat for a few minutes to allow the salt to dissolve. Drain the leeks and place in a dish. Pour the dressing over them while they are still hot. Allow them to get cold and marinate for an hour or 2. Cut some mustard greens and cress onto the leeks when serving and offer bread and butter with them.

Melon Balls with Chutney and Ham

Yield: 6 servings

dressing
3 tablespoons white wine vinegar
½ cup light olive oil
¼ cup mango chutney, finely chopped
½ teaspoon salt
⅛ teaspoon cayenne
½ teaspoon curry powder

salad
4 cups melon balls such as cantaloupe, honeydew, cranshaw, or watermelon, cut with the small end of the melon baller
½ head romaine, shredded
½ cup toasted pecans
¼ pound Virginia ham or prosciutto, very thinly sliced

Beat together the wine vinegar, olive oil, chutney, salt, cayenne, and curry powder. Set aside at room temperature for 1 to 2 hours to develop flavor. Just before serving, place melon balls in a bowl, pour on the dressing, and toss gently.

Line a shallow serving bowl with romaine. Toss the melon balls again and arrange them on the lettuce, making a mound in the center. Sprinkle with the pecans. Loosely roll the slices of ham or proscuitto and arrange them in a border around the melon.

Yogurt Stuffed Mushrooms

Yield: 6 to 8 servings

24 medium-sized whole fresh mushrooms
2 cups ham, finely chopped or ground
½ cup plain yogurt mixed with 1 tablespoon flour
⅓ cup walnuts, chopped
1 tablespoon fresh parsley leaves, chopped

Remove the stems from the mushrooms. Combine ham, yogurt, walnuts, and parsley. Place a heaping tablespoon of this mixture in the center of each mushroom cap. Place on a lightly greased baking sheet; bake at 400°F about 12 minutes. Serve hot.

Toasted Mushroom Rolls

Yield: 15 to 20 servings

½ pound mushrooms
¼ cup butter
3 tablespoons flour
¾ teaspoon salt
1 cup light cream
2 teaspoons chives, minced
1 teaspoon lemon juice
1 family-sized loaf sliced fresh white bread

Clean and finely chop mushrooms. Sauté for 5 minutes in butter. Blend in flour and salt. Stir in light cream. Cook until thick. Add chives and lemon juice; cool. Remove crust from the white bread. Roll slices thin and spread with mixture. Roll up. Pack and freeze, if desired.

When ready to serve, defrost, cut each roll in half, and toast on all sides in 400°F oven. Makes 3½ dozen.

Spinach Buns

Yield: 12 servings

1 package frozen spinach, chopped, well drained
2 eggs, beaten
1 cup feta cheese or large curd cottage cheese
½ teaspoon salt
2 packages refrigerated dough (24 biscuits)

Combine the first 4 ingredients. Set aside. Roll out each biscuit on greased cookie sheet. Place 1 teaspoon of filling in each one. Pinch together edges so that the spinach is almost all covered. Bake at 350°F for 10 minutes.

Note: Leftover filling can be baked in a casserole dish. Makes 24 buns.

Stuffed Pepper Slices

Yield: 4 to 6 servings

1 red pepper
1 green pepper
8 ounces cottage cheese
2 tablespoons milk
1 tablespoon pimiento, chopped
1 tablespoon parsley, chopped
1 tablespoon watercress, chopped
1 tablespoon chives, chopped
¼ teaspoon salt
⅛ teaspoon white pepper
1 teaspoon lemon juice
1 envelope (1 tablespoon) unflavored gelatin
⅓ cup cold water
Lettuce leaves

Cut tops off peppers. Remove seeds; wash.

Cream cottage cheese in blender (thin with milk if necessary); remove. Add pimiento, parsley, watercress, chives, salt, pepper, and lemon juice.

Soak gelatin in cold water; dissolve completely over simmering water. Add to cheese mixture. Fill peppers with mixture; chill in refrigerator at least 2 hours.

Cut each pepper into 4 thick slices. Serve on lettuce.

Marinated Mushrooms

Yield: 8 servings

1 pound fresh mushrooms, sliced
2 green onions, sliced
⅓ cup corn oil
⅓ cup wine vinegar
2 tablespoons parsley, minced
½ teaspoon salt
½ teaspoon dry mustard
½ teaspoon dried basil leaves
Dash pepper

Mix together all ingredients. Chill several hours. Makes about 5 cups.

Fried Mushrooms

1 pound mushrooms
¼ cup flour
1 teaspoon salt
1/16 teaspoon black pepper
2 eggs, beaten
¾ cup fine bread crumbs

Rinse, dry, and trim mushrooms. Combine flour with salt and pepper. Dredge mushrooms in flour, dip in eggs, and roll in crumbs.

Preheat fat to 365°F. Fry mushrooms for 3 minutes.

Mushroom Toast with Garlic

Yield: 6 servings

24 fine, white mushrooms
1 lemon
7 tablespoons butter, at room temperature
3 cloves garlic, crushed
1 tablespoon shallot, finely chopped
2 tablespoons parsley, chopped
Salt
Pepper
6 slices white bread, crusts removed

Clean the mushrooms and drip a small amount of lemon juice over them so that they stay white.

Mix the butter with the garlic, shallot, parsley, and juice from ½ lemon. Add salt and pepper to taste.

Fry the bread until golden brown on one side. Cut the mushrooms into thin slices and place them on the unfried side of the bread. Cover with the butter mixture and place in the oven under the broiler. Serve when the butter has started to become brown on the top.

Stuffed Mushrooms

Yield: 4 servings

8 large mushrooms
2 tablespoons butter or margarine
2 tablespoons onion, minced
1 clove garlic, minced
1 teaspoon dried parsley flakes
2 tablespoons salt
¼ cup dry bread crumbs
½ teaspoon oregano
½ teaspoon salt
2 tablespoon Parmesan cheese, grated

Remove stems from mushrooms. Melt butter. Brush caps with melted butter. Chop stems finely. Sauté onion, garlic, and chopped stems in melted butter for about 5 minutes. Add remaining ingredients. More butter may be needed if mixture is too dry.

Fill caps with mixture. Bake at 375°F for 20 minutes.

Potato Skins

Yield: 8 servings

8 medium-sized potatoes (4 to 5 pounds)
¼ cup flour
Cooking oil
Seasoned salt

Scrub the potatoes and pierce with a fork. Rub lightly with oil and bake in a 400°F oven for about 50 to 60 minutes, or until tender. Cool.

Cut the potatoes in half lengthwise and scoop out most of the white part, leaving about a ¼-inch shell. Cut the shells in half lengthwise, then in half crosswise, which will give you eight pieces from each potato. Dip in flour and shake off excess, then deep fry in oil heated to 375°F for about 2 minutes or until lightly browned.

Drain on a paper towel, sprinkle with seasoned salt, and serve. Makes about 64 potato skins.

These may be made ahead of time and reheated by placing on backing sheet in 375°F oven for about 10 minutes.

Leeks with Mustard Greens and Cress

Soups

Cold Buttermilk Soup

Yield: 6 to 8 servings

3 egg yolks
½ cup sugar
1 teaspoon lemon juice
½ teaspoon lemon rind, grated
1 teaspoon vanilla
1 quart buttermilk

Beat egg yolks lightly in a large bowl, gradually adding sugar.

Add lemon juice, lemon rind, and vanilla. Slowly add buttermilk, continuing to beat (either with an electric beater on slow or with a wire whisk) until soup is smooth.

Serve soup in chilled soup bowls.

Beer and Bread Soup

Yield: 6 to 8 servings

1 small loaf dark rye bread
3 cups water
3 cups dark beer or ale
½ cup sugar
1 whole lemon (both juice and grated rind)
Light or whipped cream

Break bread in small pieces into a mixing bowl. Mix water and beer; pour this over bread. Allow it to stand several hours.

When ready to serve, cook mixture over low heat, stirring occasionally, just long enough for it to thicken. (If the mixture is too thick, strain it through a coarse sieve.) Bring it to a boil; add sugar, lemon juice, and lemon rind.

Serve soup with a spoonful of light or whipped cream on top.

Apple Soup

Yield: 8 servings

1½ pounds tart apples
2½ quarts water
½ lemon, thinly sliced
1 stick cinnamon
4 tablespoons cornstarch
¼ cup water
Sugar to taste
¼ cup wine (optional)

Wash, quarter, and core apples; do not peel. Cook until soft in 1 quart of water with lemon and cinnamon. Put apples through a coarse sieve. Put with rest of water into pot; bring to boil.

Mix cornstarch with ¼ cup water; add to pot, stirring constantly. Add sugar and wine. Serve hot.

Apple Yogurt Soup

Yield: 4 servings

1 hard-cooked egg, chopped
½ cup raisins
6 cups plain yogurt
1 cucumber, peeled and chopped
¼ cup scallions, chopped
1 teaspoon salt
¼ teaspoon pepper
3 tablespoons curry powder (or to taste)
5 green, unpeeled cooking apples, cored and chopped
Milk
1 tablespoon fresh parsley (optional)

Combine all the ingredients except milk and parsley. Thin with milk to desired consistency. Chill. Sprinkle with parsley before serving.

Cream of Squash and Apple Soup

Yield: 8 servings

1 butternut squash (about 2 pounds) peeled, seeded, and coarsely chopped
2 Granny Smith apples, cored, pared, and coarsely chopped
1 medium onion, chopped
5 cups chicken broth
¼ pound farmer cheese
2 egg yolks
3 tablespoons Marsala wine
Salt and pepper

Combine squash, apples, onion, and chicken broth in a soup pot or large saucepan. Bring to a boil, cover, and simmer over medium heat for 30 minutes or until squash is soft. Purée in batches in blender or processor.

In a large bowl, mix farmer cheese and egg yolks together. Slowly stir them into the hot soup as it is puréed until all the soup is mixed in. Reblend or process to a smooth mixture and return to pot. Add wine and salt and pepper to taste. Reheat—do not boil.

Creamy Blueberry Soup

Yield: 4 to 6 servings

1 pint blueberries, washed and picked over
2 cups water
½ cup maple syrup
½ teaspoon cinnamon
1 pinch cardamom
1 cup sour cream

Place blueberries in a saucepan with water, maple syrup, cinnamon, and cardamom. Cook over low heat for 10 minutes; remove from heat and let cool.

Stir in sour cream and chill well before serving.

Celery and Walnut Soup

Yield: 4 servings

2 cups fresh celery sticks, cut in slices
1 medium-sized onion, chopped
3½ tablespoons butter
4 cups chicken broth
⅓ cup heavy cream
⅓ cup walnut meats
1½ tablespoons butter
Celery salt
Freshly ground pepper
A small amount of sherry

Combine the sliced celery and onion. Place the mixture in a frying pan with butter and allow to bubble slowly over low heat. Stir occasionally.

Simmer for about 10 minutes, or until the celery feels soft. Stir in 3¼ cups of the chicken broth. Bring to a boil and simmer for about 30 minutes.

Strain or mix in a food processor and pour the soup back into the pot. Beat in the heavy cream. Chop the walnut meats and fry them in butter for a few minutes; then blend them into the soup. Add celery salt, pepper and the sherry. Dilute with the rest of the chicken broth if the soup feels too thick. Serve in a heated soup bowl or in warmed individual serving bowls. Decorate with a few small leaves from the celery, which "swim" on the top of the soup.

Cherry Soup

Yield: 4 to 6 servings

1½ pounds sweet red cherries
4 cups water
½ cinnamon stick (or ¼ teaspoon ground cinnamon)
3 or 4 slivers orange or lemon rind and juice of ½ orange or lemon
1 cup red wine
1 tablespoon cornstarch
Sugar to taste

Pit cherries; put about three-quarters of them into pan. Cover with water. Add the cinnamon, rind, and orange juice. Cover; simmer gently until cherries are tender. Put through fine food mill or into electric blender or food processor; blend until smooth. Add wine.

Add cornstarch to cold water; mix until smooth. Add a little hot soup to cornstarch mixture; pour back into soup. Stir in well; bring to boil. Cook 4 to 5 minutes; add reserved cherries the last few minutes and heat through. Add sugar to taste. Serve hot with crackers, which can be crumbled into soup if desired.

Cranberry Soup

Yield: 4 servings

1½ cups sugar
3 cups water
2 cinnamon sticks
¼ teaspoon ground cloves
4 cups cranberries, fresh or frozen
2 tablespoons lemon juice
1 tablespoon grated orange rind
Sour cream

Combine sugar, water, cinnamon sticks and cloves in 4-quart Dutch oven. Cook over high heat until mixture comes to a boil, about 10 minutes. Add cranberries and cook until mixture returns to a boil, about 2 minutes.

Reduce heat to medium. Cook 5 minutes more or until cranberries begin to burst. Remove from heat and stir in lemon juice and orange rind. Cool to room temperature.

Chill in refrigerator at least 4 hours or until ready to serve. Serve with a dollop of sour cream.

Cranberry and Orange Soup

Yield: 4 to 6 servings

1 pound fresh cranberries
2 cups light chicken stock or water
1½ cups white wine
2 or 3 pieces lemon rind
Pared rind of ripe orange
½ cinnamon stick
¼ to ½ cup sugar to taste
Juice of 2 oranges
Juice of ½ lemon

Wash cranberries; put into pan with stock and wine. Add lemon and orange rind and cinnamon stick; simmer about 10 minutes, until cranberries have softened. Put fruit and juice through fine nylon sieve or fine food mill after removing cinnamon stick; sweeten to taste. Add orange and lemon juice.

Serve chilled with orange as garnish.

Orange Soup

Yield: 6 servings

1 tablespoon cornstarch
4 cups water
1½ cups orange juice
¼ cup sugar
Whipped cream
Thin orange slice

Mix cornstarch in ¼ cup of cold water. Bring rest of water to boil. Add cornstarch mixture to boiling water to thicken slightly. Add orange juice and sugar.

Serve either hot or cold, garnished with a spoonful of whipped cream and a thin orange slice.

Cream of Pumpkin Soup

Yield: 3 to 4 servings

½ cup onion, diced
2 tablespoons butter
2 cups chicken stock
2 cups canned pumpkin
1 teaspoon cinnamon
1 tablespoon sugar
½ cup cream for soup or sour cream

Sauté onion and butter in medium-sized, heavy saucepan until onion is transparent. Add 1 cup stock; simmer until onion is tender. Stir in pumpkin, blending until smooth. Add remaining stock, cinnamon, and sugar; stir until all flavors blend. Last, add cream. Serve when hot.

If you prefer sour-cream garnish, eliminate the cream and top each soup bowl with a generous spoonful of sour cream.

Strawberry Soup

Yield: 6 servings

1 quart fresh strawberries, washed, hulled, and cut
5 tablespoons sugar, sprinkled on berries
3 cups plain yogurt
1 cup fresh cream
Fresh mint leaf

In blender, place 1 pint strawberries, yogurt, and cream. Blend until smooth. Reserve ½ cup strawberries to be used as garnish. Fold remaining strawberries into mixture. Garnish with reserved strawberries and a fresh mint leaf. Serve cold.

Celery and Walnut Soup

Cod Soup with Orange

Yield: 4 servings

⅔ pound cod fillets (frozen or fresh)
4 cups fish stock
5 to 6 potatoes, cut into cubes
1 whole fennel, cut into cubes
1 leek, shredded
1 can crushed tomatoes
2 cloves garlic
Salt
Pepper
Juice from ½ orange or 2 to 3 tablespoons juice
    concentrate
2 tablespoons snipped parsley

Allow the fish to partially thaw, if frozen, and cut it into 1 to 1½ inch wide cubes.

Bring the stock to a boil in a pot. Add the vegetables, and the garlic. Season with salt and pepper, and let the soup simmer for 10 to 12 minutes until the vegetables feel soft. Add the orange juice and simmer the soup for another 3 to 4 minutes. Serve the soup piping hot with snipped parsley sprinkled on top.

Old-Fashioned Beef-Vegetable Soup

Yield: 6 servings

3 pounds shin beef with bone
3 quarts water
2 tablespoons salt
2 teaspoons Worcestershire sauce
¼ teaspoon pepper
1 medium onion, chopped
⅓ cup barley
1 cup celery, chopped
1 cup carrot, sliced
1 cup potatoes, sliced
1 cup cabbage, shredded
1 cup peas
1 turnip, peeled and cubed
3½ cups tomatoes
3 teaspoons parsley flakes

Place beef, water, salt, Worcestershire sauce, and pepper in large pot; cover and simmer 2½ to 3 hours. Remove bone, cut off the meat in small pieces, and return meat to pot.

Add remaining ingredients. Simmer about 45 minutes.

Cod Soup with Orange

Pumpkin Soup

Yield: 4 servings

2 tablespoons butter
2 tablespoons onion, chopped
½ teaspoon ginger
1 tablespoon flour
2 cups pumpkin
2 cups chicken stock
2 cups milk
Salt to season

Sauté butter, onion, and ginger. Stir in flour. Add pumpkin; cook 5 minutes. Gradually add stock and milk; simmer 5 minutes. Season with salt.

Cheese Soup

Yield: 4 servings

1 onion, finely chopped
1 tablespoon margarine
3 tablespoons flour
4 cups broth
1¼ cups grated cheese
1 egg yolk
⅓ cup crème fraîche or sour cream
Shredded celery
Chopped parsley

Sauté the onion in the margarine. Stir in the flour when the onion has become transparent. Cover with the broth, stirring constantly, and simmer for 5 to 6 minutes.

Stir in the cheese and let it melt. It should not, however, be allowed to boil. Remove the pot from the heat; stir in the egg yolk and the crème fraîche or sour cream. Serve immediately garnished with celery and parsley.

Vermont Cheddar Cheese Soup

Yield: 6 servings

½ cup carrots, finely diced
½ cup celery, finely diced
½ cup onion, finely diced
½ cup green pepper, finely diced
3 cups Vermont cheddar cheese, grated
¼ cup butter
¼ cup flour
1 quart chicken broth
2 cups evaporated milk
¼ teaspoon salt
Pepper to taste
Sherry or beer (optional)

Sauté vegetables in butter for 5 minutes only, so they remain crunchy. Stir in flour until pasty. Add broth and simmer 5 minutes. Add cheese very slowly. Add evaporated milk. Season to taste with salt and pepper and sherry or beer, if desired.

Parmesan Cheese Soup

Yield: 5 to 6 servings

2 slices bacon, chopped
1 large or 2 small onions, chopped
2 to 3 stalks celery, chopped
3 tablespoons butter
1 cup fresh white bread crumbs
4 to 5 cups stock or consommé
Salt and pepper
Pinch cayenne pepper
1 bay leaf, 3 to 4 sprigs of parsley, tied together
½ to ¾ cup Parmesan or other strongly flavored hard cheese
Pinch dry mustard

optional garnish
2 egg yolks
½ cup cream
Paprika
Croutons

Cook bacon, onions, and celery gently in melted butter, stirring frequently, until onions are golden brown. Add fresh bread crumbs; mix well before adding stock or consommé. Add salt and pepper, cayenne pepper, bay leaf, and parsley sprigs. Bring mixture to a boil, stirring constantly. Cover, simmer about 20 minutes. Remove bay leaf and parsley.

Add cheese; mix well. A little dry mustard can also be added. This soup can be made richer by adding a mixture of egg yolks and cream. Sprinkle with paprika; serve hot with croutons.

California Minestrone

Yield: 6 servings

¼ pound salt pork, cut into ½-inch cubes
1 cup onion, finely chopped
2 cloves garlic, minced
2 cans (1 pound, 4 ounces each) cannellini or white kidney beans, drained
6 cups beef broth or stock
2 carrots, pared and diced
2 ribs celery, sliced
1 28-ounce can tomatoes
4½ teaspoons lemon juice
1 bay leaf
1 teaspoon salt
1 teaspoon hot pepper sauce
½ teaspoon basil
½ teaspoon oregano

In large kettle, brown salt pork lightly. Add onion and garlic; cook until tender. Add remaining ingredients and simmer 30 minutes.

Hearty Vegetable Soup

Yield: 6 servings

½ cup dried lima beans
½ cup dried peas
2 tablespoons barley
2 tablespoons rice
2 tablespoons kidney beans
2 quarts cold water
½ cup celery, cut in pieces
2 potatoes, sliced
2 onions, sliced
1 white turnip, diced
1 cup stewed or canned tomatoes
1 teaspoon salt
¼ teaspoon pepper
1 ham bone or 1 frankfurter (optional)

Wash beans, peas, barley, rice, and kidney beans and soak overnight in cold water. Bring to boiling point. Add celery, potatoes, onions, turnip, tomatoes, salt, and pepper. Simmer slowly 2 hours. Add water as it cooks away.

About half hour before serving, add ham bone or frankfurters, if desired, and more seasoning if necessary. Remove bone before serving. This soup should be quite thick and is a meal in itself.

Spring Soup

Yield: 4 to 6 servings

4 young carrots
2 to 3 young leeks, depending on size (or 8 to 10 scallions)
3 tablespoons butter
1½ tablespoons flour
4 cups chicken stock
½ cup cauliflower florets
2 to 3 tablespoons peas
2 to 3 tablespoons young green beans, sliced
Pinch sugar
2 tablespoons mixed parsley, chervil, mint, and thyme
Salt and pepper
½ cup cream
2 egg yolks

Peel and dice carrots. Wash leeks or scallions thoroughly; cut white part into slices. Melt butter; cook these vegetables gently in a covered pan 5 to 6 minutes without allowing to brown. Sprinkle in flour, mix thoroughly, then add stock. Blend well until smooth; bring to a boil, stirring constantly. Cook a few minutes before adding cauliflower florets, peas, sliced beans, and sugar. Simmer 15 minutes. Add herbs; cook a few more minutes, to draw out flavor of herbs. Season to taste.

Mix cream with egg yolks. Take a few spoonfuls of hot soup; mix well with cream and egg-yolk mixture before straining it back into soup, stirring constantly. Reheat, being very careful not to allow soup to boil, as this causes egg to curdle and spoils texture of soup.

Red Bean/Vegetable Soup

Yield: 5 to 6 servings

2 quarts water
2 cups dried red beans
3 tablespoons oil
1 small onion, chopped
2 large cloves garlic, mashed
⅓ cup parsley, minced
1 teaspoon oregano
½ teaspoon basil
1½ cups chopped carrots
1½ cups zucchini
1 15-ounce can tomato sauce (or the equivalent of fresh tomatoes)
2 tablespoons red wine vinegar
Salt and hot pepper sauce to taste

Bring water to a boil in a soup pot. Add beans and reduce heat to simmer. Cover and cook for an hour or until tender.

Meanwhile, heat the oil in a frying pan and sauté the onion, garlic, parsley, oregano, and basil until the onions are tender. Add this to the cooked beans along with the vegetables and tomato sauce. Cover and simmer at least ½ hour, then add the vinegar, salt, and hot pepper sauce.

Cold Vegetable Soup (Gazpacho)

Yield: 6 to 8 servings

Soup
2 medium-sized cucumbers, peeled and coarsely chopped
5 medium-sized tomatoes, peeled and coarsely chopped
1 large onion, coarsely chopped
1 medium-sized green pepper, deribbed, seeded, and coarsely chopped
2 teaspoons garlic, finely chopped
2 to 3 cups French or Italian bread, trimmed of crusts and coarsely crumbled
4 cups cold water
¼ cup red wine vinegar
4 teaspoons salt
4 tablespoons olive oil
1 tablespoon tomato paste

Garnish
1 cup croutons
½ cup onions, finely chopped
½ cup cucumbers, peeled and finely chopped
½ cup green peppers, finely chopped

In a deep bowl, combine the cucumbers, tomatoes, onion, green pepper, garlic, and crumbled bread; mix together thoroughly. Then stir in the water, vinegar, and salt. Ladle the mixture, about 2 cups at a time, into blender or food processor and blend at high speed for 1 minute, or until reduced to a smooth purée. Pour the purée into a bowl and, with a whisk, beat in the olive oil and tomato paste.

Cover the bowl tightly with foil or plastic wrap and refrigerate at least 2 hours, or until the soup is thoroughly chilled. Just before serving, stir soup lightly, then ladle it into a large, chilled tureen or individual soup plates.

Place croutons, onions, cucumbers, and green peppers in separate serving bowls and let each diner add whatever garnishes he desires.

Zorn Soup

Yield: 8 servings

¾ cup dried green peas
12 cups of water
3 tablespoons salt
3 onions, peeled and cut into wedges
10 black peppercorns
2 bay leaves
2¾ to 3 pounds beef, for example shoulder roast
8 potatoes
4 carrots
1 wedge cabbage, about ½ pound
Snipped parsley

Soak the peas in 4 cups of the water and 1 tablespoon of the salt for 8 to 10 hours. Pour away the water. Place the peas in a pot with the remaining 8 cups of water. Cook the peas together with the onions and spices for about 45 minutes. Skim away all the pea skins.

Rinse the meat under running water. Stick a meat thermometer into the beef so that the point of the thermometer comes to the middle of the thickest part of the meat. The entire stick of the thermometer should be in the meat. Place the meat in the pot. Boil over low heat for 1¼ to 1½ hours, until the thermometer shows 185 to 195°F.

Peel the potatoes and the carrots about 30 minutes before the meat is done. Cut the vegetables into chunks and cook them in the soup. Add the shredded cabbage about 10 minutes before the meat is done. Season to taste.

Cheese Soup

When the meat is done, remove the pot from the stove. Let it stand, covered, for about 20 minutes. Remove the meat from the soup, cut it into slices, and serve it on a plate with the soup. Or cut pieces of the meat into the soup. Garnish with parsley and serve.

Avocado Soup

Yield: 4 servings

2 ripe, soft avocados, pitted and peeled
1 teaspoon lemon juice
1 cup cold chicken broth
1 cup light cream
½ cup plain yogurt
½ cup dry white wine
Salt to taste

Set aside a few thin slices of avocado brushed with lemon juice to use as a garnish. Place remaining avocado in a food processor or blender; blend until smooth. Add remaining ingredients; blend until smooth.

Serve soup very cold, garnished with reserved avocado slices.

Minestrone with Sausage and Greens

Yield: 4 servings

½ pound well-flavored Italian sausage, sweet, hot, or combination
1 medium onion, minced
1 cup brown stock
1-pound can imported plum tomatoes, with juices
20-ounce can cannellini (white kidney beans), undrained
½ pound escarole, swiss chard, or spinach
Salt and pepper
Grated Romano cheese

Sauté whole sausages in 3- or 4-quart saucepan over moderate heat. When they begin to take on color (about 5 minutes), add minced onion and sauté until onion is soft, about 10 minutes. Add broth, tomatoes, and beans and simmer for 10 minutes.

Wash escarole, swiss chard, or spinach and shred coarsely. Add to the soup, bring to a boil, and simmer for 15 more minutes (adding extra water if needed).

Remove sausages and cut in ½-inch slices. Return to soup and add salt and pepper to taste. Sprinkle cheese on top and serve very hot.

Zorn Soup

Sherry Bisque

Yield: 8 to 12 servings

1 small ham hock
¾ cup split green peas
1 bay leaf
6 cups beef broth
6 slices bacon, diced
¾ cup onion, chopped
1 stalk celery, diced
3 tablespoons flour
1 8-ounce can tomato purée
1 cup chicken broth
⅓ cup sherry
¼ cup butter
Freshly ground pepper to taste

Place ham hock, split peas, bay leaf, and 4 cups beef broth into 4-quart saucepan. Bring to a boil; reduce heat to simmer.

Sauté bacon until fat is rendered. Add onion and celery; cook until tender. Stir in flour; mix to blend. Add remaining 2 cups beef broth; cook until slightly thickened. Add onion mixture to split-pea mixture; continue to cook until split peas are soft, about 1½ hours.

When done, remove ham hock. Purée mixture in blender or food mill. Add tomato purée, chicken broth, and sherry. Add butter and pepper; stir until melted. Strain soup, if desired, before serving.

Cauliflower Soup

Yield: 6 servings

1 medium-sized head cauliflower, cut in small flowerets
¼ cup butter
⅔ cup onion, chopped
2 tablespoons flour
2 cups chicken broth
2 cups light cream
½ teaspoon Worcestershire sauce
¾ teaspoon salt
1 cup Cheddar cheese, grated
Chopped chives

Place cauliflower in boiling salted water and cook until tender; drain, reserving liquid. Cook onion until soft in melted butter. Blend in flour and broth, and stir until mixture comes to a boil. Stir in 1 cup liquid drained from the cauliflower (use water if needed to make 1 cup), cream, Worcestershire sauce, salt, and cauliflower. Heat to boiling. Add cheese and stir until it melts. Garnish with chopped chives.

Barley Soup

Yield: 6 to 8 servings

About 4 quarts water
1 pound brisket and/or 2 soup bones
1 onion, whole
2 stalks celery, sliced
2-3 carrots, whole
½ cup barley

Bring all ingredients to a boil. Cover and simmer over low heat 2 to 3 hours. Remove onion. Mash carrots and place back in soup.

Cream of Barley Soup

Yield: 4 servings

1 cup pearl barley
1 onion, sliced
1 carrot, sliced
2 stalks celery, sliced
1 bay leaf
3 or 4 sprigs parsley (or 1 tablespoon chopped parsley)
4 to 5 cups chicken stock
Chicken carcass or ham bone, if available
½ cup cream
1 to 2 tablespoons chopped parsley, for garnish
Croutons

Wash barley; soak overnight if possible. Otherwise, cover with boiling water and soak 2 hours. Put vegetables into pan with drained barley, herbs, stock, and chicken carcass or ham bone. Cover; cook gently until barley is tender, about 1½ to 2 hours. Discard bones and herbs. Set aside barley.

Strain soup through sieve, or blend soup and barley in electric blender or food processor. Reheat soup; adjust seasoning. Add cream just before serving. Sprinkle with parsley; serve with croutons.

Black-Bean Soup

Yield: 4 to 6 servings

1 to 1½ cups dried black beans
1 ham bone or some ham meat minus fat
5 to 6 cups water
2 medium onions, sliced
4 or 5 stalks celery, sliced
2 to 3 carrots, sliced
1 bay leaf, 5 or 6 sprigs parsley, and 1 sprig thyme, tied together
2 cloves
½ teaspoon mustard powder
Pinch cayenne pepper
Stock or milk
2 hard-boiled eggs
4 to 6 slices lemon
Croutons

Wash beans in several changes of cold water; cover with cold water. Soak overnight; drain. Put beans into large thick pan; add water and ham bone. Cover pan; cook 2 hours.

Add onions, celery, carrots, herbs, cloves, mustard, and cayenne; recover pan. Cook another 1 to 1½ hours, until beans are tender.

Remove bone and herbs. Put soup through fine sieve or blend in electric blender or processor. Reheat soup; if too thick, add enough stock or milk to make good texture. Adjust seasonings. Serve hot; garnish with eggs, lemon, and croutons.

Iced Green Bean Soup

Yield: 6 to 8 servings

1 pound fresh green beans
6 cups chicken stock
½ teaspoon thyme
¼ teaspoon savory
1 clove garlic, pressed
½ cup whipping cream
Salt and freshly ground pepper to taste

Snap the ends from the green beans and cut the beans into large pieces. Combine the beans and stock in a large saucepan, then add the thyme, savory, and garlic. Bring to a boil, then reduce heat and cover. Simmer until the beans are tender. Drain and reserve the liquid.

Pour the reserved liquid back into the saucepan and boil until reduced to 4 cups. Place the beans in a blender or processor container and process until puréed. Stir into the liquid in the saucepan and mix well. Bring to a boil, then stir in the cream and bring just to a boil. Remove from heat and season with salt and pepper. Cool, then chill until cold.

Senate Bean Soup

Yield: 8 servings

2 pounds navy beans
1½ pounds smoked ham hocks
1 medium onion, diced
1 tablespoon butter
Salt and pepper to taste

Wash beans and run through hot water until they are white again. Put in pot with 4 quarts of hot water. Add ham hocks and boil slowly for approximately 3 hours, covered.

Sauté onion in butter and when light brown, add to bean soup. Season to taste with salt and pepper, then serve. Do not add salt until ready to serve, as this toughens the beans.

Pinto Bean Soup

Yield: 6 to 8 servings

1¾ cups dried pinto beans
Water
2 cloves garlic
1 wedge onion
Salt
2 medium tomatoes, peeled
1 medium onion, quartered
3 tablespoons butter or margarine
½ teaspoon chili powder
¼ pound Muenster or Monterey Jack cheese, cut in small cubes
Crisp fried tortilla strips or garlic-flavored croutons

Soak beans overnight in hot water to cover generously. The next day, drain beans, place in large saucepan and add fresh hot water, 1 clove garlic, and onion wedge. Bring to a boil, reduce heat, and simmer loosely covered for 2 hours. Add salt to taste and simmer for 2 hours longer, or until tender.

Drain beans, reserving 2½ cups bean liquid. Measure 4 cups beans and save any extra for another use. Grind beans and reserved liquid in blender or food processor and set aside.

Combine tomatoes, remaining clove garlic, and quartered onion in blender or food processor and blend until smooth. Melt butter in a large heavy saucepan, add tomato mixture, and cook over high heat for about 5 minutes. Add puréed bean mixture and chili powder. Season to taste with salt and simmer for 15 to 20 minutes.

To serve, place a few cheese cubes in each soup bowl. Pour hot soup over cheese and garnish with tortilla strips or croutons.

Brown Bean Soup

Yield: 4 servings

⅔ pound brown beans/red kidney beans, dried
6 cups water
1 tablespoon salt
1 large leek
1 green pepper
1 can tomatoes, strained
1 clove garlic, crushed (optional)
¼ teaspoon chili powder
4 cups vegetable broth (use the cooking water)
⅔ pound lean salted pork/corned beef
1 tablespoon butter or margarine
⅓ cup watercress, snipped

Place the beans in a generous amount of water. Let stand overnight. Then pour off the water.

Place the beans in 6 cups water, add salt, and boil for 1½ hours. Pour off the water, but save it for the broth.

While the beans are boiling, prepare and rinse the vegetables. Peel and finely chop them. Stir all the ingredients, except the pork, butter, and watercress into the bean stew. Boil the soup over low heat for about 20 minutes. Stir the soup vigorously so that the beans break up. If you use a blender, the bean pieces will become too small.

Cut the pork into strips and brown them in the butter. Serve the soup hot, garnished with the pork and the watercress.

Cabbage Soup

Yield: 4 to 6 servings

1 small green cabbage, sliced
2 slices fat bacon
1 large onion, chopped
2 small leeks, white part only, sliced
2 carrots, sliced
1 potato, sliced
1 tablespoon flour
4 cups beef stock
2 tablespoons parsley, chopped
1 bay leaf
Salt and pepper
Pinch nutmeg
2 teaspoons of chopped dill or 1 teaspoon dill seeds
3-4 frankfurters

Slice and wash the green cabbage, put into a pan of boiling salted water, and cook for 5 minutes. Then drain and rinse under cold water. Meanwhile, chop the bacon and heat over gentle heat until the fat runs. Then add the onion, leeks, carrots, and potato, and stir over heat for a few minutes. Sprinkle in flour and blend well before adding stock. Add parsley, bay leaf, salt, and pepper. Bring to a boil. Then reduce heat and simmer for 10 minutes before adding cabbage. Cook for 20 minutes more, or until the vegetables are tender but not mushy.

Adjust seasoning and add nutmeg and chopped dill, or a few dill seeds. Remove bay leaf. For garnish, fry frankfurters and cut in slices, putting a few slices into each serving.

Cream of Carrot Soup

Yield: 4 to 6 servings

4 tablespoons butter
1½ cups young carrots, sliced
1 large onion, finely sliced
½ clove garlic, crushed
2 tablespoons rice

3 or 4 sprigs parsley (or 1 tablespoon dried parsley)
Thinly peeled rind from ½ orange
4 cups chicken stock
¼ teaspoon sugar
Salt and pepper
Juice of ½ orange
¼ cup cream
2 egg yolks
Finely grated rind of ½ orange
2 teaspoons chopped parsley

Melt butter. Add vegetables, garlic, and rice; mix well over gentle heat 5 minutes without browning. Add parsley, peeled orange rind, stock, sugar, and seasonings; bring to boil. Lower heat; simmer 30 to 40 minutes, until vegetables are tender.

Put into electric blender or food processor and blend until smooth, or put through food mill. Return to pot; reheat, adding orange juice. If not thick enough, add cream and egg yolks: Mix eggs yolks and cream well; add few spoons hot soup. Strain back into soup; stir constantly. Reheat soup without allowing to boil. Serve in soup cups; sprinkle with grated orange rind and parsley.

Cucumber Soup

Yield: 10 to 12 servings

2 quarts chicken broth
2 tablespoons chicken fat or butter
4 cucumbers
1 onion
¼ cup flour
Water
1 quart half and half or light cream
Dillweed, fresh or dried
Salt to taste

Peel cucumbers and onion. Chop and sauté in chicken fat or butter over medium heat for a few minutes. Purée in food processor. Add purée to heated chicken broth and cook over a medium heat for 15 minutes.

Make a paste of flour and water and slowly stir into slightly heated cream. Gradually stir cream mixture into broth. Simmer until thickened. Season to taste. Transfer to a heated tureen and garnish with minced dillweed or chill thoroughly in the freezer (do not freeze) and transfer to a chilled tureen and garnish.

Brown Bean Soup

Corn Soup

Yield: 4 servings

6 ears corn
2 cups water
2 cups milk
Butter
½ teaspoon salt
⅛ teaspoon pepper

Cut the corn from the cob. Boil it in the water for a few minutes until tender. Add the milk and bring it to a boil; then simmer for 10 minutes. Add a large lump of butter and salt and pepper.

Corn Chowder

Yield: 4 to 6 servings

3 slices bacon, chopped
3 tablespoons onion, chopped
1¼ cups potatoes, peeled and diced
1 cup water
2 cups cream-style corn
3 cups milk
½ teaspoon salt

Cook bacon in heavy pot until crisp. Remove from pan; save for later use.

Lightly brown onion in bacon fat. Add potatoes and water; boil gently 10 minutes. Add corn; cook 10 minutes longer. Stir in milk, salt, and bacon. Heat until just hot. Serve at once.

Portuguese Cucumber Soup

Yield: 6 servings

3 large cucumbers
4 tomatoes, skinned
1 small red sweet pepper
1 small green sweet pepper
1 clove garlic, pressed
2 tablespoons onion, finely chopped
5 cups chicken stock, clarified
½ teaspoon salt
1 tablespoon fresh lemon juice
½ cup dry white wine

Peel the cucumbers and remove the seeds, then grate the pulp coarsely. Place in a large glass bowl. Chop the tomatoes and add to the bowl. Remove the seeds and membranes from the peppers and chop coarsely. Add to the bowl. Add the remaining ingredients and mix. Chill before serving.

Creamy Squash and Corn Soup

Yield: 4 to 6 servings

2 cups yellow squash, grated
2 cups fresh corn
2 cups boiling water
1 cup onion, chopped
½ cup green pepper, chopped
6 tablespoons butter or margarine
5 cups milk
1 tablespoon salt
¼ teaspoon pepper

Place squash and corn in boiling water. Simmer, covered, until tender. Meanwhile, cook onion and green pepper in butter until tender. Stir in flour and milk, and stir until thickened. Add squash mixture along with seasonings. Heat thoroughly.

Carrot Soup with Peanut Butter

Yield: 4 servings

3 cups chicken stock
1 small onion, chopped
4 carrots, peeled and sliced
⅛ teaspoon nutmeg
2 tablespoons peanut butter

Soup with Red and Green Lentils

1 tablespoon Worcestershire sauce
1 clove garlic, minced
Dash Tabasco sauce

Simmer all ingredients together until tender, about 15 minutes. Remove half of carrots. Purée rest of ingredients. Add reserved carrots; reheat before serving. Garnish with chopped peanuts, apples, and green onions.

Hominy Soup

Yield: 8 to 10 servings

3 pigs feet, split, or 2 large fresh pork hocks
1 stewing chicken (about 4 pounds), cut up
1 pound lean pork (Boston butt), cut up
2 medium onions, finely chopped
2 cloves garlic, chopped
3 quarts water
1 tablespoon salt
4 red chili pods
1 29-ounce can white hominy, drained
1 cup radishes, sliced
1 cup lettuce, shredded
½ cup green onions, sliced
½ cup Jack cheese, shredded

In large kettle, combine pigs feet, chicken, pork, onions, garlic, water, salt, and chili pods; bring to boil. Reduce heat to low; cook 2 hours. Add hominy; cook until meat starts to fall off bone (3 to 3½ hours total cooking time).

Remove meat from broth; cool meat and broth in refrigerator several hours or overnight. Discard chili pods; remove meat from bones. Skim fat from surface of broth.

At serving time, add meat to broth; heat. Serve hot in soup bowls, with hot tortillas. Pass garnishes in separate bowls, so each diner can garnish his plate to his own taste.

Cream of Lettuce Soup

Yield: 8 servings

8 large outer iceberg lettuce leaves
1 10-ounce package frozen peas
1 teaspoon dried mint flakes
4 scallions, chopped
3 13¾-ounce cans chicken broth
½ teaspoon salt
1 teaspoon sugar
1 cup half-and-half

Arrange lettuce leaves in bottom of a soup pot or Dutch oven. Add peas, mint, scallions, chicken broth, salt, and sugar. Bring to a boil, cover, and simmer over medium heat for 15 minutes. Purée in blender or processor; cool and refrigerate at least 6 hours or overnight. Add cream, mix well, and serve cold.

Lentil Soup with Frankfurters

Yield: 4 servings

1 cup dried, quick-cooking lentils
6 cups water
2 slices lean bacon, diced
1 leek or green onion, finely chopped
1 large carrot, finely chopped
1 celery stalk, chopped
1 onion, finely chopped
1 tablespoon vegetable oil
2 tablespoons flour
1 tablespoon vinegar
4 frankfurters, thickly sliced
1 tablespoon catsup
1 teaspoon salt
¼ teaspoon black pepper

Wash the lentils thoroughly. In a 2½ quart saucepan, bring 6 cups of water to a boil. Add the lentils, bacon, leek or green onion, carrot, and celery. Simmer, partially covered, for 30 to 40 minutes.

Meanwhile, in a frying pan, sauté chopped onion in vegetable oil until soft. Sprinkle flour over onion and stir. Lower heat, stir constantly, and cook until the flour turns light brown. Do not burn flour. Stir ½ cup of hot lentil soup into the browned flour; beat with a wire whisk until well blended. Beat in vinegar.

Add contents of frying pan to lentil pan and stir together. Cover and simmer for 30 minutes or until lentils are soft. Add the frankfurters and catsup. Cook to heat frankfurters through. Season with salt and pepper and serve hot.

Soup with Red and Green Lentils

Yield: 4 servings

1 large onion
2 to 3 cloves garlic
1 tablespoon butter
⅓ cup red lentils
⅓ cup green lentils or the same amount of white beans
6 cups meat broth
Sour cream

Chop the onion into large pieces, and crush the garlic cloves. Melt the butter in a large pot and brown the onion and garlic.

Stir in the lentils and the broth. Let the soup simmer over low heat for 20 to 30 minutes, or until the lentils feel soft. Serve with a dab of sour cream in the soup.

Leek Soup

Yield: 6 servings

5 large boiling potatoes
10 cups water
1 teaspoon salt
5 medium-sized leeks
1 small onion, finely chopped
4 tablespoons butter or margarine
2 tablespoons flour
¾ cup half-and-half or evaporated milk
⅛ teaspoon pepper
2 egg yolks
Optional garnishes (bacon bits, minced parsley, grated cheese)

Peel and cut up potatoes. Boil in salted water about 10 minutes. Wash the leeks thoroughly and finely chop only the white portion.

Sauté leeks and onion slowly in hot butter or margarine until light golden brown. Sprinkle with flour and stir until flour is absorbed. Add enough of the potato cooking water to make a thin sauce, then turn sauce back into potatoes, stirring until well blended. Continue cooking until potatoes are soft enough to be puréed in a blender or food processor.

Return potatoes to soup pot and simmer about 5 minutes. Stir in cream or evaporated milk. Season and heat to boiling point. Beat egg yolks until frothy and spoon a little into each soup bowl. Ladle in hot soup and stir to blend in yolk. Sprinkle with garnish of your choice. Serve hot.

Fresh Mushroom Soup

Yield: 6 servings

1 pound fresh mushrooms
2 tablespoons vegetable oil
2 scallions or shallots, minced
4 cups chicken broth or bouillon
¼ teaspoon salt
½ teaspoon lemon juice
1 lemon, sliced

Wash mushrooms; pat dry with paper towels. Finely chop mushrooms, or chop in blender or processor.

Heat oil in frying pan and sauté scallions about 3 minutes or until wilted. Add mushrooms; cook stirring occasionally, about 5 minutes. Add broth, salt, lemon juice. Bring to a boil. Reduce heat to a simmer and cook uncovered 30 minutes.

Blend finished soup in blender or processor or press through a coarse sieve, pressing hard on the mushrooms to extract all liquid. Reheat before serving. Garnish with lemon slices.

Chased Mushroom Cap Soup

Yield: 4 servings

½ pound large, white, firm, fresh mushrooms
½ lemon
1½ teaspoons lemon juice
2 tablespoons butter
2 to 3 tablespoons onion, minced
2½ tablespoons cooking flour
2 cups vegetable broth
2 to 3 tablespoons Port wine
¾ cup heavy cream or crème fraîche
About ½ teaspoon salt
Dash cayenne pepper or freshly ground white pepper

Choose the 12 largest, whitest, and firmest of the mushrooms. Firmly hold the mushroom at the base of the stem. Hold on to the blade of a sharp paring knife with 4 fingers held close together under the blade and your thumb on top of the blade.

Place the middle part of the blade of the knife against the top of the mushroom cap. Let the top of your fingertips rest against the cap. Move the edge of the knife in a cutting half-arch movement toward yourself. The hold of your fingertips on the knife decides how deep a cut will be made. Continue cutting all around the mushroom.

Make sure that each cut starts at the top in the middle of the mushroom cap. Then cut off the stem of the mushroom and make a star on the top by pressing down with the tip of the knife so that you create 5 star points. Boil the caps in water so that they are just covered, together with the juice of ½ lemon.

Finely chop the remaining mushrooms and sprinkle the lemon juice over them. Sauté the chopped mushrooms together with the onion for a few minutes in the butter. Sprinkle with flour and add the broth, a little at a time. Add the cream and wine and simmer the soup so that it thickens, about 10 minutes.

Season the soup with salt and a dash of pepper. Serve in hot dishes with the chased mushrooms as garnish. The caps may be refrigerated for several days in their own juice or may even be frozen.

Charleston Okra Soup

Yield: 6 servings

1 large beef soup bone
3 quarts water
3 pounds fresh okra, finely chopped
1 piece breakfast bacon
8 large fresh tomatoes, peeled
2 medium onions, chopped
1 bay leaf
Salt and pepper, to taste

Wash meat and cook in water for 2 hours. Add okra, bacon, tomatoes, onions, bay leaf and salt and pepper to taste. Let cook another 2 hours. Add more water if needed. Remove bay leaf.

Onion Soup

Yield: 6 to 8 servings

1½ pounds or about 5 cups yellow onions, thinly sliced
3 tablespoons butter
1 tablespoon oil
1 teaspoon salt
¼ teaspoon sugar
3 tablespoons flour
2 quarts boiling beef bouillon
½ cup dry white wine
6-8 thick slices French bread
Parmesan cheese to taste
6-8 slices Swiss cheese

Cook the onions slowly with the butter and oil in a heavy-bottomed, 4-quart, covered saucepan for 15 minutes. Uncover, raise heat to moderate, and stir in the salt and sugar. Cook for 30 to 40 minutes, stirring frequently until onions have turned an even, deep golden brown. Sprinkle in the flour and stir for 3 minutes. Turn off heat; blend in the boiling bouillon. Add the wine and season to taste.

Simmer partially covered 30 to 40 minutes more, skimming occasionally. Set aside uncovered until ready to serve, then reheat to the simmer.

Spoon soup into ovenproof bowls. Place bread on top, then Parmesan cheese, and top with a slice of Swiss cheese. Place in oven or broiler until cheese melts and becomes bubbly.

Parsley Soup

Yield: 4 servings

1 tablespoon butter
2 tablespoons flour
1 teaspoon salt
2 cups milk
1 medium-sized onion, finely chopped
½ cup cream
2 egg yolks
½ cup parsley, finely chopped

Melt butter, add flour and salt gradually, then milk and onion. Cook until it starts to thicken, stirring constantly. Add ½ cup of cream which has been mixed with the egg yolks. Cook 1 or 2 minutes longer. Remove from heat. Add parsley and serve hot. To serve cold, refrigerate after cooling. This is good, nourishing soup for hot or cold weather.

Chased Mushroom Cap Soup

Fresh Pea Soup

Yield: 6 servings

4 small onions, finely chopped
½ cup butter
2 large potatoes, cut into cubes
2 pounds fresh green peas, shelled
3 teaspoons salt
2 cups milk
½ teaspoon pepper
½ cup half-and-half

Sauté the onions in ¼ cup of the butter in a saucepan over medium heat until tender, but not brown. Add the potatoes and 1 cup of boiling water and cover. Cook until the potatoes are tender.

Combine the peas, 1 teaspoon of the salt, and 1 cup of boiling water in a saucepan and cover. Cook over medium heat until the peas are tender.

Place the potato mixture and the peas in a blender container and process until puréed. Pour the mixture into a large saucepan, then stir in the milk, remaining salt, pepper, remaining butter, and cream until blended. Place over low heat until heated through, adding more milk if soup is too thick.

One-Hour Black-Eyed Pea Soup

Yield: 4 to 6 servings

1 10-ounce package frozen black-eyed peas
1 cup ham, diced
1 large onion, diced
Dash of hot red pepper
½ teaspoon salt
4 cups water
¼ cup dry red wine (optional)

Combine all ingredients in large saucepan in order given. Bring to boil, then reduce to simmer. Cook about 1 hour or until peas are tender. Add water if necessary.

Cream of Peanut Soup

Yield: 10 to 12 servings

1 medium onion, chopped
2 celery ribs, chopped
4 tablespoons butter
3 tablespoons flour
2 quarts chicken stock
2 cups peanut butter
1¾ cups light cream
Chopped peanuts

Stir onion and celery in large pot with butter until vegetables are soft but not brown. Blend in flour; stir until smooth. Add chicken stock, still stirring; bring to boil. (The onion and celery may be strained out at this point, but it's not necessary.) Remove from heat. Add peanut butter and cream; blend together until smooth. Return to low heat (do not boil) 5 minutes.

Serve soup topped with chopped peanuts.

Potato Soup

Yield: 10 servings

7 medium-sized potatoes
3 medium-sized onions
3 tablespoons butter
4 cups milk
6 cups chicken stock
1 tablespoon salt
¼ teaspoon white pepper
5 strips bacon
1 cup light sweet cream
¼ cup chopped chives

Peel and slice the potatoes and onions. Melt butter in a large saucepan. Add the sliced onions and cook over low heat until tender but not brown.

Add the potatoes, milk, chicken stock, salt, and pepper. Cover pan and cook over a very low heat for 1 hour.

Cut the bacon into small pieces and sauté until crisp. Remove from pan, drain, and set bacon bits aside. After the soup has cooked for 1 hour, put in blender at high speed. Return it to a saucepan. Add cream and cook slowly until the soup is just hot but not at the boiling point. Garnish with bacon bits and chives.

Green Potato Soup

Yield: 4 servings

4 to 5 potatoes
1 onion
4 cups chicken broth
1 teaspoon salt
Black pepper
1 10-ounce package frozen chopped kale

Peel the potatoes and the onion; cut them into pieces. Bring the broth to a boil. Add the potatoes and onion. Cover and boil for about 25 minutes, or until the potatoes become mushy.

Add the kale. When it is tender, beat the mixture with a whisk so that the potatoes get mashed. Season and serve.

Sauerkraut and Hot-Dog Soup

Yield: 6 to 8 servings

1 pound lean beef
6 ounces lean slab bacon
6 cups water
2 medium onions, chopped
1 leek or 2 scallions, sliced
1 clove garlic
2 carrots, cubed
3 stalks celery, cubed
1 pound sauerkraut, rinsed well in cold water and
 drained
Salt and pepper to taste
4 hot dogs, thickly sliced
Fresh dill leaves, chopped
Sour cream

Place beef, bacon, water, onions, garlic, carrots, celery, sauerkraut, and seasonings in soup pot. Cover and cook about 2 to 3 hours.

Remove bacon and beef. Cube and return to soup. Add hot dogs and continue cooking until heated through. Serve soup hot, garnished with dill leaves and a dollop of sour cream.

Spinach Soup

Yield: 4 to 6 servings

2 pounds fresh spinach, cooked and chopped, or
 2 10-ounce packages frozen chopped spinach
1 tablespoon lemon juice
3 tablespoons butter
3 tablespoons flour
2 cups milk
¼ cup Romano cheese, freshly grated
⅛ teaspoon nutmeg
Salt and pepper to taste

Cook the spinach according to package directions. Place the spinach and lemon juice in a blender container and process until puréed. Melt the butter in a large saucepan, then stir in the flour to make a smooth paste. Add the milk gradually, stirring constantly, and cook until thickened.

Stir in the cheese, nutmeg, and spinach. Cook until heated through. Season with salt and pepper. More milk may be added if a thinner soup is desired.

Fresh Tomato Soup

Yield: 6 servings

6 medium-sized tomatoes
1 onion, chopped
1 stalk celery, chopped
2 cups chicken broth
1 tablespoon tomato paste
½ teaspoon dried basil
¼ teaspoon freshly ground pepper
½ teaspoon salt
½ cup sour cream

Cut tomatoes into wedges; place in 1½-quart saucepan with all ingredients except sour cream. Simmer, uncovered, 30 minutes. Strain to remove tomato skins and seeds. Adjust seasonings. Garnish with spoonfuls of sour cream.

Tomato-Barley Soup

Yield: 6 to 8 servings

2-4 knuckle or marrow bones
1 cup barley, rinsed
1 carrot, cut up length-wise
4 quarts water
2 stalks celery, cut up
1 onion, whole
1-pound can tomatoes, cut up
Salt to taste

Put bones in cold water in large pot and bring to boil. Skim off fat. Reduce heat to simmer and add remaining ingredients. Cover and simmer 1½ hours.

Parsnip Soup

Yield: 4 servings

3 tablespoons butter
1 onion, chopped
1½ cups parsnips, peeled and finely sliced
1 tablespoon flour
3 to 4 cups vegetable stock
3 to 4 sprigs parsley
1 small bay leaf
Pinch thyme
Pinch nutmeg
Salt and pepper
½ cup cream
1 tablespoon chopped parsley
Croutons

Melt butter; cook onion and parsnips gently 5 to 6 minutes with a lid on pan, to soften without browning. Remove from heat; sprinkle in flour. Then blend well. Pour on stock; mix well; add herbs and seasonings. Bring to a boil; simmer 20 to 30 minutes, until parsnips are tender. Remove bay leaf.

Put soup into electric blender or food processor and blend until smooth or put through food mill. Return soup to pan; adjust seasoning. Reheat, adding cream. Serve in soup cups sprinkled with chopped parsley and croutons.

Potato, Sausage, and Cheese Soup

Yield: 6 servings

4 medium potatoes, peeled and halved
1 medium onion, sliced
4 cups boiling water
⅓ cup summer sausage, diced
½ teaspoon thyme leaves
½ teaspoon marjoram leaves
1½ teaspoons salt
Pepper
2 tablespoons butter or margarine
½ cup sharp cheese, grated

Place potatoes and onion in 2 cups boiling water and cook until tender. Do not drain.

Mash potatoes in the pot. Add sausage, thyme, marjoram, salt, pepper, butter, and remaining boiling water. Simmer 10 minutes. Add grated cheese just before serving.

Spicy Tomato Soup

Yield: 6 to 8 servings

2 tablespoons butter
2 medium onions, diced
4 cups fresh chicken stock, or 1½ tablespoons chicken stock base in 4 cups water
2 1-pound cans tomatoes, crushed
¼ cup fresh parsley, chopped, or 2 tablespoons dried
2 bay leaves
1 teaspoon basil
1 teaspoon paprika
1 teaspoon sugar
¼ teaspoon ground cloves
¼ teaspoon nutmeg
¼ teaspoon pepper
Salt to taste
½ cup heavy cream, whipped (optional)

Sauté onion in butter in large, heavy saucepan over low heat for 5 minutes, or until onion is translucent.

Add remaining ingredients except salt. Cover and simmer at least 30 minutes. Discard bay leaves. Add salt, if desired. Garnish each serving with a dollop of whipped cream, if desired.

Minted Zucchini Soup

Yield: 6 servings

6 small zucchini, trimmed and cut in chunks
1 large onion, chopped
1 teaspoon curry powder
½ teaspoon ground ginger
½ teaspoon dry mustard
2 cups chicken broth
3 tablespoons uncooked rice
¾ cup skim milk
¼ cup plain yogurt
1 cup dry white wine
Salt and freshly ground pepper to taste
¼ cup fresh basil leaves
3 or 4 fresh mint leaves

Combine zucchini, onion, and dry spices in saucepan. Add chicken broth and rice and bring to boil. Cover and simmer about 45 minutes.

Purée mixture in a blender or food processor. Add milk, yogurt, wine, salt, pepper, and herbs and blend until smooth.

Garnish with a sprig of mint. Serve hot or cold.

Country-Style Chicken Soup

Yield: 6 servings

1 small stewing chicken or 6 backs and necks
8 cups water
1 cup celery, chopped
1 cup carrots, sliced
2 medium onions, sliced
1 small bay leaf or ½ teaspoon dill seeds
1 large potato, diced
2 teaspoons salt
¼ teaspoon pepper

Simmer chicken in water 1 to 1½ hours. Add

Fish Soup

celery, carrots, onions, and bay leaf or dill. Simmer thirty minutes. Remove meat from the frame of the chicken. Allow meat and vegetables to stand in broth overnight.

Skim off excess fat; add potato and salt and pepper. Simmer 30 minutes longer. You can use left-over chicken to make this soup and omit letting it stand overnight.

Cream of Chicken Soup

Yield: 8 servings

4 cups chicken stock
2 cups celery, finely chopped
1 small clove garlic, pressed
¾ cup half-and-half
Salt and freshly ground white pepper to taste
2 cups cooked chicken, minced
½ cup Parmesan cheese, finely grated

Pour the stock into a large saucepan and bring to a boil. Add the celery and garlic and simmer for 10 minutes or until tender. Pour into a blender or food processor container and process until puréed, then return to the saucepan.

Add the cream, salt, and pepper, and bring just to the boiling point. Stir in the chicken and cheese and heat, stirring, until the cheese is melted and the soup is well blended. Serve in soup bowls. A dash of whipping cream may be poured into the center of each serving, if desired.

Chicken Barley Soup

Yield: 4 servings

2 quarts water
2 pounds chicken necks, skinned
16-ounce can sliced tomatoes
1 cup celery, sliced
1 cup onions, sliced
1 cup carrots, sliced
¼ cup fresh parsley, chopped
6 tablespoons medium barley
1 bay leaf
¼ teaspoon dried marjoram

Heat water to boiling; add chicken necks. When boiling again, skim foam from surface. Add remaining ingredients. Cover and simmer 50 to 60 minutes.

Remove chicken necks and chill quickly. When cool enough to handle, remove meat from bones; return the meat to the soup. Before serving, skim fat from surface of soup and remove bay leaf.

Chicken and Ham Soup

Yield: 4 to 6 servings

4 to 5 cups clear chicken stock
1 glass dry white wine
2 slices mild ham, shredded
½ cup fresh peas, lightly cooked
1 teaspoon fresh tarragon, chopped (or ½ teaspoon dried)
1 tablespoon parsley, chopped
1 to 1½ tablespoons gelatin for cold soup

If serving hot, heat clear chicken stock, adding at last minute a glass of white wine, shredded ham which has had all fat removed, peas, and herbs. Sprinkle with chopped parsley.

If serving cold and using chicken stock that is not already jellied, put gelatin to soak in ½ cup of stock. When it has swollen, heat gently; add to heated stock. Skim off any grease carefully; add white wine; let cool in a bowl. When it is on the point of setting, add shreds of ham and peas; spoon into soup cups. Chill well; serve garnished with chopped parsley or watercress leaves.

Creamed Turkey Soup

Yield: 4 to 6 servings

1 cooked turkey carcass
2 onions, sliced
1 carrot, sliced
1 tomato, chopped
2 stalks celery, chopped
2 sprigs parsley, chopped
1 bay leaf or bayberry leaf
1 teaspoon Worcestershire sauce (optional)
1 teaspoon salt
½ teaspoon pepper
2 tablespoons butter
2 tablespoons flour
1 cup heavy cream or evaporated milk

Put broken-up carcass, vegetables, and seasonings into a large pot or kettle with enough water to cover; bring to a boil. Cover and simmer 2 hours. Strain, and skim the fat.

In a separate pan or skillet, melt the butter. Stir in the flour until brown, then add a little of the soup, and stir until smooth. Add to the pot and cook until thickened. Add the cream, stir, and serve.

Clam Bisque

Yield: 6 to 8 servings

1 can (10½ ounces) clams
½ cup celery, chopped
¼ cup onion, chopped
4 tablespoons butter
3 tablespoons flour
1 teaspoon salt
Dash white pepper
2 cups milk
2 cups light cream
2 teaspoons lemon juice or 1 teaspoon curry powder

Drain clams, rinse, and chop. Sauté celery and onion in butter until tender, but not brown. Blend in flour, salt, and pepper. Add milk and light cream, stirring constantly. Cook and stir until sauce is smooth and has thickened.

Add chopped clams and lemon juice or curry powder and heat.

Cream of Crab Soup

Yield: 6 servings

1 quart half-and-half or light cream
1 quart milk
½ stick butter
1 tablespoon parsley
1 pound backfin crabmeat, shells removed
2 teaspoons seafood seasoning

Combine all ingredients and heat thoroughly. Do not boil!

Maryland Crab Soup

Yield: 4 to 6 servings

6 cups strong beef stock
3 cups mixed vegetables, fresh, leftover, or frozen (include chopped onions and celery, diced carrots, peas, lima beans, cut string beans, corn, okra, and tomatoes; not squash, cabbage or potatoes)
Seafood seasoning to taste
1 pound crabmeat (claw or white meat)
Claws and pieces of whole crab if available (either raw or cooked)

Heat stock in a large soup pot. Add vegetables and seasoning; simmer 1 hour. Add crabmeat and crab claws and pieces (if available) 30 minutes before serving. Simmer gently, to heat through and allow flavors to blend.

Serve hot in large soup bowls, with bread and butter or hard crusty rolls and butter as accompaniment.

Turkey Corn Soup

Yield:

10-to-12 pound roast turkey carcass (broken up), drumstick and wing bones
2 quarts water
1 medium onion, halved
2 inner ribs celery with leaves
1 large carrot, pared
2 teaspoons salt
4 peppercorns
1 small bay leaf
8¾-ounce can cream-style golden corn
12-ounce can shoe-peg whole kernel white corn, undrained
Diced remnants of roast turkey

In a large saucepot, bring all the ingredients except the corn and turkey remnants to a boil; cover and let bubble gently for 2 hours. Strain and reserve carrot. Dice carrot and reheat with broth, corn, and diced turkey.

Quick Mussel Soup

Yield: 4 servings

1 onion, chopped
1 leek, finely sliced
1 celery stalk, finely chopped
2 tablespoons butter
3 cloves garlic, crushed
1 teaspoon sage and salt mixture
⅓ cup snipped parsley
20 fresh mussels, or 1 large can
Liquid from the mussels
1¼ cups white wine
2 cups fish broth
1 tablespoon butter
1 tablespoon flour
⅔ pound salmon

Brown the onion, leek, and celery in butter in a pot; then add the garlic, sage, and parsley. Dilute with the mussel juice, wine, and broth, and bring to a boil.

Remove from the heat and make a ball from an equal amount of butter and flour. Add this in small bits to the soup and stir until it becomes smooth. Heat the soup again. Add the mussels and pieces of salmon, and serve immediately.

New England Clam Chowder

Yield: 6 to 8 servings

1 quart shucked clams with liquid
3 slices salt pork, diced
2 small onions, minced
2 medium potatoes, diced
1 bay leaf

1 cup water
3 cups milk, scalded
1½ cups half-and-half
¼ cup butter
Salt and freshly ground pepper

Drain clams, reserving liquor, then chop coarsely. Fry salt pork slowly in a kettle until all fat is rendered. Add onions; sauté until golden. Add potatoes, bay leaf, and water, then simmer until potatoes are tender.

Strain the reserved clam liquor, then stir into potato mixture with milk, half-and-half, butter, and chopped clams. Add seasonings, then simmer 15 minutes.

Dilled Crab Chowder

Yield: 10 servings

1 large onion, minced
4 stalks celery, minced
8 tablespoons butter
1 pound crabmeat
5 cups milk
1 cup half-and-half or light cream
2 cans cream of potato soup
1 16½-ounce can cream-style corn
3 tablespoons pimiento, diced
½ teaspoon salt
1 teaspoon dried dill weed
2 bay leaves
½ cup dry vermouth

In large pot, cook onion and celery in butter until soft. Add crab; stir and add milk, half-and-half, potato soup, corn, pimiento, salt, dill, and bay leaves. Mix well and heat over medium heat for 20 minutes — do not boil. Add vermouth and heat for 5 additional minutes.

Soup can be reheated and stores well in refrigerator 4 to 5 days.

Fish Soup

Yield: 3 to 4 servings

⅔ pound sole or cod fillets
1 tablespoon butter
2 tablespoons flour
4 cups fish stock
2 leeks (white part only)
About 1 teaspoon salt
¼ teaspoon white pepper
About 1 teaspoon ground fennel seed

Rinse the fish fillets and cut them into pieces.
Heat the butter and flour in a pot. Add the fish stock and bring to a boil, stirring constantly. Shred the leeks and add them to the soup. Season with

salt, pepper, and fennel. Add the fish and let it simmer 3 to 5 minutes, a little longer if the fish is frozen. Test for doneness by pricking it—it is done when soft. Fish should not cook longer than necessary. Serve the soup with French bread.

Fine Fish Soup

Yield: 4 servings

1 2- to 3-pound whole white fish
  (cod, haddock, hake)
1 to 2 leeks
1½ quarts water
1 tablespoon salt
½ teaspoon white peppercorns
2 bay leaves
1 sprig thyme
Several sprigs parsley
2 potatoes, sliced
3 tomatoes, peeled and cut in pieces
1 to 2 cloves garlic, crushed
2 tablespoons butter or margarine
½ to ¾ pound raw shrimp, shelled and deveined
½ cup white wine
Parsley and dill

Fillet the fish or ask your fish dealer to do so, saving the head, skin, and bones. Put all the trimmings in a pot. Wash the leeks carefully and put the green part in the pot. Add water, salt, peppercorns, bay leaves, thyme, and parsley. Let it boil, covered, for 20 minutes.

Sauté the potatoes, tomatoes, and garlic in the butter or margarine for 5 minutes over low heat. Add the fish broth, which has been strained. Cut the fish fillets in pieces and let them simmer with the shrimp and white wine for about 5 minutes. Sprinkle with parsley and dill and serve with crisp, warm, white bread.

Red Fish Soup

Yield: 4 servings

1 onion, chopped
1 green pepper, chopped
¼ cup celeriac (celery root), finely shredded
1 large clove garlic, crushed
2 tablespoons oil
2 cans crushed tomatoes
1 tablespoon tomato paste
½ teaspoon basil, crumbled
1 bay leaf
½ teaspoon salt
⅛ teaspoon black pepper
⅔ cup dry white wine

Red Fish Soup

⅔ pound fillets or cod, cut into pieces
12 clams with shells
¼ pound shelled raw shrimp
Snipped parsley for garnish

Sauté the onion, green pepper, celeriac, and garlic in oil over low heat for 5 minutes. Add the tomatoes and tomato paste. Stir in the seasonings. Let the tomato mixture simmer covered over low heat for about 30 minutes. Stir occasionally.

Add the wine, the fish, and the clams and simmer slowly for 7 minutes. Add the shrimp. Simmer for another 5 minutes. Sprinkle with parsley and serve the soup piping hot with a coarse bread.

Note: The soup can be made even more elegantly if halibut, salmon, and/or lobster are added, all according to taste and pocketbook.

Lobster Bisque

Yield: 6 servings

1 large, freshly boiled lobster (or 2 small, preferably female, lobsters)
5 to 6 cups fish stock
1 small onion, sliced
1 carrot, sliced
2 stalks celery, sliced
1 bay leaf, 3 to 4 sprigs of parsley, tied together
Salt and pepper
5 tablespoons butter
2½ tablespoons flour
¼ teaspoon mace or nutmeg
1 cup cream
3 to 4 tablespoons sherry (or brandy)
Paprika

Split freshly boiled lobster down back with a sharp knife; remove intestine, which looks like a long black thread down center of tail. Also remove stomach sac from head and tough gills. Crack claws, remove meat, and add this to tail meat. If lobster is female and there is red coral or roe, reserve this for garnish. Also reserve greenish curd (tamale) from head.

Break up all lobster shells; put into a pan with fish stock. Add onion, carrot, celery, herbs, salt, and pepper. Cover pan; simmer 30 to 45 minutes.

Meanwhile, cut lobster meat into chunks. Pound coral roe with 2 tablespoons butter to use as garnish and to color soup. Melt 3 tablespoons butter in a pot; stir in flour until smoothly blended; cook a minute or two before adding strained lobster stock. Blend until smooth; then bring to a boil, stirring constantly. Reduce heat; simmer 4 to 5 minutes before adding lobster meat and tamale. Remove herbs. Add mace or nutmeg; adjust seasoning. Add cup of hot cream and the sherry (or brandy).

Serve in soup cups with a piece of the coral butter in each cup and sprinkle with paprika.

Mussel Soup

Yield: 4 servings

About 48 fresh or frozen mussels
1 onion
2 shallots
¾ cup dry white wine
¼ cup water
⅓ cup snipped parsley
Pinch thyme
2 tablespoons butter
Pepper
Salt
1 clove garlic to rub into the sides of the soup dish

Allow 10 to 12 mussels per person. Wash them well and place in cold water.

Mince the onion and shallots and place in a thick-bottomed pot together with the wine, water, parsley, thyme, and butter. Bring to a boil. Place the mussels in the pot and stir well; grind pepper over the pot. Cover the pot and shake well so that the mussels move around and change places with each other. Allow to boil for several minutes so that all the mussels have opened. Season the soup with salt and pepper.

Rub a garlic clove into the sides of a serving dish. Pour the mussels and broth into the dish. Remember, however, that there is sand at the bottom of the pot, so do not pour in all the broth. Sprinkle with snipped parsley and serve immediately.

Variations: Skip the parsley and use a smaller amount of wine. Instead, pour in heavy cream, ¾ cup for 4 servings. Or, mix in 4 slices grated white bread before placing the mussels in the broth. Simmer for about 10 minutes and then add the mussels. The bread will somewhat thicken the soup.

Cream of Mussel and Saffron Soup

Yield: 5 servings

1 dozen mussels
½ cup white wine
2 to 3 cloves garlic
Pinch oregano
½ medium potato, diced
1 leek, diced
1 medium onion, diced
1 stalk celery, diced
3 tablespoons butter
1 quart fish stock
Pinch saffron
2 cups heavy cream
Saffron strands

Wash mussels, then steam them in white wine, garlic, and oregano. Pick mussels out of shell. Reserve liquor after straining through cheesecloth. Chop mussels very fine.

Lightly sauté potato, leek, onion, and celery in butter. Add fish stock, chopped mussels, and mussel juice. Cook until vegetables are very tender. Pass through a food mill.

Put puréed liquid back in pot. Add saffron and heavy cream and boil to reduce by about a quarter. If necessary, adjust thickness and seasoning. Strain through fine strainer. Garnish with saffron strands.

Bouillabaisse

Put the frying pan with the oyster juice on top of the stove and bring to a boil. By this time, the water in the bottom part of the double boiler should be boiling. Put the top section on the double boiler, then pour in the milk, cream, salt, and pepper.

Next, add the strained oysters, celery salt, and paprika to the liquid in the frying pan. Turn the heat down to medium and cook until the edges of the oysters start to curl (about 3 minutes).

Pour the oysters and juice into the cream and milk mixture in the top part of the double boiler. Put the lid on and cook for 3 minutes until the stew is hot. Do not let it come to a boil. Add the Tabasco sauce and butter and stir.

Oyster Bisque

Yield: 6 to 8 servings

1 quart fresh oysters
3 cups chicken stock
1½ cups fine bread crumbs
⅓ cup onion, finely chopped
1 cup celery, finely diced
Salt and white pepper to taste
1 quart milk, scalded
2 tablespoons butter
¼ cup sherry

Drain the oysters and reserve the liquid. Chop the oysters. Pour the chicken stock in a soup kettle. Add the reserved oyster liquid, bread crumbs, onion, celery, salt, and pepper. Boil slowly, stirring frequently, for about 30 minutes.

Spin in the blender container or food processor until onion and celery are puréed, then return to the soup kettle. Add the oysters and heat thoroughly, but do not overcook. Stir in the milk, butter, and sherry and heat through. Serve immediately.

Oyster Stew

Yield: 4 servings

2 cups water
1 pint shucked raw oysters
1 cup milk
1 cup light cream
½ teaspoon salt
¼ teaspoon ground black pepper
½ teaspoon celery salt
¼ teaspoon paprika
¼ teaspoon Tabasco sauce
4 teaspoons butter or margarine

Oyster stew is best when cooked over water in a double boiler, so it does not boil or overcook. Fill the bottom part of the double boiler with 2 cups of water and bring it to a boil.

Meanwhile, hold a strainer over a cold 8-inch iron frying pan and pour the oysters into the strainer, so the liquid falls into the pan. After they have drained, put the strainer of oysters over a medium-sized mixing bowl.

Chilled Shrimp Soup

Yield: 6 servings

1 medium cucumber
¾ pound shrimp, cooked and chopped
1 tablespoon chopped fresh dill or 1 teaspoon dried
1 tablespoon prepared mustard
1 teaspoon salt
1 teaspoon sugar
4 cups buttermilk

Peel cucumber and slice in half lengthwise; scoop out seeds and discard. Finely dice the cucumber. Combine all the ingredients and chill for 2 hours or longer.

Shrimp Soup

Yield: 4 servings

1 pound raw shrimp, shelled, deveined
Cayenne pepper to taste
Salt to taste
2 tablespoons flour
2 tablespoons oil
1 large onion, finely chopped
1 clove garlic, finely chopped
2 cups water
1 cup cooked rice
1 tablespoon fresh parsley, chopped

Sprinkle raw shrimp generously with cayenne and salt; set aside. Stir flour and oil together over medium flame until dark. Brown onion and garlic in flour-oil mixture. Add shrimp. When shrimp are pink, add water. Cover; simmer about 45 minutes.

Five minutes before serving, add rice and parsley. Add additional seasonings if needed.

Bouillabaisse

Yield: 6 to 8 servings

fish broth
2 cups dry white wine
2 cups fish stock
Shells from about 25 shrimp
1 sprig herbs and spices

the fish
3 to 4 pounds whole fish

remaining ingredients
1 carrot, peeled
1 large onion, minced
1 leek, sliced (white part only)
2 tablespoons olive oil
1 package saffron
1 teaspoon thyme
2 cloves garlic
1 cup white Loire wine, such as Muscadet
3 whole, skinned tomatoes, cut into small pieces
2 pounds fresh clams
25 shelled shrimp
1 cup cream, firmly whipped
Finely chopped parsley

rouille
6 to 8 slices of newly toasted white bread
⅓ cup mayonnaise
1 teaspoon concentrated tomato paste
2 to 3 cloves garlic, pressed
Salt
Paprika
Pinch cayenne pepper

Ask the fish dealer to give you 1 pound of fresh fish fillet plus the heads, skin and bones of the fish.

Let broth ingredients, including the fish carcasses, come to a boil and simmer for 10 minutes while covered. Place the fillets in the broth, cooking them for 2 to 3 minutes. Remove the fillets carefully with a spoon with holes in it. Refrigerate them in a little of the broth. Strain the rest of the broth.

Sauté the carrot, onion, and leek in the oil. Mix with the saffron, thyme, and the 2 crushed garlic cloves. Cover with 1 cup white wine and let boil vigorously until only enough liquid remains to just cover the bottom of the pot. Add the tomatoes and the strained fish broth. Bring to a boil again, then add the clams. Boil vigorously for about 5 minutes, or until all of the clam shells have opened. Remove most of the clams from the shells, but leave a few shelled to use for decorating the soup.

Thicken the soup with the whipped cream and let it start to simmer before carefully adding the pieces of fish, the shrimp, and the clams with and without the shells. Bring to a boil again, and let simmer before dishing out into individual, warmed bowls and garnishing with chopped parsley.

Serve with bread toasted in oil and the rouille made in the following way: Mix mayonnaise with the other ingredients and spice to taste. Spread the red mayonnaise over the slices of hot bread. Lay them in the soup and eat with a spoon.

Sherried Seafood Bisque

Yield: 8 servings

5 cups water
5 medium-sized potatoes, peeled and diced
½ cup onion, coarsely chopped
4 teaspoons Worcestershire sauce
1 clove garlic, crushed
½ teaspoon thyme leaves
½ teaspoon salt
1 10½-ounce can minced clams
2 cups flaked, cooked fish
¼ pound medium-sized shrimp, drained
2 tablespoons dry sherry
2 egg yolks
½ cup heavy cream

In a large saucepan, bring water to boiling point. Add potatoes, onion, 2 teaspoons of the Worcestershire sauce, garlic, thyme, and salt. Reduce heat and simmer uncovered 15 to 20 minutes or until potatoes are almost soft. Add clams, fish, shrimp, sherry, and remaining 2 teaspoons Worcestershire sauce. Cook 5 minutes longer or until seafood is hot. Remove from heat. Combine egg yolks and cream; stir into fish mixture. Heat only until hot. Do not boil. Serve hot or cold. Garnish with paprika, if desired, or minced chives.

Quick Bouillabaisse

Yield: 4 servings

1 onion
2 tablespoons margarine
½ teaspoon paprika
¾ quart fish stock
1 can chopped tomatoes
Juice of ½ lemon
2 cups frozen peas
1¼ pounds cod
2 teaspoons salt
1 clove garlic
⅓ cup mayonnaise

Chop the onion and fry until transparent in margarine in a large saucepan. Dust with paprika, then add the fish stock. Bring to a boil and add the tomatoes.

Squeeze in the lemon juice and add the peas, fish, and salt. Simmer for 5 minutes, or until the fish portions are just cooked.

Meanwhile, crush the garlic and add to the mayonnaise. Serve the hot soup with a spoonful of the garlic mayonnaise and a hot, crusty bread.

Quick Bouillabaisse

Eggs and Cheese

Bacon and Egg Cake

Yield: 4 servings

½ pound bacon
6 eggs
1 tablespoon flour
½ teaspoon salt
½ cup milk or cream
3 tablespoons chives, finely cut

Cut each bacon slice in half. Fry lightly, not too crisp. Drain; set aside. Remove all but about 1 tablespoon fat from skillet.

Combine eggs, flour, and salt in a bowl. Gradually add milk. Warm fat in a skillet over moderate heat. Pour in egg mixture; turn heat to low. Do not stir — let eggs set firm. This takes about 20 minutes. When mixture is firm, remove from heat.

Arrange bacon slices and chives on top. Serve directly from the pan.

Egg and Bacon Muffin Puffs

Yield: 8 servings

1 cup mayonnaise
1 egg white, stiff-beaten
8 English muffins, split and toasted
8 hard-cooked eggs, sliced
Crisp bacon slices
Crisp pickle slices

Fold the mayonnaise into the egg white. Spread lightly on toasted muffin halves. Place a sliced egg on top of each muffin. Cover with mayonnaise mixture. Brown 1 minute under a broiler. Top with crisp bacon slices. Serve at once. Garnish with pickle slices.

Baked Eggs

Yield: 4 servings

4 eggs, separated
1 tablespoon butter
Salt and pepper
4 slices toast

Preheat the oven to 350°F and heat a baking pan. Melt the butter in the hot pan. Beat the egg whites until stiff; then arrange them on the pan in four "nests" by swirling with a spoon. Slide the egg yolks one at a time into the centers of the nests.

Place pan in oven and cook until egg whites have begun to color and the yolks are set. Season and serve on buttered toast with a little butter on top.

Eggs Benedict

Yield: 12 servings

6 English muffins, split and toasted
1 pound Canadian bacon, thinly sliced and cooked
12 poached eggs
4 egg yolks
1 cup butter, cut into bits
2 tablespoons lemon juice
¼ teaspoon salt
Dash of cayenne pepper
Dash of white pepper

On large baking sheet, cover each English muffin half with several slices of Canadian bacon and a poached egg. Place in oven to keep warm. Over very low heat, beat egg yolks constantly, until they begin to thicken slightly. Beat in butter, bit by bit.

When thick, remove from heat and stir in lemon juice, salt, and pepper. Cover poached eggs with sauce. Serve immediately.

Eggs in Bread Rings

Yield: 10 to 12 servings

12 slices bread
Butter
12 eggs
Salt
Pepper

Cut a hole in the center of each bread slice. Butter bread rims on 1 side, then toast.

In a skillet, break an egg into each toast ring; season with salt and pepper. Cook until eggs are set, 12 to 15 minutes. This goes well with coleslaw and ham.

Curry Spiced Egg

Yield: 4 servings

8 eggs
1 large onion
1 tablespoon margarine
1 tablespoon curry
1¼ cups chicken broth
½ teaspoon salt
¼ teaspoon black pepper
2½ teaspoons arrowroot flour
⅓ cup crème fraîche
Juice from ½ lemon

Hard-boil the eggs for 10 minutes. Meanwhile, peel the onion and finely chop it. Melt the margarine in a saucepan; add the curry and the onion. Cook the onion so that it slowly softens over low heat for several minutes. Add the chicken broth, salt, and pepper and simmer for about 10 minutes.

Mix the crème fraîche with the arrowroot and lemon juice and fold into the sauce. Bring to a boil quickly, then pour the sauce over the eggs, which have been shelled and cut in half. Sprinkle a little parsley on top, if desired.

Southern Cheesed Eggs with Vegetables

Yield: 5 to 6 servings

3 tablespoons oil
½ cup green pepper, minced
½ cup red pepper, minced
½ cup zucchini, minced
½ cup green onion, minced
1 cup cooked corn
½ teaspoon salt
½ teaspoon dillweed
8 eggs, beaten
1 cup sharp Cheddar cheese, grated
Pepper

Heat oil in a large frying pan and sauté pepper, zucchini, and onion in it until slightly softened. Stir in corn, salt, dillweed, eggs, and cheese. Stir and cook until eggs reach desired doneness. Sprinkle with pepper.

Chicken and Egg Scramble

Yield: 4 to 5 servings

2 to 3 slices bacon
⅓ cup green onions, sliced
1 clove garlic, minced
½ teaspoon basil, crushed
1 10½-ounce can cream of chicken soup or creamy chicken mushroom soup
8 large eggs, slightly beaten
1 5-ounce can chunk white chicken
Freshly ground black pepper to taste
¼ cup pimiento, chopped

In skillet, cook bacon until crisp; remove and let drain on paper towel. Reserve 2 tablespoons of fat in the skillet; discard rest of fat.

Add onions, garlic, and basil to fat in skillet and cook until vegetables are soft. In medium bowl, add soup to lightly beaten eggs and stir until mixed. Pour on top of onion mixture in skillet and cook over low heat, lifting and turning with large spatula, until eggs are set but still moist. Break up chicken with hands and add to eggs with pimiento. Season to taste with pepper and crumble reserved bacon over all.

Creamed Eggs

Yield: 4 servings

6 eggs, hard-cooked and shelled
2 tablespoons butter
1 tablespoon flour
½ cup milk
Salt and pepper
Tabasco sauce
Chopped parsley
Paprika
6 slices toast

Remove the egg yolks and dice the whites. Make sauce with butter, flour, milk, and seasonings. Stir the egg whites into the sauce.

Heap the mixture on toast slices. Put the yolks through a sieve and sprinkle over the creamed egg whites. Dust with chopped parsley and paprika. Thin slices of baked ham may be browned in a skillet and placed on top of the toast before the creamed eggs are added. Creamed eggs are also good over hot biscuits, rice, baked potatoes, broccoli, or asparagus.

Deviled Eggs

Yield: 6 servings

6 hard-cooked eggs, peeled
½ teaspoon salt
½ teaspoon dry mustard
¼ teaspoon pepper
3 tablespoons salad dressing, vinegar, or light cream

Cut peeled eggs in half lengthwise. Slip out yolks; mash them in small bowl with fork. Mix in seasonings and salad dressing. Pile the egg mixture into the egg whites.

For flavor variation, mix in 2 tablespoons snipped parsley or ½ cup grated cheese.

Hot Deviled Eggs

Yield: 4 servings

2 tablespoons butter or margarine
½ green pepper, finely chopped
⅓ cup celery, finely chopped
1 small onion, finely chopped
1 tablespoon flour
1⅓ cups cooked or canned tomatoes
1 teaspoon salt
1 teaspoon Worcestershire sauce

2 drops hot pepper sauce
⅔ cup cold milk
6 hard-cooked eggs, sliced
Bread or cracker crumbs, mixed with melted butter or margarine

Heat butter or margarine and cook chopped vegetables in it until they are tender. Blend in the flour. Add tomatoes and seasonings and cook until thickened, stirring constantly. Stir the hot-tomato mixture into the milk and carefully add the eggs.

Turn into a greased baking dish and top with crumbs. Dot with butter or margarine and bake at 375°F until the crumbs are brown and the mixture is hot, about 10 to 15 minutes.

Farmer's Breakfast

Yield: 3 or 4 servings

4 medium-sized potatoes
4 strips bacon, cubed
3 eggs
3 tablespoons milk
½ teaspoon salt
1 cup small cubes cooked ham
2 medium-sized tomatoes, peeled
1 tablespoon chopped chives

Boil unpeeled potatoes 30 minutes. Rinse under cold water. Peel and set aside to cool. Slice potatoes. Cook bacon in large frying pan until transparent. Add potatoes; cook until lightly browned.

Meanwhile, blend eggs with milk and salt; stir in cubed ham. Cut tomatoes into thin wedges; add to egg mixture. Pour over potatoes. Cook until eggs are set. Sprinkle with chives and serve at once.

Ham and Egg Patties

Yield: 6 servings

Pastry for a 2-crust, 9-inch pie
1½ cups cooked ham, ground
2 hard-cooked eggs, chopped
Salt and pepper to taste
⅛ teaspoon prepared mustard
2-3 tablespoons medium cream sauce
Egg or milk to glaze

Roll out the pastry to ⅛-¼ inch thickness and cut into rounds about 4½-5 inches across. Mix the ham with the eggs; add salt, pepper, mustard, and enough sauce to bind.

Divide the mixture evenly between the pastry rounds, moisten the edges, and fold over. Press and crimp the edge, glaze with egg or milk, and bake for about 25 minutes in a 425°F oven.

Curry Spiced Egg

Grilled Corned-Beef Hash with Eggs

Yield: 8 servings

3 cups mashed potatoes
2¼ cups canned corned beef, shredded
2 tablespoons tomato purée
Dash of pepper
4 eggs, beaten

Poached Eggs
8 eggs
Salt
Pepper

Combine potatoes, corned beef, tomato purée, pepper, and eggs. Shape into 8 patties. Place on shallow dish and cover with plastic wrap. Refrigerate overnight.

Place patties in skillet. Cook about 4 minutes on each side or until heated thoroughly. Be careful when turning patties.

In a shallow pan, bring 2 inches of water to simmer. Break eggs, 1 at a time, into cup; transfer to pan by holding cup with egg on surface of water; gently pour egg into water. Cook 3 to 5 minutes, to desired degree of doneness. Remove from water with slotted spoon; sprinkle with salt and pepper.

Serve corned-beef patties with the poached eggs.

Egg Hexel

Yield: 4 servings

6 eggs
½ cup milk
½ cup cream
¾ cup baked ham, cut up
6 slices bacon, cooked and shredded
¼ cup blanched chestnuts, chopped
3 small to medium onions, chopped
Salt and pepper
Pinch thyme

Beat eggs lightly with milk and cream. Add ham, bacon, and chestnuts.

Brown onions in bacon fat. Pour off excess fat from pan; add egg mixture, season, and stir gently. Cover, cook well, serve with parsley garnishing.

Eggs in a Nest

Yield: 4 servings

2 cups cold mashed potatoes
5 tablespoons hot milk
½ cup chopped ham or fried bacon bits
3 tablespoons parsley, chopped
4 eggs
Salt and pepper to taste
1 tablespoon butter

Soften mashed potatoes with hot milk. Add ham and parsley; mix well. Place in greased baking dish. With back of tablespoon, form 4 large hollows on top. Break 1 egg into each hollow. Sprinkle with salt and pepper; dot with butter. Bake at 325°F about 12 minutes or until egg whites are firm. Serve at once.

Scrambled Country Corn

Yield: 4 to 6 servings

6 slices lean bacon, diced
1 medium onion, chopped
1 green pepper, chopped
2 cups corn kernels, fresh preferred, but canned may be used
1 large tomato, chopped
6 eggs
1 teaspoon Worcestershire sauce
1 teaspoon salt
Dash of freshly ground pepper

Cook bacon in deep skillet until almost crisp. Pour off excess fat. Add onion, green pepper, corn, and tomato. Sauté until onion is transparent.

Beat eggs and seasonings in bowl until light and frothy. Add to skillet vegetables; stir until eggs are set. Serve this with your favorite sweet rolls.

Scrambled Eggs and Sausage

Yield: 6 servings

½ pound pork sausage
8 eggs
¼ cup milk
1 teaspoon salt
¼ teaspoon freshly ground black pepper

Sauté sausage in skillet until cooked and brown. Drain off fat. Beat eggs, milk, salt, and pepper together. Pour egg mixture over sausage; stir until eggs are cooked.

Sour-Cream and Ham Pie

Yield: 4 to 6 servings

5 eggs, separated, whites beaten stiffly
1 cup sour cream
¼ teaspoon salt
1 cup cooked ham, finely chopped
2 tablespoons butter

Beat egg yolks until well mixed. Add half the sour cream and salt. Fold in stiffly beaten egg whites and ham.

Heat butter in medium-sized skillet. Gently pour in egg mixture. Cook over low heat about 5 minutes. Place skillet in 325°F oven; cook about 12 minutes more. Top should be golden brown and firm. Slice pie into wedges; garnish each slice with sour cream.

Roquefort Souffle

Yield: 4 servings

¼ pound Roquefort cheese
3½ tablespoons butter
Slightly less than ⅓ cup flour
About ⅓ cup milk
5 eggs, separated
1 teaspoon potato flour
½ teaspoon salt
¹⁄₁₆ teaspoon cayenne pepper
1½ tablespoons Armagnac

This soufflé is made best if the Roquefort is so dry that it can be grated. If this is not the case, freeze it for a short while so that it is easy to grate. Melt the butter, add the flour, then the milk, a little at a time, stirring constantly until the mixture becomes creamy. Remove from the heat and allow to cool for a few minutes.

Beat the egg yolks, one at a time, into the batter. Blend in the grated cheese, potato flour, cayenne pepper, and the Armagnac.

Preheat the oven to 425°F. Beat the egg whites into very stiff peaks and fold them extremely carefully into the soufflé batter without stirring too much. Grease and flour a soufflé dish and fill it with the batter. Flatten the surface of the soufflé with a knife.

Bake in the middle of the oven on a rack for about 25 to 30 minutes, or until the soufflé has risen to almost double its original height and has become a golden brown.

Roquefort Soufflé

Top Hatters

Yield: 6 servings

6 squares cornbread
12 tomato slices
3 egg whites
3 egg yolks
1 cup sharp cheese, grated
¼ cup cooked bacon, crumbled

Cut the squares of cornbread in half crosswise to make 12 thin squares. Brush with melted butter or margarine and place in the broiler for 3 minutes or until the cornbread is delicately browned. Top each square with a tomato slice and set aside for a moment.

Beat egg whites until stiff but not dry. Beat egg yolks until thick and lemon colored. Fold egg yolks into egg whites, then fold in cheese and bacon. Place a spoonful of this mixture on each tomato slice. Return to the broiler for a few minutes or until the topping is puffed and brown. Serve immediately.

Spinach and Egg Bake

Yield: 4 to 6 servings

4 tablespoons flour
Dash of cayenne pepper
1 teaspoon salt
4 tablespoons butter, melted
1½ cups milk
1 cup bread crumbs or cracker meal
2 10-ounce packages frozen chopped spinach, cooked and drained
2 hard-cooked eggs, peeled and thinly sliced
1 cup Cheddar cheese, grated
1 strip bacon, cut into 1-inch lengths

Add flour, cayenne, and salt to melted butter. Gradually stir in milk over low heat until mixture is slightly thickened and smooth.

In 1½-quart, greased baking dish, layer half of the bread crumbs, half of the spinach, slices of 1 egg, ⅓ of the sauce, and half of the cheese. Repeat process with remaining spinach, egg, ⅓ of the sauce, and cheese. Pour on rest of sauce; top with rest of bread crumbs, then bacon bits. Bake at 350°F 40 to 45 minutes.

Eggs in Spinach Cups

Yield: 8 servings

2 10-ounce packages frozen chopped spinach, cooked and drained
1 can condensed cream of mushroom soup
¼ teaspoon onion salt
8 eggs
Paprika

Preheat oven to 325°F.
Combine spinach, soup, and onion salt. Grease 8 (6-ounce) baking cups, then line them with spinach. Break an egg into each cup. Bake 15 minutes; sprinkle with paprika.

Eggs Supreme

Yield: 4 to 6 servings

1 cup American cheese, grated
2 tablespoons butter
1 cup light cream
½ teaspoon salt
Dash of freshly ground pepper
1 teaspoon prepared mustard
6 eggs, slightly beaten

Spread cheese in greased, 8-inch-square baking dish. Dot with butter.
Combine cream, salt, pepper, and mustard. Pour half of cream mixture over cheese, followed by beaten eggs. Add rest of cream mixture. Bake at 325°F about 40 minutes or until set and firm.

Eggs in Toast Cups

Yield: 6 servings

12 slices fresh bread, crusts removed
Melted butter or margarine
8 eggs
2 teaspoons salt
1 teaspoon pepper
¼ cup heavy cream
Fried bacon bits (optional)

Preheat oven to 400°F. Press bread slices into muffin-pan cups; brush with butter. Bake in oven 20 minutes.
Beat eggs until fluffy; add salt, pepper, cream, and bacon. Pour eggs into greased skillet. Cook over low heat until set, lifting occasionally with spatula to let uncooked portion run underneath. Spoon into toast cups and serve immediately. Garnish with more bacon.

Mushroom-Stuffed Oven Omelet

Yield: 4 servings

1½ cups fresh mushrooms, sliced
4 tablespoons green onions, minced
2 teaspoons butter or margarine
¼ teaspoon salt
¼ teaspoon thyme
5 eggs, separated
¼ cup water
½ teaspoon salt
¼ teaspoon dry mustard
⅛ teaspoon pepper
4 teaspoons oil

In a small skillet, sauté mushrooms and onions in butter or margarine until both are tender. Add salt and thyme. Set mushroom mixture aside. Beat egg whites until stiff; in a separate bowl, beat yolks until thick. Stir water and seasonings into yolks and fold very carefully into whites.

Heat oil in a 10-inch frying pan or omelet pan, making sure the sides and bottom are greased. When pan is hot, pour in egg mixture and cook over low heat until browned on the bottom (5 to 6 minutes). Lift the sides gently to check. Place pan in a preheated 325°F oven for 10 minutes or until the omelet has risen and center is set.

Loosen omelet with a spatula and spread mushrooms gently over one side. Fold over the other side and slide out onto a serving platter. Serve immediately.

Turkey Ham Omelet

Yield: 1 serving

2 eggs
2 tablespoons water
⅛ teaspoon salt
Dash pepper
1 tablespoon butter
½ cup turkey ham, diced
Choice of grated cheese, sliced mushrooms, green onions, or alfalfa sprouts
2 tablespoons sour cream or yogurt

Mix eggs, water, salt, and pepper with a fork. Heat butter in an 8-inch omelet pan or skillet until just hot enough to sizzle a drop of water. Pour in egg mixture, which should set at edges at once. Carefully push cooked edges to center so uncooked egg can flow to bottom. While top is still moist and creamy-looking, arrange turkey ham and other filling and turn out onto warm platter. Top with sour cream or yogurt and diced turkey ham.

Cheese Griddle Omelets

Yield: 2 servings

4 eggs, separated
White pepper to taste
½ cup Parmesan cheese, freshly grated
Salt to taste
Butter

Beat the egg yolks until thick and lemon colored, then stir in the pepper and cheese. Season with a very small amount of salt, as the Parmesan cheese imparts a salty flavor. Beat the egg whites in a large bowl until stiff peaks form. Push the egg whites to one side of the bowl, then turn the cheese mixture into the bowl next to the egg whites. Fold and cut the cheese mixture into the egg whites with a rubber spatula until well blended.

Melt a small amount of butter on a griddle over medium-high heat. Spoon half the cheese mixture onto the hot griddle to form an oblong loaf, then repeat with remaining cheese mixture. Reduce heat to medium-low. Shape omelets into neat ovals with a table knife and cook until bottoms are lightly browned and set. Turn the omelets with a spatula and cook until lightly browned. Drizzle with melted butter.

Country Omelets

Yield: 12 servings

½ cup butter
¼ cup green pepper, seeded and finely chopped
¼ cup onion, finely chopped
2 pounds chicken livers (about 24)
36 eggs
¾ cup light cream
Salt and pepper to taste
¼ cup vegetable oil

Use 2 to 3 skillets to make the omelets quickly. Melt ¼ cup of the butter over medium heat. Add the green pepper and onion and sauté until soft. Set aside.

Melt the remaining butter in another skillet and sauté the chicken livers, then chop them coarsely. Beat eggs and cream together; add salt and pepper.

Use ¾ cup egg mixture for each omelet. For each omelet, heat 1 teaspoon each butter and oil in a skillet and add the eggs. Before the eggs begin to set, add 2 teaspoons green pepper and onion. When eggs begin to set, lift edges with spatula so uncooked egg will run to the bottom of the pan. When egg mixture is completely set, top with 2 to 3 tablespoons chopped chicken livers and fold omelet over. Serve immediately.

Cheese Pie

Cheese Pie

Yield: 6 servings

pastry
14 tablespoons butter
1⅔ cups flour
3 tablespoons water

filling
⅔ cup light cream
⅔ cup sour cream
4 eggs
⅓ cup grated Parmesan cheese
¼ teaspoon black pepper
1 teaspoon salt
½ teaspoon paprika
1 cup aged Cheddar cheese, cubed
1 cup Swiss cheese, cubed
⅓ cup onion, minced

Combine all the pastry ingredients in a bowl. Mix the dough together using your fingertips until it is well blended. Let stand in a cool place for about ½ hour.

Preheat oven to 425°F. Flatten the dough with the palm of your hand into a thin baking dish with a detachable bottom with a diameter of 11 inches so that the bottom and sides of the dish are evenly covered. Make sure that the dough goes all the way up to the edge of the baking dish and that there are no holes in the dough. Place the dish in the oven and bake the pie shell for about 10 minutes.

Meanwhile, mix together the cream, sour cream, and eggs and beat well. Season with the grated Parmesan cheese, salt, pepper, and paprika. Combine and lay out the 2 kinds of cheese in the pie shell. Sprinkle the minced onion on top. Finally pour the egg mixture over the cheese cubes and place the pie on a rack in the middle of the oven. Bake for 35 minutes. If the pie gets too dark, cover the top with a piece of aluminum foil.

Cottage Cheese-Corn Rolls

Yield: 8 servings

2 8-ounce cartons creamed cottage cheese
1 egg, slightly beaten
1 cup fine dry bread crumbs
2 tablespoons onion, finely chopped
1 12-ounce can niblet corn with peppers and pimiento, drained
¾ teaspoon salt
¼ teaspoon black pepper
½ teaspoon Worcestershire sauce
3 tablespoons butter

Combine all ingredients except ¼ cup of the bread crumbs and the butter. Divide mixture into 8

equal portions. Shape each portion as a cylinder or log and roll in crumbs until all surfaces are coated. Refrigerate at least ½ hour.

Heat butter in frying pan until bubbling; place rolls in frying pan and fry, turning as needed, until golden brown. Serve with sour cream or tomato sauce.

Cheese Croquettes

Yield: 3 to 4 servings

3 tablespoons butter
¼ cup flour
⅔ cup milk
1½ cups cheese (combine two hard cooking cheeses such as old Cheddar, Swiss, Gruyère, or Parmesan), grated
2 egg yolks, beaten
Salt and pepper
Ground red pepper
1 whole egg, beaten
Bread crumbs
Butter or oil for frying

Melt butter in large skillet. Add flour and stir about 1 minute over medium heat. Add milk, stirring constantly, so mixture thickens without lumps. Add cheese and stir until it melts. Remove from heat, stir a little of the mixture into beaten egg yolks, and then stir the yolks into cheese mixture. Season with salt and peppers and set aside to cool.

When cool and firm, shape portions into cylinders (or cut the mixture into squares or rectangles). Dip croquettes into beaten egg and then in bread crumbs. Sauté in butter or deep-fry in hot fat (375°F) until golden. Serve with stewed tomatoes.

Ham-Flavored Cheese Pudding

Yield: 6 servings

6 slices boiled ham, shredded
2 cups Swiss cheese, grated
2 cups heavy cream
3 eggs, well beaten
1 teaspoon salt
Nutmeg for garnish

Preheat oven to 350°F. Distribute the ham evenly over the bottom of 1½-quart greased casserole. Mix all ingredients except the nutmeg. Pour over ham. Sprinkle top lightly with nutmeg. Bake uncovered for 40 minutes or until set.

Small Cheese Pies with Green Pepper Sauce

Cheese Fritters

Yield: 40 small fritters

1 egg, beaten
½ cup milk
1 teaspoon Worcestershire sauce
1 small onion, finely minced
Dash of hot pepper (optional)
2 cups biscuit mix
1½ cups American cheese, diced
Fat for deep-frying
Jelly or jam

Mix egg, milk, Worcestershire sauce, onion, pepper, and prepared biscuit mix in bowl; blend well. Stir in cheese.

Preheat fat in skillet; drop mixture by teaspoonfuls into hot fat. Fry until golden brown; drain on paper towels. Serve next to dish of jelly or jam for dipping.

Small Cheese Pies with Green Pepper Sauce

Yield: 6 servings

2 cups milk
Nutmeg
Salt
Freshly ground pepper
¼ pound Swiss cheese, preferably Gruyère, freshly grated
3 egg yolks plus 2 whole eggs
Butter

sauce
2 tablespoons butter
1 medium onion, minced
1 medium green pepper, finely diced
½ teaspoon paprika
⅔ cup dry white wine
1¼ cups crème fraîche
Salt
Pepper

Bring the milk to a boil together with the spices. As soon as the milk begins to boil, stir in the cheese so that it will melt, at the same time removing the pot from the heat. Have the egg yolks and eggs next to the stove, already beaten together. Stir the boiled milk, by the spoonful, into the beaten eggs.

Grease 6 individual custard dishes generously and pour the batter into them. Place in a pan of water (a waterbath) and bake for about 30 minutes in a 350°F oven.

For the sauce, sauté the onion and green pepper in the butter so that it becomes soft but not brown. Add the paprika and allow to bubble for a moment before adding the wine and the crème fraîche. Let

boil until only half the amount of liquid remains. Season with salt and pepper. Serve the sauce with the small cheese pies. This dish will look more elegant if the pies are turned upside down out of the custard dishes and served in a "mirror" of sauce.

Ham and Cheese Rarebit

Yield: 6 servings

1 tablespoon butter or margarine
1½ tablespoons flour
1 cup milk
1½ teaspoons Worcestershire sauce
½ teaspoon prepared mustard
⅛ teaspoon salt
3 cups Cheddar cheese, shredded
½ cup tomato, diced
½ cup ham, diced
1 egg, lightly beaten

In a medium saucepan, melt butter. Stir in flour. Gradually add milk, Worcestershire sauce, mustard, and salt. Cook, stirring constantly, until thickened. Blend in cheese, tomato, and ham; cook and stir until cheese is melted. Mix in egg. Heat, but do not boil, stirring. Serve on crisp crackers or toast triangles.

Cheese and Potato Omelet

Yield: 2 to 4 servings

4 tablespoons peanut, vegetable, or corn oil
2 medium-sized potatoes, peeled and thinly sliced
Salt, if desired
Freshly ground pepper
6 eggs
¾ cup Gruyère or Swiss cheese, finely diced
2 tablespoons parsley, chopped
2 tablespoons chopped chives (optional)
2 tablespoons butter

Heat the oil in a skillet and add the potatoes. Add salt and pepper to taste. Cook, shaking the skillet and redistributing the potatoes so that they cook on all sides, about 8 to 10 minutes, or until golden brown on the bottom and top. Drain well.

Beat the eggs in a mixing bowl and add salt and pepper to taste, cheese, potatoes, parsley, and chives. Heat the butter in an omelet pan or nonstick skillet and add the egg mixture, stirring. Cook until the omelet is done on the bottom. Invert the omelet onto a hot, round platter and serve.

Herb and Cottage Cheese Pie

Herb and Cottage Cheese Pie

Yield: 6 servings

pie crust
5¼ tablespoons butter
Salt
1½ cups flour, sifted
1 egg yolk
1 tablespoon cold water

filling
2 leeks
2 tablespoons butter
1 package frozen or 1½ pounds fresh spinach
2 tablespoons parsley, chopped
2 tablespoons chives, chopped
Salt
Pepper
3 eggs, separated
⅓ pound cottage cheese

First make the pie crust. Place the butter in a warm bowl, and soften the butter with a wooden spoon. Add the salt to the flour and shape it into a pyramid in the bowl. Make a hole in the middle and fill it with the butter, egg yolk, another dash of salt, and the water. Stir with a spoon. Dip your fingers in a small amount of flour and knead the dough. Add more water, if needed. Place the dough in a piece of waxed paper so that it is totally covered. Refrigerate. Remove the dough from the refrigerator 15 minutes before it is to be rolled out.

Cut the white part of the leeks into thin rings. Melt the butter in a frying pan, and place the leek rings in the butter. Stir until they have become soft. Add the spinach and the herbs. Season well and mix. Add more melted butter if the mixture seems too dry. Let cool.

Roll out the dough and line a pie tin with detachable sides or 4 individual tart pans with it. Cut away any extras around the edge with a sharp knife.

Preheat the oven to 375°F. Cover a baking sheet with foil and place it in the oven. Place the herb mixture in the bottom of the forms. Separate the egg yolks and the whites. Strain the cottage cheese through a sieve; beat the egg yolks and the cottage cheese together and season well. Beat the whites into stiff peaks and fold them carefully into the cheese mixture. Pour into the pie forms.

Bake for about 30 minutes until the pie has risen and become golden brown. Serve warm or cold.

Salads

Stuffed Apple-Jerusalem Artichoke Salad

Yield: 6 servings

6 large red apples
Juice of 1 medium-sized orange
3 medium-sized Jerusalem artichokes
¼ cup celery, finely chopped
2 tablespoons walnuts, coarsely chopped
3 tablespoons mayonnaise
½ teaspoon celery salt

Remove the apple cores with a corer, then cut a thin slice about 1½ inches in diameter from the stem end of the apple. Scoop out the apple pulp with the corer or a sharp knife, leaving a shell about ½ inch thick. Chop the removed apple pulp coarsely and drop immediately into the orange juice to prevent discoloration.

Grate the artichokes coarsely and drop into the orange juice. Add the celery, walnuts, mayonnaise, and celery salt; then toss with a fork to mix well. Pack the salad mixture into the hollowed out apples and chill until serving time.

Molded Apple Salad

Yield: 6 servings

6 apples
3 cups water
1 cup sugar
Red vegetable coloring
½ cup crushed pineapple
¼ cup raisins
¼ cup chopped nuts
1 package lemon-flavored gelatin

Peel and core the apples. Combine water, sugar, and a few drops of red vegetable coloring. Drop apples in syrup and cook gently until apples are tender. Do not overcook so apples lose their shape. Remove apples from syrup and place each in a large cup.

Combine pineapple, raisins, and nuts. Stuff centers of apples with this mixture. Make up gelatin according to directions on package. When cool, pour gelatin over apples. Chill well until set. Unmold on crisp lettuce and serve with mayonnaise.

Apple-Bacon Salad

Yield: 8 servings

½ pound bacon
1 head lettuce, cut into bite-sized chunks
3 red apples
⅔ cup garlic oil (place 2 or 3 cloves in oil, let stand overnight)
2 teaspoons lemon juice
½ cup Parmesan cheese, grated
1 bunch scallions, trimmed and sliced
1 cup croutons
½ teaspoon coarsely ground black pepper
¼ teaspoon salt
1 egg, unbeaten

Cook bacon until crisp, drain on absorbent paper, and break into small pieces. Quarter and core apples, but do not peel. Cut apples into thin slices and drop into garlic oil. Stir in lemon juice. Combine all ingredients in salad bowl. Toss until all traces of egg disappear.

Apricot Ring Mold

Yield: 4 servings

1 can (1-pound, 4-ounce) apricots
1 cup pineapple juice
1 envelope unflavored gelatin
2 tablespoons water
1 3-ounce package cream cheese
1 tablespoon whipped cream
½ small green pepper, blanched, finely chopped
Pinch paprika
Pinch salt
Watercress or lettuce

Drain apricots; finely chop enough to make ¼ cup and reserve rest. Mix 1 cup apricot syrup with pineapple juice; heat to boiling.

Soften gelatin 5 minutes in water; dissolve in hot fruit juice. Add chopped apricots to half the gelatin; pour into small ring mold. Refrigerate until set. Chill remaining gelatin until it begins to thicken.

Blend cream cheese with cream. Add green pepper, paprika, and salt; spread on firm gelatin. Cover with remaining thickened gelatin; set aside until firm. Unmold and fill center with watercress and remaining apricots.

Melon and Ham Salad

Banana Mold

Yield: 4 to 6 servings

1 package pineapple-flavored gelatin
½ pint hot water
½ pint cream
4 large bananas

Dissolve gelatin in hot water. When nearly cold, but before set, gradually stir in cream.

Peel bananas; mash with fork. Beat until light and smooth. Stir lightly but thoroughly into gelatin and cream. Pour into glass dish; let set.

Note: If mixing is done before gelatin is sufficiently cool, gelatin, banana, and cream will separate into layers.

Cranberry Holiday Salad

Yield: 6 servings

2 cups raw cranberries
1 orange, thinly sliced
1 cup water
¾ cup sugar
1 envelope unflavored gelatin
¼ cup cold water
½ cup seedless grapes, sliced
1 cup celery, diced
¼ cup chopped nuts

Cook cranberries, orange, and water in covered saucepan until cranberry skins pop open. Press through fine sieve; add sugar and heat to boiling. Soften gelatin in cold water, add hot cranberries, and stir until gelatin is dissolved. Chill until syrupy.

Add remaining ingredients and turn into a ring mold. Chill in refrigerator until firm. Unmold and garnish as desired.

Molded Cranberry Salad

Yield: 10 servings

1 package lemon-flavored gelatin
¼ cup cold water
1 cup boiling water
1 quart cranberries
1 whole orange, unpeeled
¾ cup chopped celery
1 apple, peeled, cored, and diced
½ cup chopped nuts
1 cup sugar

Soften gelatin in cold water; mix with hot water and stir until gelatin is dissolved. Chill until syrupy. Pick over cranberries and put through food chopper with unpeeled orange. Add celery, apple, and nuts to cranberry mixture; cover with sugar and let stand while gelatin cools. Stir fruit into gelatin, pour into mold, and chill until firm. Serve on salad greens.

Cinnamon-Spiced Orange Salad

Bing-Cherry Mold

Yield: 4 to 6 servings

1 1-pound can bing cherries, pitted
1 6-ounce package lemon gelatin
2¾ cups hot water
½ cup chopped nuts

Drain cherries; reserve 1 cup juice. Dissolve gelatin in hot water; add reserved cherry juice. Allow mixture to set slightly 1 hour in refrigerator. Add cherries and nuts; pour into ring mold. Refrigerate several hours or overnight.

Turn out mold onto bed of crisp greens.

Great Grape Waldorf

Yield: 8 to 10 servings

½ pound seedless grapes
¾ cup mayonnaise
½ cup sour cream
3 tablespoons sugar
Pinch salt
3 apples
2 cups celery, chopped

1 cup walnuts, coarsely chopped
Lettuce

Combine grapes, mayonnaise, sour cream, sugar, and salt. Blend gently.

Core apples and cut into ½-inch cubes. Immediately add to grape mixture. Mix in celery and walnuts. Cover and chill until serving time. Serve on lettuce-lined bowl.

Honeyed Salad

Yield: 4 to 5 servings

4 dessert apples
½ cup seedless raisins
¼ cup walnuts, chopped
1½ cups carrots, cooked and diced
Pinch of salt
1 tablespoon clear honey
3 tablespoons lemon juice

Peel, core, and dice 3 apples; combine with raisins, nuts, and carrots. Add salt. Add honey and lemon juice blended together; toss lightly. Set aside in cool place about 1 hour.

Arrange in salad bowl or on platter; garnish with remaining apple—unpeeled, cut into slices, and brushed with lemon juice.

Melon and Ham Salad

Yield: 4 servings

1 melon, large enough for 4 servings
6 slices smoked ham
6 slices Swiss cheese
½ cucumber
2 tablespoons raspberry vinegar or red wine vinegar
2 tablespoons Dijon mustard
1 tablespoon snipped chives
Salt
Pepper
⅓ cup oil
Lettuce

Cut the melon in half and scrape out the fruit with a spoon. Cut the fruit into wedges, peel them, and cut them into thin slices. Attractively place the slices on plates.

Cut the ham, cheese, and cucumber into thin strips. Mix the vinegar, mustard, chives, salt, and pepper—preferably in a blender. Then slowly drip the oil into the mixture while vigorously stirring. The dressing should be rather thick, but it can be thinned slightly with water if necessary. Blend with lettuce and place on plates with the slices of melon. Sprinkle snipped chives on top.

Orange and Onion Salad

Yield: 6 servings

4 large oranges
1 Bermuda onion, sliced
1 medium-sized cucumber, sliced
1 small green pepper, peeled, seeded, chopped
⅓ cup vegetable oil
¼ cup wine vinegar
1 teaspoon sugar
½ teaspoon salt
¼ teaspoon chili powder

Peel oranges; remove as much white membrane as possible. Slice; remove seeds. Alternate layers of oranges, onion, and cucumber in serving dish. Sprinkle with green pepper. Refrigerate.

Combine the oil, vinegar, sugar, salt, and chili powder and pour over salad. Refrigerate until serving time.

Cinnamon-Spiced Orange Salad

Yield: 4 servings

8 oranges
About ⅓ cup sugar
2 teaspoons cinnamon

Peel 7 of the oranges with a knife, so that even the outer membrane around the orange fruit is removed. Slice the oranges.

Mix the sugar and cinnamon; put the sliced oranges and the sugar mixture in layers in a glass bowl. Squeeze the last orange and pour the juice over the fruit. Let stand in a cold place until the salad is to be served.

Valencia Salad

Yield: 4 to 6 servings

6 oranges
2 cups water
¾ cup sugar

Brush the oranges with warm water. Peel them with a potato peeler and cut the peels into thin strips, or pull off the peels with a peel-shredder. Boil the peel strips in 2 cups water with ¼ cup of the sugar for 3 minutes. Strain.

Thinly slice the peeled oranges. Place them overlapping on a plate, sprinkle with ¼ cup of sugar, and let them stand for several hours.

Melt ¼ cup sugar in a frying pan. Pour out onto greased aluminum foil when the sugar has melted and become golden brown. Let the candy become firm. Then place the candy in a plastic bag and hammer it into crumbs. Sprinkle the strips of peel and the crushed candy over the orange salad before serving.

Valencia Salad

Stuffed Pears

Yield: 6 servings

3 large ripe pears
Lemon juice
2 red dessert apples, cored and diced but not peeled
2-3 stalks celery, diced
1 can crabmeat
1 tablespoon onion, finely chopped
1 tablespoon parsley, chopped
French dressing
Lettuce

Wipe the pears but do not peel them. Cut in halves, remove the cores, and scoop out some of the flesh. Brush the pear halves with lemon juice. Put the scooped-out flesh into a bowl and add apples, celery, crabmeat, onion, and parsley. Add enough French dressing to moisten; mix well and check the seasoning.

Spoon into the pear halves, arrange on a bed of lettuce, and garnish with thin slices of unpeeled apple brushed with lemon juice.

Plum Summer Salad

Yield: 6 to 8 servings

1 6-ounce package lemon-flavored gelatin
3 cups carbonated lemon-lime soda
2 cups fresh plums (about ¾ pound), sliced
1 cup fresh peaches, diced
Sweetened whipped cream
Chopped nuts

In saucepan, dissolve gelatin in 1 cup of the soda which has been heated to boiling. Stir in remaining soda. Chill until slightly thickened.

Fold in prepared fruit; pour mixture into a 1½-quart mold. Chill until firm. To serve, unmold on platter; garnish with whipped cream and chopped nuts. Serve at once.

Raspberry Mold

Yield: 8 to 10 servings

1 10-ounce package frozen raspberries, thawed
2 3-ounce packages raspberry gelatin
2 cups boiling water
1 pint vanilla ice cream, softened
1 16-ounce can pink lemonade, thawed
½ cup pecans or walnuts, chopped

Drain raspberries and reserve syrup. Dissolve gelatin in boiling water; add ice cream by spoonfuls, stirring until melted. Stir in lemonade concentrate and raspberry syrup. Chill in a 6-cup ring mold until partially set. Add raspberries and nuts. Chill until firm. Unmold on platter.

Springtime Strawberry Salad

Yield: 4 servings

Lettuce Leaves
1 pint fresh strawberries, stems removed
1 orange, peeled and sliced
1 cup pineapple chunks
⅓ cup orange juice
⅓ cup yogurt
1 teaspoon sugar

Arrange lettuce, strawberries, orange, and pineapple on serving platter or individual serving plates; chill.

In small bowl, make a dressing by mixing together orange juice, yogurt, and sugar; chill. Serve separately with the strawberry salad.

Strawberry Gelatin Salad

Yield: 8 to 10 servings

1 large package strawberry gelatin
1 cup boiling water
20 ounces sliced frozen strawberries, thawed
1 pound can crushed pineapple, drained
1 cup chopped pecans
2 medium-sized ripe bananas, mashed
1 pint sour cream

Dissolve gelatin in water; add sliced strawberries with liquid. Mix well. Add pineapple, pecans, and bananas. Spread half the mixture in 13 × 9 inch pan. Chill until firm.

Spread sour cream as a layer and then add remaining mixture on top. Chill well. Keeps for days in refrigerator.

Waldorf Salad

Yield: 3 to 4 servings

½ cup mayonnaise
½ cup sour cream
1 tablespoon honey
1½ cups tart apples, peeled, cored, and diced
1 cup celery, diced
½ cup walnuts, coarsely chopped
1 cup grapes, halved and seeded

Combine mayonnaise, sour cream, and honey. Add apples; mix well to prevent apple discoloring. Add celery, walnuts, and grapes; mix lightly. Chill well before serving.

Fruit Bowl Salad

Yield: 6 servings

2 red apples, cored and diced
1 pear, peeled, cored, and diced
1 banana, peeled and sliced
1 cup celery, diced
½ cup walnuts, coarsely chopped
½ cup mayonnaise
2 tablespoons lemon juice
1½ teaspoons sugar
1½ teaspoons Worcestershire sauce

In a salad bowl, combine apples, pear, banana, celery, and walnuts. Mix remaining ingredients. Pour over salad; toss gently. Serve in lettuce-lined salad bowl, if desired.

Fruit Salad

Yield: 5 to 6 servings

1 ripe honeydew melon
1 small fresh pineapple
2 ripe red grapefruits
3 kiwi fruits
1 papaya fruit

Cut the melon in half and remove the seeds and peel. Cut the fruit into cubes. Slice the pineapple and cut away the peel edges. Cut the slices into smaller pieces. Peel the grapefruits with a knife, also cutting away the white membrane under the peel. Then cut out the wedges of the grapefruit so that only grapefruit "meat" gets into the salad.

Peel the kiwi fruits and slice them across. Peel the papaya, cut it in half, and remove the black seeds. Cut the fruit into long slices.

Carefully mix the fruits together and serve in a pretty bowl.

Coleslaw

Yield: 10 servings

1 large head cabbage
1 cup mayonnaise
1 cup sour cream
1 teaspoon prepared mustard
1 tablespoon lemon juice
Salt and pepper to taste
1 tablespoon sugar

Slice cabbage very thin. Mix other ingredients; stir into cabbage. Chill about 4 hours.

Peanut Crunch Slaw

Yield: 6 to 7 servings

4 cups white cabbage, shredded
1 cup celery, diced

dressing
½ cup sour cream
½ cup mayonnaise
¼ cup scallions, chopped
¼ cup green pepper, chopped
¼ cup cucumber, chopped

topping
½ cup salted peanuts, coarsely chopped
1 tablespoon butter
2 tablespoons Parmesan cheese, grated

Combine cabbage and celery. Sprinkle with a little salt and pepper and set aside to chill.

Combine all ingredients for the dressing, season and chill.

Brown the peanuts in the butter and stir in the cheese. Toss the vegetables and dressing together and sprinkle the nuts and cheese on top.

Red Cabbage Slaw

Yield: 4 servings

4 cups red cabbage, finely shredded
1 cup apple, chopped
¼ cup raisins
2 tablespoons onion, chopped
½ cup mayonnaise
½ teaspoon salt
⅛ teaspoon ground cloves

In large bowl, toss together all ingredients. Chill.

Mixed Green Salad

Yield: 4 servings

1 head Bibb lettuce or ½ head iceberg lettuce
2 green peppers, cleaned, seeded, cut into strips
4 small tomatoes, sliced
2 small onions, sliced, separated into rings
2 hard-cooked eggs, sliced
½ cup stuffed green olives, sliced
½ medium cucumber, peeled, seeded, cut into chunks

salad dressing
4 tablespoons olive oil
3 tablespoons tarragon vinegar
½ teaspoon salt
¼ teaspoon freshly ground pepper
1 clove garlic, crushed
¼ teaspoon crushed oregano
1 tablespoon fresh parsley, chopped

Wash lettuce; dry. Tear into bite-size pieces and place in salad bowl. Add peppers, tomatoes, onions, eggs, olives, and cucumber; refrigerate.

Combine all dressing ingredients; mix well. At serving time, toss salad at table with prepared dressing.

Fruit Salad

Avocado with Bacon and Roquefort Dressing

Yield: 2 to 4 servings

1 avocado
Lettuce
Bacon
Roquefort cheese
Vinaigrette (See index)
Parsley and chives

Cut the avocado in half, peel it, and cut the halves into slices. Place on lettuce leaves. Cut the bacon into small pieces, fry them until crisp, and then sprinkle over the avocado once they have drained completely. Mash the Roquefort cheese in Vinaigrette dressing and drip it over the salad. Chop chives and parsley and sprinkle on top.

Salad with Oregano

Yield: 4 servings

6 cups mixed salad greens such as romaine, arugula, Boston lettuce, cut into large, bite-sized pieces
½ cup onion rings, thinly sliced
1 teaspoon dried oregano
1 tablespoon imported mustard
1 tablespoon shallots, finely chopped
2 tablespoons red wine vinegar
½ cup olive oil
Salt and freshly ground pepper to taste

Rinse the greens well and dry them in a spin dryer or with paper towels. Put the greens and onion rings in a salad bowl. Sprinkle with the oregano.

Put the mustard, shallots, and vinegar in a mixing bowl. Gradually beat in the oil. Add salt and pepper. Pour the sauce over the greens and toss well.

Garden Salad

Yield: 6 servings

3 ripe avocados, skinned and pitted and cut into ½-inch chunks
3 ripe tomatoes, cut in sixths
1 medium-sized Bermuda onion, diced finely
1 teaspoon fresh oregano or 2 teaspoons dried oregano
½ teaspoon fresh basil or 1 teaspoon dried basil
1 clove garlic, finely diced
Juice of 1 lemon
½ teaspoon Worcestershire sauce

Mix ingredients together in a bowl. Pour clear Vinaigrette dressing (see Index) over the salad and marinate for ½ hour before serving.

Serve on a bed of leaf lettuce or Boston lettuce.

Marinated Vegetable Salad

Yield: 6 servings

2 cups cooked carrots, diagonally sliced
2 cups cooked cauliflowerettes
1 cup cooked asparagus, diagonally sliced, or 1 package frozen broccoli spears, thawed, cooked, and sliced in 1-inch chunks
1½ cups tomato or vegetable juice
¼ cup red wine vinegar
1 tablespoon honey
1 teaspoon dry mustard
½ teaspoon dried dillweed, crushed
1 cup radishes, sliced
1 small red onion, sliced

Cook carrots, cauliflowerettes, and asparagus (or broccoli) just until fork-tender—but not mushy.

In shallow dish, combine tomato juice, vinegar, honey, mustard, and dill. Add cooked vegetables, radishes, and onion. Cover. Chill 6 hours or more. Stir occasionally. Use slotted spoon to serve.

Avocado Salad with Bacon

Yield: 4 servings

1 package of bacon
3 to 4 ripe avocados
4 tender stalks celery
A piece of leek
3 to 4 hard-cooked eggs
2 tomatoes, cut in wedges

dressing
5 tablespoons oil
2 tablespoons tarragon vinegar
1 clove garlic, crushed
2 teaspoons light French mustard
1 to 2 teaspoons Italian salad spices, or 1 teaspoon herb salt

Mix the dressing together and adjust the seasonings. Fry the bacon in a dry pan until crisp. Place the bacon on a paper towel so that the fat drains off. Divide the avocados in half and remove the pits. Peel the halves and cut them into slices.

Alternate in a salad bowl sliced avocado, celery, leek, bacon, egg slices, and tomato wedges.

Mix the dressing ingredients together and adjust the seasonings. Shake up the dressing and pour it over the salad.

Avocado Salad with Bacon

Hot Slaw

Yield: 4 to 6 servings

2 tablespoons salad oil
4 cups cabbage, shredded
½ teaspoon salt
½ teaspoon celery seeds
¼ teaspoon pepper
2 tablespoons vinegar

Heat oil in medium-sized skillet. Add cabbage and seasonings, but not vinegar. Cover; cook over medium heat about 3 minutes. Be sure to stir occasionally to mix flavors. Add vinegar and stir again.

Serve hot slaw at once.

Molded Asparagus Salad

Yield: 4 servings

2 envelopes unflavored gelatin
1½ cups water
1 tablespoon sugar
½ cup lemon juice
½ teaspoon salt
¼ cup pimientos, chopped

1 1-pound can asparagus tips, drained
2 teaspoons onion, grated
1 cup celery, chopped

Soften the gelatin in ½ cup water. Combine the sugar, 1 cup water, and lemon juice in a saucepan and bring to a boil. Remove from heat, add the gelatin and salt, and stir until dissolved. Chill until partially set.

Fold in the pimientos, asparagus tips, onion, and celery and spoon into a 1-quart ring mold. Chill until firm, then unmold onto a serving plate.

Green Beans with Mint

Yield: 6 servings

1½ pounds fresh string beans (or 2 boxes frozen whole green beans)
4 tablespoons extra virgin olive oil
3 teaspoons lemon juice, freshly squeezed
3 tablespoons mint, freshly chopped
Pinch garlic powder
Pinch black pepper
Salt

Fantasy Salad

Steam string beans just long enough to ensure that they are firm to the bite. Allow to cool. Place in a bowl and dress with the olive oil, lemon juice, mint, garlic powder, and black pepper. Salt to taste. Toss gently.

Three-Bean Salad

Yield: 6 to 8 servings

1 cup red kidney beans, freshly cooked or canned
1 cup white kidney beans, freshly cooked or canned
1 cup chickpeas, freshly cooked or canned
¾ cup onion or scallions, finely chopped
½ teaspoon garlic, finely chopped
2 tablespoons parsley, finely chopped
1 small green pepper, seeded and coarsely chopped (optional)
1 teaspoon salt
Freshly ground black pepper
3 tablespoons wine vinegar
½ cup olive oil

If you plan to use canned cooked beans and chickpeas, drain them of all their canning liquid, wash them thoroughly under cold running water, drain again, and pat dry with paper towels. If you plan to cook the beans yourself, soak the beans overnight in water, drain them, cover them with fresh water, then bring them to a boil; boil them for 10 minutes and then simmer for 1½ hours until they are tender. One-half cup of dry uncooked beans yields approximately 1¼ cups cooked.

In a large bowl, combine the chickpeas, red and white kidney beans, onion or scallions, garlic, parsley, and green pepper if you plan to use it. Add the salt, a few grindings of pepper, and wine vinegar, and toss the ingredients gently with a large spoon; pour in the olive oil and toss again. This salad will be greatly improved if it is allowed to rest for at least 1 hour before serving.

Broccoli Salad

Yield: 6 servings

1½ pounds fresh broccoli spears
¼ cup vegetable oil
6 tablespoons cider vinegar
¼ cup water
½ cup apple juice
Salt and pepper to taste
6 lettuce leaves
2 hard-cooked eggs, chopped

Cook the broccoli in a small amount of boiling, salted water until tender, then drain and cool. Place in a shallow dish. Place the oil, vinegar, ¼ cup of water, apple juice, salt, and pepper in a small bowl and mix well. Pour over the broccoli; marinate in the refrigerator, carefully turning the broccoli occasionally, for at least 2 hours.

Place the broccoli in the lettuce leaves on individual salad plates, then sprinkle the eggs over the top. Garnish with tomato wedges.

Carrot Salad

Yield: 10 to 12 servings

1 small onion, finely chopped
1 medium pepper, finely chopped
3 ribs celery, finely chopped
2 1-pound cans sliced carrots, drained
1 cup tomato soup, undiluted
1 cup sugar
¼ cup oil
¾ cup cider vinegar
1 tablespoon dry mustard
1 tablespoon Worcestershire sauce
Lettuce leaves, washed, drained

Add onion, pepper, and celery to drained carrots; set aside. Put soup, sugar, oil, vinegar, mustard, and Worcestershire sauce into small saucepan. Bring to boil, so that all ingredients blend. Pour over vegetables. When cool, refrigerate to chill thoroughly, at least overnight.

Serve salad on crisp lettuce leaves.

Cauliflower Salad

Yield: 8 servings

1 head cauliflower
¼ cup green onions, minced
½ cup celery leaves, minced
½ cup sour cream
½ cup Vinaigrette (see recipe below)
2 teaspoons caraway seed
Salt to taste
Lettuce leaves

Separate the cauliflower into flowerets and place in a large bowl, then chill. Place the onions, celery leaves, sour cream, Vinaigrette, caraway seed, and salt in a small bowl and mix until blended. Add the onion mixture to the cauliflowerets and mix well.

Line a salad bowl with lettuce, then place the salad in the bowl over the lettuce.

To make Vinaigrette, combine 2 teaspoons salt, ½ teaspoon freshly ground pepper, 1 teaspoon prepared mustard, 1 cup olive oil, ¼ cup red wine vinegar.

Pickled Corn Salad

Yield: 4 to 6 servings

½ cup onions, chopped
½ cup green peppers, diced
4 tablespoons pimiento, chopped
3 tablespoons sugar
¾ teaspoon salt
½ teaspoon celery salt
½ teaspoon dry mustard
½ cup cider vinegar
½ cup water
3 cups frozen whole-kernel corn

Combine all ingredients except corn and bring to boil. Lower heat; cover pan. Simmer 12 minutes, stirring occasionally.

Add frozen corn; raise heat. When boiling resumes, lower heat. Simmer until corn is just tender (2 or 3 minutes); drain. Serve salad hot, or refrigerate and serve on lettuce leaves.

Macaroni Salad

Carrot-Lentil Salad

Yield: 2 servings

2 medium carrots, grated
1 medium tomato, chopped
1 tablespoon grated coconut
1 small bunch coriander leaves, chopped
1 tablespoon lentils, previously soaked in water for
    several hours or overnight
Salt to taste
1 tablespoon oil
1 teaspoon mustard seeds
Few drops lemon or lime juice

Mix together the carrots, tomato, coconut, coriander leaves, lentils, and salt.

Heat oil. When it is hot, but not sputtering, add mustard seeds. When seeds start sputtering, add oil and seeds to the salad. Add a few drops of lemon or lime juice.

Dilled Cucumbers and Sour Cream

Yield: 4 servings

2 cucumbers
1 cup sour cream
2 teaspoons onion, grated
2 tablespoons lemon juice
1 tablespoon wine vinegar
½ teaspoon dillseed
1 teaspoon salt
Lettuce leaves

Peel the cucumbers, then slice paper-thin. Place in a bowl and chill well. Place the sour cream, onion, lemon juice, vinegar, dillseed, and salt in a medium-sized bowl and blend thoroughly. Add the cucumbers and toss lightly until coated.

Line a salad bowl with lettuce, then add the cucumber mixture.

Pepper Salad

Yield: 6 servings

2 medium-sized green sweet peppers
3 large firm ripe tomatoes, thinly sliced
Salt and freshly ground pepper to taste
½ cup olive oil
1 to 2 tablespoons red wine vinegar
1½ teaspoons chopped chives
1½ teaspoons chopped parsley

Cut the peppers in half and remove the seeds and membrane. Cut into thin, lengthwise slices. Arrange the tomatoes and peppers in a serving dish and sprinkle with salt and pepper. Pour the oil evenly over all. Sprinkle the vinegar, chives, and parsley over the top.

Cucumber Salad

Yield: 4 to 6 servings

1 cup water
½ cup sugar
⅓ cup white vinegar
2 large cucumbers, pared and thinly sliced
4 tablespoons olive oil

Bring water, sugar, and vinegar to a heavy boil. Add cucumbers. Simmer 2 to 3 minutes. Remove from heat and add olive oil. Chill.

Potato Salad

Yield: 6 to 8 servings

6 cups cooked potatoes, diced
3 or 4 green onions (scallions), chopped
4 hard-cooked eggs, chopped
1 teaspoon celery seed
1½ teaspoons salt
¼ teaspoon pepper
1 teaspoon curry powder
1 cup sour cream
½ cup mayonnaise
2 tablespoons vinegar
Chopped parsley

Mix potatoes, onions, eggs, and seasoning (except curry powder) together in bowl. Set aside to chill.

Mix curry powder with sour cream. Add mayonnaise and vinegar. When ready to serve, add to potato mixture. Toss together lightly; sprinkle with parsley. Serve cold.

German Potato Salad

Yield: 10 servings

1 pound bacon
5 pounds potatoes, boiled and sliced
1 large Spanish onion, minced
3 tablespoons flour
½ cup vinegar
1¼ cups water
½ cup sugar
1 tablespoon salt
½ tablespoon pepper

Fry bacon until crisp. Crumble it and place in a bowl with potatoes and onion. Add flour to the pan with the hot bacon grease and mix. Add the remaining ingredients to the pan and mix thoroughly until sugar is dissolved and mixture thickens slightly.

Immediately pour contents of the pan over the potatoes, onion, and bacon and mix thoroughly until most of the juice has soaked into the potatoes.

Fantasy Salad

Yield: Varies

Fresh spinach leaves
Lettuce
Sliced mushrooms
Finely shredded spring onions
Shrimp or shredded crab
Shredded cucumber
Lime
Soy sauce
Vinaigrette (See index)
Basil or mint leaves

This is an elegant, fresh salad with many different shades of green. Mix spinach with lettuce, mushrooms, spring onions, shrimp or crab, and cucumber.

Mix a small wedge of finely chopped lime (both the fruit and the peel) with the salad, and drip a small amount of soy sauce on top. Garnish with leaves of basil or mint. Serve with Vinaigrette sauce.

Rice Salad with Ham

Easy Tomato Aspic

Yield: 6 servings

3½ cups tomato juice
1 6-ounce package lemon gelatin
1 teaspoon lemon juice
4 drops Tabasco sauce
3 stalks celery, chopped fine
5 stalks scallions, finely chopped
1 cucumber, finely chopped
7 radishes, finely chopped

Bring 1½ cups tomato juice to boil. Add gelatin and stir. Add 2 cups cold tomato juice, then lemon juice and Tabasco and stir. Pour into mold or glass bowl and refrigerate.

When beginning to thicken, add vegetables. Refrigerate until firm.

Hot Potato Salad

Yield: 4 servings

3 large potatoes
2 tablespoons vinegar
1 teaspoon salt
Pepper to taste
½ pound bacon, chopped
3 eggs, hard-cooked
¼ cup scallions, chopped
Lettuce

Scrub the potatoes and cook in boiling salted water. Then drain, peel, and dice potatoes. Add vinegar, salt, and pepper.

Fry the bacon until crisp. Combine the potatoes, bacon, 2 tablespoons of the bacon fat, chopped eggs, and onion and mix well. Serve hot on a bed of lettuce.

Sauerkraut Salad

Yield: 6 servings

1 1-pound can sauerkraut
1 cup green pepper, chopped
1 cup onion, chopped
1 small can pimientos, chopped (optional)
1 cup sugar
1 cup white vinegar

Drain sauerkraut thoroughly. Add chopped vegetables; mix well. Bring sugar and vinegar to boiling point, but do not boil. This will thoroughly dissolve sugar. Pour over mixture; toss thoroughly.

Chill in covered bowl in refrigerator at least several hours. Overnight is even better. This dish will keep well several days.

Fresh Raw Spinach Salad

Yield: 6 servings

½ pound raw spinach
¼ cup sweet green pepper, chopped
½ cup onion rings
1½ tablespoons fresh lemon juice
1 tablespoon salad oil
½ teaspoon tarragon leaves
½ teaspoon salt
⅛ teaspoon ground black pepper
Hard-cooked eggs
Anchovies

Thoroughly wash spinach; drain and wrap in a clean towel to absorb excess water. Tear leaves into bite-sized pieces and put into a salad bowl. Add chopped green pepper, onion rings, lemon juice, salad oil, tarragon leaves, salt, and black pepper. Toss lightly. Garnish with hard-cooked eggs and anchovies.

Spinach Salad

Yield: 6 servings

1 pound fresh spinach
⅓ cup red wine vinegar
⅔ cup oil
2 eggs
2 teaspoons Dijon mustard
1 teaspoon dried tarragon
1 teaspoon parsley flakes
1 dozen fresh mushrooms
6 pieces bacon, cooked and crumbled

Wash spinach thoroughly. In blender or food processor, combine red wine vinegar, oil, eggs, mustard, tarragon, and parsley flakes. Blend until well mixed. Pour over spinach; add the sliced mushrooms and crumbled bacon.

Tomato, Avocado, and Onion Salad

Yield: 6 servings

6 large ripe tomatoes
4 ripe avocados, peeled and sliced
1 Bermuda onion, cut into rings
Lemon juice (or lime juice)
Salt and freshly ground pepper
Olive oil

Slice tomatoes and arrange on a plate. Top with slices of avocado and onion rings. Squeeze a generous amount of lemon (or lime) juice over the top. Sprinkle salt and pepper and top with a thin drizzle of oil.

Dilled Zucchini Salad

Yield: 4 to 6 servings

⅓ cup oil
½ cup lemon juice
1½ teaspoons salt
1½ teaspoons onion, grated
1 teaspoon dillweed
¼ teaspoon freshly ground pepper
5 cups zucchini (about 4 medium), sliced
2 medium-sized carrots, cut in very thin strips
½ cup ripe olives, sliced
¼ cup pimiento, minced
Bibb lettuce leaves

Combine oil, lemon juice, salt, onion, dill, and pepper in a small, covered jar. Shake well.

Mix zucchini, carrots, olives, and pimiento in a large bowl. Toss gently. Add about ¼ cup dressing and toss again. Cover and chill.

At serving, arrange lettuce leaves on serving plates. Spoon portions of marinated vegetables atop lettuce leaves. Pass remaining salad dressing.

Seafood and Fresh Asparagus Salad

Yield: 6 servings

1 pound fresh asparagus
1¼ cups Vinaigrette (see recipe below)
½ cup fresh avocado strips
2 tablespoons fresh lemon juice
1 cup boiled shrimp
1 cup cooked lobster chunks
1 cup lump crabmeat
Fresh lettuce leaves

Cook the asparagus, then drain. Place in a shallow dish and add ½ cup of the Vinaigrette. Chill thoroughly. Combine the avocado and lemon juice in a small bowl and chill well.

Combine the shrimp, lobster, and crabmeat in a bowl and add the remaining Vinaigrette, then chill. Arrange the lettuce leaves on a serving tray. Drain the shrimp mixture and combine with the avocado, then place in the center of the tray. Drain the asparagus and arrange at each end of the tray.

To make Vinaigrette, combine 2 teaspoons salt, ½ teaspoon freshly ground pepper, 1 teaspoon prepared mustard, 1 cup olive oil, and ¼ cup red wine vinegar.

Festive Crab Salad

Mississippi Rice Salad

Yield: 6 servings

3 cups rice, cooked and cooled
½ cup onions, finely chopped
½ cup sweet pickles, finely chopped
1 teaspoon salt
¼ teaspoon pepper
1 cup mayonnaise
1 teaspoon prepared mustard
1 2-ounce can pimiento, diced
4 hard-cooked eggs, chopped

Blend all ingredients thoroughly. Chill. Serve on lettuce leaves.

Garden Tomatoes

Yield: 8 servings

6 large very ripe tomatoes, sliced
Salt
Sweet basil leaves
Olive oil

Arrange tomato slices on a large serving platter. Sprinkle with salt and basil. Drizzle olive oil over tomatoes and serve at room temperature or chilled.

Macaroni Salad

Yield: 4 servings

1⅔ cups macaroni
4 tablespoons oil
1½ tablespoons vinegar
½ teaspoon salt
1 teaspoon thyme
¼ pound smoked sausage, cubed
About 1 cup cheese, cubed
½ cucumber, cubed
Part of 1 leek, shredded
Tomatoes
Lettuce

Boil the macaroni according to the directions on the package. Combine the oil, vinegar, salt, and thyme. Pour the dressing over the hot macaroni. Let cool.

Mix the sausage, cheese, cucumber, and leek with the cold macaroni. Season. Serve with tomatoes and lettuce.

Cold Pasta Salad

Yield: 6 servings

½ pound cold cooked ruotini or medium pasta shells
1 or 2 tomatoes, diced
2 to 4 scallions, diced
1 cucumber, peeled, seeded, and diced
1 red onion, diced
1 Spanish onion, diced
2 green and/or red peppers
2 to 4 red potatoes, cooked and diced
5 ounces cold steamed broccoli, diced
6 ounces steamed green beans, diced
Fresh basil to taste
¼ cup parsley, minced

dressing
¼ cup low-acid vinegar (balsamic or similar)
⅛ teaspoon Dijon-style mustard
Pinch oregano
½ teaspoon pepper
1 tablespoon frozen apple juice concentrate

Toss all vegetables with cold pasta, adding more or less of each to taste. Mix dressing ingredients together; shake and pour over salad.

Variation: Dice or shred a skinned and boned chicken breast and poach in mixture of 2 tablespoons of white wine, 1 tablespoon lemon juice, 2 tablespoons water, and lots of dried basil. Cover while poaching just until poached through. Cool and add to salad.

Lobster and Wild Rice Salad

Yield: 4 to 6 servings

3½ to 4 cups wild rice, cooked
2 cups lobster meat, cooked and cut into bite-sized cubes
2 medium-sized unblemished avocados
1 tablespoon lemon juice
½ cup red onion, coarsely cubed
1 tablespoon imported mustard
2½ tablespoons red-wine vinegar
½ cup corn, peanut, or vegetable oil
½ teaspoon garlic, finely minced
Salt to taste, if desired
Freshly ground pepper to taste
2 tablespoons parsley, finely chopped

Put the rice in a mixing bowl; let cool and add the lobster.

Peel the avocados and slice in half. Remove the pits. Cut the avocados into cubes and sprinkle with lemon juice to prevent discoloration. Add the cubes to the mixing bowl. Sprinkle with onion.

Put the mustard and vinegar in a small mixing bowl and beat lightly with a wire whisk. Gradually add the oil, beating briskly with the whisk. Add the garlic, salt, pepper, and parsley. Pour over the salad and toss. Serve at room temperature.

Mussel Salad (lower right)

Rice Salad with Ham

Yield: 4 servings

⅔ cup rice
1½ tablespoons vinegar
½ teaspoon salt
¼ teaspoon black or white pepper
1 clove garlic, crushed
1 teaspoon tarragon (optional)
3 tablespoons oil
2 tablespoons water
1 pound ham, cut into cubes
¼ cup parsley, finely chopped

Boil the rice according to the directions given on the package. Mix together the vinegar, spices, oil, and water, and pour the dressing over the hot rice. Let stand until the rice becomes cold.

Mix the cold rice with the ham and the parsley.

Festive Crab Salad

Yield: 4 servings

crab salad
4 meaty crabs
4 hard-cooked eggs
⅓ cup celery, cut into ¼-inch pieces

garnish
Lettuce
2 avocados, pits removed
Mushrooms
Tomatoes
A small amount of Vinaigrette (See index)

dressing
¾ cup mayonnaise
2 tablespoons snipped chives
2 tablespoons snipped parsley
2 tablespoons snipped dill
1 tablespoon capers, slightly chopped
1 clove garlic, crushed
Several drops Tabasco sauce
Squeezed lemon
1 teaspoon Worcestershire sauce
1 teaspoon chili sauce

Lift away the shell of the crab and carefully remove the roe with a fork. Try to remove it in one piece, cut it into slices, and place it decoratively on individual plates. Crack the claws and the legs with a nutcracker, and scrape all the meat out into a bowl. Also scrape out as much of the rest of the crabmeat as possible.

Cut the eggs into pieces and mix with the crabmeat and the celery. Divide the salad up onto the plates and sprinkle with a small amount of snipped chives. Cut the lettuce, pitted avocados, mushroom caps, and tomatoes into slices and divide them up

among the plates. Drip a small amount of Vinaigrette dressing over the vegetables.

Mix all the dressing ingredients together and season to taste. It should be quite strong. Salt and pepper if necessary.

Mussel Salad

Yield: 4 to 6 servings

40 mussels, fresh or frozen
⅓ cup white wine
1 tablespoon shallot, finely chopped
Water
¼ cup mayonnaise
½ lemon
1 tablespoon capers
1 tablespoon parsley, finely chopped
1 tablespoon chives, finely chopped
1 teaspoon dried tarragon
3 tomatoes
Salt
Pepper
1 drop hot sauce
Lettuce leaves

Boil the mussels in the wine, water, and shallots, covered, until they open. Remove the mussels from their shells. Save the largest shells, about 4 to 5 per person.

Chop the mussels and mix with the mayonnaise, juice from ½ lemon, capers, and the herbs. Divide the tomatoes into wedges, remove the seeds, and cut the tomato fruit into small pieces. Mix into the mussel mixture.

Season the salad to taste with salt, pepper, and hot sauce. Fill the mussel shells and arrange them attractively on plates with leaves of lettuce.

Swedish Raw Spiced Salmon with Mustard Dressing

Yield: 4 servings

mustard dressing
3 tablespoons mustard
2 tablespoons vinegar
1 teaspoon salt
¼ teaspoon black pepper
¾ cup oil
¼ cup water
1 tablespoon sherry (optional)
⅓ cup chopped dill

salad
½ head iceberg lettuce
¼ leek
1 cucumber
¼ pound fresh mushrooms

Mixed Green Salad and Swedish Raw Spiced Salmon

1 bunch radishes
⅓ pound raw spiced salmon (graulax)
1 lemon

Remove all the dressing ingredients from the refrigerator so that they become room temperature. This is especially important for the oil so that the dressing will "pull" together.

When the ingredients have become room temperature, mix the mustard, vinegar, salt, and pepper; add the oil a drop at a time, while beating constantly. Finally add the water, sherry, and chopped dill.

Finely shred all the salad ingredients. It is easiest to use a vegetable shredder on a food processor. Choose the fine cutter. Alternate all the ingredients on individual plates or on a large serving plate.

Cut the salmon into thin slices without removing the skin. Immediately before serving, turn the slices very quickly in a piping hot pan, and then place the slices on the salad. Squeeze with lemon juice.

The dressing is served with the salad, in generous proportions.

Molded Chicken Salad

Yield: 6 servings

1 envelope unflavored gelatin
¼ cup cold water
1 cup hot chicken broth
2 tablespoons green pepper, chopped
2 cups cooked chicken, diced
1 tablespoon onion, chopped
1 cup celery, chopped
1 cup cooked rice
1 teaspoon salt
¼ cup French dressing
½ cup mayonnaise

Combine gelatin and cold water, let stand 5 minutes. Add chicken broth and stir until gelatin is dissolved.

Place chopped green pepper in bottom of 2-quart mold. Cover with 2 tablespoons of the gelatin and chill until firm. Combine remaining ingredients and stir into remaining gelatin. Pour into mold over firm green pepper and gelatin. Chill until firm. Unmold and serve on salad greens.

Salmon Mold

Yield: 6 servings

1 envelope unflavored gelatin
¼ cup water
1 pound red salmon, skin and bones removed
1 cup plain yogurt
¼ cup chili sauce
½ cup minced celery
2 tablespoons grated onion
2 tablespoons diced cucumbers
1 tablespoon prepared mustard
1 tablespoon lemon juice

Soften gelatin in water in small saucepan. Heat gently until gelatin dissolves. Combine salmon with yogurt, chili sauce, celery, onion, cucumbers, mustard, and lemon juice. Blend in gelatin. Pour into 1 quart mold and chill until firm.

Unmold salad onto lettuce leaves.

Papayas with Shrimp

Yield: 4 servings

1½ cups cooked shrimp, cut in chunks
½ cup mayonnaise
2 tablespoons lemon juice
⅛ teaspoon curry powder
1 tablespoon chutney, minced
Salt and pepper to taste
2 ripe papayas
Lime wedges

Mix all the ingredients except the papayas and limes to make a shrimp salad. Cut the papayas in half, remove the seeds, heap with the shrimp salad. Garnish with lime wedges when ready to serve.

Chicken and Grape Salad

Yield: 6 to 8 servings

3 cups cooked chicken, diced
1 cup seedless white grapes, halved
1 cup celery, diced
1½ cups blanched, salted almonds
1 cup green pepper, diced
½ cup sour cream
1 tablespoon fresh lemon juice
¼ teaspoon tarragon (optional)
¼ teaspoon chervil (optional)
¼ teaspoon nutmeg
1 cup mayonnaise

Combine ingredients and chill several hours. Serve on lettuce and garnish with cantaloupe, peaches, or strawberries.

Chef's Salad

Yield: 8 servings

1 head lettuce
1 head romaine
1 cup cooked ham, cut into strips
1 cup cooked chicken, cut into strips
4 hard-cooked eggs, sliced
1 can anchovies
8 to 10 sweet pickles, sliced
Vinaigrette (see Index)

Wash and drain lettuce and romaine; arrange on 8 salad plates. Spread remaining ingredients over tops of greens. Pour salad dressing over all; serve chilled.

Chicken Salad with Avocado Mayonnaise

Yield: Varies

Cooked chicken, skin and bones removed
Chopped walnuts
Chopped onion
Snipped parsley
Lettuce
Salt

Chicken Salad with Avocado Mayonnaise

Pepper
Paprika
Lemon
1 ripe avocado
Mayonnaise (homemade or store-bought mixed
   with a raw egg yolk)
Rosemary or oregano
Several whole walnuts

Cut the chicken into small pieces. Mix the chicken meat with the walnuts, parsley, and onion. Place on a leaf of lettuce in an individual serving bowl. Lightly season with salt, pepper, and paprika. Sprinkle with a little lemon juice.

Mash the avocado and blend it with mayonnaise, pressed lemon, salt, and freshly ground black pepper, and a small amount of rosemary or oregano. Pour the avocado mayonnaise over the salad; garnish with several whole walnut meats and pieces of lettuce. Serve with warm, crisp French bread.

Wintry Turkey Salad

Yield: 4 servings

2 cups leftover turkey, chopped
¼ cup celery, cut in thin crescents
2 tablespoons pimiento, finely chopped
2 tablespoons capers
1 tablespoon green onion, finely chopped
1 tablespoon parsley, finely chopped
½ cup mayonnaise
1 teaspoon Dijon mustard
Salt to taste
A few drops Tabasco sauce
½ lemon
Bibb lettuce

Toss the ingredients together, except for the lemon and Bibb lettuce, adjusting seasoning. Squeeze lemon juice to taste.

To serve, arrange on Bibb lettuce leaves.

Smoked Turkey Salad

Yield: 8 servings

1 cup smoked turkey, diced
1 cup Swiss cheese, diced
2 cooked beets, diced
2 cold boiled potatoes, diced
1 pimiento, chopped
1 cup romaine, shredded
1 teaspoon chopped chives
French dressing
Watercress
Hard-cooked eggs

Combine all ingredients, adding enough French dressing to moisten. Season to taste and garnish with watercress and sliced hard-cooked eggs.

Blue Cheese Dressing

Yield: About 2 cups

1 cup mayonnaise
1 cup plain yogurt
1 tablespoon Worcestershire sauce
½ small onion, finely chopped or grated
1 clove garlic, minced
2 ounces blue cheese, crumbled

Combine all ingredients. Allow to stand overnight, if possible.

Creamy Garlic Dressing

Yield: 1 cup

1 cup mayonnaise
3 tablespoons skim milk
2 tablespoons cider vinegar
½ teaspoon sugar
¼ teaspoon salt
⅛ teaspoon pepper
1 clove garlic, crushed

Stir together all ingredients. Cover; chill.

French Dressing or Vinaigrette

Yield: 1⅓ cups

2 teaspoons salt
½ teaspoon freshly ground pepper
1 teaspoon prepared mustard
1 cup olive oil
¼ cup red wine vinegar

Place the salt, pepper, and mustard in a medium-sized bowl; then add several drops of olive oil. Blend with a wooden spoon. Add several drops of vinegar, blending well. Add remaining oil and vinegar gradually, stirring constantly, until the total amount is used. Store in covered jar in refrigerator. Shake well before using.

Italian Dressing

Yield: 1⅓ cups

1 cup oil
⅓ cup red wine vinegar
½ teaspoon salt
½ teaspoon dry mustard
¼ teaspoon paprika
⅛ teaspoon cayenne pepper
½ teaspoon oregano
½ teaspoon marjoram
½ clove garlic

Combine all ingredients and chill. Remove garlic before serving.

Curry Mayonnaise

Yield: 1¼ cups

1 cup mayonnaise
3 tablespoons catsup
2 tablespoons sweet pickle or India relish
1 teaspoon prepared spicy brown mustard
1 teaspoon curry powder

With a fork or a whisk, mix together all the ingredients. Store, tightly covered, in the refrigerator.

Lemon-Basil Dressing

Yield: 1 cup

⅔ cup olive oil
3 tablespoons lemon juice
2 cloves garlic, minced
1 tablespoon minced fresh basil or ¾ teaspoon dried leaf basil
1 teaspoon salt
¼ teaspoon freshly ground pepper

Combine all ingredients in a small bowl or jar. Mix well. Cover. Refrigerate until ready to use. Serve with pasta salad.

Homemade Roquefort Dressing

Yield: 1¾ cups

1 cup sour cream
2 tablespoons mayonnaise
2 tablespoons lemon juice
¾ teaspoon Tabasco sauce
2 green onions, chopped
½ cup Roquefort cheese, crumbled
Salt

Mix together sour cream, mayonnaise, lemon juice, and Tabasco sauce. Fold in green onions and cheese. Salt to taste. Refrigerate several hours.

Sour Cream Dressing

Yield: 1¼ cups

1 cup sour cream
¼ cup lemon juice
1 teaspoon sugar
½ teaspoon salt
Cayenne pepper to taste
¼ teaspoon celery salt
½ teaspoon paprika
1 teaspoon dry mustard
¼ teaspoon garlic salt

Combine all ingredients in a small mixer bowl and beat until smooth.

Thousand Island Dressing

Yield: 1⅔ cups

2 tablespoons chili sauce
1 cup mayonnaise
⅓ cup milk
2 tablespoons sweet pickle relish
1 hard-cooked egg, chopped

Gradually stir chili sauce into mayonnaise. Add milk, pickle relish, and egg; stir until well blended. Chill. Serve on tossed salad greens.

Chicken Bread with Autumn's Harvest

Poultry

Skillet Apricot Chicken

Yield: 4 servings

1 3-pound broiler or frying chicken, cut up
2 tablespoons flour
½ teaspoon salt
¾ teaspoon garlic powder
¼ teaspoon ginger
1 tablespoon vegetable oil
¾ cup orange juice
¼ cup honey
2 chicken bouillon cubes, crumbled
½ teaspoon rosemary, crushed
1 3-inch stick cinnamon
½ cup dried apricots
½ cup scallions, sliced

Wash and dry the chicken. Mix the flour, garlic powder, salt, and ginger. Roll chicken pieces in the flour mixture. Heat the oil in a large skillet and add the chicken. Sauté until browned on both sides.

Combine the orange juice, honey, bouillon, and rosemary. Pour over the chicken. Add the cinnamon stick, apricots, and scallions. Heat to boiling. Reduce heat, cover, and simmer for 25 minutes. Uncover and cook over medium heat 3 to 5 minutes, spooning sauce over chicken frequently until chicken is glazed.

Barbecued Chicken

Yield: 4 to 6 servings

1 2½- to 3-pound frying chicken, cut into serving pieces
2 tablespoons butter
1 cup catsup
½ cup chili sauce
1 teaspoon dry mustard
Dash Tabasco sauce
⅓ cup vinegar
2 teaspoons Worcestershire sauce
3 tablespoons brown sugar
1 medium onion, grated

Disjoint chicken; place in casserole dish with cover.

Place the rest of the ingredients in a saucepan; bring to a boil. Simmer 5 minutes, until all flavors blend. Pour sauce over chicken. If possible, marinate several hours. Cover casserole; bake at 350°F 1½ hours. Uncover for last 15 minutes of baking.

Barbecued Chicken with Herb Butter

Yield: 4 servings

½ cup dry white wine
2 tablespoons oil
Juice of ½ lemon
1 small onion, peeled and chopped
½ teaspoon tarragon
1 3-pound chicken

herb butter
½ cup butter or margarine
4 tablespoons parsley, chopped
2 teaspoons rosemary

Combine wine, oil, lemon, onion, and tarragon. Cut chicken into 8 pieces; put into wine mixture. Leave several hours; turn frequently. Drain.

Put herb butter ingredients into a small pan; heat just enough to melt the butter. Use half to baste the chicken; put the rest into the refrigerator to firm.

Brush the chicken with half the Herb Butter. Cook on rack over glowing coals; baste several times. Cook until chicken is crisp and golden.

Cut the rest of the butter into pats and serve it on the chicken.

Lemon Barbecued Chicken

Yield: 6 to 8 servings

2 broilers
½ cup butter or margarine
1 clove garlic, mashed
1½ teaspoons salt
¼ cup salad oil
½ cup lemon juice
2 tablespoons onion, minced
½ teaspoon pepper
½ teaspoon dried thyme

Split chicken in half. Rinse in cold water and dry. Melt butter in a heavy skillet or pan. Brown chicken on both sides; combine rest of ingredients and pour the sauce over the chicken. Cover tightly. Cook over low heat about 40 minutes or until chicken is tender.

Beer Batter Chicken

Yield: 3 to 4 servings

2 eggs, well beaten
⅔ cup beer or ale
1 cup flour
½ teaspoon salt
2 tablespoons oil or melted shortening for frying
1 2½- to 3-pound chicken, cut into serving pieces

Combine eggs and beer. Slowly beat in flour, salt, and 2 tablespoons oil until batter is smooth. Dip chicken into batter; drain. Drop into heated oil at 375°F and fry 15 to 20 minutes.

Leftover Chicken with Biscuit Topping

Yield: 4 servings

filling
2 tablespoons vegetable oil
1 small onion, peeled and chopped
½ green pepper, finely chopped
⅔ cup mushrooms, sliced
2 tablespoons cornstarch
1½ cups milk
1½-2 cups cooked chicken, cut into cubes

biscuits
2 cups flour
1 teaspoon salt
2½ teaspoons baking powder
⅓ cup shortening
About ⅔ cup milk

Heat the oil in a skillet; add onion, green pepper, and mushrooms and sauté for a few minutes. Add cornstarch and cook for 1 minute, stirring constantly. Gradually add milk; stir until boiling, then add chicken and seasoning. Turn into a deep 8-9 inch pie plate.

Sift flour, salt, and baking powder together; cut in shortening with a pastry blender until mixture looks like coarse bread crumbs. Using a fork, stir in enough milk to make a soft but not sticky dough. Knead lightly on a floured board, roll out about ½ inch thick and cut into 1½-inch rounds with a cookie cutter. Place the rounds on top of the chicken mixture; brush with milk and bake for 10-15 minutes at 450°F.

Chicken Bread with Autumn's Harvest

Yield: 6 servings

1 round bread, country-style
2 tablespoons butter or margarine, melted
1 beaten egg

Filling
1 onion
1 tablespoon butter or margarine
1 to 2 tablespoons flour
¾ cup vegetable broth
3 juniper berries, crushed
½ teaspoon thyme
½ teaspoon salt
⅛ teaspoon black pepper
1 pound cooked chicken meat
1 can chanterelles (mushrooms)
¼ pound fresh mushrooms

Cut a lid off the bread and dig out well. (Save the bread and dry it to use as bread crumbs.) Brush the bread, both inside and out, first with the melted butter and then with the beaten egg. Heat at 350°F for about 5 minutes.

Peel and thinly slice the onion. Brown it lightly in butter. Sprinkle with flour and cover with the broth. Add the seasoning and simmer over low heat for a few minutes. Cut the chicken into pieces and stir into the sauce. Put aside.

Pour the liquid from the chanterelles into a pot. Chop the chanterelles and add them to the liquid. Brush any dirt off the mushrooms. Avoid rinsing them. Slice and simmer them with the chanterelles until the liquid has been absorbed. Season, if desired, with salt and pepper.

Cover the bottom of the bread with half of the mushroom mixture. Place the chicken mixture over the mushrooms, and finally cover the chicken with the rest of the mushroom mixture. Cover with the bread lid and warm the bread in the oven for another 7 to 10 minutes. Serve the bread warm with a salad or fresh vegetables.

Brunswick Stew

Yield: 4 to 6 servings

1 3- to 4-pound stewing or roasting chicken
1 teaspoon salt
3 potatoes, sliced
1 large onion, sliced
1 cup green lima beans
1 cup canned tomatoes (or 5-6 sliced fresh tomatoes)
1 tablespoon sugar
1 cup corn
1 tablespoon catsup or Worcestershire sauce
4 tablespoons butter

Cut chicken into pieces and put it in a casserole with enough boiling water to cover; add a little salt. Simmer for about 45 minutes. Add sliced potatoes, sliced onion, lima beans, tomatoes, and sugar to casserole. Cook for 45 minutes, until beans and potatoes are tender.

Remove as many bones as possible from the chicken; add the corn. Cook for 10 minutes. Then season to taste and add catsup or Worcestershire sauce, if desired. Add butter and stir well.

Brandied Cherry Chicken

Yield: 4 to 5 servings

1 8-ounce can pitted Bing cherries
¼ cup port wine
1 3-pound broiler or frying chicken, quartered
1 tablespoon vegetable oil
¼ cup brandy
¾ cup hot water
1 large onion, thinly sliced
½ teaspoon salt
Few grains pepper
1½ tablespoons cornstarch

Drain cherries; reserve ¼ cup syrup. Pour reserved syrup and wine over cherries; cover. Marinate in refrigerator 2 hours.

Remove excess fat from chicken. Heat oil in a large skillet over moderately high heat; add chicken. Cook until lightly browned on all sides. Remove from heat. Pour brandy over chicken and ignite with match. When flame goes out, add water, onion, salt, and pepper. Cover and cook over moderately low heat 40 to 45 minutes, until chicken is fork-tender. Remove chicken to platter.

Pour juices into a measuring cup; remove as much fat as possible. Drain marinated cherries; reserve liquid. Blend cherry syrup into cornstarch; pour into a skillet. Add chicken juices; cook over moderate heat, stirring constantly, until sauce is thickened. Add cherries; cook 2 to 3 minutes to heat cherries. Pour over chicken.

Chicken in Cider and Mustard

Yield: 4 servings

1 spring chicken
½ tablespoon margarine
1 large onion, peeled and thinly sliced
½ to 1 teaspoon salt
½ teaspoon black pepper
⅔ cup apple cider
1 tablespoon light French mustard
½ teaspoon dried, or 2 sprigs fresh, thyme
⅔ cup light cream

Divide the chicken into 6 to 8 pieces. Brown the chicken on all sides in margarine. Add the sliced onion, salt, pepper, and cider. Mix the mustard and thyme with the light cream and pour it into the pot.

Mix thoroughly and let the chicken simmer for 30 to 35 minutes. Serve with chopped parsley, boiled potatoes, and tender boiled carrots.

Chicken in Cider and Mustard

Spiced Cranberry Chicken

Yield: 4 servings

½ cup flour
1 teaspoon salt
⅛ teaspoon pepper
6 frying chicken legs and thighs
¼ inch salad oil
2 tablespoons brown sugar
1 tablespoon cornstarch
¾ cup cranberry juice cocktail
1-pound can whole cranberry sauce
1 teaspoon ground nutmeg
1 teaspoon ground marjoram
1 tablespoon onion, minced

In a paper bag, mix flour, salt, and pepper together. Shake chicken pieces in seasoned flour mixture to coat. Brown chicken on all sides in hot oil. Cover tightly. Reduce heat and cook gently 20-30 minutes, turning occasionally, until tender. Drain on paper towels.

Mix brown sugar and cornstarch together in a saucepan. Slowly stir in cranberry juice cocktail until smooth. Add whole cranberry sauce, spices, and minced onion. Cook over medium heat, stirring, until mixture comes to a boil. Spoon over top of chicken.

Creamed Chicken and Ham

Yield: 4 servings

1½ tablespoons flour or cornstarch
1½ tablespoons butter
¾ cup chicken stock
¼ cup cream
½ cup cooked chicken, diced
½ cup cooked ham, diced
¼ cup celery, chopped
1 tablespoon parsley
1 egg, beaten
1 or 2 tablespoons sherry (optional)

Add flour to melted butter; stir until blended. Slowly stir in soup stock, then cream. When sauce is smooth and at boiling point, add chicken, ham, celery, and parsley.

Mix 2 tablespoons of the sauce with the beaten egg. Reduce heat to low; return egg mixture to heat. Stir constantly until it thickens slightly. If you like, add 1 or 2 tablespoons sherry just before serving.

Creole Chicken

Chicken Crisps

Yield: 4 servings

4 tablespoons butter
2 tablespoons flour
1 cup milk
8 mushrooms, sliced
4 tablespoons stock
2 cups cooked chicken, chopped or diced
½ cup cooked peas or corn
5 thick slices white bread
1 cup oil
1 tablespoon parsley, chopped

Melt 3 tablespoons of the butter; blend in flour. Gradually add milk. When smooth, bring to a boil, stirring constantly. Boil 3 minutes, then cool slightly.

Cook mushrooms in stock 3 to 4 minutes. Add chicken and cooked vegetables. Add mixture to cream sauce and season well. Heat thoroughly; keep warm.

Remove crusts from bread; with a small cutter, cut 4 crescent-shaped pieces from 1 slice.

Heat oil; add remaining 1 tablespoon of butter. When foaming, fry bread slices and crescents until golden brown on both sides; drain on paper towel.

Arrange bread slices on a serving dish; spoon hot chicken mixture onto bread. Decorate with crescents and chopped parsley.

Creole Chicken

Yield: 4 servings

1 2½-pound chicken
6 to 7 slices of bacon
⅓ cup flour
1 tablespoon olive oil
¾ cup onion, sliced
1 clove garlic, chopped
2 to 3 celery stalks
1 green pepper, shredded
2 14-ounce cans crushed tomatoes
2 teaspoons thyme
1 teaspoon black pepper
¼ teaspoon cayenne pepper
1 bay leaf
Juice from ½ lemon

Divide the chicken into 8 pieces. Fry the bacon slices until brown and crispy in a stew pot. Take them out and let them drain on a paper towel.

Dredge the chicken pieces in flour and fry them in the bacon fat so that they become golden brown all over. Take them out of the pot. Pour the olive oil into the pot and add the onion and garlic. After about 5 minutes, add the celery and the green pepper.

After another 3 minutes, add the canned tomatoes and the rest of the spices. Let the mixture come to a boil. Place the chicken pieces on the vegetable mixture, cover, and let simmer for 30 minutes. Add a little water if the mixture becomes too dry.

Just before serving, add the lemon juice. Then sprinkle with the bacon slices, which also can be slightly crumbled. Serve with rice.

Batter-Fried Chicken Breasts

Yield: 4 to 6 servings

6 to 8 chicken breasts, boned
2 teaspoons salt
Dash pepper
1 egg, lightly beaten
½ cup milk
2 tablespoons flour
1½ cups flour for dredging chicken
Oil for deep-fat frying

Divide each chicken breast in half to make 12 to 16 pieces. Sprinkle each piece with salt and pepper.

Mix egg and milk in a shallow bowl or pie dish. Add flour and mix until very smooth. Dip each chicken piece in batter; dredge generously in flour. Put 4 or 5 chicken pieces into preheated 375°F oil; deep-fry 12 to 15 minutes or until chicken is golden brown on all sides. Drain on paper towels. Keep warm in a very low oven until all the chicken is fried.

Fried Chicken with Cream Gravy

Yield: 4 to 6 servings

Salt, pepper, and garlic salt
1 cup flour
1 2½- to 3-pound frying chicken, cut into serving pieces
Fat for deep frying

cream gravy
2 tablespoons cornstarch
¾ cup hot chicken broth
½ cup milk at room temperature
1 teaspoon salt
¼ teaspoon pepper

Mix seasonings with flour; coat each chicken piece.

Heat fat in a skillet; fry the chicken, a few pieces at a time. Cook about 25 minutes per batch of chicken, so that pieces are crisp and crusty. Drain on paper towels; set on a warmed platter.

Pour off most of the fat in the skillet; leave about 2 tablespoons.

Mix cornstarch with chicken broth. Add to the hot fat, stirring constantly. Gradually add milk, salt, and pepper. When slightly thickened, gravy is ready. Serve with the chicken.

Chicken Croquettes

Yield: 4 to 6 servings

4 cups cooked chicken, put through meat grinder
1 cup celery, chopped
1 tablespoon onion, grated
4 tablespoons butter
4 tablespoons flour
1 cup milk
1 teaspoon salt
Generous dash of freshly ground pepper
1 egg, beaten with 1 tablespoon milk
1 cup cracker meal
Oil for deep frying
2 cans cream of mushroom soup

Mix chicken and celery in a large bowl; set aside. Sauté onion in butter in a small saucepan until onion is transparent. Blend in flour. Add milk and heat, stirring constantly. When slightly thickened, add salt and pepper; simmer just 3 minutes. Add sauce to chicken and celery and chill several hours.

Shape chicken into rolls about 3 inches long. Dip rolls into egg; coat with cracker meal. Place croquettes on a waxed-paper-lined baking sheet; chill in refrigerator at least 3 hours.

Fry croquettes in deep fat, a few at a time, until brown on all sides; drain on paper towels. Keep warm in very low (250°F) oven until ready to serve.

For a quick sauce, heat cream of mushroom soup over low heat; stir until piping hot. If you prefer a thinner sauce, add milk by ¼ cups; stir until desired consistency is reached.

Chicken in Crumb Baskets

Yield: 6 servings

crumb baskets
5 cups soft bread crumbs
¼ cup onion, minced
1 teaspoon celery salt
⅛ teaspoon pepper
½ cup melted butter or margarine
chicken filling
⅓ cup butter or margarine
⅓ cup flour
½ cup light cream
1½ cups chicken broth
½ teaspoon salt
⅛ teaspoon pepper
1 teaspoon Worcestershire sauce
1 cup cooked peas
3 cups cooked chicken, chopped

Mix the bread crumbs with the onion, seasonings, and butter. Grease 6 individual casseroles and line with the crumb mixture. Press into place. Bake in a 375°F oven for 15 minutes, or until the crumbs are brown.

To make the filling, blend the flour in melted butter. Stir in the cream, broth, and seasonings. Keep stirring and cook until thickened. Then add the peas and chicken. Serve the chicken mixture in the baked crumb baskets.

Cucumber-Filled Chicken

Yield: 3 to 4 servings

1 2½-pound chicken
Salt
Pepper
3 tablespoons pink pepper, crushed
1 cucumber
1 tablespoon soy sauce
1 tablespoon pressed lemon juice
⅓ cup dry white wine
1½ crumbled chicken bouillon cubes
½ container crème fraîche or heavy cream
2 tablespoons flour stirred into 2½ tablespoons light cream

Cucumber-Filled Chicken

Remove the skin and the fat from the chicken. Salt and pepper the inside. Crush 2 tablespoons of the pink peppercorns. Peel the cucumber and cut into thin slices. Mix the cucumber slices with the crushed pepper. Fill the chicken with the mixture and tie up the chicken with kitchen string.

Mix together the soy sauce, lemon juice, and the remaining 1 tablespoon of pepper, crushed. Brush the chicken with the mixture. Place the chicken in an ungreased, ovenproof dish that has a lid (preferably an earthenware dish) and pour the wine over the bird. Add the crumbled chicken bouillon cubes. Place the dish in a cold oven and set the temperature for 425°F. Bake for about 1 hour after the oven has reached this temperature.

Remove the chicken from the dish, take away the string, and remove the cucumber stuffing, which is to be added to the sauce. Allow the cucumber mixture to drain. Keep the chicken warm by wrapping it in aluminum foil and placing it back in the oven.

Strain the gravy and pour it into a pot. There should be about 1 ¼ cups of gravy. Stir in the crème fraîche and bring to a boil. Stir in the flour with a whisk. Add the well-drained cucumber mixture into the sauce, which should have a creamy consistency. This is not a thick sauce.

Chicken Florentine Au Gratin

Yield: 4 servings

1 package frozen spinach leaves
2 chicken breasts, skinned and boned
½ teaspoon salt
Dash grated nutmeg

cheese sauce
1½ tablespoons margarine
3 tablespoons wheat flour
1⅔ cups chicken bouillon
4 twists of ground black pepper from the mill
1 egg yolk
⅔ cup single cream
¾ cup cheese (preferably strong cheese), grated

Cover an ovenproof dish with the thawed and well-drained spinach leaves. Cut the breast into bits but place them so that they still look whole on top of the spinach leaves. Season with salt and nutmeg.

Melt the margarine in a saucepan on a low heat. Add the flour and make a roux for the sauce. Then add the chicken bouillon, turn up the heat, and stir until the sauce comes to the boil. Reduce the heat again and cook for 3 minutes. Season with the black pepper.

Stir the egg yolk in the cream. Remove the saucepan from the heat and stir the egg mixture quickly into the sauce. Add the grated cheese and pour the sauce over the chicken meat and spinach leaves.

Bake in a preheated 425°F oven for 15 minutes. Serve with boiled rice or potatoes.

Fruit and Nut Stuffed Chicken Breasts

Yield: 6 servings

¾ cup butter
1 cup apple, diced
½ cup nuts, coarsely chopped
½ cup golden raisins
1 can (1 pound, 4 ounces) crushed pineapple
1 cup soft bread crumbs, toasted
1 teaspoon salt
1 teaspoon cinnamon
½ teaspoon nutmeg
¼ teaspoon ginger
¼ teaspoon ground cloves
6 whole chicken breasts, boned

fruit sauce
1 tablespoon sugar
1 tablespoon cornstarch
⅛ teaspoon salt
½ teaspoon cinnamon
¼ teaspoon nutmeg
⅛ teaspoon ginger
1 cup orange juice
Pineapple and syrup reserved from stuffing
¼ cup golden raisins
1 tablespoon butter
Sections and slivered peel of 1 orange

Melt ½ cup of the butter in a skillet; sauté the apple and nuts 10 minutes. Remove from heat. Add raisins, ½ cup drained pineapple (reserve remaining pineapple), toasted bread crumbs, ½ teaspoon salt, cinnamon, nutmeg, ginger, and cloves.

Sprinkle inside of chicken breasts with ½ teaspoon salt. Place ⅓ cup of the fruit stuffing on the inside of each breast; fold the sides over and fasten with skewers or string.

Place remaining ¼ cup butter in a 9 × 13-inch baking pan lined with foil; place in moderate oven (375°F) until melted, about 5 minutes. Place breasts top side down in the melted butter; return pan to oven and bake chicken 25 minutes. Turn chicken over and bake 20 minutes more.

Combine sugar, cornstarch, salt, cinnamon, nutmeg, and ginger. Stir in orange juice; add pineapple and pineapple syrup, raisins, butter, and slivered peel. Cook, stirring constantly, over medium heat until mixture comes to a boil and thickens. Add orange sections and heat. Serve with the chicken breasts.

Chicken Florentine au Gratin

Oven-Fried Chicken

Yield: 4 to 5 servings

1 young chicken, cut into serving pieces
4 tablespoons flour
Salt
Black pepper
Paprika
1 egg, beaten
Fine bread crumbs
3 to 4 tablespoons oil

Preheat oven to 400°F.

Toss chicken lightly in flour to which a little salt, pepper, and paprika have been added. Brush with a beaten egg, then coat with bread crumbs.

Heat oil in a roasting pan; put in chicken. Brush lightly with hot oil and bake about 30 minutes.

Glazed Chicken

Yield: 4 servings

1 10-ounce jar apricot preserves
6 chicken breasts
1 package onion soup
1 bottle red Russian dressing

Cover the chicken with the preserves, then sprinkle on the onion soup. Pour on the Russian dressing. Take the bottle of dressing, after emptying it, and fill with water; pour the water over the chicken. Bake about 1 hour at 350°F. You may baste during baking.

Honey Chicken

Yield: 4 servings

½ cup flour
1 teaspoon salt
3 or 4 chicken breasts, boned
1 stick butter
¼ cup honey
¼ cup lemon juice
1 tablespoon soy sauce

Combine the flour and salt. Dip chicken in the flour-salt mixture. Melt butter and pour over chicken. Bake ½ hour at 350°F. Mix the rest of ingredients and pour over chicken. Bake 30 minutes longer, basting often. Serve over rice.

Groundnut Stew

Yield: 8 to 10 servings

1 2- to 3-pound frying chicken, cut into small
    pieces
Salt and pepper to taste
1 pound beef cubes, 1-inch size
2 tablespoons oil (peanut oil is good)
1 teaspoon salt
1 cup onions, chopped
1 green pepper, chopped
2 large tomatoes, peeled and diced
1½ teaspoons cayenne pepper
2 cups water
1½ cups peanut butter

Season chicken with salt and pepper; set aside.

Brown the beef cubes in hot oil in a large skillet. Add salt, ½ the onions, ½ the pepper and tomatoes, cayenne, and water. Simmer this gently for 30 minutes.

Mix 1 cup of cooking liquid with peanut butter to make a smooth paste. Add to skillet; cook 15 minutes more. Add chicken pieces and remainder of vegetables. Simmer 30 minutes, until all is tender.

Chicken Hot Pot

Yield: 4 to 5 servings

1 2½- to 3-pound frying chicken
1 tablespoon flour
4 tablespoons butter or margarine
1 large onion, peeled and sliced
1 can tomatoes (2 cups)
2 teaspoons brown sugar
2 teaspoons prepared mustard
4 medium-sized potatoes, peeled and sliced
2 apples, peeled, cored, and sliced

cream slaw
1 small head firm white cabbage, shredded
1 small green pepper, seeded and shredded
2 teaspoons prepared mustard
½ teaspoon paprika
2 teaspoons lemon juice
½ cup sour cream

Disjoint the chicken, dredge with flour mixed with a little salt and pepper, and brown on all sides in the butter. Remove from the pan.

Lightly brown the onion in the remaining butter. Add tomatoes, sugar, and mustard and heat gently. Arrange the potatoes in the bottom of a buttered casserole, season lightly, and add the apples; cover with the tomato mixture. Put the chicken pieces on top; cover and cook in a 350°F oven for about 1½ hours.

Mix the cabbage and green pepper. Add the other ingredients to the sour cream, blend well, and toss the cabbage and pepper lightly in the sour-cream dressing. Serve with the chicken.

Orange Chicken

Yield: 4 to 6 servings

3-pound frying chicken, quartered and
    skinned
4 teaspoons Dijon mustard (optional)
1 teaspoon salt
¼ teaspoon pepper
2 tablespoons butter
1 small onion, chopped
1 cup orange juice
¼ cup brown sugar, lightly packed

Spread mustard on the meaty side of the chicken and sprinkle with salt and pepper. Place meaty side down in a 10 × 6 × 1¾-inch baking pan. Add butter, onion, and orange juice. Bake in a preheated 375°F oven, for 20 minutes, basting midway. Turn chicken over.

Stir the sugar into juices in the pan. Continue baking approximately 40 minutes, basting several times, until the chicken is golden brown and tender. Remove chicken and keep hot.

Pour the juice into a 1-quart saucepan and boil gently, stirring often until reduced and thickened. Spoon this glaze over the chicken.

Jambalaya

Yield: 6 servings

1 3-pound frying chicken, cut into serving
    pieces
Salt and pepper
3 tablespoons bacon drippings or vegetable oil
2 cups celery, sliced
2 cups green onions with tops, sliced
1 cup green peppers, chopped
1 cup uncooked rice
2 cups boiling broth
1 teaspoon salt
½ teaspoon garlic salt
¼ teaspoon black pepper
¼ teaspoon red pepper

Season chicken with salt and pepper. Brown on all sides in drippings in a large skillet or Dutch oven. Remove chicken. Pour off all but 2 tablespoons of the drippings. Add celery, onions, and green peppers. Sauté until tender. Stir in rice, broth, and seasonings. Return chicken to pan. Cover and bake at 375°F for 30 minutes or until chicken is tender. Fluff with a fork.

Chicken in Lemon-Dill Butter

Yield: 4 to 6 servings

¼ pound butter
2 tablespoons lemon juice
1 teaspoon salt
1 clove garlic, minced
½ teaspoon paprika
1 can sliced mushrooms, drained
1 tablespoon dillweed
2½- to 3-pound frying chicken, cut into serving pieces

Melt the butter in a large skillet. Add all ingredients, except the chicken. Bring to a boil. Add chicken, bring to the boiling point, but do not actually boil. Cover skillet. Lower heat; simmer 30 minutes or until chicken is tender.

Remove chicken to a platter; serve with noodles or rice, covered with the remaining liquid.

Lemon and Garlic-Filled Chicken Breasts

Yield: 4 servings

8 chicken breasts
Salt
Pepper
7 tablespoons butter, at room temperature
3 cloves garlic, crushed
Juice of 1 lemon
2 tablespoons parsley, finely chopped
Flour
1 egg, beaten
Bread crumbs
Oil

Remove the bones and pound the breasts so that they become quite thin. Salt and pepper them slightly. Mix the butter with the garlic, lemon juice, parsley, salt, and pepper. Spread the butter mixture on the chicken breasts, fold in the edges, and roll them together. Fasten with a toothpick.

First roll the breasts in flour, then dip them in a beaten egg. Finally roll in the bread crumbs. Fry them rather slowly in hot oil until they have become golden brown and are cooked through.

Serve with peeled, seeded cucumbers, which have simmered slightly in the rest of the butter, and rice.

Chicken and Lobster Marengo

Yield: 8 to 10 servings

2 pounds boned chicken breasts, cut into bite-sized pieces
1 onion, sliced
1 clove garlic, crushed
½ cup olive oil
2 cups chicken broth (undiluted)
2 16-ounce cans Italian-style tomatoes or 5 medium-sized tomatoes, peeled and chopped
¾ cup celery, diced
1 bay leaf
2 tablespoons fresh parsley, minced
¾ teaspoon thyme
¾ teaspoon basil
¾ teaspoon tarragon
¼ cup dry sherry
Salt and pepper to taste
3 cups fresh mushrooms
1 jar pearl onions
1 pound cooked lobster meat (or shrimp)
1 jigger brandy

In a skillet, brown the chicken, onion slices, and garlic in olive oil. Set aside. In a saucepan, combine the broth, tomatoes, celery, and bay leaf. Bring to a boil; cover and simmer about 30 minutes.

Add parsley, herbs, sherry, salt, and pepper. Cook about 5 minutes more. Add mushrooms, pearl onions, chicken mixture, lobster, and brandy. If sauce seems too thin, thicken it with a little flour and water.

Simmer until thickened and transfer to a casserole dish. Bake for 20 to 30 minutes at 350°F. Serve over rice. This tastes better if served the next day.

Mint Julep Chicken

Yield: 4 to 6 servings

6 tablespoons butter
4 whole chicken breasts, skinned and boned
¼ cup shallots, chopped
½ pound mushrooms, sliced
Juice of ½ lemon
Salt and pepper to taste
¼ cup bourbon
1 cup heavy cream
2 tablespoons mint, finely chopped

Melt 4 tablespoons of the butter in a pan; sauté the chicken breasts 1 minute on each side. Remove the chicken and keep it warm. Add shallots and cook for 3 minutes. Add the remaining 2 tablespoons of butter and sauté the mushrooms with lemon juice, salt, and pepper for 3 minutes. Add the bourbon and heavy cream and bring to a boil.

Put chicken breasts back in the dish, cover, and cook for 10 minutes. If the sauce is too thin, remove the chicken and reduce the sauce, stirring, until it coats a spoon. Garnish with chopped mint.

Nutty Chicken

Yield: 4 servings

1 cup dry roasted, skinless peanuts,
    finely chopped
½ cup fine dry bread crumbs
1¼ teaspoons salt
½ teaspoon poultry seasoning
Pepper to taste
4 broiler drumsticks
4 broiler wings
¼ cup chicken broth

Mix peanuts, crumbs, and seasonings together.

Dip chicken pieces in the broth, then in the peanut mixture; coat all over. Place in a single layer on a foil-lined pan. Bake at 400°F 40 minutes or until tender. Do not turn chicken during baking.

Chicken and Oyster Casserole

Yield: 4 servings

1 frying chicken, cut up
1 cup water
½ cup vinegar
1 clove garlic
1 pinch dried thyme
1 bay leaf
1 teaspoon salt
1 pint oysters
2 tablespoons butter
1 tablespoon flour
2 tablespoons sherry
1 tablespoon parsley, minced
3 tablespoons bread or cracker crumbs

Simmer the chicken in water and vinegar with garlic, thyme, bay leaf, and salt for 30 minutes, or until tender. Cool and strip the meat from the bones, reserving liquid. Discard bones and skin and cut the chicken meat into bite-sized pieces.

Drain the oysters, adding oyster liquor to the liquid in which the chicken was cooked. In a frying pan, melt 1 tablespoon butter and stir in flour. Stir in the chicken-and-oyster liquid and simmer until slightly thickened. Add sherry and parsley; pour the sauce over the chicken and oysters in a 2-quart baking dish. Top with crumbs and the remaining tablespoon of butter; cut in small bits. Bake 15 minutes at 350°F. Serve on hot biscuits.

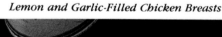

Lemon and Garlic-Filled Chicken Breasts

Marinated Chicken

Yield: 4 servings

1 chicken, about 2½ pounds

marinade
2 cups yogurt
1 onion, peeled and sliced
2 teaspoons curry
1 teaspoon ginger
2 teaspoons paprika
1 teaspoon caraway
1 to 2 cloves garlic, crushed

cucumber salad
2 cups yogurt
½ to ¾ cucumber
¼ cup chives, finely snipped
1 teaspoon salt
Black pepper

Divide the chicken in half. Mix all the marinade ingredients together. Place the chicken halves in a deep plate. Cover with the marinade. Refrigerate for 6 to 8 hours. Turn the chicken several times while it is marinating.

Preheat the oven to 350°F. Place the chicken halves in an ovenproof dish. Pour the marinade over the chicken and brush the chicken well. Bake for about 45 minutes. Brush the chicken occasionally with the marinade while it is baking.

When making the cucumber salad, allow the yogurt to drain through a coffee filter for about 15 minutes. Thinly slice the cucumber. It is easiest to do this with a cheese slicer. Mix with the yogurt. Add the chives; season with salt and pepper. Serve with brown rice.

Marsala Chicken

Yield: 4 servings

1 chicken, cut into serving pieces
⅔ cup Marsala (Port wine or Madeira can be used)
1½ tablespoons butter
1 shallot, peeled and chopped
About 1 teaspoon salt
¼ teaspoon black pepper
⅓ cup water
2 teaspoons flour
⅓ cup crème fraîche or heavy cream
Chopped walnuts

Marinated Chicken

Place the pieces of chicken in a plastic bag in a bowl. Pour the wine into the bag. Fold up the bag and refrigerate for 2 to 3 hours. Turn the bag occasionally while it is in the refrigerator. Remove the chicken but save the wine. Dry off the chicken.

Brown the pieces of chicken in a deep frying pan in a little butter. Add the shallot and slightly brown. Season with salt and pepper. Add the wine and water. Cover and cook the chicken for about 15 to 20 minutes, until the chicken is done. Place the pieces of chicken in a warm, deep dish.

Prepare the gravy by stirring the flour into the frying pan. Allow the sauce to boil for a few minutes, then add the cream.

Season to taste and possibly dilute the sauce slightly more. Pour over the chicken (if you prefer, strain the sauce before pouring it over the chicken). Sprinkle with the chopped nuts.

Chicken Delaware

Yield: 6 servings

6 pieces frying chicken
4 tablespoons flour mixed with salt, pepper, and a
 pinch of cayenne pepper
1 egg
1 teaspoon oil
1-1½ cups fresh, white bread crumbs
2 tablespoons oil
7 tablespoons butter
3 bananas, halved
6 slices bacon

fritters
1 cup canned corn kernels
Salt and pepper to taste
1 egg, separated
⅔ cup flour
½ teaspoon baking powder
½ teaspoon curry powder
Fat for deep frying

tomato sauce
3 tablespoons butter
1 onion, sliced
1 clove garlic, crushed
1 cup canned tomatoes
2 tablespoons mixed herbs
Salt and pepper to taste
1 teaspoon sugar
1 teaspoon paprika
½ cup cider or stock

Marsala Chicken

Roll chicken pieces in seasoned flour, then brush all over with egg beaten with oil. Coat well with fresh, white bread crumbs. Heat oil and add 4-5 tablespoons butter. When foaming, put in the chicken pieces and fry gently for 20-25 minutes, turning frequently until brown and crisp all over.

Meanwhile, prepare the corn fritters. Drain the corn and mix it with 1 egg yolk and seasoning. Sift flour, baking powder, and curry powder together; stir into corn mixture. Just before frying, beat the egg white and fold it into the corn mixture. Heat the fat until very hot but not smoking. Drop the fritter mixture into the fat by tablespoonfuls and fry until light brown. Drain on paper towels. Keep warm.

Fry bananas in 2 tablespoons butter until golden brown. Keep warm. Cut bacon slices in half and roll up carefully. Thread onto skewers and broil until crisp all over. Keep warm.

Prepare tomato sauce: Cook the onion and crushed garlic in melted butter for 5-6 minutes. Add tomatoes, herbs, seasoning, sugar, paprika, and cider or stock. Bring to a boil, then strain or blend in an electric blender or food processor and serve hot with the chicken.

Easy Paella

Yield: 4 to 6 servings

¼ pound bacon
½ onion, chopped
1 clove garlic
1 red or green pepper, cubed
2 cups chicken broth
¼ teaspoon saffron
Salt
Pepper
1 cup rice
1 broiled chicken, cut up into smaller pieces
1 can clam meats
1 10-ounce package frozen peas
About 20 large shrimp with shells
Oil
Garlic powder
Lemon wedges

Cut the bacon into smaller pieces and brown them in a pot together with the onion, garlic, and red or green pepper. Pour over the broth which has been flavored with the saffron, and season with salt and pepper. Bring to a boil. Add the rice and cover the pot. Simmer for about 25 minutes.

Warm the pieces of chicken in the rice mixture: add the clams and the peas. Dip the shrimp in a little oil that has been seasoned with garlic powder and salt. Sauté them quickly in a hot frying pan, and then place them in and on top of the rice.

Garnish with wedges of lemon.

Chicken-Peach Casserole

Yield: 6 servings

1 3½-pound frying chicken or 6 to 8 chicken joints
2 tablespoons butter or margarine
1 tablespoon oil
1 large onion, peeled and sliced
1 green pepper, seeded and cut into strips
1 large can (about 30 ounces) sliced peaches
1 tablespoon cornstarch
1 tablespoon soy sauce
3 tablespoons white wine vinegar
2 tomatoes, peeled and thickly sliced

Preheat oven to 375°F.
Disjoint and skin chicken. Heat butter and oil in a skillet. Brown chicken pieces on all sides. Cover; reduce heat. Cook about 10 minutes. Remove the chicken and arrange in a large casserole.

Sauté the onion and pepper in the remaining fat until the onion is transparent. Drain the peaches; reserve syrup.

Mix cornstarch smoothly with soy sauce and vinegar. Add 1 cup peach syrup. Pour into a skillet.

Stir until boiling; boil until clear. Add peaches and tomatoes. Pour skillet contents over the chicken. Cover casserole and cook 30 to 40 minutes. Remove lid the last 5 minutes. Adjust seasoning.

Serve with wild rice to which some cooked green peas and a few strips of red pepper have been added.

Chicken Pot Pie

Yield: 6 servings

1 5-pound stewing chicken
1½ quarts water
2 teaspoons salt
1 small onion
1 carrot
1 rib celery
½ cup flour
½ teaspoon onion salt
½ teaspoon celery salt
1 teaspoon thyme
Dash pepper
3½ cups chicken broth
2 tablespoons sherry
1 egg white, slightly beaten
Pastry for 1-crust pie

Place the chicken in a large pot and add water, 1 teaspoon salt, onion, carrot, and celery. Simmer, covered, until tender, about 2½ hours. Remove chicken and cut the meat from the bones in large pieces. Refrigerate the chicken and broth to cool.

Combine flour, onion salt, celery salt, thyme, pepper, and remaining salt with ½ cup cooled chicken broth. Mix until smooth.

Put 3 cups chicken broth in a skillet; heat and add the flour mixture, stirring constantly to prevent lumps. Cook over medium heat, stirring, until mixture is thickened. Stir in sherry. Add chicken and blend well. Cool.

Pour filling into a 9-inch, deep-dish pie pan. Roll out pastry and brush underside with egg white. Cover filling with pastry and crimp edges. Cut vents in top. Freeze, then bake at 400°F for 45 minutes to an hour.

Chicken Pie with Biscuit Topping

Yield: 8 servings

1 5-pound stewing chicken, cut in serving pieces
2 small onions
1 teaspoon salt
¼ teaspoon pepper
Chicken giblets
4 tablespoons butter
4 tablespoons flour

2 cups chicken stock
¼ cup celery, diced
2 tablespoons parsley, chopped
1 onion, minced

biscuit dough
1½ cups flour, sifted with 1½ teaspoons baking
  powder
Pinch of salt
1 scant tablespoon butter
¼ cup milk, scant

Place the chicken in a large pot; add water to cover and onions and cook until the chicken is tender, about 2½ hours. Season; remove the chicken from the broth and cut the meat from the bones.

Cook the giblets in salted water until tender; drain and mince. Melt the butter in a skillet, then add flour and a little of the broth. Add the celery, parsley, minced onion, giblets, and more chicken stock; cook all together for a few minutes. Season to taste.

Place the chicken in a buttered baking dish, pour the sauce over all, and drop teaspoonfuls of biscuit dough on top (not too close together) to make the crust.

To make the biscuit dough, sift the flour, baking powder, and salt 3 times. Cut the butter into the flour, mix, and stir in the milk. Roll out lightly on a floured board; cut in shapes.

Bake the pie in a 450°F oven for 15 minutes, or until the biscuit crust has browned.

Poached Chicken and Mushrooms
Yield: 4 servings

4 whole chicken breasts, boned and skinned
1 cup water
1 sprig fresh dillweed or 1 teaspoon dried dillweed
½ pound fresh mushrooms, sliced
2 carrots, scraped and thinly sliced
½ teaspoon salt

Arrange the chicken breasts in a large skillet. Pour water around the chicken. Add dill, mushrooms, carrots, and salt. Cover and simmer gently for 15 to 20 minutes, until chicken is cooked through.

Easy Paella

Chicken and Oyster Pie

Yield: 4 servings

12 oysters
2 tablespoons butter or margarine
1 large chicken breast, cut into strips
1 cup mushrooms, sliced
Oyster liquor, made up to ¼ cup with water
Pinch salt
Pinch cayenne pepper
Pinch sugar
½ cup light cream
1 teaspoon cornstarch
Milk
1 egg yolk
1 8-inch baked pastry shell
Chopped parsley
1-2 pimientos (can or jar)

Open the oysters and retain their liquor. Heat the butter in a sauté pan, add the strips of chicken, and mushrooms and cook quickly for a few minutes. Heat the oyster liquor and water, put in the oysters, and let sit for 7-8 minutes off the heat. Lift out into a bowl. Add the chicken, mushrooms, salt, cayenne pepper, and sugar.

Stir all but 1 tablespoon of the cream into the oyster liquor; add the cornstarch, mixed until smooth with a little milk. Stir until boiling, and boil for 1 minute.

Mix the remaining 1 tablespoon cream with the egg yolk; stir a little of the hot sauce into the cream-yolk mixture, then return to the pan. Add all the other ingredients, check the seasoning, and heat through. Pour into the warm pastry shell, sprinkle with parsley, and decorate with strips of pimiento.

Chicken in Apricot-Cinnamon Yogurt Sauce

Yield: 4 to 6 servings

4-6 chicken pieces, about 2 pounds or more
2 tablespoons oil
7-8 tablespoons butter
1 large onion, sliced
1 cup dried apricots, chopped
½ teaspoon cinnamon
Salt and pepper to taste
Grated rind of 1 lemon
1 cup yogurt
1½ cups long-grain rice
2 tablespoons almonds

Heat the oil and 2 tablespoons of butter. When foaming, fry the chicken pieces until golden brown.

Remove and let cool. Cook onion in the same oil and butter until golden. Add apricots; sprinkle with cinnamon, lemon rind, salt, and pepper. Remove bones from chicken pieces and shred meat. Mix yogurt with onion mixture and soak chicken in this while rice is cooking.

Cook rice in boiling salted water for 10-12 minutes. Drain and rinse with boiling water. Dry for a few minutes. Heat 3 tablespoons butter in thick pan or casserole; put half rice into pan and mix well with butter and seasoning. Spoon chicken mixture over rice, and put remaining rice on top. Sprinkle with salt and pepper.

Melt the remaining butter and spoon over the rice. Cover the pan with cloth and a lid and cook gently for 15-20 minutes, until all the flavors are blended; the cloth absorbs extra moisture. (This process can be done in a 350°F oven but cloth should not be used.)

Brown slivers of almonds, sprinkle on top of the rice, and serve at once.

Popovers with Creamed Chicken

Yield: 6 servings

1 cup flour
½ teaspoon salt
2 eggs
1 cup milk
3 tablespoons butter or margarine
2 tablespoons flour
¾ cup chicken broth
1 cup cooked or canned chicken, cubed
⅓ cup canned mushrooms, drained and chopped
½ teaspoon salt or seasoned salt
Dash nutmeg
1 egg
¼ cup cream
1 tablespoon sherry

Sift 1 cup flour; measure and sift again with the salt. Beat eggs with a rotary beater until thick and lemon colored; gradually add milk and 1 tablespoon melted butter. Stir in salted flour. Beat until mixture is smooth. Fill buttered custard cups a little less than half full. Bake in an oven preheated to 425°F about 40 minutes.

Meanwhile, melt the remaining 2 tablespoons butter and blend in 2 tablespoons flour; slowly add broth. Cook and stir until thickened. Add chicken, mushrooms, salt, and nutmeg; heat through. Beat egg, cream, and sherry together, then add to chicken mixture. Split sides of hot popovers and fill with creamed chicken.

Chicken in Port Wine

Pot-Roasted Chicken

Yield: 4 servings

1 whole broiler or frying chicken
2 tablespoons vegetable oil
2 tablespoons butter or margarine
1 clove garlic, minced
4 medium-sized onions, quartered
4 medium-sized potatoes, quartered
6 carrots, pared and cut in 2-inch pieces
1 can condensed chicken broth
1 soup can water
1 teaspoon rosemary, crumbled
⅓ teaspoon pepper
1 teaspoon salt

Using kitchen string or heavy white thread, tie legs to tail of prepared chicken. Hook wing tips under back. Heat oil, butter, and garlic in a Dutch oven. Brown the chicken; remove from pot. Add onions, potatoes, and carrots to pan drippings and sauté. Remove vegetables and reserve. Stir broth, water, rosemary, and pepper into pan drippings.

Return the chicken to the pan; surround with vegetables. Baste with liquid; sprinkle vegetables with salt and cover. Bake at 350°F for 1 hour, basting twice with sauce, or until chicken is fork-tender. Serve chicken and vegetables with sauce.

Chicken in Port Wine

Yield: 4 servings

1 spring chicken
¼ cup flour
1½ teaspoons salt
1 teaspoon paprika
¼ teaspoon black pepper
1 tablespoon margarine
⅔ cup Port wine
1 clove garlic, minced
⅓ pound mushrooms, sliced
⅓ cup heavy cream

Cut the chicken into 8 pieces. Mix the flour, salt, paprika, and pepper in a plastic bag. Dredge the chicken pieces in the bag.

Brown the chicken on all sides in the margarine. Add the Port wine and let the chicken simmer for about 15 minutes.

Add the garlic, the mushrooms, and the cream. Let simmer for another 10 minutes.

Chicken in a Potato Nest

Yield: 4 servings

2 cups cooked mashed potatoes
2 tablespoons butter or margarine
2 tablespoons flour
Salt to taste
½ teaspoon pepper
1 cup chicken broth
¼ cup heavy cream
1 small can (about 3 ounces) sliced mushrooms
2 cups cooked chicken, diced
2 tablespoons Parmesan cheese, grated

Line a buttered 8-9 inch pie plate with the potatoes. Melt the butter in a pan, stir in the flour and seasonings. Add the broth gradually; stir until boiling. Add cream and mushrooms and cook for a few minutes.

Put the chicken into the prepared pie plate, cover with the sauce, and sprinkle with the cheese. Bake in a 400°F oven for 25-30 minutes.

Chicken in Red Wine with Carrots and White Onions

Yield: 4 servings

1 3½-pound frying chicken, cut into serving pieces
3 tablespoons oil
1 clove garlic, minced
¼ teaspoon thyme
Salt and pepper to taste
1 cup dry red wine
2 sprigs parsley
12 small white onions, peeled
6 carrots, cut in 1-inch pieces

Wash the chicken and pat it dry. Heat the oil. Add garlic and cook briefly. Brown the chicken quickly on all sides. Add seasonings and red wine and simmer until nearly done (about 25 minutes.)

Add vegetables and cook until tender.

Chicken Stew with Brandy

Yield: 4 servings

1 2½-pound chicken or 2 small chickens
Olive oil
Butter
¼ cup brandy
⅔ cup white wine
1¼ cups heavy cream
4 tomatoes, peeled, seeded, and chopped into pieces
1 apple, cubed
10 green olives

10 small onions
Salt
Pepper
Tarragon
1 teaspoon curry
1 teaspoon chervil
1 teaspoon thyme
1 bay leaf
20 small mushroom caps
1 tablespoon parsley, chopped
Chopped chives

Cut the chicken into pieces. Brown the pieces in olive oil and a little butter. Pour off the fat when the pieces have become brown, add the brandy, and ignite. Pour in the white wine. Add the tomatoes, apple, olives, and onions into the stew. Season with salt, pepper, tarragon, curry, chervil, thyme, and the bay leaf. Bake in a 350°F oven one hour or until the pieces are tender. Saute the mushroom caps.

Remove the bay leaf. Transfer the chicken stew to a deep platter. Garnish with the mushroom caps and sprinkle with the parsley and chives. Serve with boiled noodles or rice.

Chicken Skewers

Yield: Varies

skewer
Pieces of chicken liver wrapped up in bacon slices
Small pieces of chicken
Small onions
Tomato wedges
Pieces of pineapple
A couple of strips of green pepper

marinade
1 tablespoon brown sugar
1 tablespoon orange juice
1 teaspoon lemon juice
½ teaspoon ginger
⅔ cup oil
Salt
Pepper
Pinch cayenne pepper

Alternate the meat and vegetables on a skewer. Combine the marinade ingredients and baste the meat and vegetables. Grill over coals or in the oven for 6 to 7 minutes on each side.

Serve with rice, preferably cooked in broth with chopped onion and seasoned with saffron. Also serve small bowls with the rest of the marinade and with peanut butter sauce in them.

To make peanut butter sauce, beat together 1 ¼ cups sour cream and 3 to 4 tablespoons chopped salted nuts. Spice with plenty of onion powder.

Chicken Stew with Brandy

Summer Chicken with Fresh Tarragon

Yield: 3 to 4 servings

1 2½-3 pound chicken
1 lemon
1 teaspoon salt
¼ to ½ teaspoon freshly ground black pepper
Several sprigs tarragon
2 tablespoons butter
Cream (optional)

Rub the chicken both inside and out with lemon, salt, and pepper. Fill the chicken with sprigs of tarragon, perhaps even with a whole lemon, and the butter. Bind the chicken together and sprinkle finely chopped tarragon on top.

Roast the chicken in a preheated 350°F oven on a rack over a roasting pan. Baste the chicken with water several times during baking. Cooking time varies, about 1 to 1¼ hours. When the drumstick can be turned in its joint, the chicken is done.

Stir a little water into the juice in the pan and bring the gravy to a boil. Add a little cream, if you'd like.

Chicken Surprise

Yield: 5 servings

2 medium-sized marrows or zucchini
Butter
3 slices white bread, with crusts removed and cut into cubes
1 large egg
⅓ cup cheese, grated
Salt
Pepper
1 2½-3 pound broiler, cut into 4 pieces
Honey

Grate the washed and then dried marrows or zucchini on the coarsest side of a grater. Sauté them in 1 tablespoon butter for 1 minute, making sure that they don't change color. Then place them in a dish. Add the bread cubes, eggs, grated cheese, salt, and pepper. Stir and season well.

Make a pocket between the skin and the meat on the chicken pieces by inserting your fingers. Place the bread filling into these pockets. Salt and pepper. Place the chicken pieces in a buttered oven dish and brush them with melted butter.

Chicken Skewers

Bake them in the oven at 400°F for 50 minutes. Brush them with honey when 15 minutes remain of cooking time. Serve with fried potatoes, slightly cooked tomatoes, and salad.

Chicken with White Wine

Yield: 5 servings

About 3½ pounds chicken parts
Salt
White pepper
1 tablespoon paprika
Butter
Oil
⅓ cup cognac or whisky
1½ tablespoons light French mustard
1 packet grated cheese
1¼ cups dry white wine
¼ cup heavy cream
¾ cup cheese, grated

Sprinkle salt, pepper, and paprika over the chicken pieces. Brown them lightly in equal amounts of butter and oil. Pour warm cognac or whisky over them, ignite, and allow them to burn out on their own.

Mix the mustard, cheese, and wine and pour this mixture over the chicken. Allow to simmer slowly, covered, for 12 minutes. Strain the sauce, thicken it with the cream, and pour it over the chicken again. Sprinkle with grated cheese.

Bake in oven at 450°F for 8 minutes. Serve with freshly cooked, butter-tossed spaghetti.

Chicken Breasts in Sour Cream

Yield: 6 servings

1 package dried chipped beef, finely chopped
6 chicken breasts, boned, skinned, and split
6 slices bacon, cut in half
2 cans condensed mushroom soup, undiluted
1 pint sour cream

Place the beef in the bottom of a casserole dish. Wrap each chicken piece with a half-slice of bacon, then place on the bed of chipped beef. Mix the soup and sour cream together; pour over the chicken. Bake at 275°F 2½ to 3 hours.

Serve chicken on a bed of hot rice or mashed potatoes.

Stuffed Chicken Breasts

Yield: 6 servings

1 tablespoon butter
1½ cups zucchini, shredded
1 tablespoon dillweed
Salt and freshly ground pepper to taste
6 chicken breast halves, boned, skinned, and pounded thin
1 egg, beaten
Bread crumbs

Melt butter in a large skillet. Add the zucchini, dill, salt, and pepper. Cook over medium heat until zucchini becomes tender and loses moisture. Divide the zucchini mixture among the chicken breast halves, using only enough filling so the chicken can be drawn up around it. Fold over the sides of the chicken to totally enclose the zucchini. Secure with a toothpick.

Dip the chicken breasts in egg, then coat with bread crumbs. Place in a lightly greased baking dish and bake at 450°F about 15 minutes. Serve with boiled new potatoes and spinach.

Chicken Breasts with Celery Salad

Yield: 4 servings

4 chicken breasts
1 lemon
Salt
Pepper
Butter
6 stalks celery
¼ cup walnuts, coarsely chopped
3 tablespoons Roquefort cheese
⅓ cup Vinaigrette (See index)
Lettuce
Snipped chives

Place the chicken breasts in a bowl with the juice from 1 lemon. Add salt and pepper. Allow the chicken to marinate while the salad is being made.

Cut the celery into small pieces and chop up the walnuts into fairly large pieces. Mash the cheese into the Vinaigrette or mix it in a blender. Blend with the celery and the nuts. Place leaves of lettuce on individual plates or a large serving plate.

Fry the chicken breasts in butter. When they have become golden brown and are cooked through, cut them into slices and place them, warm, on the lettuce leaves. Place the salad on top of the chicken, sprinkle with snipped chives, and decorate with water cress, if you have it on hand. Serve immediately while the chicken is warm.

It is also tasty to serve cold chicken leftovers, which have been sprinkled with lemon juice, in this manner.

Chicken or Turkey Cutlets with Savory Tomato Sauce

Yield: 4 servings

1 tablespoon butter or margarine
1 pound chicken or turkey cutlets
2 cups tomato juice
2 tablespoons onion, minced
½ teaspoon dried savory
Salt or garlic salt to taste
Pepper to taste
Parsley

Melt butter in a nonstick skillet. Add the chicken cutlets in a single layer. Cook over moderate heat, 1 to 2 minutes on each side, just until cooked through. Remove to a platter and keep warm. Drain skillet.

Combine the remaining ingredients, except the parsley, in the skillet. Raise heat to high and cook uncovered until juice is reduced by half. Pour the sauce over the cutlets and garnish with fresh parsley.

Curried Chicken Breasts

Yield: 4 servings

⅓ cup flour
1 teaspoon salt
1 teaspoon curry
½ teaspoon crushed rosemary
4 chicken breasts
Margarine or butter

curry sauce
½ onion, chopped
1 tablespoon margarine or butter
1 small green apple, diced
1 clove garlic, crushed
1 to 2 teaspoons curry
2½ tablespoons flour
1 cup chicken broth, made from bouillon cube
¼ cup pineapple juice (from the canned pineapples)
⅓ cup heavy or light cream
½ teaspoon salt

garnish
2 large bananas
1 can pineapple slices in their own juices
Sliced red peppers
Roasted almond slivers

Mix the flour and spices together. Roll the chicken in the mixture. Brown in margarine in a frying pan. Place in a cooking pot. Add a little water and let simmer about 20 minutes.

For the sauce, sauté the chopped onion in margarine. Add the apple, garlic, and curry. Sauté several minutes. Sprinkle the flour on top. Pour in the broth and pineapple juice; boil several minutes. Beat in the cream. Season to taste with salt and possibly more curry.

Peel the bananas. Divide them into bite-sized pieces. Roll them in the flour mixture you rolled the chicken in. Fry for several minutes in margarine. Pour the sauce onto a serving plate. Lay out the pineapple slices and place the chicken breasts over these. Garnish with banana pieces, sliced peppers, and roasted almond slivers. Serve with boiled rice.

Baked Chicken Livers

Yield: 4 servings

3 or 4 medium-sized onions, sliced ¼ inch thick
10 or 12 chicken livers
3 strips bacon
Salt and pepper to taste
½ cup sherry

Arrange onion slices in a flat, oblong baking dish. Put 1 chicken liver on top of each onion; salt lightly. Cut each bacon strip into quarters and place 1 quarter on each chicken liver. Sprinkle with salt and pepper. Pour sherry over all.

Bake at 350°F about 45 minutes or until bacon is crisp. Baste occasionally during baking time. Serve 2 or 3 livers per portion.

Roast Capon with Orange Pecan Stuffing

Yield: 6 to 8 servings

1 5- to 6-pound capon
¼ cup butter or margarine
1 cup celery, thinly sliced
¼ cup onion, chopped
¾ cup water
5 cups toasted, crust-free bread cubes (½ inch)
¾ cup oranges, sectioned, and diced
⅓ cup pecans, coarsely chopped
1 teaspoon orange rind, grated
1 teaspoon salt
½ teaspoon curry powder (optional)
Orange slices for garnish
Watercress for garnish

Wash, drain, and dry the capon.

Prepare the stuffing: Melt butter in a skillet. Add the celery, onion, and water; cook over moderate heat until the vegetables are tender. Combine the bread cubes, orange pieces, pecans, orange rind, ½ teaspoon salt, and curry powder; mix. Add vegetables and mix carefully.

Sprinkle the remaining salt over the neck and body cavities of the capon. Stuff neck and body cavities loosely with the bread mixture. Skewer neck skin to back. Return legs and tail to tucked position. Place capon, breast side up, in an open roasting pan. Do not add water to the pan. Brush with melted butter or margarine. Cover the capon loosely with foil, crimping it to the edges of the pan. (Foil should not touch capon.) Place in a 325°F oven for about 3 hours. Remove the foil 45 minutes before the end of the roasting time to allow the bird to brown. Brush again with melted butter. Test for doneness; continue roasting if not done.

Roast Cornish Hens with Savory Stuffing

Yield: 4 servings

4 Cornish hens (about 1 pound each)
8 thick slices home-style white bread, crusts removed
1½ tablespoons parsley flakes
¾ teaspoon salt
½ teaspoon poultry seasoning
¼ teaspoon freshly ground pepper
¾ cup butter
1 cup onions, finely chopped
4 Cornish hen livers
Salt and pepper to taste
3 tablespoons melted butter

Remove the giblet packs from the hens; reserve the livers. Wash the hens and pat dry.

Cut the bread into ½-inch cubes; place on a cookie sheet. Bake at 350°F until golden, stirring occasionally. Remove from oven. Combine cubes with parsley, ¾ teaspoon salt, poultry seasoning, and ¼ teaspoon pepper; set aside.

Melt ¾ cup of butter in a heavy skillet. Add the onions and livers; cook until the livers are lightly browned and the onions tender. Remove livers; chop. Add the livers, onions, and butter from the pan to the bread-cube mixture; toss to mix well.

Salt and pepper the hens lightly. Pack tightly with stuffing; truss. Place in an ovenproof baking dish, breast side up; brush with melted butter. Roast at 375°F. Turn ever 15 minutes and baste with butter and pan juices. Cook a total of 45 minutes to 1 hour, until the juices run clear when the tip of a knife is inserted in the hen. Serve hot with wild rice and a green vegetable.

Summer Chicken with Fresh Tarragon

Herbed Game Hens

Yield: 6 servings

6 Cornish hens, 1 to 1¼ pounds each
2 cups herb-seasoned croutons
½ cup ripe olives, sliced
¼ cup lemon juice
¼ cup vinegar
¼ cup vegetable oil
1 clove garlic, crushed
½ teaspoon dried thyme leaves
¼ to ½ teaspoon salt
Grape clusters

Dry the cavities of the hens (do not rub cavities with salt). Mix the croutons and olives. Stuff each hen loosely with ⅓ cup crouton-olive stuffing; fasten openings with skewers and lace shut with string. Place the hens, breast side up, in an ungreased, shallow baking pan.

Mix lemon juice, vinegar, oil, garlic, thyme, and salt; pour on hens. Bake uncovered in a 350°F oven for 2 hours, spooning the lemon mixture onto the hens every 20 minutes.

Place the hens on a warm platter. Garnish with grape clusters and parsley sprigs.

Cornish Hens with Orange Sauce

Yield: 4 servings

2 Cornish hens, split in half
1½ cups orange juice
⅓ cup orange marmalade
⅓ cup currant jelly
2 tablespoons cornstarch
1 can mandarin oranges (optional)

Roast Cornish hens in a 350°F oven for 45 minutes.

In a saucepan, combine the orange juice, marmalade, and jelly. Heat, mixing until smooth. Add cornstarch and stir until thick. Add drained mandarin oranges, if desired. Pour the sauce over the Cornish hens and cook another 30-45 minutes.

Apricot Duck

Yield: 4 to 6 servings

1 4- to 5-pound roasting duck
1 pound fresh apricots
1 orange
1 onion, finely chopped
Salt and pepper
2 to 3 tablespoons oil
3 tablespoons honey
1 to 1½ cups stock made with duck giblets
3 to 4 tablespoons apricot brandy

Chicken Surprise

Stuff the duck with half-seeded apricots and 3 strips of orange zest (the thin outer skin of the orange), onion, and seasonings. Prick the skin of the duck with a fork to allow the fat to run out while cooking; season with salt and pepper.

Heat the oil in a roasting pan. When very hot, add the duck; baste all over with oil. Roast in a preheated 400°F oven; allow 20 minutes per pound. Half an hour before cooking is completed, spoon melted honey and juice of the orange over the duck. Ten minutes before the end of cooking, add the rest of the apricots to pan; heat through and brown slightly. Remove duck to warm dish; remove stuffing to bowl. Arrange roasted apricots around the duck.

Pour off fat from roasting pan. Put in stuffing; bring to a boil, stirring all the time. Taste for seasoning. Strain or blend in a blender or food processor. Return to heat and add apricot brandy. Serve at once with duck and apricots.

Brandied Duck

Yield: 4 to 6 servings

1 5- to 6-pound duck
2 large onions, chopped
¼ cup parsley, minced
1 bay leaf
½ teaspoon thyme
2 cloves garlic, crushed
3 jiggers brandy
2 cups red wine
¼ cup olive oil or butter
¾ pound mushrooms, sliced
Salt and pepper

Clean the duck, then cut it into serving pieces. Place the duck pieces in a deep dish. Add onions, parsley, bay leaf, thyme, garlic, brandy, and wine. Marinate at least 4 hours, preferably overnight.

Heat the oil; brown the pieces of duck about 15 minutes. Add marinade, mushrooms, and seasonings. Cover tightly; simmer over low heat at least 1 hour.

Barbecued Game Birds

Yield: 2 to 4 servings

2 plump game birds, (partridge, grouse, quail, etc.)
1 clove garlic
Salt
2 small onions, quartered
2 celery tops
2 sprigs parsley
¼ cup olive oil
1 lemon, juice and grated rind
Dash Tabasco sauce
1 teaspoon onion juice
¼ teaspoon thyme

Clean birds thoroughly and rinse in cold water; pat dry. Rub inside and out with garlic and salt. Insert an onion, celery top, and parsley sprig into each cavity. Shake oil, lemon juice and rind, Tabasco sauce, onion juice, and thyme in a wide-mouth jar.

Place the birds on a rack in a covered roasting pan; roast in a 375°F oven until done to your liking, basting with sauce every 10 minutes, or grill over faintly glowing coals on your outdoor grill, turning and basting frequently until thoroughly done and tender.

Game Pie

Yield: 4 to 6 servings

2 grouse (or other game)
½ pound steak
½ pound bacon
1 large onion, finely chopped
4-6 mushrooms
2 tablespoons chopped herbs
Salt and pepper
Pinch nutmeg
1 cup red wine
1 cup stock
1 package frozen puff pastry
1 egg

Cut the meat off the grouse (or other game birds), then cut the steak into small pieces and dice the bacon. Arrange them in layers with the onion, mushrooms, herbs, and seasoning between each layer. Add 1 cup of red wine and enough stock to barely cover the meat. Cover with foil and bake very slowly in a preheated 325°F oven for about 1½ hours, until all meat is tender. Let cool completely.

Roll out the pastry and place a strip moistened with water, around the edge of the dish. Moisten the pastry strip and place a large piece of pastry on top. Press edges together. Cut off surplus and crimp edges. Make slashes in top to release steam and decorate with pastry leaves.

Put into a 425°F oven and bake for about 30 minutes. Serve hot or cold.

Fried Duckling

Yield: 4 to 6 servings

1 3- to 4-pound duckling, cut into serving pieces
1 cup flour
2 teaspoons salt
¼ teaspoon pepper
2 teaspoons paprika
¼ cup butter or margarine
Shortening
1 cup water

Place 2 or 3 pieces of duckling in a paper bag with the flour, salt, pepper, and paprika. Shake until thoroughly coated; repeat with the rest of the duckling pieces.

In a skillet, heat the butter and enough shortening to make a ¼-inch layer. Place the duckling in the hot fat, skin side down. Brown and turn. Add water and cover tightly.

Reduce the heat and cook slowly or bake in a 350°F oven about 1 hour. Uncover and continue to cook about 30 minutes, until duckling pieces have crisp crusts.

Roast Goose with Apple-Sausage Stuffing

Yield: 6 servings

¾ pound sausage, hot or mild
5 tablespoons butter
1 medium-sized onion, chopped
2 stalks celery, chopped
5 cups toasted white bread cubes
1 large apple, peeled and chopped
½ teaspoon crumbled dried marjoram
3 teaspoons salt
½ teaspoon pepper
1 8-pound goose
Juice of 1 lemon

giblet stock
Goose giblets and liver (including neck if available)
4 cups water
2 celery tops
1 small onion
2 cloves
Salt and pepper

gravy
6 tablespoons rendered goose fat or drippings
6 tablespoons flour
Salt and pepper
1 teaspoon brown-gravy seasoning
4 cups giblet stock

Fry the sausage in a heavy skillet until well browned, breaking into bite-sized pieces as it cooks. Drain well; reserve. Melt butter in a skillet. Add the onion and celery; cook until tender. Combine the sausage, onion, celery, butter, bread cubes, apple, marjoram, 1 teaspoon salt, and pepper in a mixing bowl. Mix well and set aside.

Remove giblet pack from the goose; set aside. Remove and discard loose fat in body cavity; reserve for rendering, or discard. Wash goose well; pat dry. Rub the goose inside and out with the lemon juice and 2 teaspoons salt. Stuff neck cavity loosely; skewer shut. Spoon remaining stuffing into body cavity; truss. Be sure to tie wings and legs closely to the bird. Place the goose on a rack, breast side up; prick well on breast and thighs so that the fat will drain. Roast at 325°F 3 to 3½ hours, or until a meat thermometer registers 185°F when inserted into the breast.

While the goose cooks, prepare the broth. Combine giblets, water, celery, onion, and seasonings in a small saucepan; bring to a boil. Cover and simmer 30 minutes. Remove the liver; cook 30 minutes. Strain the broth and cool. Chop the liver and giblets; reserve.

Remove the goose to a platter when done; cover with a tent of aluminum foil while making the gravy. Combine goose drippings and flour in a medium-sized saucepan; cook over low heat, stirring constantly, until lightly browned. Add salt, pepper, and gravy seasoning. Slowly stir in giblet stock; cook, stirring constantly, over low heat until thickened. Add the reserved giblets and heat through.

Carve the goose; spoon dressing into a serving dish. Serve with gravy and red cabbage or sauerkraut and applesauce.

Roasted Duck

Yield: 2 to 4 servings

1 4- to 5-pound duck, fresh, or frozen and thawed
Boiling water
Salt and pepper
2 small apples, oranges, or lemons, or a combination, quartered

Remove the giblets and neck from inside the duck. Immerse the duck in boiling water to cover 1 minute. Remove; drain. Pat dry with paper towels. Sprinkle the cavity lightly with salt and pepper and stuff fruit into the cavity.

Truss the duck; place on a rack in a roasting pan. Roast at 350°F 30 minutes; remove from oven. Pierce the duck all over (except breast) with a fork. Return duck to oven; continue roasting, draining off the fat and piercing every 30 minutes, until a meat thermometer placed in the meatiest part reads 170°F, about 1½ to 2 hours. Remove and discard trussings and fruit. Cut the duck in half or quarter to serve.

For a crisper skin, roast the duck at 500°F during the last 15 minutes of cooking.

Roast Goose with Giblet Stuffing

Yield: 8 servings

1 9- to 11-pound goose with giblets, fresh, if possible
2½ cups water
⅓ cup onion, sliced
¼ cup celery, diced
2 chicken bouillon cubes
Salt and pepper to taste
½ cup butter
½ cup onion, minced
½ cup celery, minced
2 tablespoons parsley, chopped
1 tablespoon poultry seasoning
7 cups cubed day-old bread
½ cup milk
2 tablespoons cornstarch

Put goose giblets, neck and liver, if desired, water, sliced onion, diced celery, bouillon cubes, salt, and pepper in a small saucepan. Bring to a boil; reduce heat. Simmer until tender; remove from heat. Drain and reserve broth. Chop the meat from the neck, giblets, and liver.

Meanwhile, melt butter in a large saucepan; add minced onion and celery, parsley, poultry seasoning, salt, pepper, and half of the chopped meats. Stir to blend. Cover and simmer 12 minutes. Stir in bread cubes and milk; toss well.

Rinse the goose and pat dry. Pull off all inside fat. Rub inside and out with salt and pepper. Fill breast cavity loosely with stuffing. Put on a rack in a large roasting pan, breast side down. Cover with aluminum foil; roast at 400°F 1 hour.

Remove the foil. Turn goose breast side up; lower heat to 350°F and continue roasting 2 hours, uncovered. Remove goose from oven and prick surface area all over with fork tines. Return to oven and continue roasting 1 more hour, until browned and drumsticks move easily. The internal temperature of the breast should register 170°F to 175°F. Transfer to a warm serving platter. Let stand 15 minutes before carving; temperature will increase 10 degrees.

Pour off fat from the pan drippings. Dissolve cornstarch in reserved giblet broth. Stir into pan drippings, scraping up little bits that cling to the pan. Cook and stir over medium heat until thickened. Add remaining chopped meats. Taste and adjust seasonings.

American Pheasant

Yield: 4 servings

1 pheasant
Salt and pepper
1 cup butter
1½-2 cups fresh white bread crumbs
Pinch cayenne pepper
4 tomatoes, halved and seasoned
4 slices bacon
8 flat mushrooms

Cut the pheasant open along its back with a sharp knife. Remove back bone. Open it out and flatten with a heavy rolling pin. Season with salt and pepper. Melt butter in a large pan and, when hot, sauté pheasant on both sides. Remove from heat.

Make plenty of fresh, white bread crumbs and cover the pheasant with these; sprinkle with a little cayenne pepper. Heat broiler and broil slowly so that the crumbs do not become too brown before the bird is cooked. Test with a skewer in the thickest part of the leg. At the same time, broil the tomatoes.

Chicken with White Wine

Also broil the bacon and mushrooms filled with butter and seasonings.

When the pheasant is done, serve it on a platter surrounded by broiled accompaniments and some butter balls rolled in parsley.

Quail on Toast

Yield: 4 servings

4 quail, split
½ cup flour
½ teaspoon salt
⅛ teaspoon pepper
4 tablespoons butter or margarine
1 cup boiling water
1 pint half-and-half
⅓ cup sherry
Buttered toast

Roll each piece of quail in flour seasoned with salt and pepper. Brown in butter on all sides. Pour boiling water over; cover. Let simmer until tender (15 to 20 minutes); remove cover. Add cream and sherry and simmer 10 minutes.

Place birds on pieces of buttered toast. Taste sauce for seasoning and pour it over the quail.

Chicken Breasts with Celery Salad

Sautéed Pheasant with Herbs

Yield: 4 servings

1 2-pound pheasant, cleaned and cut into serving
  pieces
Salt to taste, if desired
Freshly ground pepper to taste
2 tablespoons butter
2 whole cloves garlic, peeled
1 bay leaf
2 sprigs fresh thyme or ½ teaspoon dried thyme
¾ cup dry white wine
3 tablespoons cold butter
2 tablespoons parsley, finely chopped

Sprinkle the pheasant pieces with salt and pepper. Heat the butter in a skillet and add the pieces, skin side down. Cook about 2 or 3 minutes until the skin is golden brown. Turn the pieces and continue cooking about 3 minutes more. Add the garlic, bay leaf, thyme, and wine. Cover and cook 20 minutes or until the pheasant is tender.

Transfer the pheasant pieces to a serving dish. Swirl the 3 tablespoons of cold butter into the pan sauce. Pour and scrape the sauce (including garlic and thyme sprig) over the pheasant and serve sprinkled with chopped parsley.

Roast Guinea Hens

Yield: 4 servings

2 2- to 3-pound dressed guinea hens
1½ teaspoons salt
1 lemon, quartered
2 small onions
4 slices country-style bacon, sliced

Rub hens inside and out with salt and lemon wedges. Insert an onion in each hen; place bacon over the backs of the hens. Roast in a 325°F oven 40 minutes, back sides up. Turn hens over in roasting pan; rearrange bacon over the breasts of the hens. Cook 35 to 40 minutes or until fork-tender.

Squabs Stuffed with Almonds and Raisins

Yield: 4 servings

4 tender squabs
1 cup cooked rice
2 onions, cooked
3 tablespoons butter
3-4 tablespoons peeled, flaked almonds
1 tablespoon chopped herbs
4 tablespoons raisins

2-3 tablespoons sherry
4 slices fat bacon
2-3 tablespoons oil
1-2 teaspoons flour
½ cup red wine
½ cup stock

Boil the rice until tender; drain and let cool. Cook the onions until soft in the butter. Add the almonds and cook until all are golden brown. Add 8 table-spoons of rice to the pan; cook for 1 minute, then remove from heat. Add chopped herbs, raisins that have been soaking in sherry, and seasonings. Stuff mixture into the squabs.

Tie a slice of fat bacon around the breast of each bird. Heat oil in a 400°F oven, add the squabs, and baste thoroughly. Roast in the oven for about 35-40 minutes, basting and turning every 10 minutes. Remove the bacon for the last 15 minutes, to brown the breast. Remove to a serving dish and keep warm.

Pour off the oil and sprinkle flour into the pan; blend with the pan drippings and add wine and stock. Stir until smooth and boiling, add seasonings, and pour into a sauce boat.

Barbecued Turkey

Yield: 10 to 12 servings

½ cup onion, chopped
1½ tablespoons butter
1½ cups catsup
¼ cup brown sugar, packed
1 clove garlic, pressed
1 lemon, thinly sliced
¼ cup Worcestershire sauce
2 teaspoons prepared mustard
1 teaspoon salt
¼ teaspoon freshly ground pepper
1 12-pound fresh or frozen turkey
2 to 3 tablespoons barbecue or seasoned salt

Sauté the onion in butter in a small saucepan until lightly browned. Add remaining ingredients, except the turkey and barbecue salt; simmer 20 minutes. Remove lemon slices. Store the sauce in a covered jar in the refrigerator if not used immediately.

Thaw turkey, if frozen. Rinse and pat dry.

Start a charcoal fire 20 to 30 minutes before cooking turkey, allowing about 5 pounds charcoal for beginning the fire. During the cooking period, push burning charcoal to the center; add more briquettes as needed around the edge.

Sprinkle the cavity of the turkey with barbecue salt. Insert a spit rod in front of its tail; run it diagonally through the breast bone. Fasten tightly with spit forks at both ends. Test for balance; re-adjust spit rod, if necessary. Insert a meat thermometer into the thickest part of the thigh; make sure the thermometer does not touch the bone or spit rod and that the thermometer will clear the charcoal as the spit turns.

Brush off gray ash from coals; push coals to back of firebox. Place a drip pan made of heavy-duty foil directly under the turkey in front of the coals. Attach spit; start rotisserie. Cook 25 minutes per pound or to 180 to 185°F on the meat thermometer; baste frequently with barbecue sauce during the last 30 minutes of cooking.

Turkey, Ham, and Oyster Casserole

Yield: 6 to 8 servings

½ cup butter or margarine
¼ cup flour
2 cups milk
½ teaspoon salt
⅛ teaspoon pepper
¼ teaspoon dry mustard
2 cups cooked turkey, diced
1 cup cooked ham, ground
1 pint oysters, preheated in juice
3 cups mashed potatoes
Paprika

In a saucepan, melt the butter; stir in the flour and blend. Add milk, salt, pepper, and mustard. Cook over low heat, stirring, until smooth and thickened. Add turkey, ham, and oysters.

Pour the mixture into a greased, 1½-quart casserole. Make a border around the casserole with mashed potatoes; sprinkle with paprika. Bake in a 350°F oven for 30 minutes.

Baked Turkey Hash

Yield: 2 servings

1½ cups turkey, diced
1 medium-sized onion, diced
1 medium-sized potato, diced
1 pimiento, diced
2 medium-sized carrots, coarsely grated
1 teaspoon salt
2 teaspoons parsley, minced
¼ teaspoon poultry seasoning
½ cup seasoned thin gravy

Combine all the ingredients except the gravy. Mix lightly to distribute seasoning evenly throughout the mixture. Blend in gravy and stir until all ingredients are moistened. Spoon into a greased 1-quart casserole. Cover and bake in a 350°F oven for 45 minutes. Remove cover and continue to bake uncovered for 15 minutes. Serve with reheated extra gravy.

Turkey Gratin

Yield: 4 to 6 servings

2-3 cups cooked turkey, chopped
3 tablespoons butter
1 onion, chopped
2-3 large mushrooms, chopped
2½ tablespoons flour
1½ cups turkey or chicken stock
1-2 cups cooked vegetables (peas, beans, corn, chopped carrots, pimiento, etc.) or 1 cup cooked noodles
3-4 tablespoons thick cream
1 tablespoon chopped parsley and thyme
4-5 tablespoons Cheddar cheese, grated

Melt the butter and cook the onion until tender. Add the mushrooms and cook for 1 minute. Sprinkle in flour and blend well. Add the stock and bring to a boil, stirring constantly. Add the chopped turkey and any available cooked vegetables or cooked noodles. Stir well into the sauce. Add cream and herbs.

Turn into a buttered baking dish and sprinkle thickly with grated cheese and a little paprika. Broil until crisp and brown all over. Serve with cooked noodles, rice, or potatoes.

Turkey Fricassee

Yield: 4 servings

6 tablespoons butter
3 tablespoons flour
1½ cups mixed turkey stock and milk
½ teaspoon onion powder
1 tablespoon parsley, chopped
1 tablespoon thyme
1 tablespoon powdered bay leaf
¼ teaspoon mace
2 egg yolks
3-4 tablespoons cream
1 pound cold turkey meat
4 slices bacon, cut in half
8 mushroom caps

Melt 3 tablespoons of butter; add flour and pour on mixed chicken stock and milk. Blend well. Then bring to a boil, stirring constantly. Simmer for a few minutes. Then add onion powder, herbs, and seasonings. Beat egg yolks with a little cream. Add a little sauce. Then add the egg yolk to the sauce.. Do not allow to boil.

Cut the cold turkey into slices. Place it in a buttered, ovenproof dish. Cover with buttered paper and heat in a preheated 325°F oven for 10-15 minutes. Spoon the sauce over the turkey and return to oven for 10 minutes, being careful not to boil the sauce.

Meanwhile, roll up the bacon slices and put them on skewers. Broil until crisp. Put the mushrooms into a buttered dish with seasoning and a pat of butter on each. Cook in the oven for 15 minutes at the same time as the turkey. Arrange mushrooms around the sides of the dish and bacon rolls down the center and serve hot, with rice or mashed potatoes.

Curried Chicken Breasts

Meat

Boiled Beef and Carrots

Yield: 6 servings

3-4 pounds round beef roast
1 large onion, stuck with 2 cloves
4-6 small onions, whole
6 peppercorns
1 bay leaf
Some parsley stems
Sprig of thyme
8-10 medium-sized carrots
2 small turnips
3 celery stalks
2 cups flour
8 tablespoons suet (or butter)
3 tablespoons parsley, chopped
½ tablespoon thyme
½ tablespoon marjoram

Put the beef, large onion, peppercorns, bay leaf, parsley stems, sprig of thyme, enough water to cover the meat, and a little salt in a large pot. Bring to a boil slowly; remove any scum that rises to the surface, put a lid on the pot, and simmer for 1 hour.

Peel and quarter the carrots and turnips lengthwise. Remove the herbs and the single onion from the pot; add the carrots, turnips, celery, and small onions. Simmer for another hour.

Sift the flour with a pinch of salt. Mix in finely shredded suet, parsley, thyme, marjoram, and pepper. Mix in enough water to make a light dough. Divide the dough into pieces about the size of a small walnut, rolling it between your hands. Bring the liquid the meat has been cooking in to a boil. Drop the dumplings into the boiling liquid, cover the pot, and cook them for about 15-20 minutes.

Serve the beef on a large dish with the vegetables and dumplings, and serve the gravy in a separate sauceboat.

Vegetable-Stuffed Flank Steak

Yield: 6 servings

1 2-pound flank steak
¼ cup butter or margarine
½ cup onion, finely chopped
½ cup carrot, finely chopped
½ cup celery, finely chopped
1 cup apple, chopped, pared and cored
2 tablespoons parsley, chopped
1 teaspoon salt
½ teaspoon ground sage
½ teaspoon marjoram
1 cup fresh bread cubes
1¾ cups water
2 teaspoons cornstarch

Lay the flank steak flat on a board; trim any excess fat; score the top side with a sharp knife. In a Dutch oven, melt 3 tablespoons of butter; sauté the onion, carrot, and celery until tender, about 5 minutes. Add the apple, parsley, and seasonings; cook 3 minutes longer. Add the bread cubes; mix well.

Spread the stuffing on the unscored side of the meat, leaving a 1-inch margin all around. Roll up lengthwise; tie in several places with string. In the same Dutch oven, melt the remaining butter; brown the meat on all sides. Add 1½ cups of water. Cover and cook in a 350°F oven for 1½ hours or until the meat is tender.

Remove the meat to a heated serving platter; remove the string. Blend the cornstarch and remaining ¼ cup water together; add to the drippings in the Dutch oven. Cook, stirring, until the gravy is thickened. Slice the meat into ½-inch slices. Serve with hot gravy.

Brisket and Beer

Yield: 4 to 6 servings

1 3½-pound boneless beef brisket, flat half
1 teaspoon seasoned salt
1 teaspoon paprika
1 clove garlic, crushed
1 cup chili sauce
1 12-ounce can beer
1 onion, sliced
4 medium-sized potatoes

Trim the excess fat from the brisket. Sprinkle seasoned salt, paprika, and garlic over both sides of the brisket.

Place the meat in a shallow roasting pan and broil, 4 to 5 inches from the heat, for 20 minutes. Turn the brisket and continue broiling 20 minutes. Reduce the heat to 350°F. Add the chili sauce, beer, and onion; cover tightly and bake at 350°F for 1 hour.

Meanwhile, pare the potatoes and cut them into 1-inch thick slices. Add the potatoes to the brisket and continue baking, covered, 1 hour or until tender. Carve the meat diagonally across the grain into thin slices. Serve the cooking liquid with the carved roast.

Barbecued Brisket

Yield: 4 to 6 servings

1 onion, diced
1 clove garlic, diced
2 pounds brisket, cut into 1-inch pieces
½ pound mushrooms, sliced
½ cup beef stock
½ cup barbecue sauce
1 tablespoon cornstarch (optional)

Place the onion, garlic, and mushrooms in a heavy baking dish. Top with the meat; add the stock and barbecue sauce. Bake at 300°F about 3 hours, until the meat is fork-tender. Remove the fat from the gravy.

If you prefer a slightly thickened gravy, remove 1 cup of gravy from the pot; mix with 1 tablespoon of cornstarch. Return the gravy to the pot; stir until slightly thickened. Serve the brisket with hot buttered noodles or over rice.

Exotic Steak

Fillet Steak with Garlic Butter

Company Corned Beef

Yield: 8 to 10 servings

4 to 5 pounds corned beef
2 bay leaves
5 peppercorns
2 sprigs parsley
1 branch celery, cut in chunks
1 small onion, sliced
Whole cloves
2 tablespoons butter or margarine, melted
1 tablespoon prepared mustard
⅓ cup brown sugar, firmly packed
⅓ cup catsup
3 tablespoons vinegar
3 tablespoons water

Wash the corned beef and place it in a large pot. Add enough cold water to cover, bay leaves, peppercorns, parsley, celery. and onion. Cover and simmer about 45 minutes to a pound, or until tender. Drain.

Place the beef in a shallow baking dish. Stick a few whole cloves in it and season. Combine the remaining ingredients; cook over medium heat until well blended. Pour the sauce over the corned beef and bake in a 350°F oven 30 minutes, basting with the sauce several times.

Barbecued Chuck Roast

Yield: 8 servings

3 pounds chuck roast, ½-2 inches thick
⅓ cup wine vinegar
¼ cup catsup
2 tablespoons soy sauce
1 teaspoon salt
2 teaspoons Worcestershire sauce
1 teaspoon prepared mustard
¼ teaspoon garlic powder
¼ teaspoon pepper

Trim the fat from the chuck roast. Place the meat in a clear plastic bag; set in a deep bowl. Mix the vinegar, catsup, soy sauce, salt, Worcestershire sauce, mustard, garlic powder, and pepper; pour the sauce over the meat. Close the bag. Marinate 2-3 hours at room temperature or overnight in the refrigerator. Turn the bag occasionally to distribute the marinade. Remove the roast from the bag; reserve the marinade. Place the meat in a broiler pan. Broil 6-8 inches from the heat, about 50-60 minutes. Turn the meat every 10 minutes. Baste with marinade the last 15-20 minutes.

Chuck Steak

Yield: 6 to 8 servings

3 tablespoons oil
3- to 3½-pound boneless chuck, round, or
  shoulder steak
3 tablespoons Worcestershire sauce
½ teaspoon salt
3 tablespoons butter or margarine
2 cloves garlic, halved
Water
1 cup onion rings, sliced

In a large, heavy, ovenproof skillet or Dutch oven, heat the oil until very hot. Pat the meat dry and add it to the skillet. Brown it well, about 3 minutes on each side. Pour off the oil in the skillet.

Combine the Worcestershire sauce and salt; brush it over both sides of the meat. Spread 1 tablespoon of the butter over the steak. Place the garlic around the meat. Bake, uncovered, in a preheated 350°F oven 15 to 20 minutes for medium rare or longer if a more well-done piece is desired. Remove the steak from the skillet; keep warm. Pour off and measure the pan drippings, discarding the garlic. Add water to the pan drippings to measure ¾ cup; set aside.

Melt the remaining 2 tablespoons of butter. Add the onions and sauté 5 minutes. Add the reserved pan drippings. Bring to the boiling point. Slice the steak across the grain and serve with sauce.

Skillet Hash

Yield: 4 servings

2 cups cooked beef, chopped
4 small potatoes, cooked and chopped (about 2
  cups)
1 medium-sized onion, chopped
1 tablespoon parsley, minced
½ teaspoon salt
⅛ teaspoon pepper
¼ cup shortening

Mix the beef, potatoes, onion, parsley, salt, and pepper. Heat the shortening in a 10-inch skillet over medium heat until melted. Spread the beef mixture evenly in a skillet. Fry, turning frequently, until browned, 10 to 15 minutes.

Broth-Cooked Roast Beef

Exotic Steak

Yield: 6 servings

2 tablespoons oil
2 tablespoons butter
6 thick tomato slices
4 cloves garlic, minced
6 eggplant slices, sliced lengthwise
6-12 thin slices filet mignon
Salt
Pepper

Heat the fat in a skillet and sauté the tomatoes and garlic over medium heat for 8 to 10 minutes, turning the tomatoes from time to time. Remove the tomatoes to a heated platter and sauté the eggplant in the same skillet until tender and lightly browned on both sides. Place the tomatoes back in the pan. Season with salt and pepper. Keep very warm.

Heat another skillet. Sprinkle both sides of the beef slices with salt and pepper and sauté them 1 minute on each side. Serve the meat on a heated platter surrounded with eggplant and tomato.

London Broil

Yield: 8 servings

2 2-pound flank steaks
1 cup salad oil
1 cup dry red wine
4 tablespoons soy sauce
2 tablespoons green onions, chopped
1 clove garlic, chopped
1 teaspoon salt
¼ teaspoon pepper

Place the flank steaks in a shallow pan; combine the remaining ingredients and pour them over the meat. Marinate at least 4 hours. Broil 5 to 7 minutes on each side 3 inches from the heat; baste frequently. Slice thinly on the diagonal.

Fillet Steak with Garlic Butter

Yield: 4 servings

8 to 10 potatoes
2 tablespoons butter or margarine
1 teaspoon salt
1½ to 2 pounds fillet steak, middle piece
1 tablespoon butter or margarine
¾ teaspoon salt
Black pepper
Water
2 tomatoes

garlic butter
4 tablespoons butter
2 cloves garlic

Lettuce
Parsley

Preheat oven to 450°F. Peel and slice potatoes and spread them out in a greased, ovenproof dish. Season with salt; dot with butter. Cover with foil and place in the center of the oven for 15 minutes. Remove the foil and cook for an additional 30 minutes, moving them around gently from time to time.

Trim away the long tendons from the meat. Melt the butter in a frying pan or casserole and brown the meat slowly on all sides. Season with salt and pepper. Lower the heat and cook, covered, for 10 to 15 minutes. Lift out the meat and allow it to rest for a short while. Add a little water to the pan juices and stir. Pour the gravy over the potatoes.

Carve the meat into slices when the potatoes are ready and arrange on a serving plate. Cut the tomatoes in half and use as garnish.

Make the garlic butter: Melt the butter in a saucepan and add the crushed garlic. Pour the garlic butter over the meat, potatoes, and tomato. Up to this stage, the dish can be prepared in advance.

Shortly before serving, place the dish on the top shelf of the oven at 450°F and heat through. Serve with lettuce and parsley.

Roast Beef with Nobis Sauce

Old Fashioned Beef Mold

Yield: 4 to 6 servings

1 pound steak
½ pound bacon
1½ cups fresh bread crumbs
Grated nutmeg
1 tablespoon Worcestershire sauce
1 egg
2 tablespoons butter
2 tablespoons flour
1 cup milk
2 teaspoons English mustard (or more if strong
    flavor is desired)
1 tablespoon white wine vinegar
Dash of Tabasco sauce
Salt and pepper

Grind the beef and bacon and combine with the bread crumbs, nutmeg, and Worcestershire sauce. Mix with the beaten egg. Put the mixture into a well-greased mold, covering the mold with a double layer of grease-proof paper or foil. Tie the paper on tightly and steam for 2 hours.

Make a mustard sauce: Melt the butter. Remove the pan from the stove and add flour and milk. Bring to a boil, stirring constantly; boil for 2 minutes. Add the mustard, mixed with vinegar and a dash of Tabasco, and seasoning to taste. Turn out the meat mold and serve with mustard sauce.

Beef Pot Pie

Yield: 4 servings

1 medium-sized onion, peeled and chopped
2 tablespoons oil
1½ pounds chuck roast, trimmed and cut into
    1-inch pieces
⅓-cup flour
Salt and pepper
1 teaspoon crushed thyme
2 teaspoons dill
1 cup dry red wine
3 cups beef bouillon
½-pound fresh mushrooms, thickly sliced
Pastry for 1-crust pie, unbaked
1 egg white, slightly beaten

Sauté the onion in oil in a heavy skillet; remove it from the pan and set aside. Dredge the beef cubes in flour seasoned with salt and pepper. Brown the cubes in hot oil on all sides, a few cubes at a time, adding more oil as needed.

Return the beef and onions to the skillet and add the thyme and dill. Add the wine, cover the skillet, and simmer for 3 minutes. Add the bouillon and mushrooms and stir well. Simmer, uncovered, for 1 hour or until the beef is tender and the gravy is thickened.

If a thicker gravy is desired, blend 1 tablespoon of flour with ½ cup of water and add, a little at a time, until the gravy reaches the desired consistency. Cool to room temperature.

Standing Rib Roast

Yield: 10 to 16 servings

1 3-rib standing rib roast, about 8 pounds
Salt and pepper

Stand the roast, fat side up, on a rack in a shallow pan. Add no water. Insert a meat thermometer into the center of the roast, making sure point rests on meat. Roast uncovered in a 325°F oven until the thermometer registers 140°F for rare, 160°F for medium, and 170°F for well done; about 23 to 25 minutes per pound for rare, 27 to 30 minutes for medium, and 32 to 35 minutes for well done.

Remove the roast from the oven and place it on a large, warm platter. Slice as desired. Season with salt and pepper.

Roast Beef with Nobis Sauce

Yield: 8 servings

3¾ pounds tender roast beef
2½ teaspoons salt
½ to 1 teaspoon freshly ground black pepper

Preheat oven to 375°F. Season the meat on all sides with salt and pepper. Stick a meat thermometer into the roast so that the tip of the thermometer is in the middle of the roast. Place the roast in a lightly greased pan or dish and put it in the oven. Cook 1 hour to 1¼ hours. Serve with Nobis Sauce (see below).

Nobis Sauce

Yield: 4 servings

1 egg
2½ to 3 teaspoons vinegar
¾ cup oil
½ teaspoon salt
¼ teaspoon black pepper
1 teaspoon light French mustard
1 tablespoon snipped chives
¼ to ½ garlic clove, crushed

Boil the egg for 3 minutes — no more, no less. Break open the egg and scrape out the insides with a spoon into a bowl. Alternate adding drops of vinegar and oil while beating constantly so that the sauce is well blended before adding the next drops. The sauce should thicken to the consistency of mayonnaise.

Season with salt, pepper, mustard, chives, and garlic, and refrigerate before serving.

Burgundy Beef Stew

Hungarian Beef Stew

let it simmer until it feels done, about 7 to 10 minutes per pound. Pick up the meat and cut a slice to see if it is pink inside. Add more broth, if necessary. The meat should be pink on the inside.

When the meat is done, take it out of the broth and remove the string. Cut into thin slices.

Meanwhile, place the vegetables in the broth, and make sure that they become well heated. Place the ingredients in a large, deep serving bowl, and pour the broth over them. Serve immediately. On the table, you should have different kinds of mustard, pickles, grated horseradish, a peppermill, and coarse salt.

Leftover broth makes an excellent soup for the next day.

Savory Pot Roast

Yield: 8 servings

1 4-pound pot roast
½ teaspoon salt
¼ teaspoon pepper
2 tablespoons flour
4 tablespoons butter
3 onions, sliced
3 carrots, peeled and sliced
2 stalks celery, sliced
½ cup tomato sauce
2 cups water
1 bay leaf
½ cup red wine

Wipe the meat with a damp cloth. Combine the salt, pepper, and flour. Rub the seasoned flour on the roast.

Melt the butter in a Dutch oven. Brown the roast on all sides. Add the onions; brown. Add the carrots, celery, tomato sauce, water, bay leaf, and red wine. Cover and simmer 3 hours.

Slice the meat. Serve with pan juices, accompanied by rice or potatoes.

Broth-Cooked Roast Beef

Yield: 6 to 8 servings

1 tenderloin of beef, about 2½ pounds
Salt
Pepper
1½ to 2 quarts strong beef broth
12 leeks (white part only)
6 carrots, cut into pieces
6 medium onions, peeled
12 potatoes, all the same size, peeled
2 fresh fennels, well trimmed and sliced
Cauliflower
24 Brussels sprouts
Parsley

Place the broth in a large pot. Add the carrots and onions when it starts to boil. Cook for several minutes, then add the leeks and fennels.

Boil the potatoes and cauliflower separately in salted water. Do the same with the Brussels sprouts.

Bind the roast beef up well, leaving a long piece of string hanging from the meat. Season with salt and pepper. When all the vegetables are cooked, remove them with a slotted spoon and keep them warm. Place the meat in the simmering broth, and

Sweet-Sour Pot Roast

Yield: 8 to 10 servings

2 tablespoons shortening
5 pounds pot roast
½ cup onion, sliced
1 cup vinegar
¾ cup brown sugar
¼ teaspoon nutmeg
½ teaspoon salt

Melt the shortening in a heavy kettle. Brown the meat in the melted fat. Remove the meat. Add the onions and cook until transparent. Return the meat to the kettle. Add the remaining ingredients. Cover and simmer over low heat until the meat is tender, about 3½ hours. If desired, thicken the broth with a butter and flour ball and cook 5 minutes.

Hungarian Beef Stew

Yield: 4 servings

1 to 1½ pounds boneless stew meat
4 to 5 onions
1 14-ounce can crushed tomatoes
1 to 2 cloves garlic, crushed
1½ teaspoons salt
¼ teaspoon black pepper
1 teaspoon thyme
About 1 tablespoon paprika
2 tablespoons tomato paste
Water (optional)

Cut the meat into sugar-cube size. Peel and cut the onions into large pieces. Mix the meat, onions, tomatoes with juice, and spices together in a pot.

Simmer, covered, for about 45 minutes or until the meat feels tender. Add water, if necessary, while simmering. Season to taste and serve the stew with boiled potatoes or rice.

Steak with Seasoned Butter

Yield: 6 servings

1 pound butter
⅛ teaspoon white pepper
1 tablespoon parsley, finely chopped
2 tablespoons lemon juice
1 tablespoon fresh horseradish
1 teaspoon sugar
½ teaspoon dry mustard
1 tablespoon onion, finely grated
6 individual steaks of your choice

Soften the butter at room temperature for 1 hour. Transfer to a small mixing bowl. Add all the other ingredients, except the steaks. Cream the mixture with the back of a spoon, then beat until mixed thoroughly.

Preheat the broiler. Spread seasoned butter over one side of each steak. Place under the broiler, butter side up. Cook to preferred doneness. Remove from the broiler and spread seasoned butter on the other side of each steak. Return to the broiler until cooked to your liking.

Serve the steaks with toast spread with the remaining seasoned butter. Leftover butter may be refrigerated for later use.

Beef Stew with Pastry Crust

Oven Baked Short Ribs with Garden Vegetables

Yield: 4 servings

3 pounds beef short ribs
1 teaspoon salt
¼ teaspoon pepper
1 pound carrots, cleaned and halved
1 pound potatoes, pared and halved
½ pound fresh green beans
4 small white onions
1 13¾-ounce can beef broth
2 tablespoons horseradish
2 teaspoons prepared mustard
2 tablespoons cornstarch
¼ cup water

Trim excess fat from the meat. Place the meat in a 13 × 9 × 2-inch baking pan; sprinkle with salt and pepper. Bake uncovered in a 350°F oven 2 hours; drain the fat. Add the next 4 ingredients. Mix the broth, horseradish, and mustard; pour over meat and vegetables. Cover with foil; bake 1 to 1½ hours longer, or until tender.

Arrange the meat and vegetables on a serving platter; keep warm. Strain the broth; remove excess

fat. Add water, if necessary, to make 2 cups and return to the baking pan. Mix cornstarch and ¼ cup cool water; stir into the pan. Bring to a boil over medium heat, stirring constantly, and boil 1 minute. Serve the gravy with meat and vegetables.

Barbecued Short Ribs

Yield: 4 servings

4 pounds beef short ribs
2 teaspoons salt
¼ teaspoon pepper
1 8-ounce can tomato sauce
¼ cup catsup
⅓ cup brown sugar
¼ cup vinegar
2 tablespoons prepared mustard
½ cup onion, chopped
1 clove garlic, minced
1 tablespoon chili powder

Place the short ribs in a covered frying pan and cook slowly for 1½ hours, turning occasionally. Season with salt and pepper. Combine the tomato sauce, catsup, brown sugar, vinegar, mustard, onion, garlic, and chili powder in a saucepan and simmer 5 minutes. Remove each short rib from the pan, dip in sauce to coat all sides, and place on a grill, brushing with sauce and turning occasionally for 20 to 30 minutes, or until done.

Buck's County Beef Stew

Yield: 6 servings

3 tablespoons corn oil
2 pounds stewing beef, cut in 2-inch cubes
1 beef bouillon cube
2 teaspoons salt
1 bay leaf
¼ teaspoon dried thyme leaves, crushed
4½ cups water
6 carrots
12 small white onions
¼ cup cornstarch

In a skillet, heat the corn oil over medium heat. Add the beef; brown on all sides. Add the next 4 ingredients and 4 cups of the water. Cover; bring to a boil. Reduce the heat and simmer 1½ hours. Add the carrots and onions. Simmer ½ hour or until tender.

Mix the cornstarch and ½ cup of water, stir into the beef mixture. Bring to a boil, stirring constantly; boil 1 minute.

Hamburger Stew with Green Peppers

Burgundy Beef Stew

Yield: 6 to 8 servings

2½ pounds stew meat
3 tablespoons butter
½ teaspoon coarsely ground black pepper
2 teaspoons salt
2 large onions, chopped
6 cloves garlic, crushed
⅓ pound lightly salted side of pork
¼ cup brandy
2 tablespoons tomato paste
2 tablespoons flour
1 cup water
1 bottle Burgundy red wine
1 carrot, cut into pieces
1 piece celeriac (celery root)
2 teaspoons thyme
1 bay leaf
1 sprig parsley
Soy sauce
25 small onions
⅔ pound fresh mushrooms
Noodles with butter

Cut the meat into 1½-inch cubes and brown it in butter in a hot stew pot. Add salt and pepper. Add the onions to the stew together with the garlic cloves. Take strips of rind from the pork meat and fry it in the stew.

Flambé with the brandy but NOT under the kitchen fan! Add the tomato paste, flour, water, and wine. Stir in the pieces of carrot and celeriac, and the thyme, bay leaf, and parsley. Place the pot over low heat and simmer, uncovered, for 2 hours. Add a little more water if necessary.

When the meat is done, remove it from the stew and place in a serving dish. The sauce may be thickened using a butter-flour ball and should be allowed to boil for another 5 minutes. Flavor with a few tablespoons of soy sauce and strain it over the meat.

Cut the pork into very small cubes and fry it for 10 minutes. Boil the small onions for several minutes, peel them, and glaze them with a few spoonfuls of the sauce before serving. Brush the mushrooms and brown them in butter. Cook the noodles, rinse them quickly in cold water, and gloss them with butter in a hot pot. Serve the pork, onions, mushrooms, and noodles with the stew.

Hunter's Stew

Yield: 8 servings

3 pounds stewing-beef cubes
1 quart water
8 peppercorns
8 whole cloves
2 whole bay leaves
2 teaspoons salt
1 teaspoon marjoram
3 pounds chicken, cubed
½ cup butter
2 medium-sized onions, peeled and cut into rings
5 large carrots, peeled and sliced
2 sprigs parsley, chopped
4 celery stalks, chopped
3 leeks, chopped
½ teaspoon white pepper
3 sprigs dill, chopped
½ bunch parsley, chopped

Cover the beef with water; bring to a boil. Tie the peppercorns, cloves, and bay leaves in a cloth bag; drop into the boiling beef. Sprinkle 1 teaspoon of salt and marjoram over the beef; simmer 2 hours in a covered kettle. Add the chicken; simmer, covered.

Put the butter into a pan. Add the vegetables, 1 teaspoon of salt, and pepper; sauté over low heat until wilted. Take the cloth bag out of the meat; discard. Remove the meat from the water. Add the wilted vegetables to the meat stock; simmer until tender. Add the meat. Pour into a serving dish; sprinkle with chopped dill and parsley.

Sunday Stew

Beef Stew with Pastry Crust

Yield: 6 servings

2½ pounds stew meat
Butter for frying
1½ tablespoons flour
1 teaspoon salt
¼ teaspoon black pepper
1 large onion, chopped
1 large eggplant, sliced and peeled
¼ pound fresh mushrooms
1 can crushed tomatoes
1¼ cups beef broth
2 cloves garlic, crushed
2 teaspoons marjoram
3 to 4 tablespoons red wine
2 to 3 teaspoons arrowroot, mixed with a little water
Pimiento-filled olives, cut in half
Snipped parsley
3 to 4 frozen pastry crust patties, just thawed
1 egg, beaten

Cut the meat into 1¼-inch cubes, dredge them in flour, and brown them in butter in a frying pan. Season with salt and pepper. Place the meat in a stew pot. Brown the onion, eggplant, and mushrooms, each separately, in the frying pan, and place them in the stew pot. Pour over the crushed tomatoes and broth. Bring to a boil and season with the garlic and marjoram.

Simmer the stew for about an hour, or until the meat feels very tender. Season with red wine toward the end of the simmering time. Thicken with the arrowroot, which has been mixed with a little water, so that the stew has a fine consistency. Pour the stew into an ovenproof dish. Garnish with sliced olives and snipped parsley.

Place the pastry crust patties together and roll them out into a ¼-inch thick crust. Brush the edges of the pan with a beaten egg. Place the crust over the stew. Press well around the edges of the pan, make a hole in the crust for the steam to escape, and place in a 400°F oven for about 20 to 25 minutes.

Hamburger Stew with Green Peppers

Yield: 8 servings

1⅓ pounds ground chuck or ground round
About 2½ tablespoons butter or margarine
3 onions, peeled and chopped
2 14-ounce cans crushed tomatoes
2½ teaspoons salt
½ teaspoon ground black pepper
2 to 3 tablespoons tomato paste
4 to 5 green peppers
1½ to 2 tablespoons snipped fresh thyme (or 1½ teaspoons dried thyme)

Dash cayenne pepper (optional)
1 small beef bouillon cube (optional)

Brown the meat in a little butter or margarine in a large frying pan or stew pot. Stir so that the meat crumbles into little pieces. Peel and chop the onions, and brown them with the meat toward the end of the browning process.

Place the meat and onion in a stew pot if they have been browned in a frying pan. Add the tomatoes, salt, pepper, and tomato paste. Cover and simmer over fairly low heat for 10 minutes.

In the meantime, remove the seeds and membranes from the peppers. Cut into thin strips, then divide the strips into pieces. Add the peppers and the thyme to the stew. Simmer the stew for another 5 to 8 minutes so that the peppers become somewhat soft.

Adjust the seasoning if necessary; melt a bouillon cube in the stew, if desired, or if the stew has a weak flavor. When served with noodles, the stew might need to be thinned with a small amount of water.

Sunday Stew

Yield: 4 servings

2 large onions
1 small piece celeriac (celery root)
¾ pound ground meat
About 1 teaspoon salt
¼ teaspoon white or black pepper
2 teaspoons paprika or chili powder
1 bouillon cube
3 tablespoons tomato paste
About ¾ cup water
Pasta (shells or penne)

Peel and chop the onions and cut the celeriac into small cubes. Brown the meat in a pot while stirring, so that it evenly crumbles. Sauté the onion and celeriac with the meat when the meat is almost all brown. Season and add the bouillon cube, tomato paste, and water. Stir well and simmer for several minutes.

Prepare the pasta according to the directions on the package (make enough for 4 servings). Add the cooked pasta to the stew.

Stew with Vegetables and Meatballs

Yield: 4 servings

3 onions, peeled and sliced
6 potatoes, peeled and quartered
⅓ cup celeriac, cut in small cubes
2 to 3 carrots, thinly sliced
1 14-ounce can crushed tomatoes
⅓ cup vegetable broth
2 tablespoons tomato paste

1 teaspoon salt
½ teaspoon lemon pepper
¼ teaspoon cayenne pepper
1 green pepper, seeded and cut in strips
1 red pepper, seeded and chopped
1 leek, finely chopped

meatballs
⅔ pound ground veal or hamburger meat
1 tablespoon bread crumbs
⅓ cup milk
½ teaspoon salt
⅛ teaspoon pepper
1 egg

yogurt salad
2 cups natural yogurt
¼ fresh cucumber
1 clove garlic, crushed
¼ teaspoon salt
⅛ teaspoon pepper

Place the onion, potatoes, celeriac, and carrots in a pot. Add the crushed tomatoes, broth, tomato paste, and spices, and simmer until the vegetables begin to feel soft. Add the peppers and leek.

Mix the meatball ingredients together and shape them into small balls. Place them in the vegetable stew and let them simmer with the vegetables during the final 5 minutes.

Serve with yogurt salad. To make the salad, drain the yogurt for about 2 hours in a paper coffee filter. Grate the cucumber coarsely and press as much liquid out of it as possible. Mix it with the yogurt right before serving. Season with the garlic, salt, and pepper.

Beef Barbecue

Yield: 4 servings

1 pound ground beef
½ cup onions
½ cup green pepper (optional)
¼ cup catsup
1 tablespoon vinegar
1 tablespoon sugar
1 tablespoon Worcestershire sauce
8 ounce tomato sauce

Brown the beef, onions, and green peppers; set aside. Put the remaining ingredients in a large saucepan and simmer. Add the beef mixture to the sauce. Simmer for 1 hour.

Stew with Vegetables and Meatballs

Swiss Steak

Yield: 6 servings

2 pounds boneless rump, round, or chuck steak, cut into 6 pieces
¼ cup flour
1¼ teaspoons salt
3 tablespoons oil
½ cup onion, chopped
1 1-pound can peeled Italian plum tomatoes, broken up
4 tablespoons Worcestershire sauce
6 carrots, halved lengthwise and cut in thirds
2 green peppers, cut into 1-inch pieces

Dredge the meat with flour mixed with ¾ teaspoon of the salt. Pound the flour into both sides of the meat with the edge of a heavy plate.

In a large, heavy pot or Dutch oven, heat the oil. Add the meat and brown well on both sides. Add the onion; sauté until transparent. Stir in the tomatoes and 2 tablespoons of the Worcestershire sauce. Cover; reduce heat and simmer 45 minutes.

Add the carrots and green peppers. Cover and cook 45 minutes longer or until the vegetables and meat are tender. Stir in the remaining 2 tablespoons of Worcestershire sauce and ½ teaspoon of salt.

Barbecued Meatballs

Yield: 3 to 4 servings

meatballs
1 pound ground beef
¾ cup bread crumbs
½ cup milk
½ cup onions, chopped
1 teaspoon salt
½ teaspoon pepper
½ teaspoon oregano
1 egg

barbecue sauce
1 10½-ounce can tomato purée
¼ cup molasses
¼ cup brown sugar
¼ cup vinegar
1 teaspoon sweet basil;

Combine the meatball ingredients; form into 1-inch balls. Brown in a skillet; drain.

Combine the sauce ingredients; simmer, covered, in the skillet used for the meatballs, about 15 minutes to allow flavors to blend.

Hamburger-Filled Cabbage

Yield: 4 servings

1 small head of cabbage
½ teaspoon salt per cup of water
¼ cup round-grained rice
1 celery stalk, thinly sliced
1 onion, minced
⅓ pound ground chuck meat
⅓ pound ground pork meat
1 clove garlic, crushed
1 egg
1 14-ounce can crushed tomatoes
1½ teaspoons salt
½ teaspoon black pepper
¼ teaspoon herb seasoned salt
¼ cup parsley
⅓ cup vegetable broth

Remove the outer leaves of the cabbage head. Rinse the cabbage head and cut a cross in the cabbage root. Place the cabbage head in boiling salted water—it should be totally covered—and simmer for 10 minutes. Pour off the water and let the cabbage cool enough so that the leaves can be turned out, one by one, into a water-lily. (See the picture.)

Boil the rice. Mix the rice, celery, and onion in a large bowl and add the ground meat together with the crushed garlic, egg, half of the crushed tomatoes, spices, and parsley. Blend well.

Hamburger-Filled Cabbage

Gorgonzola Hamburgers

Spoon the meat mixture in between the leaves of the cabbage head. Start in the middle and fold up the leaves as you go along. Tie the cabbage head up into a package using shrunken cotton string and place in a stew pot.

Mix the rest of the crushed tomatoes with the broth. Pour it over the cabbage and simmer for 2 hours, so that the cabbage becomes cooked all the way through. Baste the cabbage now and then with the broth. This dish may be prepared in advance, as it is easy to warm up.

Pink Pepper Hamburgers

Yield: 4 servings

1½ pounds ground beef
5 tablespoons onion, minced
2 eggs
½ plus 1 container crème fraîche
Salt
Pepper
2 tablespoons plus ½ teaspoon pink pepper
Butter or margarine for frying
1¼ cups strong meat broth
1 teaspoon light French mustard
1 to 2 teaspoons soy sauce

Mix the ground beef, onion, eggs, ½ cup crème fraîche, salt, and pepper together. Blend well into an even mixture. Crush the pink peppercorns. This spice has a very mild flavor, which is why so much is needed.

Shape the meat into 8 hamburgers. Sprinkle with 2 tablespoons ground pink pepper and flatten the hamburgers with your hands, pressing the pepper into the patties.

Brown the hamburgers in the butter or margarine in a large frying pan. Decrease the heat and add the broth, a little at a time. Let the hamburgers simmer in the gravy until they are done. Remove the patties.

Mix the mustard and 1 cup of crème fraîche in the gravy. It should not be boiling. The gravy will first look as though it has curdled but it will become the right consistency after it comes to a boil. Season with soy sauce and ½ teaspoon pink peppercorns which have been crushed. The sauce should have a creamy consistency and a fairly strong flavor.

Place the hamburger patties back into the sauce and let it come to a boil.

Gorgonzola-Filled Hamburgers

Yield: Varies

Ground beef
Salt
Pepper
Minced onion
Soda water
1 tablespoon Gorgonzola cheese for each hamburger patty
Oil

Blend ground beef with salt, pepper, onion, and a little soda water. Fold so that all becomes well mixed.

Shape the meat into hamburger patties. Make a hole in the middle of each patty and fill it with Gorgonzola cheese. Press the meat around the cheese so that it thoroughly covers the cheese, and brush with oil.

Broil the hamburgers for about 10 minutes on each side and serve with a mixed salad.

Green Pepper Hamburgers

Yield: 4 servings

1½ to 2 pounds ground hamburger meat
1 teaspoon salt
1 egg
¼ cup water
⅛ cup heavy cream
1 to 1¼ tablespoons dried or preserved green peppercorns or 1 tablespoon coursely ground black pepper
About 1½ tablespoons butter

gravy
About ⅓ cup beef broth
⅓ cup heavy cream
½ tablespoon mustard

Mix the ground meat with salt. Add the egg and moisten with the water and cream. Mix well.

Pound the dried peppercorns or chop the preserved ones. Make 8 hamburgers. Dredge them in the pepper, making sure it gets evenly spread. Push in the pepper so that it goes into the meat.

Sauté the hamburgers in a little butter in a frying pan. Place on a warm dish.

Make the gravy by pouring the broth and cream into the frying pan. Add the mustard. Let simmer for a few minutes.

Croquettes

Yield: 4 servings

1 pound cooked potatoes, mashed
1 small onion, finely chopped
2-3 cups cooked ground beef
1 tablespoon chutney
1 tablespoon chopped herbs
½ teaspoon salt
⅛ teaspoon white pepper
Tomato purée (optional)
2-3 tablespoons flour
2 eggs, beaten
Dry white crumbs
Fat for deep frying
Bunch of parsley

Mix the potatoes and onion with the meat, chutney, herbs, and seasonings. Add a little tomato purée if the mixture is too dry. Put the mixture on a floured board. Make into a long roll; cut into sections about 1 inch thick and 3 inches long. Roll in seasoned flour. Brush all over with eggs; roll in bread crumbs.

Deep-fry in smoking-hot fat until well browned; drain. Serve with parsley fried in deep fat a few seconds and pass a well-flavored sauce.

Green Pepper Hamburgers

Beef Hedgehog

Yield: 4 to 6 servings

1 pound ground beef
½ pound ham (or bacon), chopped
5-7 tablespoons oil
1 small onion, finely chopped
2 tablespoons flour
1 cup strong beef stock
¾ cup fresh bread crumbs
1 egg
2 tablespoons catsup (or 1 tablespoon soy sauce)
2 tablespoons chopped mixed herbs, mainly parsley
2 pounds old potatoes
2 tablespoons butter or margarine
½ cup milk
12 pickling onions
12 small button mushrooms

Mix the ground beef and chopped ham in a bowl. (If using bacon, chop and cook for a few minutes before adding the beef.) Heat 3-4 tablespoons of oil in a fairly large pan. Cook the onion with the lid on the pan for 5 minutes. Add the beef and ham. Mix in the flour and blend well. Add the stock and bring to a boil, stirring all the time. Cook for a minute or two; then cool slightly. Add the bread crumbs, then the beaten egg and sauce. Mix well, adding herbs and seasoning to taste.

Butter a loaf tin or oval baking dish well and turn the meat mixture into it. Cover with a lid or foil and bake for about 1 hour.

Peel and boil the potatoes; drain and dry them before mashing. Beat in butter and enough milk to make a dryish mixture. Season well and keep warm. Heat 2-3 tablespoons of oil and cook pickling onions for about 10 minutes sprinkling with a little sugar to help the browning. Remove and keep warm. Add the button mushrooms to the pan and cook these for 3-4 minutes.

When the beef roll is cooked, turn it onto an ovenproof dish, reserving any juice to make gravy. Coat the meat roll all over with an even layer of mashed potato and mark with a fork. Press the onions and mushrooms into the potato in rows to represent the hedgehog's spines. Then return the roll to the oven for 15 minutes or until golden brown.

Pink Pepper Hamburgers

Mazetti

Yield: 10 to 12 servings

2 pounds ground beef
2½ cups celery with leaves (about ½ bunch), finely chopped
2 cups onions, chopped
2 cloves garlic, finely chopped
1 tablespoon water
1 8-ounce package medium-fine noodles
2 cans condensed tomato soup
1 6-ounce can mushrooms and liquid
2 teaspoons salt
½ teaspoon pepper
2 cups sharp Cheddar cheese, grated

Brown meat in a skillet, then add the celery, onions, garlic, and water. Cover and cook until the vegetables are tender. Remove from the heat.

Cook the noodles according to package directions; drain. Combine the noodles and beef mixture; add the soup, undrained mushrooms, salt, and pepper. Spread the mixture in a 3-quart casserole. Sprinkle with cheese on top. Place in a cold oven. Bake uncovered at 250°F about 1 hour, until bubbly. This dish may be refrigerated up to 24 hours, or frozen before cooking.

Corn Rolls

Yield: 4 servings

¾ pound ground beef
1 large yellow onion, chopped
1 14-ounce can crushed tomatoes
3 to 4 tablespoons tomato paste
6 to 8 ears fresh corn
1 green pepper, chopped
Herb salt
Black pepper
2 cups beef broth

Place the ground beef and onion in an ungreased pan; brown. Add the crushed tomatoes and tomato paste and let simmer for 25 minutes, stirring occasionally.

Shuck the corn, but save the husks. Scrape the corn from the cob and add it to the ground beef mixture. Cut the pepper into small bits and add. Season and let simmer a few minutes.

Rinse the corn husks. You'll need several for each roll. Place a spoonful of the ground beef mixture in the center of a husk. Roll into a tight package and fasten with a toothpick. Place the corn rolls together in a shallow pan. Pour boiling bouillon over the rolls. Cover and simmer for 15 minutes. Turn and baste after 7 minutes.

Ranch Beef Loaf

Yield: 8 servings

1½ cups soft bread crumbs
¾ cup milk
2 pounds ground beef
2 teaspoons salt
⅛ teaspoon pepper
1 medium-sized carrot, peeled and grated
1 small onion, peeled and minced
2 eggs, beaten
¼ cup catsup
3 tablespoons brown sugar
2 tablespoons prepared mustard

Put the bread crumbs in a large bowl and pour milk over them. Stir in the ground beef, salt, pepper, carrot, onion, and beaten eggs. Mix thoroughly with a spoon or fork. Lightly shape the meat mixture with your hands to make an oval loaf. Put in a shallow baking pan, such as a 13 × 9 × 2-inch pan. Gently smooth the loaf to make it even and neatly shaped. The loaf will be juicier if you don't handle the mixture much.

Mix the catsup, brown sugar, and mustard; spread over the loaf. Bake at 325°F for 1½ hours. Remove the meatloaf from the oven. Loosen the

Corn Rolls

bottom of the loaf from the pan and lift it with a wide spatula onto a warm platter. Slice to serve.

Stuffed Bacon with Ground Meat

Yield: 4 servings

1 pound ground chuck
1 tablespoon onion, chopped
1 tablespoon parsley, chopped
3 tablespoons heavy cream
½ teaspoon salt
Pepper
¼ pound sliced bacon
Juice from 1 orange
1 to 1¼ cups beef broth
2 tablespoons red wine
1 tablespoon black currant juice or jelly
1 teaspoon thyme
1 teaspoon arrowroot mixed with a little water
1 teaspoon lemon juice (optional)
Orange peel
Finely chopped parsley

Mix together the meat, onion, parsley, and cream. Season with salt and pepper and form into rolls. Wrap the rolls up in thin bacon slices.

Fry the stuffed bacon slowly in a frying pan until evenly brown. Add the orange juice, broth, red wine, and currant juice or jelly. Season with thyme, salt, pepper, and lemon juice. Thicken with the arrowroot mixed with a little water. Simmer for 4 to 5 minutes. Heat up thin strips of orange peel in the sauce. Sprinkle with parsley when it is time to serve the meal.

Western Meatballs and Franks

Yield: 6 servings

1 pound ground beef
1 egg, slightly beaten
¼ cup dry bread crumbs
1 medium-sized onion, grated
1 teaspoon salt
¾ cup chili sauce
¼ cup grape jelly
2 tablespoons lemon juice
⅔ cup water
1 pound frankfurters, cut diagonally in ½-inch slices

Mix the beef, egg, crumbs, onion, and salt together. Shape the mixture into small balls. Place the chili sauce, grape jelly, lemon juice, and water in a large skillet. Heat; add the meatballs and simmer until the meat is cooked.

Just before serving, add the frankfurters and heat.

Stuffed Bacon with Ground Meat

Ground Beef Gratin with Mushrooms

Yield: 4 servings

1 eggplant, pared
1 teaspoon salt
About 2 cups fresh mushrooms, rinsed and chopped
1 tablespoon margarine
1 pound ground beef
1 teaspoon salt
Black pepper
2 teaspoons paprika
1 to 1¼ cups boiled rice
1 onion, finely chopped
1 green pepper, cubed
¾ cup broth
About 1 cup coarsely grated cheese

Cut the eggplant into slices and place on the bottom of a greased, ovenproof dish. Season with salt. Sauté the mushrooms in margarine until the liquid has soaked back into the vegetables. Place the mushrooms over the eggplant.

Mix the ground beef with salt, pepper, and paprika. Add the boiled rice, which has been allowed to become cold, and the onion. Add the green pepper and the broth. The beef should be rather loose in consistency.

Spread the meat out in the dish. Sprinkle with the grated cheese. Place the dish in a preheated 350°F oven for about 30 minutes, or until the meat is cooked through.

Deviled Lamb Chops

Yield: 4 to 5 servings

1½-2 pounds rack of lamb
Salt and pepper
Butter or margarine
1 onion, peeled and chopped
¼ cup celery, finely chopped
1 clove garlic, crushed
1 10-ounce can tomato soup
1 tablespoon Worcestershire sauce
1 tablespoon lemon juice
2 tablespoons sherry
1 tablespoon brown sugar
2 teaspoons prepared mustard

Trim and cut the meat into chops and arrange in a buttered casserole. Sprinkle with salt, pepper, onion, celery, and garlic. Cover and cook for about 20 minutes. Remove any excess fat.

Heat the tomato soup; add all the other ingredients and mix well. Adjust seasoning. Pour the sauce over the chops. Cover and cook in a preheated 350°F oven for about 1 hour, basting occasionally.

Serve with some chutney or pickled pears.

Porcupine Meatballs

Yield: 4 servings

1 pound ground beef
¼ cup uncooked rice
¼ cup onion, finely chopped
1 teaspoon salt
⅛ teaspoon pepper
1 egg
1 10½-ounce can condensed tomato soup
½ cup water
1 teaspoon Worcestershire sauce

Combine the ground beef, rice, onion, salt, pepper, and egg in a bowl. Mix lightly but well. Shape the mixture into 24, 1-inch meatballs.

Blend the tomato soup, water, and Worcestershire sauce in a 10-inch skillet. Cook over medium heat until the mixture comes to a boil, about 3 minutes. Add the meatballs to the simmering sauce, spooning sauce over all. Return the mixture to a boil. Reduce heat to low. Cover and simmer 45 minutes, turning meatballs once or twice during cooking.

Bitter-Sweet Lamb Casserole

Yield: 4 to 6 servings

2-2½ pounds rack of lamb
2 tablespoons oil
3 tablespoons vinegar
1 6-8 ounce can orange juice
2 teaspoons Worcestershire sauce
½ teaspoon salt
⅛ teaspoon freshly ground pepper
Pinch dry mustard
Pinch paprika
½ teaspoon celery seed
½ teaspoon basil
½ teaspoon oregano
3-4 cloves
2 teaspoons sugar
Cooked rice or noodles

Trim and cut the meat into chops; brown it in hot oil and place in a casserole with 1 cup of water and the vinegar. Cover and cook in a 350°F oven for 1 hour.

Put the orange juice, Worcestershire sauce, seasonings, and flavorings into a small pan and simmer, uncovered, for 10 minutes. When the meat has cooked for 1 hour, stir in the orange juice mixture and cook for another hour.

Serve with rice or noodles.

Ground Beef Gratin with Mushrooms

Filled Green Peppers

Yield: 6 servings

6 green peppers
1 pound ground beef
Margarine or oil for frying
1 whole garlic, peeled and chopped
Salt
Pepper
1 can crushed tomatoes
2 to 3 teaspoons mixed herbs (oregano, basil, and
  chervil)

Boil the green peppers in salted, boiling water for 10 minutes. Cut a lid off of each pepper and let the peppers drain. Remove the seeds.

Brown the ground beef and garlic cloves in margarine for about 10 minutes. Season with salt and pepper, and pour the mixture into a pot with the crushed tomatoes. Simmer for 5 minutes. Season by adding oregano, basil, and chervil, according to your taste. Serve with boiled potatoes or rice.

Stuffed Meatloaf

Yield: 4 to 5 servings

1 pound lean ground beef
1 pound ground pork
1 cup dry bread crumbs
½ cup carrot, grated
¼ cup plus 1 tablespoon onion, finely chopped
2 eggs, beaten
½ cup milk
2¼ teaspoons salt
1 teaspoon Worcestershire sauce
⅛ teaspoon pepper
1 4-ounce can mushrooms, drained and chopped
2 tablespoons butter
2 cups soft bread crumbs
1 tablespoon parsley, chopped
½ teaspoon poultry seasoning

Combine the ground beef, bread crumbs, carrot, ¼ cup of the onion, and eggs. Add the milk, 2 teaspoons of salt, Worcestershire sauce, and pepper. Place the mixture on a double thick square of greased aluminum foil. Shape into a 14 × 18-inch rectangle.

Sauté the mushrooms and remaining 1 tablespoon of onion in butter over medium heat. Add the remaining ingredients. Spread the mushroom stuffing over the meat; roll up the foil, starting with the long side. Press the overlapping edge into the roll to seal. Bring the foil edges together in a tight double fold on the top. Fold ends up, using tight double folds.

Place the wrapped meatloaf on a rack in a shallow pan. Bake in a 375°F oven 1 hour. Open the foil;

continue baking for 15 more minutes, or until the loaf browns.

Broiled Lamb Chops with Vegetables

Yield: 6 servings

5 tablespoons olive oil
1 clove garlic, minced
4 tablespoons butter
½ teaspoon tarragon
½ teaspoon rosemary
1 tablespoon fresh parsley, chopped
6 double lamb chops
Salt and pepper to taste
1 pound carrots, peeled and julienned
7 tablespoons butter
24 spears asparagus

Combine the olive oil and garlic; set aside. Cream the butter with tarragon, rosemary, and parsley. Cut a slit along the back, fatty edge of the lamb chops and stuff with a little of the butter mixture, dividing it equally among the chops. Brush the chops with the olive oil mixture and place on a rack over a baking sheet. Broil 2 inches from the source of heat in a very hot broiler. Brown both sides, cooking a total of 10 minutes for rare, 15 for medium, and 20 for well done. Transfer to a warm platter. Season with salt and pepper.

Put the carrots in a saucepan. Add salt and pepper to taste and 2 tablespoons of butter. Cover and simmer for 15 to 20 minutes, until tender. Toss with ½ tablespoon of butter. Wash the asparagus, carefully scraping sand out from the sides. Steam for about 8 minutes; pat with 2 tablespoons of butter and season with salt and pepper.

To serve, put 4 asparagus spears on each plate. Place the lamb chop on top and serve the carrots next to the chops.

Pan-Fried Lamb Slices

Yield: 8 to 10 servings

1 leg of lamb
2 or 3 medium-sized onions, peeled and sliced into
  rings
4 or more tablespoons oil for frying
Salt and pepper to taste

With a sharp knife, cut the lamb into ½-inch steaks. Brown the onion rings in oil in a large skillet. Drain and set aside to keep warm. Sauté the meat slices in the same oil; season with salt and pepper.

To serve, arrange the meat on a platter. Cover the slices with drained onions.

Mini Lamb Rolls

securely with a toothpick.

Brown the rolls on all sides in the butter and then place them in a greased, ovenproof dish or pot. Add the onions. Pour in the hot broth, cover, and place in the oven for about an hour. Add the rest of the celeriac stalks when about 15 minutes of the baking time remains. Serve with boiled potatoes, sprinkled with snipped parsley or chives.

Lamb and Cheese Rolls

Yield: 6 servings

2 cups cooked lamb, cubed
1 cup Swiss cheese, grated
⅓ cup celery, diced
3 tablespoons onion, grated
1 teaspoon salt
¼ cup mayonnaise
2 tablespoons catsup or chili sauce
6 French rolls, about 6 inches long
Butter or margarine

In a mixing bowl, toss the lamb, cheese, celery, onion, and salt together. Combine the mayonnaise and catsup or chili sauce; stir into the lamb mixture, mixing thoroughly.

Slightly hollow out the center of the rolls. Spread lightly with butter or margarine and fill with the lamb mixture. These may be served immediately or wrapped in foil and heated in the oven until the cheese melts.

Mini Lamb Rolls

Yield: 4 servings

About 2½ pounds thin breast of lamb
Salt
Pepper
1 bunch parsley
1 bunch chives
1 teaspoon salt
¼ teaspoon ground black pepper
½ teaspoon thyme
1 large piece celeriac (celery root)
2 medium-sized onions, cut into large pieces
About 1 cup broth
1 tablespoon butter

Preheat oven to 400°F. Remove bones from the lamb breast. Take away the largest membranes and cut straight across where the bone sits, making 3 to 4 inch wide strips. Cut these strips down the middle.

Salt and pepper the meat. Chop the chives and parsley, mix with the thyme, and sprinkle this mixture evenly over the meat.

Cut the celeriac into ½ inch thick strips. Place one strip on each piece of meat. Roll the meat strips up tightly into small mini-rolls and fasten them

Lamb and Potato Casserole

4 servings

2 tablespoons flour
Salt and pepper
4 large loin or 8 rib lamb chops
4 tablespoons butter or margarine
½ pound onions, peeled and sliced
1 small clove garlic, crushed
4 tomatoes, peeled and sliced
1-2 sprigs fresh, or ⅛ teaspoon dried, rosemary
1 pound potatoes, peeled and sliced
3-4 tablespoons broth or water

Mix the flour with a little salt and pepper and dredge the chops well. Heat 3 tablespoons of butter in a sauté pan, brown the chops on both sides, then remove from the pan. Add the onion and garlic to the remaining fat and cook until softened.

Arrange the meat, onion, tomatoes, rosemary, and potatoes in layers in a casserole, seasoning each layer lightly and finishing with the potatoes. Add the broth or water and dot with the remaining butter. Cover, and cook for about 2 hours. About 15 minutes before the end of the cooking, remove the lid to allow the potatoes to brown.

Rolled Leg of Lamb

Yield: 6 to 8 servings

1 4- to 7-pound leg of lamb, boned, trimmed of fat, rolled, and tied
1 teaspoon salt
½ clove garlic, minced
¼ teaspoon pepper
½ small bay leaf, crushed
¼ teaspoon ground ginger
¼ teaspoon dried thyme
¼ teaspoon dried sage
¼ teaspoon dried marjoram
1 teaspoon lemon juice
1 tablespoon olive oil

With a sharp knife, cut small but deep slashes in the lamb, distributing them evenly.

In a small bowl, mix the salt, garlic, pepper, bay leaf, ginger, thyme, sage, and marjoram together. Fill the slashes with the herb mixture; then rub the surface of the lamb with lemon juice and olive oil.

Place the lamb on a rack in a roasting pan. Roast in a preheated 325°F oven for 20 minutes per pound, or until a meat thermometer indicates the desired degree of doneness. Make a gravy from the pan drippings, if desired.

Lamb Chops Marinated in Beer

Yield: 2 to 4 servings

1 12-ounce can beer
⅓ cup salad oil
1 clove garlic, minced
1 tablespoon lemon juice
1 tablespoon sugar
¾ teaspoon salt
Dash pepper
4 lamb chops

In a shallow baking dish, combine the beer, oil, garlic, lemon juice, sugar, salt, and pepper. Add the lamb chops; cover and refrigerate overnight. Remove the chops from the baking dish; drain. Broil 6 to 8 minutes on each side or until the desired degree of doneness. Serve with broiled apple rings, if desired.

Herb-Spiced Leg of Lamb

Herb-Spiced Leg of Lamb

Yield: 8 servings

1 5½ to 6 pound leg of lamb
¼ cup vegetable oil
2 teaspoons salt
1 teaspoon thyme
1 teaspoon marjoram
1 teaspoon black pepper

Rub the oil and spices into the lamb. Let the meat stand while the oven is preheating so that it can take in the seasoning. Preheat the oven to 350°F.

Stick a meat thermometer into the thickest part of the meat but not against the bone. Bake the lamb until the thermometer shows 158 to 161.5°F. The meat is then a pretty pink inside. This takes about 1¾ to 2 hours. Let the meat stand for 10 minutes before slicing it.

Lamb with Dill

Yield: 4 servings

About 2½ pounds lamb meat with the bone— shoulder, breast, rib
Water
2 teaspoons salt per quart water
Dill stalks
6 white peppercorns
2 unpeeled cloves garlic
1 small carrot, cut into small pieces
1 leek or onion, cut into small pieces

sauce
1½ tablespoons butter or margarine
2½ tablespoons flour
1⅔ to 2 cups broth
3 tablespoons snipped dill
1 tablespoon pressed lemon juice
1 egg yolk
¼ cup cream

Place the meat in a pot. Measure and pour over as much water as needed to cover the meat. Add salt and bring to a boil. Skim well and add dill, pepper, garlic, carrot, and leek or onion. Let the meat simmer over low heat until it feels tender, 1 to 1 ½ hours.

To make the sauce, melt the butter in a pot, stir in the flour, and dilute with the liquid. Let the sauce boil for several minutes. Season with the dill and lemon juice.

Remove the pot from the heat and add the yolk, which has been beaten first together with the cream. The sauce should not be allowed to boil again as it can curdle.

Cut up the meat and serve it with the sauce, boiled potatoes, and vegetables.

Lamb with Dill

Lamb Pie with Sweet Potato Topping

Yield: 6 servings

2 cups cooked lamb, cut into 1-inch cubes
1 cup rich lamb gravy
1 cup bouillon
12 small cooked white onions
2 cups peas
1 cup celery, diced
¼ teaspoon thyme
¼ teaspoon ground allspice
Salt
Pepper
2 cups sweet potatoes, mashed
½ cup buttermilk
¼ teaspoon baking powder
1 tablespoon brown sugar

Combine the lamb, gravy, bouillon, onions, peas, celery, thyme, and allspice. Season to taste with salt and pepper. Turn the mixture into a 2½-quart, greased casserole or 6 individual, greased casseroles. Bake uncovered in a preheated 400°F oven for 15 minutes.

Beat the potatoes, buttermilk, baking powder, ½ teaspoon salt, and brown sugar together. Arrange the mixture on top of the cassrole. Return to the oven and continue to bake for 15 to 20 minutes, or until the topping is heated through and lightly browned.

Lamb Stew

Yield: 4 servings

1½ to 2 pounds lamb meat with bone—back, shoulder, or cracked breast
8 small onions
4 tomatoes, cut into pieces
About 1 teaspoon salt
½ teaspoon black pepper
1 to 2 cloves garlic, crushed
Slightly less than 1 teaspoon thyme
¼ cup parsley, chopped
¼ cup snipped chives
1 to 1¼ cups broth
1 tablespoon flour
⅓ cup crème fraîche or sour cream

Cut the meat into pieces and brown them in a small amount of butter in a frying pan. Pour into a stewing pot. Peel and brown the onions and mix them with the meat; add the tomatoes. Season and pour in the broth. Cover and simmer until the meat feels tender, about 45 minutes.

Stir the flour into a small amount of water, and mix in with the stew together with the crème fraîche or sour cream. Simmer for another 5 to 10 minutes. Season to taste. Serve with boiled potatoes.

Lamb with Vegetables

Yield: 10 servings

1 large onion, chopped
1 large carrot, sliced
2 large leeks, sliced
Butter or oil
1 large meaty lamb roast
1 can consommé plus 1 bouillon cube
Water
Salt
Pepper
Mustard seeds
Bay leaf
Sprigs of parsley

Brown the onion, carrot, and leeks in butter or oil in a thick-bottomed pot. Insert a cooking thermometer in the well-trimmed lamb roast. Place the roast on the vegetables, cover with the consommé, bouillon cube, and enough water to come more than halfway up the roast. Salt lightly, season with the pepper, mustard seeds, bay leaf, and sprigs of parsley. Cover and cook slowly until the ther-

Lamb with Vegetables

mometer shows 150 to 160°F. Remove the roast, wrap it up in aluminum foil, and keep it warm.

Strain the roast juice and simmer it so that it becomes a thick gravy. Then mix in more mustard seeds to make a strong sauce.

Serve the roast with potato cakes and applesauce.

Baked Ribs of Lamb

4 servings

1 2½-pound strip of lamb ribs
Salt and freshly ground pepper to taste
2 tablespoons vegetable oil
1 tablespoon soy sauce
1 tablespoon tomato purée
1 clove garlic, pressed
Salt and pepper

Have a thick, bony side of lamb strip cut through in several places when purchasing ribs.

Sprinkle the ribs with salt and pepper; place on a rack in a roasting pan, meat side down. Bake in a preheated 350°F oven 30 minutes. Turn; bake 30 minutes more.

Combine the oil, soy sauce, tomato purée, garlic, salt, and pepper in a small bowl; brush over the ribs. Bake 30 minutes. Cut the ribs into serving pieces.

Lamb Fricassee

the flour, then the broth. Let the sauce boil for several minutes.

Remove the pot from the heat, and stir in the egg yolk which has been mixed with the cream. The sauce should not be allowed to boil after this step as it will curdle. Season with the dill and the lemon, if desired. Cut up the meat and serve it with the sauce, boiled potatoes, and the season's vegetables.

Lamb Shanks with Horseradish

Yield: 4 servings

4 lamb shanks
2 tablespoons oil
1 teaspoon paprika
1 large onion, peeled and sliced
1 cup mushrooms, sliced
1 cup water
1 tablespoon prepared horseradish
1 teaspoon parsley, chopped
¼ teaspoon dried rosemary
¼ teaspoon sweet basil
¼ teaspoon oregano
1 cup sour cream

Heat the oil in a heavy skillet. Sprinkle the lamb shanks with paprika; brown the lamb and the onion in the oil. Add the mushrooms and cook for a few minutes; then remove all to a casserole.

Add 1 cup of water to the pan drippings, scrape up all the brown particles, and bring to a boil; then pour into the casserole. Add horseradish, herbs and seasonings. Cover and cook in a preheated 325°F oven for 1½ hours, or until the meat is quite tender.

Remove the shanks from the casserole and cut off all the meat. Stir the sour cream into the casserole and adjust the seasoning. Put the meat back and leave it just long enough for it to reheat.

Lamb and Sausage Roll

Yield: 4 servings

3 pounds boned breast of lamb
Salt
Pepper
½ pound bulk pork sausage
2 tablespoons fat
½ cup catsup
¾ cup water
½ cup onion, chopped

Rub the lamb with salt and pepper and spread with the sausage. Roll lengthwise; tie or fasten with skewers. Cook the roll in hot fat until browned.

Combine the catsup, water, and onion; pour over the lamb. Cover and simmer about 1½ hours, or until the lamb is tender and sausage cooked through. Add more water during cooking as

Lamb Fricassee

Yield: 4 servings

About 2½ pounds lamb meat with bone, cut shoulder or breast
Water
2 teaspoons salt per quart of water
10 white or black peppercorns
1 carrot, cut into pieces
1 leek, cut into pieces
Sprigs of dill

sauce
2 tablespoons butter or margarine
2 tablespoons flour
1⅔ cups broth
1 egg yolk
¼ cup heavy cream
¼ cup dill, finely chopped
Pressed lemon juice (optional)

Place the meat in a pot. Measure and pour in enough water to cover the meat. Add the salt and bring to a boil. Skim well, and add the peppercorns, vegetables, and the dill. Simmer over low heat until the meat feels tender, about 1 to 1½ hours.

To make the sauce, melt the butter in a pot. Stir in

needed. Skim off the fat, then slice the roll and serve with the sauce.

Apple-Sweet Shoulder of Lamb

Yield: 4 servings

1 4- to 5-pound lamb shoulder, presliced and tied
Salt
Pepper
1 apple, thinly sliced
⅓ cup tart red jelly
1 tablespoon lemon juice
⅓ cup seedless raisins soaked in 2 tablespoons water
¼ cup onion, finely chopped

Place the lamb in a roasting pan. Sprinkle generously with salt and pepper. Cook in a preheated 325°F oven for 1½ hours. Press rows of apple slices between the meat slices.

In a small saucepan, bring the remaining ingredients to a boil; brush over the lamb. Return the lamb to the oven for 30 minutes, or until a meat thermometer registers 160°F for medium or 170°F for well-done, brushing occasionally with sauce. Remove the strings, free the lamb slices from the bone, and serve with the remaining sauce.

Baked Glazed Ham

Yield: 4 to 6 servings

1 2- to 3-pound canned ham
2 tablespoons honey
Grated rind of 1 orange
1 teaspoon dry mustard
4 tablespoons brown sugar
½ cup cider or pineapple juice
1 tablespoon butter
1 small can pineapple rings
Dusting of sugar
6 to 8 canned sweet cherries

Scrape the jelly off the ham; reserve. Place the ham in a baking pan. Melt the honey; spread it over the ham. Mix the orange rind, mustard and brown sugar together; sprinkle over the meat. Pour the cider over the ham. Add the jelly from the ham. Bake in a preheated 400°F oven 30 minutes; baste after 15 minutes.

Melt the butter in a frying pan. Sprinkle the pineapple slices with sugar; brown in butter on both sides. Serve around the ham with cherries in the center of each ring.

Use the liquid from the baking pan to make a sauce; add water and a squeeze of lemon if too sweet.

Grilled Ham with Raisin and Cranberry Sauce

Yield: 4 to 5 servings

1½ to 2 pounds 1-inch-thick ham slices
Few cloves
½ cup brown sugar
2 tablespoons cornstarch
1½ cups cranberry juice
½ cup orange juice
½ cup raisins

Score the fat edges of ham at intervals of about 2 inches; insert 2 or 3 cloves in the fat.

Mix the sugar and cornstarch with the cranberry juice; put into the pan. Add the orange juice and raisins; bring to a boil. Stir constantly until the mixture thickens.

Put the ham on a grid over hot coals, away from the hottest part; cook about 15 minutes. Turn; brush liberally with glaze. Cook 10 minutes. Turn; brush the other side. This can be put on a broiler rack in an open pan 3 inches below heat. Allow 10 to 12 minutes on each side; brush with glaze as above. Brush again just before serving; serve any remaining glaze with the ham.

Lamb Stew

Ham Hocks in Sauerkraut

Yield: 4 servings

3 large ham hocks
2 cups sauerkraut
1 large onion, sliced into thin rings
1 tablespoon granulated sugar
¼ teaspoon black pepper

Cover the ham with water. Simmer 1 hour; drain.

Add the sauerkraut, onion, sugar, and pepper; place on the stove again and simmer 1½ to 2 hours, until the meat falls off the bone.

Spicy Ham Loaf

Yield: 6 servings

3 cups ground cooked ham
½ cup fine bread crumbs
¼ cup onion, finely chopped
2 tablespoons green pepper, finely chopped
½ teaspoon dry mustard
⅛ teaspoon allspice
⅛ teaspoon ground cloves
2 eggs, slightly beaten
½ cup milk

Combine the ham, bread crumbs, onion, green pepper, mustard, allspice and cloves. Add the eggs and milk and mix until combined. Pack the mixture into a 1-quart loaf pan. Bake in a 350°F oven for 45 minutes. Unmold and serve hot.

Southampton Ham

Yield: 20 to 24 servings

1 10- to 12-pound Smithfield or Virginia country ham
6 to 7 cups cold water (5½ cups cold water plus 1½ cups dry sherry optional)

Soak the ham overnight or for about 8 hours in water to cover. Rinse the ham under running water and scrub off its pepper coating with a stiff brush. Place it in a roaster and add the water or water and sherry. Place a tightly fitting lid on the roaster, making sure that any vents are shut. Put the ham in a 500°F oven and cook 15 to 20 minutes. Turn off the oven and leave the oven door shut; for the entire cooking time of the ham, the oven door must remain closed at all times to retain the heat necessary to cook the ham.

Let the ham sit in the oven for 3 hours, then turn heat back on to 500°F. Cook the ham 20 to 25 minutes, turn the heat off again and allow the ham to sit in the oven undisturbed for another 3 hours or overnight.

To make this a simple, one-day affair, soak the ham in the morning. Around 6:00 p.m. begin the first phase of cooking; at about 9:30, turn the heat back on to complete the cooking. Turn off the oven and leave the ham undisturbed in the oven until the next morning. At this time, the rind and excess fat can be cut away and the ham glazed, if desired. Be sure to slice it wafer-thin.

Note: You should not attempt to use this cooking method with a ham larger than 12 pounds.

Ham with Sweet Potatoes

Yield: 5 to 6 servings

1½ pounds ham, sliced
3 cups raw sweet potatoes, sliced
2 tablespoons sugar
1 cup hot water
1 tablespoon drippings or other fat

Cut the ham into pieces for serving. Brown the meat lightly on both sides and arrange the pieces to cover the bottom of a baking dish.

Spread the sliced sweet potatoes over the meat; sprinkle with sugar. Add the hot water to the drippings in the frying pan and pour over the sweet potatoes and meat.

Cover the dish and bake at 325°F until the meat and sweet potatoes are tender, basting the sweet potatoes occasionally with the gravy. Toward the end of the cooking time, remove the lid and let the top brown well.

Pork with Cider

Yield: 4 servings

1½ pounds lean boneless pork, cut into 1-inch cubes
⅓ cup flour
⅓ cup vegetable oil
1½ cups apple cider or apple juice
2 carrots, sliced
1 small onion, sliced
½ teaspoon rosemary
1 bay leaf
1 teaspoon salt
½ teaspoon pepper

Thoroughly dredge the pork with flour. Heat the oil in a large frying pan. Carefully add the pork; cook until browned on all sides. Remove the pork and drain on paper towels. Place in a casserole.

Drain the oil for the pan. Pour in the cider; heat and stir to remove browned pieces from the pan. Add the carrots, onion, rosemary, bay leaf, salt, pepper, and hot cider to the casserole; cover. Bake in a 325°F oven 2 hours, until the meat is tender. Remove the bay leaf.

Pork or Veal with Artichoke Hearts

Yield: 4 servings

4 artichokes
4 boneless loin of pork steaks or 4 veal chops
2 teaspoons salt
Black pepper
2 tablespoons margarine
4 slices cheese
¾ cup chili sauce
1 to 2 tablespoons grated horseradish

Twist off the stalks of the artichokes and remove the outermost leaves. Place the artichokes in lightly salted, boiling water. Cover and boil for 30 to 45 minutes. They are ready when the leaves come off easily. Remove the leaves from the artichokes. Place them in a pot with the cover on so that they keep warm. Save the artichoke hearts.

Brown the meat on both sides in margarine. Add salt and pepper. Sauté until the meat is cooked all the way through. Place an artichoke heart on each slice of meat. Cover with a slice of cheese. Place a lid over the frying pan. Allow the cheese to melt.

To make the sauce, mix the chili sauce with the grated horseradish. Place the meat on plates, putting the artichoke leaves decoratively around each slice. Dip the leaves in the sauce.

Pork Loin with Cabbage in Beer Sauce

Yield: 6 servings

1 head cabbage
8 cloves garlic
10 tablespoons butter
2½ pounds pork loin
¼ teaspoon black pepper
½ to 1 teaspoon salt
¾ cup dark beer
¾ cup beef broth
½ teaspoon caraway seeds

Rinse the cabbage. Cut away the larger membranes and shred the leaves. Quickly place the cabbage in boiling water, let the water come to a boil again, remove the cabbage right away, and dip it into cold water so that the cabbage remains an attractive green. Drain. Parboil the garlic cloves separately but in the same way.

Trim the pork and place in a deep frying pan. Sprinkle it with pepper and brown all around in some of the butter. Cover and cook until it registers 170°F on a meat thermometer. Sprinkle with salt. Remove meat from pan.

Pour beer and broth into the frying pan. Add the cabbage, peeled garlic cloves, and caraway seeds. Bring to a boil and season to taste.

Pork or Veal with Artichoke Hearts

Remove the pan from the heat, push the cabbage over to one side, and add the rest of the butter by dabbing it into the sauce so that the mixture becomes slightly thickened. Cut up the meat and place it on top of the cabbage. Serve with potatoes.

Ham Potato Cakes

Yield: 4 to 6 servings

1 cup mashed potatoes
1 cup cooked ham, finely ground
1 egg, slightly beaten
¼ cup onion, minced or grated
¼ teaspoon dry mustard
¼ teaspoon lemon pepper
Flour for batter
Fat for frying

Mix the potatoes, ham, egg, onion, and seasonings together. Form into flat cakes about 3 inches in diameter. Dip each cake lightly in flour, coating both sides. Set aside.

Melt the fat in a medium-sized skillet. Lightly brown each cake on both sides. Drain on paper towels; put on a warming plate in the oven until all are cooked and ready to serve.

Pork, Apples, and Sauerkraut

Yield: 4 servings

4 pork chops, ½-inch thick
2 tablespoons butter
1 teaspoon salt
⅛ teaspoon pepper
1 tablespoon prepared mustard
1 tablespoon horseradish
1 1-pound, 13-ounce can sauerkraut, drained
2 medium-sized apples, chopped
½ cup onion, chopped
1 teaspoon caraway seeds

Brown the pork chops in the butter; pour off the excess fat. Season the chops with salt and pepper.

Combine the mustard and horseradish and spread over the chops. Combine the sauerkraut, apples, onion, and caraway seeds and place in a 2-quart baking dish. Arrange the chops over the top of the sauerkraut and apple mixture; cover tightly and bake in a preheated 350°F oven 30 minutes. Uncover and bake 30 minutes longer.

Barbecued Pork Tenderloin

Yield: 8 servings

2 whole pork tenderloins
2 tablespoons butter or margarine
½ cup flour
¼ cup vinegar
½ teaspoon salt
½ teaspoon dry mustard
2 teaspoons celery seed
1½ teaspoons chili sauce
½ cup catsup
2 tablespoons sugar
2 tablespoons paprika
Pepper

Cut each tenderloin lengthwise and crosswise. This will make 8 pieces. Melt the butter in a skillet. Coat the meat with flour and brown in the hot butter. Combine the remaining ingredients and pour over the meat. Cover and simmer over very low heat about 2 hours.

Baked Stuffed Pork Chops

Yield: 4 servings

¼ cup butter or margarine
½ cup onion, finely chopped
2 tablespoons celery, finely chopped
½ cup water, stock, or canned broth
3½ cups croutons
4 pork chops, 1½ inches thick, cut with pockets
Salt
Pepper

Melt the butter in a medium-sized saucepan over low heat. Add the onions and celery. Cook, stirring frequently, until tender. Add the water; bring to a boil. Remove the pan from the heat. Add the croutons all at one time, tossing lightly until evenly moistened.

If necessary, extend the pocket in each pork chop to the bone. Fill with the crouton mixture. Fasten the edges with wooden toothpicks. Place the stuffed chops, flat side down, in a shallow baking pan. Do not crowd. Sprinkle with salt and pepper. Cover pan tightly with foil.

Bake in 350°F oven about 55 minutes. Uncover and bake about 30 minutes longer, or until the chops are browned and tender.

Smoked Pork Loin with Rice

Yield: 4 servings

1 cup long-grain rice
1 teaspoon salt
2 cups meat stock (from cubes)
1 can sweet corn
About 1½ pounds smoked pork loin, cut in 6 to 8 slices
1 can whole, peeled tomatoes
1½ teaspoons sage or basil
½ teaspoon lemon pepper
½ teaspoon garlic salt (optional)

Place rice, salt, and stock in a wide, shallow pan and bring to a boil. Simmer slowly, covered, for about 15 minutes. Drain the sweet corn and mix with the rice. Place the pork slices in a ring on top of the rice. Finally, place the tomatoes, with some of the liquid, in the center.

Mix the sage, lemon pepper, and garlic salt and sprinkle the mixture over all the ingredients in the pan. Cover and simmer slowly for 5 to 8 minutes more. Serve immediately.

Spareribs and Sauerkraut

Yield: 4 servings

2 pounds spareribs
1 teaspoon salt
4 cups sauerkraut

Have the spareribs divided into serving pieces. Wipe them with a cold, damp cloth; sprinkle with salt. Put the ribs in a kettle; cover with cold water. Bring to a boil; cover. Reduce heat and simmer 30 minutes.

Add the sauerkraut. Bring to a boil, then reduce the heat and simmer, uncovered, 30 minutes. Serve hot.

Pork Loin with Cabbage in Beer Sauce

Breaded Pork Scallops

Yield: 4 servings

1½ pounds boneless loin of pork, trimmed of almost all fat
Salt to taste, if desired
Freshly ground pepper to taste
1 egg
3 tablespoons water
½ cup plus 1 tablespoon corn, peanut, or vegetable oil
⅓ cup flour
1 cup fine fresh bread crumbs
3 tablespoons butter (optional)
Lemon wedges for garnish

Cut the meat or have it cut crosswise into 12 slices of equal thickness. Pound each lightly with a flat mallet. Arrange on a flat surface and sprinkle with salt and pepper on both sides.

In a dish, combine the egg, water, 1 tablespoon of oil, salt, and pepper. Beat well to blend. Put the flour in a second dish and the bread crumbs in a third. Dip the pork slices in flour to coat thoroughly, shaking off excess. Then dip each slice in the egg mixture and then in crumbs to coat well. Pat to help the crumbs adhere.

Heat about ¼ cup of oil in a large, heavy skillet and add a few breaded slices to fill the skillet without crowding. Cook about 5 minutes on one side until golden brown. Turn and cook about 5 minutes or slightly longer on the other side. Transfer to a warm platter. Continue adding oil and pork until all are cooked.

Heat the butter until lightly browned and pour over the meat. Serve with lemon wedges.

Grilled Marinated Spareribs

Yield: 4 servings

2½ pounds spareribs, preferably thinly cut so that it takes less time to grill them

marinade
1 14-ounce can crushed pineapple
1 tablespoon vinegar
1 tablespoon soy sauce
2 tablespoons oil
1 teaspoon salt
1 teaspoon ginger
Juice from 1 orange or ⅓ cup orange juice

Mix all the marinade ingredients together. Place the ribs in a thick plastic bag. Pour in the marinade; tie a knot. Place the bag in the refrigerator for at least 3 hours, preferably overnight.

Place the ribs on the grill. Grill about 20 minutes for thinly sliced ribs, 40 minutes otherwise. Turn occasionally. Make sure the ribs are not too near the coals, as they easily can burn without being thoroughly cooked inside. Baste with the marinade.

Boil the rest of the marinade and serve as a sauce. Serve the ribs with baked potatoes and corn-on-the-cob.

Garlic-Spiced Pork Loin with Green Pepper Sauce

Yield: 6 servings

2½ pounds fresh pork tenderloins
6 cloves garlic, sliced lengthwise
3 tablespoons butter
½ teaspoon coarsely ground black pepper
¾ teaspoon salt
1 package frozen puff pastry
1 egg

mushroom filling
¼ pound smoked ham
5 to 6 shallots
1 pound fresh mushrooms
1 tablespoon butter
¾ teaspoon salt
⅛ teaspoon coarsely ground black pepper

green pepper sauce
4 shallots, chopped
1 teaspoon dried green peppercorns, crushed
⅓ cup red wine vinegar
1 cup beef broth
⅔ cup heavy cream
1 tablespoon flour
2 tablespoons soy sauce
Salt
1 teaspoon whole green peppercorns
Butter

Trim the meat well, make tiny holes in it with a sharp knife, and stick garlic cloves into the holes. Sauté the pork in butter until golden brown on all sides. Season with salt and pepper. Do not overdo the cooking—the fillets should just be done, which takes about 7 to 8 minutes. Allow to cool.

Finely chop the ham, shallots, and mushrooms for the filling. The mushrooms may be chopped in a food processor if they are done quickly and in several batches. Melt butter in a wide frying pan and add the chopped ingredients. Let them "perspire" and then become dry. Salt and pepper and let cool.

Allow the puff pastry patties to thaw, and place 4 patties next to each other sideways. Dampen the "seams," allowing the patties to overlap each other. Roll the patties out into one large dough, which is big enough to cover both the meat and the filling.

Spread the filling over the dough. Place the meat fillets one on top of the other in the center of the filling. Spoon the filling up onto the fillets and onto their sides.

Wrap up the dough, pinching the seams together well. Trim off extra pastry. Decorate the "package" with stripes or squares or with a flower and leaves made with the remaining puff pastry. Everything up to this point may be prepared in advance; keep refrigerated.

Preheat the oven to 400°F. Brush the dough with a beaten egg and bake in the middle of the oven for 20 to 30 minutes.

Make the Green Pepper Sauce. Place the shallots in a pot together with the green peppercorns and vinegar. Simmer until the vinegar has almost totally evaporated. Then add the broth and bring to a boil.

Strain off the shallots and beat in the cream, flour, and soy sauce. Simmer, stirring constantly, for a few minutes. Season with salt and finally mix in a teaspoon whole green peppercorns and a dab of butter. Serve the sauce piping hot.

Garlic-Spiced Pork Loin with Green Pepper Sauce

Texas Pork Chops

Yield: 2 servings

1 can condensed chili beef soup
1 cup cooked rice
2 tablespoons green pepper, finely chopped
2 tablespoons ripe olives, sliced
4 pork chops, ¾-inch thick
1 1-pound can tomatoes
1 medium-sized onion, sliced
1 medium-sized clove garlic, minced

Combine ¼ cup of soup, rice, green pepper, and olives. Trim excess fat from the chops, Slit each chop from the outer edge toward the bone, making a pocket; stuff with the rice mixture and fasten with toothpicks.

In a skillet, brown the chops; pour off the fat. Add the remaining ingredients. Cover and cook over low heat 1¼ hours. Stir now and then to break up the tomatoes. Uncover and cook to desired consistency.

Pork Chops and Sweet Potatoes

Yield: 4 servings

4 center-cut pork chops
Salt and pepper to taste
¼ cup flour
2 tablespoons butter
½ cup currant jelly
½ cup orange juice
1 tablespoon lemon juice
1 teaspoon dry mustard
1 teaspoon paprika
½ teaspoon ground ginger
3-4 medium-sized sweet potatoes, boiled, sliced

Season the chops with salt and pepper; coat with flour. Brown on both sides.

Melt the butter in a small saucepan. Add the remaining ingredients, except the sweet potatoes, stirring constantly, to make a sauce.

Arrange the sweet potatoes and pork chops in an ovenproof dish. Pour ¾ of the sauce over the potatoes and chops; keep the remainder for basting while baking. Bake, uncovered, at 350°F for 45 minutes.

Gorgonzola Pork Loin

Yield: 4 servings

1 onion plus butter
1 tablespoon flour
1 can broth
⅓ cup heavy cream or crème fraîche
Tarragon
Dark French mustard

Gorgonzola Pork Loin

Salt
Black pepper
Gorgonzola cheese, according to own taste
3 green peppers, preferably 2 different shades
1½ pounds pork loin, finely trimmed
Butter
A few drops of sherry, port, brandy, or other kind of dessert wine
¼ cup chopped walnuts

Chop the onion and sauté it in butter in a small pot. Skip the flour if crème fraîche is to be used. Otherwise, sprinkle the flour into the pot. Alternate beating in the cream or crème fraîche with ⅓ cup broth, and let the mixture simmer until it has a pleasant sauce consistency. Season with tarragon, mustard, salt, and a little black pepper. Finally, add a large dab of Gorgonzola cheese. Let it melt while stirring constantly. Season to taste. Let the sauce stand and thicken on the side of the stove.

Slice the peppers and simmer them in the rest of the canned broth until they are almost soft. Then let the liquid simmer down to half the original amount.

Grease an ovenproof dish. Pour in the simmered-down broth, mixed with a little dessert wine. Place the pork, which has been cut into several pieces, on a bed of the soft peppers. Season the meat lightly and dab on a little butter. Place high up in a hot oven or under the broiler 2 to 3 minutes. Lower the rack and open the oven door a little so that the temperature quickly sinks to 350°F. Total time in the oven: about 8 minutes for pink meat, otherwise longer. Cut the meat up into thinner slices and place it back on the peppers.

Keep the sauce ready and warm. Right before serving, add the nuts and swirl the thick sauce over the pork slices. The dish can be garnished with watercress if desired.

Japanese-Style Pork Loin

Yield: 4 servings

About 1 pound thick pork loin

marinade
⅓ cup oil
2 tablespoons not-too-salty soy sauce
2 onions, minced
¼ teaspoon black pepper
1 clove garlic, crushed
1 tablespoon vinegar
5 coriander seeds, crushed

Trim and cut the loin into thick (½-inch) slices. Mix the marinade ingredients together. Place the pork in a greased pan and cover with the marinade. Let stand in a cool place for about 24 hours.

Preheat oven to 400°F. Place the plate with the meat and the marinade in the oven for about 20 minutes if pink and juicy meat is desired, somewhat longer if the meat is to be well done. Baste several times with the marinade while baking. Serve immediately with rice mixed with sliced mushrooms or raisins.

Pork Roast with Cranberry Stuffing

Yield: 6 servings

1 6- to 7-pound pork loin roast
Salt and pepper
Poultry seasoning
1 cup boiling beef broth
½ cup butter
1 8-ounce package herb-seasoned bread stuffing
1 cup cranberries, knife-chopped
1 small red apple, unpeeled, cored and diced
¼ cup celery, finely chopped
¼ cup parsley, minced
1 large egg

Have the butcher saw off the backbone (chine) of the roast. Place the meat, rib ends up, on a cutting board. Holding the meaty side of the roast with one hand, and starting 1 inch from one end of roast and ending 1 inch from the other end, cut a slit between the meat and rib bones almost to the bottom of the roast. With your fingers, pull the meaty part slightly away from the ribs to form a pocket. Sprinkle the inside of the pocket and outside of the roast with salt, pepper, and poultry seasoning.

Pour boiling broth into a large skillet or medium saucepan, off the heat. Add butter; over very low heat stir until melted. Remove from the heat. Add the bread stuffing, cranberries, apple, celery, and parsley; mix well.

Beat the egg until thick and pale-colored; mix with the stuffing. Spoon the stuffing into the pocket in the roast; put any leftover stuffing into a small baking dish. Roast the pork on a rack in a shallow roasting pan in a 350°F oven 35 minutes per pound. About half an hour before the roast is ready, put the baking dish of extra stuffing in the oven to heat.

After the roast has been removed to a hot serving platter, pour off the fat in the roasting pan. Spoon some drippings over the top of the stuffing in the roast and some over the small baking dish of extra stuffing.

Japanese-Style Pork Loin

Pork Pie

Yield: 6 servings

1 medium-sized head of cauliflower
1 tablespoon oil
2 small onions, peeled and very finely chopped
1 clove garlic, crushed
3½ cups canned tomatoes
Pinch thyme
Salt and pepper
¼ teaspoon paprika
3 tablespoons flour
3 cups cooked pork, diced
Pastry for a 9-inch, 1-crust pie

Cook the cauliflower until just tender in boiling, salted water. Drain and divide into small flowerets.

Heat the oil in a skillet; add the onion and garlic and sauté for a few minutes. Add the tomatoes, thyme, salt, pepper and paprika. Simmer for 10 minutes, then press through a sieve. Blend the flour with a little cold water; add it to the sauce and stir until boiling.

Put the pork and cauliflower into a deep dish (about 2 quarts) and pour the sauce over them. Cover with the pastry and bake for about 25 minutes in a preheated 450°F oven or until the crust is well browned.

Pork Stroganoff

Yield: 4 servings

1½ pounds shoulder of pork
4 onions
Butter or margarine for frying
Salt
Pepper
1⅔ cups strong beef broth
2 tablespoons tomato paste
1½ cups crème fraîche or sour cream
1 to 2 teaspoons soy sauce

Cut the meat into strips. Peel and slice the onions. Brown the meat in the butter in a stew pot. Add salt and pepper. Add the onions so that they also become brown.

Decrease the heat and gradually add the beef broth. Add the tomato paste. Simmer the meat and the onions in the gravy for about 25 minutes, or until the meat is tender and thoroughly cooked. Cover the pot when simmering the meat.

Remove the pot from the heat and stir in the crème fraîche. Bring to a boil and add the soy sauce. This dish should have a rich and rather strong taste. Serve with rice.

Muckalica

Yield: 4 servings

1¾ pounds boneless loin of pork
2 tablespoons butter or margarine
2 green peppers, seeded and cubed
2 onions, chopped
4 tomatoes, chopped
4 pepperoni (fresh), cubed
2 teaspoons soy sauce
1¼ teaspoons salt
½ teaspoon black pepper
¾ cup sour cream
1 onion, chopped

Trim the meat by cutting away any extra pieces of fat, then cut the meat into strips. Brown it well in the butter. Mix the green peppers, onions, tomatoes, and pepperoni with the meat, decrease the heat, and add the soy sauce, salt, and pepper. Cover and simmer for about half an hour. If the stew begins to look dry, add ¼ cup water.

Serve with sour cream, chopped raw onion, and boiled rice.

Smoked Pork Loin

Barbecued Pork Ribs

Yield: 6 servings

1½ cups catsup
1½ cups water
¾ cup chili sauce
½ cup vinegar
6 tablespoons Worcestershire sauce
6 tablespoons light brown sugar, firmly packed
3 tablespoons fresh lemon juice
1 tablespoon paprika
3¼ teaspoons salt
1 clove garlic, crushed
¼ teaspoon hot-pepper sauce
5 pounds pork back ribs
½ teaspoon pepper
Thin slices of onion and lemon (optional)

Combine the catsup, water, chili sauce, vinegar, Worcestershire sauce, brown sugar, lemon juice, paprika, 2¼ teaspoons of salt, garlic, and hot-pepper sauce in a large saucepan. Heat to boiling; reduce heat. Simmer 30 to 45 minutes, until the sauce is good basting consistency.

Cut the meat into 3 to 4 rib portions. Sprinkle with 1 teaspoon of salt and pepper. Put it on a rack in a shallow baking pan. Bake at 450°F 30 minutes. Remove the meat from the rack; drain off excess fat.

Put the ribs in a baking pan, meaty side down; brush with sauce. Reduce the oven temperature to 300°F; bake 30 minutes. Turn the ribs meaty side up; brush with sauce. Top each rib with an onion slice. Bake about 1 hour, brushing frequently with some remaining sauce, until the ribs are tender and nicely browned. Add lemon slices to the ribs during the last half hour of baking. Serve the remaining sauce on the side.

Roast Pork with Oranges

Yield: 6 servings

4 pounds pork loin roast
1 teaspoon sage
Salt and pepper
1 cup water
Juice of 1 orange
½ cup sherry
1 tablespoon red currant jelly
Grated rind of 1 orange
3-6 oranges, peeled and sectioned

Rub the pork with sage, salt, and pepper. Put it on a rack in a shallow roasting pan. Add the water. Roast at 325°F 2 hours or until a thermometer registers 170°F.

About 45 minutes before the meat is done, pour off the fat; leave the pan juices. Pour orange juice and sherry over the meat. Spread jelly over the

Grilled Marinated Spareribs

meat; sprinkle with orange rind. Baste a few times. When done, put the meat on a platter; surround it with oranges.

Savory Pork in Sweet Potato Nests

Yield: 4 servings

2 cups sweet potatoes, mashed
Milk
1 tablespoon butter or margarine, melted
1½ cups cooked pork, finely chopped
1 cup peas
½ cup pork gravy
½ teaspoon salt
⅛ teaspoon thyme

To the mashed sweet potatoes, add enough milk to make the mixture smooth and easy to shape. Divide in mounds on a baking sheet. Make a well in the center of each mound with the back of a spoon. Brush with melted butter.

Combine the remaining ingredients in a baking dish. Place the pork mixture and sweet potato mounds in a 350°F oven for 15 to 20 minutes. Spoon the pork into the sweet potato nests and serve at once.

Rolled Shoulder with Ham and Cheese

Yield: 4 servings

½ tablespoon butter
8 thin slices of lean pork shoulder, about 1 pound
¼ pound smoked ham, in thin slices
5 to 6 slices cheese
¾ teaspoon salt
¼ teaspoon black pepper
½ to ¾ teaspoon crushed sage (optional)
Tomato halves (optional)

Grease a roasting pan, placing a wide strip of butter along the middle of the pan. Place the shoulder slices in the middle of the roasting pan. The slices should be placed in a row, slightly overlapping. Sprinkle with most of the salt, pepper, and sage, if desired. Place the ham and cheese on top.

Roll up the meat, first from one side and then from the other, so that it becomes a long roll. Fasten with toothpicks. Salt.

Bake in the middle of a preheated 350°F oven until a toothpick goes easily through the meat, about 45 minutes. Toward the end of the baking time, brush the roll with a small amount of the gravy and fat which has collected in the bottom of the pan. If you wish, place tomato halves around the meat when 15 minutes of the baking time remains.

Cut the roll up into slices and serve with boiled potatoes. Lightly salt and pepper the tomatoes.

Swedish-Style Pork

Yield: 4 servings

1¼ pounds lean, boned pork shoulder
1 tablespoon soy sauce
1 tablespoon oil
Black pepper
1½ pounds frozen potatoes, diced
3 tablespoons butter
1 onion, finely chopped
1½ teaspoons salt
4 raw egg yolks (optional)

Cut the meat into small cubes and mix with soy sauce, oil, and black pepper. Sauté the potatoes in 2 tablespoons of the butter in a large frying pan until soft and browned, about 10 minutes. Cook the onion with the potatoes for the last 3 to 4 minutes. Season with about 1 teaspoon salt.

Finally, sauté the meat quickly in butter in a large, very hot pan—cook about 3 to 4 minutes. Season the meat with ½ teaspoon salt.

Serve the meat and potatoes with a raw egg yolk, if desired.

Sausage and Apple Casserole

Yield: 4 to 6 servings

8 cups white bread (about 15 slices), cubed
1 pound country sausage
1 large onion, diced
1 green pepper, diced
½ cup water
2 large apples, pared, cored, and chopped
1 teaspoon salt

Use stale white bread for the cubes, or stale them by putting the bread in a 250°F oven for 10 minutes. Brown the country sausage in a large skillet. Cook until there is no trace of pink in the meat. Add the onion and green pepper; cook for 2 minutes more. Stir in the bread cubes, water, apples, and salt. Mix together until evenly moist.

Turn out the cooked mixture into a well-greased casserole. Cook in a 350°F oven 30 minutes or until the top crusts.

Boston Baked Sausage and Rice

Yield: 6 servings

1 pound smoked country-style link sausage
¾ cup onion, chopped
½ cup catsup
2 tablespoons brown sugar, firmly packed
1 teaspoon prepared mustard
1 teaspoon liquid smoke
½ teaspoon salt
¼ teaspoon ground black pepper
3 cups cooked rice

Simmer the sausage in water to cover for 10 minutes. Remove the sausage and cut it in 1½-inch pieces. Combine with the remaining ingredients. Turn into a greased, shallow, 2-quart casserole. Bake, uncovered, at 350°F for 20 to 25 minutes.

Barbecued Hot Dogs

Yield: 4 to 6 servings

¼ cup onion, chopped
2 teaspoons sugar
¾ teaspoon paprika
¼ teaspoon salt
⅛ teaspoon pepper
⅓ cup catsup
⅓ cup water
3 tablespoons vinegar
2 teaspoons Worcestershire sauce
1 pound hot dogs

Combine all the ingredients and pour the sauce over the hot dogs in a baking dish. Bake at 400°F for 30 minutes.

Muckalica

Veal Breast with Herb Stuffing

Yield: 6 servings

herb stuffing
3 strips bacon
1 medium-sized onion
1 4-ounce can mushroom pieces
¼ cup fresh parsley, chopped
1 tablespoon fresh dill, chopped
1 teaspoon dried tarragon leaves
1 teaspoon dried basil leaves
½ pound lean ground beef
½ cup dried bread crumbs
3 eggs, beaten
⅓ cup sour cream
½ teaspoon salt
¼ teaspoon pepper

veal
3-4 pounds boned veal breast or leg
½ teaspoon salt
¼ teaspoon pepper
1 tablespoon vegetable oil
2 cups hot beef broth
2 tablespoons cornstarch
½ cup sour cream

Prepare the stuffing: Dice the bacon and onion. Cook the bacon in a skillet until partially cooked. Add the onion; cook 5 minutes.

Drain and chop the mushrooms; add to the skillet. Cook 5 minutes; remove from the heat. Let cool; transfer to a mixing bowl. Add the herbs, beef, crumbs, eggs, and sour cream; mix thoroughly. Season with salt and pepper.

With a sharp knife, cut a pocket in the veal; fill it with the stuffing. Close the opening with toothpicks. (Tie with string if necessary.) Rub the outside with salt and pepper.

Heat the oil in a Dutch oven or heavy saucepan; place the meat in the pan. Bake in a preheated 350°F oven about 1½ hours; baste occasionally with beef broth. When done, place the meat on a preheated platter.

Pour the rest of the beef broth into the Dutch oven; scrape any brown particles from the bottom. Bring to a simmer. Thoroughly blend the cornstarch with the sour cream; add to the pan drippings, stirring. Cook and stir until thick and bubbly. Slice the veal breast. Serve the sauce separately.

Pork Stroganoff

Batter-Dipped Hot Dogs

Yield: 6 servings

½ cup cornmeal
½ cup flour
1 teaspoon salt
½ teaspoon pepper
½ cup milk
1 egg, beaten
2 tablespoons oil
12 hot dogs
Fat or oil for deep frying

Mix the cornmeal, flour, salt, and pepper in a bowl. Add the milk, egg, and oil. Stir until smooth. Dip the hot dogs into batter; drain over a bowl. Fry in deep fat 2 to 3 minutes, until golden brown, turning once. Remove from the fat; drain.

Frank and Bean Casserole

Yield: 4 to 6 servings

4 cups baked beans
¼ cup catsup
¼ cup molasses
¼ cup onion, minced
1½ teaspoons prepared mustard

¼ teaspoon Worcestershire sauce
1 pound hot dogs

Combine all the ingredients except the hot dogs and place them in a 1½-quart casserole. Slash the top of the hot dogs in 3 or 4 places and arrange them on top of the bean mixture. Bake in a 350°F oven for 25 to 30 minutes.

Sausage and Apple Pie

Yield: 6 to 8 servings

1 pound link sausages
3 apples, peeled, cored, and sliced
2 tablespoons sugar
6 tablespoons butter or margarine
1 cup flour
1 teaspoon salt
1 egg, beaten
Milk

Grease a large pie tin. Place the sausages in a skillet; prick each sausage with a fork. Cover with water; bring to a boil. Simmer 5 minutes; drain off the water. Brown the sausages; place in the pie tin. Spread apple slices over the meat. Sprinkle the apples with sugar.

Mix the butter and flour; add the salt. Stir in the egg and enough milk to make a stiff dough. Spread the dough over the apples, using your fingers. Brush with butter (or some of the egg). Make a hole in the center for the steam to escape. Bake 25 to 30 minutes in a 400°F oven. Serve as is or with tomato sauce.

Veal Chops with Rosemary

Yield: 6 servings

6 veal chops
Granulated flour
1 large clove garlic, minced
2 tablespoons butter
2 tablespoons olive oil
Rosemary to taste
Salt and freshly ground pepper

Dust the veal chops lightly with flour. Set aside on a paper towel. Add the garlic to the melted butter and oil in a sauté pan large enough to hold all the chops without crowding or overlapping. When the oil begins to sizzle, add the chops and sauté quickly on both sides until well browned.

When the chops have browned on first side, sprinkle with rosemary. Season to taste with salt and pepper. Cover the pan and let the chops cook until cooked through. Do not overcook or chops will dry out and toughen. Serve with some of the garlic butter spooned on each chop.

Veal with Onions

Yield: 6 servings

2 onions
2 tablespoons butter
6 carrots, sliced
4 tablespoons butter, additional
2½ pounds veal stew meat
Salt and pepper
½ cup water
1 tablespoon flour (optional)

Peel the onions and slice into rings. Sauté the onion rings in 2 tablespoons of butter until brown. In a large, covered skillet, melt 4 tablespoons of butter until light brown. Add the sautéed onions, carrots, veal, and salt and pepper to taste. Mix well; add ½ cup of water. Mix; cover and simmer over low heat for 30 minutes.

Serve over rice or noodles. If a thicker sauce is desired, mix 1 tablespoon of flour with 3 tablespoons of cold water and add to sauce; mix to thicken.

Braised Liver and Vegetable Rings

Yield: 6 servings

1½ pounds liver
2 tablespoons flour
2½ teaspoons salt
⅛ teaspoon pepper
2 tablespoons cooking fat
4 medium-sized turnips, thinly sliced
4 medium-sized carrots, thinly sliced
1 large onion, sliced
¼ teaspoon marjoram
½ cup water
Paprika

Cut the liver in 6 serving-size pieces. Combine the flour, 1 teaspoon salt, and pepper; dredge the liver slices. Brown the liver in the cooking fat and remove from the pan. Pour off the drippings. Add the turnips, carrots, and onion to the pan and sprinkle with 1½ teaspoons salt and marjoram.

Place the liver on top of the vegetables; add the water, cover tightly, and cook slowly 20 minutes or until done. Place the liver and vegetables on a platter and sprinkle with paprika.

Rolled Shoulder with Ham and Cheese

Piccata with Rice and Saffron Sauce

Veal Stew with Sweet Potatoes

Yield: 6 servings

1 pound veal, thinly cut
2 tablespoons flour
2 tablespoons salad oil
1 clove garlic, minced
1 10-ounce can condensed tomato soup
1 cup beef broth
1 teaspoon salt
1 teaspoon paprika
2 bay leaves
4 tomatoes, peeled and quartered
2 medium-sized onions, sliced
1 12-ounce package frozen mixed vegetables, partly thawed
2 cups sweet potatoes, mashed and seasoned
2 tablespoons butter or margarine, melted
⅓ cup milk
1 seasoned dried mint

Cut the veal in 1-inch strips. Dredge in flour. Brown in hot oil with garlic. Combine with the tomato soup, broth, and seasonings. Turn into a 2½-quart casserole. Add the tomatoes, onions, and mixed vegetables. Bake covered in a 350°F oven for 45 minutes.

Meanwhile, whip the sweet potatoes, butter, milk, and mint until fluffy. When the veal is tender, spoon in mounds over the casserole. Bake uncovered 15 minutes or until the potatoes are heated through.

Piccata with Rice and Saffron Sauce

Yield: 4 servings

1 pound fillet of pork or veal

batter
2 to 3 eggs
⅔ cup grated Parmesan cheese
2½ tablespoons water
½ teaspoon paprika
½ teaspoon salt
⅛ teaspoon white pepper
¼ cup flour
2 to 3 tablespoons butter

saffron sauce
1⅔ cups crème fraîche or sour cream
Pinch saffron, crushed
½ to ¾ teaspoon salt
About 1 tablespoon butter

Trim the fat and membranes from the meat; cut the meat into 8 pieces. Flatten each using a pounder or a small, thick-bottomed pot.

Mix the eggs, cheese, water, and spices into a batter. Pour the flour out on a plate and dredge the slices of meat in the flour In the meantime, heat a large frying pan to medium temperature.

Lightly brown the butter in the pan. Dip the meat slices in the egg batter, turning the slices so that both sides get covered, and place them in the frying pan. Sauté 1 to 2 minutes on each side, making sure that the pan does not get too hot. Cook the slices in several batches if the pan is not large enough.

Make the saffron sauce. Bring the crème fraîche to a boil. Season with the saffron and the salt. Boil the sauce for several minutes and then beat in 1 tablespoon cold butter.

Serve the piccata on warm plates with a pool of saffron sauce and with rice as a side dish. Allow 2 meat slices per person.

Veal Schnitzel with Spinach and Sherry Sauce

Yield: 2 servings

1 10-ounce box frozen spinach
½ pound asparagus tips
½ teaspoon salt
⅛ teaspoon pepper
⅛ teaspoon garlic powder
¼ teaspoon crushed basil
2 veal cutlets
2 teaspoons butter
1½ teaspoons soy sauce
1 teaspoon arrowroot, potato flour, or cornstarch
2 tablespoons sherry

Cook the spinach in its own juice over medium heat. When tender, drain and reserve the liquid. Cook the asparagus tips in ½ cup boiling salted water for 4 to 5 minutes. Drain and combine the liquid with the spinach broth.

Combine the spices; rub half of them into the cutlets and season the spinach with the rest.

Heat a skillet, preferably of the nonstick variety; add the butter and sauté the cutlets, 1 to 2 minutes on each side. Place the cutlets on a heated platter along with the asparagus and the spinach. Cover with foil and keep warm while making the sauce.

Boil the vegetable broth until it measures approximately ⅔ cup. Add the soy sauce. Mix the thickener with the sherry and add it to the broth, stirring constantly. Bring to a boil and season with salt and pepper. Pour the sauce around the meat and serve immediately.

Marinated Liver with Tomato-Crush

Yield: 4 servings

¾ cup red wine
1 teaspoon thyme
4 to 6 slices calf liver
4 tomatoes
1 small onion
1 tablespoon olive oil
2 cups celery, cut in strips
½ teaspoon basil
1½ teaspoons salt
⅓ cup flour
¼ teaspoon black pepper
1 tablespoon butter or margarine

Mix the wine and thyme in a bowl. Place the liver slices in the mixture and marinate for 1 hour in the refrigerator.

Dip the tomatoes in boiling water, then peel. Remove the seeds and cut the tomatoes into large pieces. Peel and mince the onion. Heat the oil in a little pot and lightly sauté the onion. Add the tomato pieces, celery, basil, and ½ teaspoon of the salt. Simmer for a few minutes.

Dry off the liver. Dredge the slices in flour that has been mixed with the remaining salt and pepper. Brown the butter in a frying pan and sauté the liver slices for about 3 minutes on each side.

Divide the tomato mixture over the liver slices and serve immediately.

Autumn Stew with Tongue

Rabbit Stew

Yield: 6 servings

1 4- to 5-pound rabbit or 1 package frozen rabbit, thawed
4 tablespoons bacon fat or butter
3 tablespoons flour
2 cups chicken stock
2 cups dry white wine
1 clove garlic, crushed
2½ tablespoons tomato paste
Salt
Pepper
1 teaspoon tarragon
1 bay leaf, crushed
½ teaspoon thyme
3 tablespoons sour cream

Have the butcher cut the rabbit into serving pieces. Heat the fat; brown the rabbit pieces on all sides. Sprinkle with flour; blend in well. Add the stock, wine, garlic, tomato paste, and seasonings. Simmer, covered, over low heat 1½ hours. Transfer the meat to a warm serving platter.

Reduce the sauce if necessary. Stir in the sour cream; heat, but do not let the sauce boil. Pour the sauce over the rabbit.

Autumn Stew with Tongue

Yield: 4 servings

1½ pounds tongue
Water
1 bay leaf
10 white peppercorns
1 pound potatoes
1 leek
¼ pound celery root (celeriac)
2 carrots
1 teaspoon mustard seeds
⅓ cup snipped green herbs

Place the tongue in a pot, and pour over enough water so that it is just covered. Add the bay leaf and the peppercorns. Cover and simmer over low heat for about 1 hour. Test to see if the tongue is done by pricking it with a toothpick. If the toothpick goes easily through, the meat is done.

Remove the cooked tongue from the pot and skin it while still warm. Place the meat back in the broth.

Peel and prepare the vegetables by cutting them into pieces. Cut the celery root into thinner pieces as it takes longer to cook. Place all the vegetables and spices in a pot and cover with enough broth to cover the vegetables. (Add more broth, if necessary.)

Cut the tongue into strips or cubes. Place them in the pot and cover. Cook the stew for about 15

Marinated Liver with Tomato-Crush

minutes or until the potatoes and vegetables feel soft. Add the mustard seeds and sprinkle with the snipped herbs (parsley, dill, etc.) just before serving.

Venison Loaf

Yield: 8 to 10 servings

2 pounds ground venison
2 pounds bulk pork sausage
2 medium-sized onions, finely chopped
1½ cups cracker crumbs
1 cup evaporated milk
3 eggs, lightly beaten
2 cups barbecue sauce
1 teaspoon salt
½ teaspoon freshly ground pepper

Place the venison, sausage, onions, and crumbs in a large bowl and mix will. Add the milk, eggs, 1 cup of the barbecue sauce, salt, and pepper and blend well. Chill for 15 minutes.

Shape into 2 loaves, then place the loaves in a large, greased baking pan. Bake in a preheated 350°F oven for 30 minutes. Spoon the remaining barbecue sauce over the loaves and bake for 45 minutes longer.

Seafood

Grilled Bluefish Fillets

Yield: 6 servings

2 pounds bluefish fillets
½ cup catsup
¼ cup melted fat or oil
3 tablespoons lemon juice
2 teaspoons liquid smoke
2 tablespoons vinegar
1 teaspoon salt
1 teaspoon Worcestershire sauce
½ teaspoon powdered mustard
½ teaspoon onion, grated
¼ teaspoon paprika
1 clove garlic, finely chopped
3 drops liquid hot pepper sauce

Cut the fillets into serving-size pieces and place in a single layer in a shallow pan. Combine the remaining ingredients. Pour the sauce over the fish and allow it to stand 30 minutes, turning once. Remove the fish; reserve the sauce for basting.

Place the fish in a well-greased, hinged wire grill. Cook about 4 inches from moderately hot coals for 8 minutes. Baste as needed. Turn and cook 7 to 10 minutes longer, or until the fish flakes easily with a fork.

Fried Catfish

Yield: 6 servings

3 pounds catfish fillets
2 eggs
2 tablespoons water
2 cups stone-ground white cornmeal
2 teaspoons salt
Freshly ground pepper
Lard for deep frying

Beat the eggs and water together; then mix the salt, pepper, and cornmeal together. Dip the fillets in the egg mixture, then in the cornmeal to coat.

In a heavy, preferably cast-iron skillet, heat about ½-inch of lard. Fry the fillets until they are a crusty golden brown, turning once. Drain and serve very hot with wedges of lemon, coleslaw, and hush puppies.

Parmesan-Baked Halibut with Zucchini

163

Pike with Tomato and Anchovy

Fillet of Flounder with Clam and Mushroom Sauce

Yield: 4 servings

4 flounder fillets, 6 ounces each
Butter or margarine

clam and mushroom sauce
3 tablespoons butter or margarine
3 tablespoons flour
1½ cups plain yogurt
1 8-ounce can minced clams, undrained
½ cup mushrooms, sautéed in butter
Salt and freshly ground black pepper to taste

Fresh dill leaves for garnish

Sauté the flounder in butter or margarine in a large skillet until the fish can be separated into flakes with a fork.

Prepare the sauce. Melt the butter in a saucepan. Add the flour; stir to form a smooth paste. Add the yogurt; heat and stir over moderate heat just until the mixture comes to a boil and is thickened. Add the clams, mushrooms, and salt and pepper. Reheat briefly.

Place the fish on a warm serving platter. Ladle the sauce over the fish. Serve at once garnished with sprigs of dill leaves.

Baked Bluefish

Yield: 6 servings

2 pounds bluefish fillets
3 tablespoons lemon juice
½ cup milk
Salt and pepper
1 cup dried bread crumbs
¼ pound butter
2 tablespoons lemon juice
Seafood seasoning to taste (about ½ cup)

Place the fillets into a large pot of cold water with about 3 tablespoons of lemon juice. Cover the pot; place in the refrigerator overnight. This draws the oil out of the bluefish. Bluefish tend to taste oily, so it is important to do this before baking.

Dip the fillets in milk; lightly salt and pepper. Dip into the bread crumbs. Place ½ teaspoon of butter on each fillet; sprinkle with lemon juice. Sprinkle with seafood seasoning. Place in a well-buttered pan. Bake uncovered 10 to 12 minutes in a pre-heated 500°F oven, until the fish flakes easily.

Cape Cod Turkey

Yield: 4 to 6 servings

1 pound salt cod
4 large red or yellow onions, finely sliced
⅔ cup white vinegar
⅔ cup water
2½ tablespoons sugar
Salt and pepper to taste
¾ pound lean salt pork, finely diced
4 pounds medium-sized boiling potatoes

Cover the cod with cold water and let it soak overnight. Drain and rinse well.

Combine the onions, vinegar, water, sugar, salt, and pepper in a bowl and let stand for about 2 hours before serving time.

Place the diced pork in an iron skillet and cook slowly over medium-low heat until golden brown.

Peel the potatoes and cut them in half, then place in a 5-quart pan. Place the cod over the potatoes and add enough water to cover. Cover and bring to a boil. Reduce the heat and simmer for about 40 minutes or until the potatoes are tender.

Pour the diced pork and fat into a gravy boat. This is the sauce. Drain the potatoes and cod and arrange on a platter. Spoon the pickled onions over the potatoes and cod.

Lemon Flounder

Yield: 4 to 6 servings

2 large (2-2½ pound) flounder, scaled and cleaned
½ lemon, thinly sliced
¾ tablespoon poultry seasoning
Salt and pepper
2 tablespoons lemon juice
1 tablespoon parsley, chopped
3 spring onions, diced, including greens
¼ pound butter, melted

Score the flounder with a sharp knife. Lay the lemon slices in the slits. Add the remaining ingredients to the melted butter; simmer 3 minutes.

Place the flounder in an ungreased oven dish. Pour the sauce over the fish. Broil the flounder about 20 minutes, or until the fish is flaky to a fork. Baste several times with the sauce while the fish is cooking.

Poached Haddock with Mussels

Yield: 6 servings

2 pounds haddock, cod, or other thick fillets
4 pounds mussels in shells (about 4 dozen)
1 cup dry white wine
1 cup water
1 small onion, sliced
½ teaspoon salt
½ cup whipping cream
¼ cup margarine or butter
Dash white pepper
Dash nutmeg
2 tablespoons parsley, chopped

Cut the fillets into serving-size portions.

Clean the mussels in cold water; scrub the shells with a stiff brush, rinsing thoroughly several times. Combine the wine, water, and onion in a large pan; bring to a simmer. Add the mussels. Cover and steam about 5 minutes or until the shells open. Remove the mussels from the shells; set aside.

Strain the cooking liquid into a large skillet. Add the fillets and salt. Cover; simmer 8 to 10 minutes or until the fish flakes easily. Transfer the fillets to a warm platter; keep warm.

Reduce the cooking liquid to ½ cup. Stir in the whipping cream, ¼ cup of margarine or butter, pepper, and nutmeg; simmer until the sauce thickens slightly. Add the mussels and parsley; heat. Spoon the mixture over the fillets.

Sole Fillets in Orange Sauce

Parmesan-Baked Halibut with Zucchini

Yield: 6 servings

1½ pounds fillets of halibut
2 cups fish broth
1 zucchini

sauce
¾ cup broth from the above
¼ cup dry white wine
⅓ cup heavy cream

garnish
⅓ cup Parmesan cheese, freshly grated
⅓ cup day-old white bread
1 egg yolk plus ⅓ cup heavy cream

Boil the fish broth in a low, wide pan and poach the fish fillets in the broth for 2 to 4 minutes. Then place them on a large, ovenproof plate or on individual serving plates.

Thinly slice the zucchini and prepare the slices by placing them in salted boiling water, letting the water come to a boil again, draining off the water, and finally cooling off the slices in cold water.

Prepare the sauce by mixing the fish broth, wine, and cream in a pan. Bring the sauce to a boil, then let simmer until it has a thick, creamy consistency. Pour the sauce over the fish. Place the zucchini slices on top. Mix the cheese and white bread crumbs together and cover the entire dish with them.

Preheat oven to 450°F. Beat the egg yolk and cream together and sprinkle drops of this mixture over the crumb mixture, using a fork to mix it in. Finally sprinkle a little more Parmesan cheese on top and bake in the oven until the dish has browned.

Pike with Tomato and Anchovy

Yield: 4 servings

About 3 pounds pike fillets
½ teaspoon salt
Freshly ground white pepper
1 cup sieved tomatoes
¼ cup onion, finely chopped
1 2-ounce can anchovy fillets, chopped
1 teaspoon chervil or thyme
¾ cup mild Cheddar cheese, grated
2 tablespoons grated Parmesan
1 cup fish stock
4 tablespoons butter
About ¼ cup parsley, chopped

Grease an ovenproof dish and place the fish on it with the flesh side facing up and the belly parts slightly overlapping. Season well with salt and a few turns of the pepper mill. Combine the tomatoes, onion, anchovies, and thyme or chervil in a bowl. Divide the tomato mixture evenly over the fish. Blend the 2 cheeses and sprinkle over the tomato mixture.

Bring the stock to a boil and pour it carefully around the fish. Place the dish in a preheated 450°F oven for 15 to 20 minutes. Then carefully pour off most of the liquid into a saucepan and beat in 3 to 4 tablespoons butter and the chopped parsley. Heat the sauce and pour around the fish on a serving dish. Serve with freshly boiled potatoes or boiled rice.

Sole Fillets in Orange Sauce

Yield: 4 servings

¼ cup soy sauce
½ teaspoon ground ginger
1 teaspoon salt
Juice of 2 oranges
1 pound sole fillets
1 large onion, chopped
1 tablespoon margarine
4 leaves Chinese cabbage, finely shredded

Cold Sole Plate

¼ cup water
½ tablespoon arrowroot or cornstarch
Pepper

Mix the soy sauce, ginger, salt, and orange juice in a bowl. Cut each plaice fillet into 3 strips lengthwise and place in the mixture.

Fry the onion in the margarine in a wide pan, then add the cabbage. Lift out the fish and arrowroot or flour into the soy sauce mixture and pour this over the fish. Cover and allow to come to a boil while shaking the pan. Season with salt and pepper and serve with boiled rice.

Festive Cold Sole Plate

Yield: 6 servings

4 bay leaves
1 teaspoon whole allspice
2 to 3 pounds sole fillets
½ bottle dry white wine

sauce
1¼ cups whipped cream
1 jar salmon caviar
3 tablespoons chili sauce
Several dashes of Tabasco
About ⅔ cup snipped dill
1 large can clam meats
Shrimp, as much as you want but at least 14 ounces, with the shells still on.
Lemon slices

Place the bay leaves and the allspice in a piece of gauze and tie it together into a little spice bag. Thaw the fish, if frozen, and place it with the wine and the spice bag in a pot. Simmer for 10 minutes.

Remove the spice bag and allow the fish to become cold in the wine. (The fish may be prepared in advance up to this step and then refrigerated overnight.) Pour off the wine and place the fish on a serving plate.

Whip the cream. Mix in all the ingredients except the clams and the shrimp. Pour off the clam juice from the can. Shell the shrimp. Add both clams and shrimp to the mixture, saving a few shrimp with which to garnish the dish.

Pour the sauce over the fish and garnish with the saved shrimp, lemon slices, and sprigs of dill.

Baked Salmon

Yield: 6 servings

1 5-pound salmon (whole or piece), scaled and fins removed
Salt and pepper
Flour
6 tablespoons butter, melted

Sole Pie

1 large onion, minced
1 clove garlic, minced or pressed
1 tablespoon Worcestershire sauce
2 tomatoes, peeled, drained of juice, seeded, and chopped, or 1¼ cups canned tomatoes, drained
¼ cup (approximately) light cream
1 tablespoon butter and 1 tablespoon flour kneaded together, if necessary
Lemon wedges
Parsley

Rub the salmon inside and out with salt and pepper, dredge with flour, and put it into a well-greased narrow baking pan. Bake in a preheated 425°F oven for 15 minutes, then add the butter, onion, garlic, Worcestershire sauce, and tomatoes and reduce heat to 375°F. Bake for 30 minutes longer, basting frequently. A meat thermometer, inserted into the thickest part of the fish, should reach 160°F.

Remove the fish to a hot platter and keep warm. Add a little cream, about ¼ cup, to the sauce in the pan and stir well until smooth. If sauce is too thin, thicken with the butter kneaded with flour. Garnish the fish with lemon wedges and parsley and serve the sauce in a separate dish.

Sole Pie

Yield: 6 servings

pie pastry
1¼ cups flour, preferably a slightly coarser variety
7 tablespoons butter or margarine
⅓ cup cottage cheese

filling
1 pound fillet of sole
3 tablespoons flour
1 teaspoon dried parsley
1 teaspoon tarragon
½ teaspoon salt
½ pound frozen broccoli, thawed and drained

sauce
1 tablespoon flour
¾ cup crushed tomatoes
½ teaspoon French mustard
¼ cup grated mild Cheddar cheese
¼ teaspoon salt
⅛ teaspoon nutmeg

Mix together the pie pastry and refrigerate it for 30 minutes. Roll out the dough and line a pie plate with it. Prick with a fork and bake in a 400°F oven for 7 minutes.

If the fish fillets are large, they should be cut up into smaller pieces. Dredge with the flour, which has been mixed with the spices and salt. Lightly dry the broccoli with a paper towel. Alternate the fish and the broccoli in the baked pie shell. Bake the pie for another 10 minutes.

Mix the flour for the sauce in a little of the crushed tomatoes, to avoid lumping. Add the rest of the ingredients. Divide the sauce evenly over the fish and bake the pie for another 10 minutes, or until the pie has an attractive color. Serve hot or slightly warm.

Note: The pie can also be made from leftover, cooked fish. Bake the pie shell so that it is almost done. Cover the fish with the sauce, right from the beginning. Fish that is already cooked can easily become dry if it stays in the oven too long.

Poached Salmon

Yield: 8 to 10 servings

Water to fill fish poacher halfway
2 cups dry white wine
2 tablespoons peppercorns
1 tablespoon salt
2 onions, sliced
½ cup white wine vinegar
1 cup celery tops
1 5- to 6-pound whole salmon (or one that fits your poacher)
Lemon slices

Place all of the ingredients in the poacher except the salmon and boil for 15 minutes. Strain the mixture (it's now called a court bouillon) and let it cool to room temperature.

Wash the salmon, make sure the scales are removed, and trim off all of the fins. Place the salmon in the poacher to size it. If the fish is a bit too long, trim off a little of the tail. If your fish is much too long, borrow another poacher and cut the fish in half. Rejoin the fish after it is cooked, hiding the seam with a garnish of lemon slices.

Measure depth of the thickest part of the fish with a ruler. After measuring the fish, wrap it in cheese cloth. Put in the poacher and place over high heat. When the court bouillon comes to a boil, begin timing the cooking. The fish should cook for 10 minutes per inch of thickness. A 2-inch-thick fish would cook for 20 minutes, a 2½-inch-thick one for 25 minutes. Figure the time to the tenth of an inch and remove the fish promptly.

Place the fish on a warm platter and remove the skin. Under the skin is a brownish fatty layer that can be lifted off the fish to reveal the coppery flesh beneath.

Salmon Slices in Herb Sauce

Yield: 4 servings

⅛ cup water
⅔ cup dry white wine
4 tablespoons olive oil
2 cloves garlic, chopped
6 to 8 slices fresh salmon (2 pounds)
Salt
Pepper
⅓ cup heavy cream
2 tablespoons parsley, chopped
1 rounded teaspoon of each: oregano, basil, thyme, and tarragon
⅓ cup crème fraîche or sour cream

Simmer the water, wine, oil, and garlic together. Salt and pepper the salmon slices; then place the fish in the pan. Cover and simmer for about 10 minutes. Pick up the fish with a slotted spoon and place it in a deep, warm plate.

Mix the cream with the salmon broth and let it boil vigorously for a few minutes, uncovered, before adding all the herbs. After a few minutes, beat in the crème fraîche and season with salt, pepper, and perhaps a little more of the bouillon cube, crumbled. Serve immediately with boiled rice and a green salad.

Salmon Slices in Herb Sauce

Sole in Vermouth Sauce

Fillets of Pompano with Orange

Yield: 4 servings

4 pompano fillets
Bones from the fish
2 navel oranges
Juice of 1 lemon, strained
3 tablespoons butter
⅓ cup sherry
1 cup heavy cream
Salt and pepper
½ teaspoon paprika
3 egg yolks, well beaten
1 cup white wine
1 shallot, finely chopped

Wash the fillets in cold water and dry on paper towels. Place the fish bones in an enamel pan, cover with 1 cup of cold water, and simmer 15 minutes. Strain and save the fish stock.

Wash the navel oranges and, with a sharp knife or a potato peeler, cut off the orange part only of the rind. Cut it in thin slivers and cover immediately with strained lemon juice. With a sharp knife, cut off the remaining white pith from the oranges, and cut between sections to extract the pulp in neat, crescent-shaped pieces.

Melt 2 tablespoons of butter in the top part of a small double boiler over boiling water. Add the sherry. When hot, stir in the heavy cream. Season to taste with salt and pepper and the paprika. Cook for a minute or two, then pour the hot mixture over the egg yolks, stirring hard. Return to the top of a double boiler and cook, stirring constantly, until the sauce is smooth and thick like custard, about 2-3 minutes. Remove the top pan and set it aside to keep warm.

Put the white wine in a shallow enamel pan, add the shallot, 1 tablespoon of butter, the fish stock, and the prepared orange peel, drained of lemon juice. Season lightly to taste with salt and pepper and lay the 4 fillets on this bed. Poach very gently until opaque, about 10 minutes, turning the fillets over once with a pancake turner when half done. Transfer the fillets gently to a hot platter and keep warm.

Reduce the stock in the fish pan to ⅓ its original quantity by boiling rapidly. Add this gradually to the egg sauce, place over hot water, and stir constantly until warm, not hot. Pour the sauce over the fish, garnish with the orange sections, and serve at once, accompanied by tiny boiled potatoes.

Crab-Stuffed Red Snapper

Yield: 4 servings

⅓ cup onion, minced
3 tablespoons butter
1 cup crabmeat, picked over
½ cup fresh bread crumbs
¼ cup fresh parsley, chopped
¼ cup heavy cream
¼ teaspoon thyme
1 4-pound red snapper, dressed for stuffing
Salt and pepper
⅓ cup dry white wine mixed with ⅓ cup melted
  butter

Sauté the onion in butter until golden. Remove from the heat and mix in the crabmeat, bread crumbs, parsley, heavy cream, and thyme. Sprinkle the cavity of the fish lightly with salt and pepper. Stuff the fish and skewer edges securely.

Place the fish in a greased baking pan; pour the wine-butter mixture over the fish. Bake in a 400°F oven, uncovered, for 30 minutes, or just until the flesh is opaque. Baste frequently with the wine sauce.

Baked Shad

Yield: 6 to 8 servings

1 (3- to 3½-pound) shad
Salt
Ice-cold water
Good cooking oil

stuffing
Shad roe
1 tablespoon onion, grated
1 tablespoon parsley, chopped
⅔ cup soft bread crumbs
2 tablespoons soft butter
½ teaspoon salt
⅛ teaspoon white pepper

Split the fish down its back; remove the backbone, viscera, and roe (reserve the roe). Pull out the rib bones with pliers. Wash; cover with a salt solution made in the proportion of 1 tablespoon salt to 1 cup ice-cold water. Let stand ½ hour or more. Drain; dry.

Scald the roe in boiling water for 2 minutes; drain. Scrape the eggs into a bowl. Add the onion, parsley, bread crumbs, butter, salt, and pepper; mix until well blended.

Stuff fish. Wrap with string to keep the stuffing in. Place on a greased baking pan; sprinkle the top of the fish with oil. Bake in a preheated 500°F oven 10 minutes. Lower the heat to 400°F; cook 15 to 20 minutes. Serve with a sauceboat of melted butter; garnish with lemon wedges.

Deep-Fried, Batter-Coated Sole

Yield: 4 servings

1 egg
1 cup flour
Salt to taste, if desired
1 cup beer at room temperature
1 egg white
1½ pounds small fillets of sole
Corn, peanut, or vegetable oil for deep-frying

Put the egg in a mixing bowl and beat it briskly until foamy. Add the flour and salt and stir to blend. Beat in the beer. Beat the egg white and fold it in. Let stand until ready to use.

Meanwhile, split the fillets lengthwise in half. There may be a small bone line running down the center of each fillet. If so, trim it away and discard it. Cut the sole pieces crosswise in half. Add the fish to the batter and stir to coat.

Heat the oil in a kettle, wok, or deep-fryer. Add the fish pieces. When brown on one side, turn with a slotted spoon and continue cooking until crisp and brown all over. Cooking time is about 2 or 3 minutes. Drain on absorbent paper towels. Serve with tomato or tartar sauce.

Fillet of Turbot with Wine-Onion and Tomato-Butter

Salmon Cakes

Yield: 4 servings

1 pound can of salmon
½ cup onion, chopped
¼ cup oil
⅓ cup salmon liquid
2 eggs, beaten
½ teaspoon pepper
⅓ cup dry bread crumbs
1 teaspoon parsley, chopped
½ teaspoon mustard
½ teaspoon seafood seasoning (optional)

Drain and flake the salmon; save the liquid. Cook the onion in oil until soft. To the salmon, add the eggs, pepper, bread crumbs, parsley, mustard, seafood seasoning, and onion. Use enough liquid to keep the mixture together. Form into 4 or 8 cakes. Fry or broil.

Broiled Shad

Yield: 6 servings

3-4 pound whole boned shad
Watercress
Lemon slices

Place the shad, skin side down, on greased broiler. Spread it with melted butter; sprinkle with salt and pepper. Broil 20 to 25 minutes, depending on the size of the fish. Remove it to a hot platter; garnish with watercress and lemon slices.

Shad Roe

Yield: 4 servings

1-1¼ pounds shad roe
Water
Salt and pepper to taste
Flour
2 tablespoons butter or margarine
Lemon
Parsley

Wash and dry the shad roe, using care not to break the skin. Let it stand 5 minutes in ice water; drain. Simmer in salt water 5 minutes; sprinkle with salt, pepper, and flour.

Melt the butter or margarine in a frying pan. When hot, put in the roe; cook it slowly until brown on one side. Turn; brown the other side. Cook 20 to 30 minutes. Garnish with lemon and parsley.

Sole in Vermouth Sauce

Yield: 4 servings

4 large sole fillets
Salt
Pepper

Easy-to-Bake Fish

1 tablespoon shallot, finely chopped
About 7 tablespoons butter
⅓ cup white bread crumbs
¾ to 1 cup dry vermouth
1 beef bouillon cube stirred into 1 tablespoon hot water
Beurre manié (1 tablespoon butter blended with 1 tablespoon flour)
1 tablespoon parsley, chopped

Season the fish with salt and pepper. Grease a roasting pan or ovenproof dish, and sprinkle it with ½ tablespoon of the shallots. Then place the fish fillets in the pan so that they look like a whole fish. Brush the top side with melted butter—use a generous amount. Then sprinkle with the grated bread in an even layer.

Carefully pour a small amount of butter over the crumbs. Pour in enough vermouth so that the bottom of the pan is just covered. Place in a 450°F oven and bake until the sole has become a pretty golden brown with a crispy surface. This usually takes about 15 minutes but can vary depending on the size of the fish.

In the meantime, make the sauce. Pour the rest of the vermouth, about ⅓ cup, in a pot with the rest of the shallots and the broth. Allow this to boil until a little more than half remains. Thicken with a small amount of beurre manié. Remove the pot from the stove and slowly stir in the butter in nut-sized pieces until ¾ cup of sauce has been made.

Place the pot in hot water (or over a double-boiler) so that it remains warm. Should there be any vermouth left in the bottom of the roasting pan when the fish is done, add this also to the sauce. Season with pepper. Add the chopped parsley.

Place the fish on a serving plate or on individual plates. Pour a small amount of sauce around the fish and pour the rest into a warm gravy bowl. Serve with small, boiled potatoes.

Fillets of Sole with White Grapes

Yield: 6 to 8 servings

1½ cups white seedless grapes
1 cup dry white wine
3 pounds sole fillets
4 tablespoons butter
Juice of 1 lemon
3 bay leaves
2 small shallots, peeled and sliced
12 white peppercorns
2 tablespoons flour
½ cup milk, warmed
½ cup heavy cream
Salt
Cayenne pepper

Peel the grapes and soak them immediately in the white wine. Wash the sole fillets and pat dry. Butter a large, flat, ovenproof glass or enamel dish with about ½ tablespoon of butter. Lay the fillets in the dish. Pour ½ cup of cold water, the strained lemon juice, and the white wine in which the grapes have been soaking over the fillets. Cover the grapes and put them aside until ready to use.

Scatter the bay leaves, shallots, and whole peppercorns over the fish. Dot with 1½ tablespoons of butter. Bake in a preheated 350°F oven until the fish is opaque throughout, about 25 minutes, basting occasionally. When done, remove the fish from the oven and carefully strain the juices into a small pan. Keep the fish warm while you make the sauce.

Make a white roux by cooking 2 tablespoons of butter and the flour together over very low heat, stirring constantly with wooden spoon. Cook very slowly for 5 minutes, then gradually add the strained juice reserved from the fish. Continue cooking for about 5 minutes longer. Remove from the heat and stir in the warm milk. Put the pan back on the heat and bring to a boil, stirring vigorously,

Fish in Foil with Tomato-Filled Zucchini or Squash

then gradually add the heavy cream. Do not allow the sauce to boil after the cream has been added. Season to taste with salt and a very small pinch of cayenne. Add the grapes to the sauce, and pour it over the fish. Serve at once.

Fried Trout

Yield: 6 servings

6 small trout
1 cup milk
½ teaspoon celery salt
½ teaspoon onion salt
½ teaspoon garlic salt
¼ teaspoon black pepper
⅔ cup white cornmeal
12 slices bacon
⅓ cup butter or margarine
1 lemon

Clean and split the trout; remove the heads and tails. Dip the fish in milk. Combine the seasonings and sprinkle them over the fish. Dip the fish in cornmeal.

Fry the bacon until crisp; drain. Add butter to the bacon fat; heat. Fry the fish gently in the hot fat until crisp and brown. Serve the fish garnished with bacon and lemon.

Skewered Swordfish

Yield: 6 to 8 servings

2 pounds swordfish
½ cup olive oil
¾ cup lemon juice
¼ cup onion, grated
2 teaspoons salt
½ teaspoon freshly ground pepper
1 teaspoon paprika
12-16 bay leaves
2 tablespoons parsley, chopped

Rinse the fish and pat it dry. Cut the fish into 1½-inch cubes. In a glass or pottery bowl, mix ¼ cup of olive oil, ¼ cup of lemon juice, the grated onion, 1½ teaspoons of salt, the pepper, paprika, and bay leaves. Toss the fish in the mixture, then cover and marinate in the refrigerator 6-8 hours. Turn and baste the fish frequently.

Drain and divide the fish among 6 or 8 skewers, putting a couple of bay leaves on each skewer. Broil 15 minutes, or until the fish is browned and tender, turning the skewers so as to be sure to brown all sides evenly.

Mix the remaining oil, lemon juice, salt, and parsley together. Serve in a sauceboat.

Swordfish Steamed with Herbs

Yield: 4 to 6 servings

2 slices swordfish, about ¾ inch thick (about 2½ pounds)
Coarse salt
Freshly ground pepper
Extra virgin olive oil
Fresh lemon juice
Fresh basil and parsley, chopped
Dried oregano

Arrange the swordfish in a single layer on one of two round, heavy porcelain plates or platters. Sprinkle with salt and pepper and trickle olive oil over both slices of the fish; then sprinkle with lemon juice, basil, parsley, and oregano, placing one slice on top of the other. Cover with the second plate and set on a steamer in a large stockpot over boiling water. When the fish is white, it is done.

The fish can be served hot, cold, or at room temperature.

Fillets of Sole with Lobster Stuffing

Yield: 6 servings

1 cup soft bread crumbs
1 rock lobster tail, cooked, shelled, and minced
3 tablespoons olive oil
Salt
¼ cup and 1 teaspoon parsley, minced
1 tablespoon onion, minced
Pinch oregano
6-8 toasted almonds, crushed
6 fillets sole
2 scallions, minced
1 clove garlic, crushed
2 medium-sized tomatoes, peeled, seeded and chopped
2 tablespoons sherry

Combine the bread crumbs, lobster, 2 tablespoons of oil, ¼ teaspoon of salt, ¼ cup of parsley, minced onion, oregano, and almonds. Place 1-1½ tablespoons of the mixture on each fillet and roll up. Place on individual squares of foil with the overlapped side of the fillet underneath.

Combine the scallions, garlic, tomatoes, sherry, remaining parsley and oil and salt to taste. Spoon some over each stuffed fillet. Crimp the edges of the foil together to seal. Bake in a 350°F oven for 25-35 minutes.

Fish au Gratin on a Bed of Broccoli

Fish Kebabs, Two Different Ways

Broiled Lake Trout

Yield: 2 servings

1 whole lake trout
¼ cup oil
¼ teaspoon pepper
Butter
Lemon slices
Parsley

Split the trout into 2 fillets; remove the backbone. Wash thoroughly; remove all traces of blood or membrane. Place in a salt solution made in the proportion of 2 tablespoons salt to 1 cup water; let stand 8 to 10 minutes.

Preheat the broiler about 10 minutes. Oil the heated broiler pan.

Brush the fish with oil mixed with pepper. Amount of oil required will be about ¼ cup with ¼ teaspoon pepper. Place the trout on the broiler pan, skin side up, about 2 inches below the heat. After 5 minutes, the skin should be turning brown; baste. Cook until the skin is well browned, then turn the fish flesh side up. Baste again; cook until the flesh side is well browned. Remove to a hot platter; butter the top of the fish.

Garnish with lemon slices and parsley. Allow ⅓ to ½ pound fish per person.

Baked Fish in Wine

Yield: 3 servings

1 pound fish fillets (sole, flounder, or red snapper)
1 tablespoon parsley, chopped
1 tablespoon lemon juice
¾ teaspoon seasoned salt
3 tablespoons olive oil
1 medium-sized onion, thinly sliced
1 clove garlic, minced
1 large tomato, chopped
3 slices lemon
2 tablespoons white wine

Arrange the fish in an 8- or 9-inch square baking dish. Sprinkle with parsley, lemon juice, and seasoned salt.

Heat the oil in a small skillet; fry the onion and garlic until limp.

Top the fish with the onion mixture, including the oil from the skillet. Arrange the tomatoes on top of the onion mixture; place the lemon slices on top of the fish. Pour wine over all; bake at 350°F 30 to 35 minutes or until the fish flakes with a fork.

Trout with Lemon and Parsley

Yield: 4 to 8 servings

8 5-ounce trout or 4 8- to 10-ounce trout
½ cup milk
¼ cup flour
Salt and freshly ground pepper
½ to 1 cup peanut, vegetable, or corn oil
Juice of 1 lemon
8 tablespoons butter
8 lemon slices, seeded
¼ cup parsley, finely chopped

Put the trout in a shallow dish and add the milk. Turn the fish in the milk. Drain the trout one at a time, but do not pat dry. Blend the flour with salt and pepper to taste. Dip each trout in the mixture and shake off any excess flour.

Heat half a cup of oil in a skillet (or use 2 skillets, using half a cup of oil in each). Fry 4 trout at a time in 1 skillet, or cook all 8 in 2 skillets. The oil must be quite hot when the trout are added.

When the trout are browned on one side, about 2 to 3 minutes, turn them. Spoon the oil over the trout as they cook. A 5-ounce trout should be cooked in about 5 minutes (total cooking time, about 1 minute per ounce).

When all the trout are cooked, transfer them to a serving platter. Squeeze the juice of a lemon over the trout.

Heat the butter in a clean skillet, swirling it around until it foams. Continue cooking, swirling it around, until the butter is hazelnut-colored. Pour this over the trout. Garnish each trout with 1 lemon slice topped with finely chopped parsley.

Texas Tuna

Yield: 4 servings

1 9¾-ounce can tuna in oil
¾ cup onion, chopped
½ cup celery, chopped
¾ cup catsup
¾ cup water
1 tablespoon sugar
1 tablespoon vinegar
1 tablespoon Worcestershire sauce (optional)
1 teaspoon prepared mustard
¼ teaspoon salt
Pepper to taste

Drain and flake the tuna, but save the oil and put it in a saucepan. Cook the onion and celery in tuna oil until soft but not brown.

Add the remaining ingredients, except the tuna, and simmer uncovered about 10 minutes. Fold in the tuna and heat.

Serve on noodles, spaghetti, toast, or rice, or make hot sandwiches on rolls.

Fillet of Turbot with Wine-Onion and Tomato-Butter

Yield: 4 servings

wine-onion
1 large onion
1 cup red wine
¼ cup red wine vinegar
1¾ tablespoons butter
Salt
Pepper
1 tablespoon honey

tomato-butter
7 to 8 medium-large tomatoes
⅓ cup heavy cream
4 tablespoons butter
Salt
Pepper

fish
4 turbot fillets
1 tablespoon oil
Salt
Pepper
Cayenne pepper
Snipped parsley

Shred or finely chop the onion. Place in a pot with the wine and vinegar, cover, and simmer for 10 minutes. Then simmer uncovered so that all the liquid evaporates. Add the butter and seasonings and stir until the butter has melted. Add the honey and mix well. This may be done in advance and then reheated.

Boil and peel the tomatoes; remove the seeds from 3 of the tomatoes. Cut the 3 seeded tomatoes into small pieces, cover, and refrigerate. Strain the other tomatoes into a tomato juice and bring it to a boil together with the cream. Simmer, uncovered, until ⅔ of the original amount of liquid remains. Add the butter and season carefully.

Dredge the fish fillets in the oil; add salt, pepper, and a dash of cayenne pepper. Heat up the tomato-butter sauce and the wine-onion. Broil the fish 2 to 3 minutes on each side. Carefully warm up the refrigerated tomatoes in the tomato sauce. Divide the wine-onion up onto 4 warm plates. Place a fish fillet on each bed of onions, and pour the decorative tomato sauce around the onion. Sprinkle with parsley and serve immediately.

Three Kinds of Fish in Red Wine Sauce

Tuna Pie

Yield: 6 servings

crust
1 cup cooked brown rice
1 cup whole-wheat flour
⅓ cup sunflower kernels
2 tablespoons wheat germ
1 teaspoon salt
⅛ teaspoon pepper
⅓ cup salad oil
⅓ cup milk

filling
4 eggs
1½ cups milk
2 7-ounce cans tuna in vegetable oil
1 cup frozen chopped broccoli, thawed
½ cup Swiss cheese, shredded
½ cup celery, chopped
⅓ cup carrot, chopped and pared
1 teaspoon salt
⅛ teaspoon pepper

Mix the cooked rice, flour, sunflower kernels, wheat germ, salt, and pepper in a bowl. Stir in the oil and ⅓ cup milk. Roll out the dough between 2 pieces of waxed paper to a 10-inch round. Remove the top piece of waxed paper and turn the pastry into a 9-inch pie plate. Remove the second piece of waxed paper. Make a rim on the edge of the crust. Bake in a 400°F oven for 20 to 25 minutes, until lightly browned. Cool.

Beat the eggs with 1½ cups milk. Add the tuna, broccoli, cheese, celery, carrot, salt, and pepper; mix well. Turn into the baked pie shell. Bake in a 350°F oven for 1 hour or until the tip of a knife inserted in the center comes out clean. Let stand 10 minutes before serving.

Fried Yellow Perch

Yield: 6 servings

2 pounds yellow perch or other small fish, split, cleaned, and boned
1½ teaspoons salt
¼ teaspoon pepper
½ cup flour
2 tablespoons cornstarch
1 cup water
1 egg yolk, slightly beaten
1 egg white, beaten until stiff
Fat for deep-frying

Sprinkle the fish with 1 teaspoon of salt and pepper; set aside.

Combine the flour, cornstarch, and ½ teaspoon of salt. Blend the water and egg yolk together; stir

into the flour mixture until smooth. Fold in the egg white.

Dip the fish into the batter; deep-fat fry at 350°F 2 to 3 minutes, until the fish is golden brown. Drain on paper towels.

Baked Fish with Cucumber Sauce

Yield: 4 servings

½ cucumber, peeled, seeded, and coarsely grated
½ teaspoon salt
1 cup plain yogurt
1 teaspoon fresh dillweed, chopped
¼ teaspoon freshly ground black pepper
1 to 1½ pounds fish fillets
Fresh parsley leaves

Prepare the sauce. Sprinkle the grated cucumber with salt; let it stand 20 minutes to withdraw some of the water present. Drain away the accumulated water; combine the cucumber with the salt, yogurt, dill, and pepper.

Place the fish on a lightly greased baking sheet. Bake at 425°F for 10 minutes for each inch of

Quick Paella

thickness, or until the fish can be separated into flakes with a fork.

Place the fish on a warm platter. Ladle the sauce over the fish; garnish with fresh parsley leaves.

Easy-to-Bake Fish with Cheese and Tomatoes

Yield: 4 servings

1½ pounds haddock or cod fillets
½ tablespoon butter
1 tablespoon flour
¾ teaspoon salt
1 tablespoon squeezed lemon juice
2 tablespoons chopped dill
¾ cup grated cheese
¼ cup milk
2 to 3 tomatoes

Rinse the fish and let the water totally drain off. Grease a pan with low sides and sprinkle flour on the bottom. Place the fish in the pan. Salt and sprinkle with lemon juice. Add the dill and grated cheese. Cover with the milk.

Bake in the middle of a preheated 425°F oven for about 20 minutes or until the fish has a nice color. Cut the tomatoes into cubes and spread them over the top of the fish.

Fish in Foil with Tomato-Filled Zucchini or Squash

Yield: 4 servings

A whole haddock, cod, pike, perch, or whitefish (3 to 3½ pounds)
2 teaspoons salt
Dill
Parsley stalks
1 sheet of oven aluminum foil
2 large zucchini or 2 small squashes
2 teaspoons salt per quart of water
1 pound tomatoes
1 small carrot, finely grated
2 onions, finely chopped
2 tablespoons tomato paste
½ teaspoon black pepper
½ teaspoon salt
½ teaspoon tarragon
¼ cup chopped parsley

Clean the fish, but let the head and fins remain. Rub salt into the fish and fill the stomach with dill and parsley. Place the fish on a sheet of oven aluminum foil. Place a ruler next to the fish and measure the back at the thickest spot.

Make a tight package with the foil around the fish and place it in a roasting pan in the oven. If the fish is 1½ inches thick, it will take 30 minutes to bake; 2½ inches thick, 40 minutes; and 3 inches thick, 50 minutes. Increase or decrease by 5 minutes for every ¼ inch.

Peel the zucchini along 4 lines with spaces in between, so that the peel remains on the spaces in between. Cut lengthwise into halves and take out the seeds. Place in salted, boiling water and boil for 10 minutes. Remove from the water and drain well.

Scald the tomatoes in the same water and peel. Cut the tomatoes into 4 pieces and place them in a saucepan together with the carrot, the onions, the tomato paste, the pepper, salt, and tarragon. Boil for about 5 minutes.

Place the zucchini halves on an ovenproof plate and pour the tomato mixture into the zucchini. Place the plate over the fish and let it sit there during the last 20 minutes of the fish baking time.

Serve the fish in the foil, surrounded by the tomato-filled zucchini. Sprinkle with parsley.

Island Fish Stew

Spicy Shellfish Stew

Broiled Fish with Fresh Tomatoes

Yield: 4 servings

2 medium-sized tomatoes, coarsely chopped
2 tablespoons onion, finely chopped
½ teaspoon dried basil leaves, crushed
½ teaspoon salt
Dash pepper
1⅓ pounds fish fillets
2 tablespoons butter or margarine, melted

Stir the first 5 ingredients together. Brush both sides of the fish with butter or margarine. Arrange the fish on a rack in the broiler pan. Top with the tomato mixture.

Broil 4 inches from the heat 4 to 6 minutes, or until the fish flakes easily.

Clam-Stuffed Fish Fillets

Yield: 6 to 8 servings

2 1-pound packages fish fillets
2 5-ounce cans minced clams
½ cup butter or margarine
¼ cup onion, chopped
¼ cup celery, chopped

4 cups soft bread crumbs
2 tablespoons lemon juice
Salt and pepper

Let the fish fillets thaw on the refrigerator shelf or at room temperature. Arrange half of the fillets, close together, in a buttered baking dish.

Drain the minced clams, reserving the liquid. Melt the butter or margarine in a skillet. Pour off about half of the butter and save. To the butter in the skillet, add the onion and celery and cook until tender. Stir in the bread crumbs until the butter is soaked up. Continue tossing the crumbs until they brown slightly.

Stir in the clams, lemon juice, and enough clam liquid to moisten. Season to taste with salt and pepper.

Spoon the stuffing over the fillets. Cover with the remaining fillets. Brush with the reserved butter. Bake in a 375°F oven 20 minutes, or until the fish flakes easily when tested with a fork. Serve in a baking dish.

Fish with Herb Sauce

Yield: 4 servings

1½ pounds fresh fish fillets
1 to 2 tablespoons lemon juice
4 tomatoes, peeled and sliced
Salt and pepper
1 strip lean bacon, diced
1 small onion, chopped
½ cup plain yogurt
1 tablespoon flour
1 tablespoon parsley leaves, chopped
1 tablespoon chives, chopped, or scallions, thinly sliced
1 teaspoon dried dillweed (optional)
½ teaspoon tarragon
½ teaspoon chervil
1 tablespoon dried bread crumbs

Sprinkle the lemon juice over the fish; set aside. Line the bottom of a greased, shallow casserole dish with the tomato slices. Season with salt and pepper. In a small skillet, combine the bacon and onion. Cook until the onion is golden.

Combine the yogurt, flour, and herbs. Season to taste with salt and pepper.

Place the fish fillets on top of the tomatoes, pour the yogurt sauce over the fish; cover with the bacon-onion mixture and sprinkle bread crumbs over all. Cover; bake at 350°F for about 20 minutes, or until the fish can be separated into flakes with a fork. Serve at once.

Shellfish Kebab

Fish Au Gratin on a Bed of Broccoli

Yield: 4 servings

1 ½-pound package frozen broccoli
1½ pounds fresh or frozen fish fillets—cod, haddock, or perch
1 teaspoon salt

au gratin
1¼ cups coarsely grated cheese
3 tablespoons bread crumbs
⅓ cup finely shredded leek or snipped chives
2 to 3 tablespoons milk, cream, or sour cream

Prepare the broccoli according to directions on the package. Place it in a greased, ovenproof dish. Cut the fish fillets in slices. Place the fish over the broccoli. Sprinkle with salt.

Mix the grated cheese with the bread crumbs and the leek or chives. Pull the mixture together with milk, cream, or sour cream.

Dab the cheese mixture over the fish. Bake in a preheated 425°F oven for 20 to 30 minutes, or until the fish is done. Serve with sliced or mashed potatoes.

Shellfish Rice Feast

Pan Fried Fish

Yield: 6 servings

6 pan-dressed fish
1 teaspoon salt
⅛ teaspoon pepper
1 egg
1 tablespoon milk
1 cup bread crumbs, cracker crumbs, cornmeal, or flour

Wash the fish and be sure that they are well cleaned inside. Sprinkle both sides with salt and pepper. Beat the egg slightly and blend in the milk. Dip the fish in the egg and roll it in crumbs.

Place the fish in a heavy frying pan which contains about ⅛ inch melted fat, hot but not smoking. Fry at moderate heat. When the fish is brown on one side, turn carefully and brown the other side. Cooking time is about 10 minutes, depending on the thickness of the fish. Drain on paper towels. Serve immediately.

Fish Kebabs, Two Different Ways

Yield: 4 servings

1 pound fillets of fish with firm meat
Salt
Pepper
¼ pound mushrooms
6 slices of bacon, cut in squares
5 tomatoes
Oil

crayfish kebabs
25 grapes
12 crayfish tails or clams from a can
4 tomatoes
Oil
Salt
Black or white pepper

Cut the fish into 1 × 1 × ½-inch cubes. Lightly salt and pepper the fish cubes. Divide each tomato into 8 pieces.

Alternate the fish, mushrooms, bacon, and tomato pieces on a skewer, making 4 skewers in all. Baste with oil before grilling for 10 to 15 minutes. Turn the skewers several times.

To make 4 skewers of crayfish kebabs, take the seeds out of the grapes without cutting them in two. Cut each tomato into eight pieces. Alternate the grapes, crayfish tails or clams, and tomatoes on a skewer. Baste with oil, salt and pepper lightly, and grill until slightly brown (4 to 8 minutes). Turn several times.

French-Style Clams

Mustard-Broiled Fish Fillets

Yield: 3 to 4 servings

1½ pounds flounder fillet or similar fish
Oil
2 tablespoons mayonnaise
1 tablespoon Dijon mustard
Chopped parsley
Ground pepper

Lay the fillets on a lightly greased broiler pan or dish in one layer; brush lightly with oil. Combine the remaining ingredients and spread them on the fish. Broil for 3-8 minutes, or until the topping is browned and the fish flakes lightly with a fork. The length of broiling depends on the thickness of the fillets.

Poached Fillet of Fish

Yield: 4 servings

3 cups water
2 slices ginger, approximately 1 inch in diameter by ⅛ inch thick, smashed with the side of a cleaver
2 stalks green onions (scallions), cut into 2-inch lengths

1 pound fish fillets, cut into 1½-inch squares
1 tablespoon wine
2½ teaspoons light soy sauce
1 teaspoon sugar
½ teaspoon sesame oil
1 tablespoon oil
½ tablespoon ginger, minced
2 stalks green onions (scallions), finely minced

Put the ginger and green onions into a pot containing the 3 cups of water. Bring the water to a boil and boil for 3 minutes. Gently add the fish slices. When the water begins to boil again, remove the fish slices immediately and set on a platter. Keep warm.

Combine the wine, light soy sauce, sugar, and sesame oil to form the sauce. Set within easy reach.

Heat the oil in a pan over high heat until hazy. Put in the minced ginger and fry for 10 seconds. Put in the minced green onions and stir-fry another 10 seconds. Pour in the sauce and heat until bubbly. Then pour the sauce over the fish slices and serve hot.

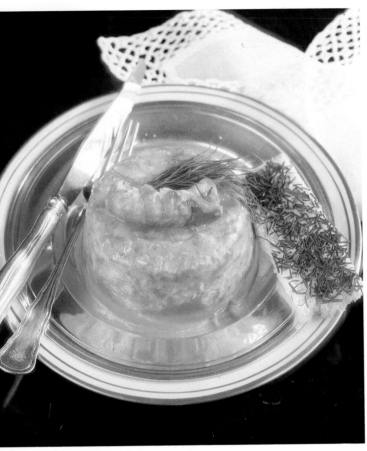

Crayfish Dish

Fish Fillets in Sour Cream

Yield: 4 to 6 servings

1 pound fish fillets
Salt and pepper to taste
Dash Tabasco sauce
1 cup sour cream
2 tablespoons dill pickle, finely chopped
2 tablespoons onion, minced
2 tablespoons green pepper, chopped
1 tablespoon parsley, chopped
1 tablespoon lemon juice
¼ teaspoon dry mustard
¼ teaspoon sweet basil
Paprika

Place the fish in a greased baking dish. Sprinkle generously with salt and pepper.

Mix the rest of the ingredients, except the paprika, together. Pour the mixture over the fish. Use a generous amount of paprika on top. Cover. Bake at 325°F 45 to 60 minutes, until the fish flakes when tested with a fork. Serve at once.

Seafood Jambalaya

Yield: 6 servings

3 tablespoons margarine
¾ cup green pepper, chopped
¼ cup celery, chopped
⅓ cup onion, chopped
½ cup fresh parsley, chopped
1 16-ounce can tomatoes, chopped
2 cups chicken bouillon
½ teaspoon salt
⅛ teaspoon pepper
½ teaspoon chili powder
2 bay leaves
2 cups cooked rice
1 pint oysters, drained
½ pound white fish, cut in chunks
1 pound regular crabmeat, cartilage removed

Sauté the green pepper, celery, and onion in margarine 5 minutes in a large saucepan. Add the parsley, tomatoes, water, bouillon, and seasonings; simmer over medium heat 30-40 minutes.

Add the rice, oysters, and fish and simmer 10 minutes. Add the crabmeat and simmer 5 more minutes.

Quick Paella

Yield: 4 servings

1 pound white fish, fresh or frozen
1 onion
2 tablespoons margarine
1 teaspoon curry powder or ½ envelope saffron
1 cup long-grain rice
2 cups chicken broth
1½ teaspoons salt
1 cup frozen peas
½ cup red pepper, frozen
1¼ cups frozen shrimp in shells

If the fish is frozen, place it in lukewarm water. Chop and fry the onion until transparent in the margarine in a wide frying pan. Dust the onion with curry powder or saffron and stir in the rice. Add the chicken broth; cover the pan and simmer for 10 minutes.

Cut the fish into pieces, season with salt, and press them into the rice which will have expanded and absorbed most of the liquid. Place the peas, red pepper, and shrimp on top of the rice, cover, and cook for 10 more minutes.

Serve in the pan or in a large dish and garnish with lemon wedges. Serve with a green salad.

Three Kinds of Fish in Red Wine Sauce

Yield: 4 to 6 servings

4 to 6 pieces of each: eel, pike, and perch—cleaned, trimmed, and skinned or scaled

marinade
⅔ cup olive oil
2 teaspoons salt
2 cloves garlic, crushed
1 shallot, chopped

red wine sauce
2 shallots, chopped
1 tablespoon butter
¼ teaspoon black pepper, coarsely ground
¼ cup brandy
1 tomato, boiled, peeled, and cut into pieces
2 tablespoons flour
1 small bottle French red wine
About ¾ cup broth from cooking the fish
Butter

for the fish
½ quart fish stock

Mix the marinade ingredients together in a plastic bag. Place the prepared fish pieces in the bag. Tie a knot and place in the refrigerator overnight. For best results, turn the bag several times while the fish is marinating.

The sauce may be prepared while the fish is marinating. Sauté the shallots and pepper in butter. Add the brandy and ignite. Add the tomato, flour, and wine. Allow the sauce to boil vigorously until the amount has decreased by ⅓. Strain the sauce.

Everything may be prepared in advance up to this point.

Bring the fish stock to a boil in a wide pan. Add the fish and let it simmer in several batches until it is just done. Remove the pieces with a slotted spoon and keep them warm.

Now beat about ¾ cup of the fish broth into the sauce. Season to taste. Add a dab of butter and pour into a wide, attractive serving dish.

Place the fish pieces in the sauce. Garnish with butter sautéed mushroom caps; and toast points fried in butter and garlic.

Crayfish-Perch

Lobster Mousse in Avocado Sauce

Island Fish Stew

Yield: 4 servings

About 1 pound cod or haddock
1 small can clams in water
4 cups fish broth
1 can whole peeled tomatoes
Salt
Freshly ground pepper
4 to 6 potatoes, peeled and boiled
¼ pound fresh shrimp, shelled
Dill

Cut the fish into large cubes. Drain the clams, reserving their juice. Mix the clam juice, fish broth, and the juice from the can of tomatoes and simmer together for about 10 minutes. Add the fish cubes and simmer in the broth for several minutes. Season with salt and freshly ground pepper.

Add the boiled potatoes, clams, shrimp, and tomatoes, and simmer for several more minutes. Chop the dill and sprinkle it over the stew.

Serve with crispy, warm French bread and a good cheese.

Seafood Rolls

Yield: 6 servings

½ cup mayonnaise
¼ cup sour cream
2 teaspoons lemon juice
¼ teaspoon dillweed
2 5-ounce cans lobster, shrimp, crab or tuna, flaked
½ cup celery, minced
12 small dinner rolls, split and buttered

Combine the mayonnaise, sour cream, lemon juice, and dillweed; mix with the seafood and celery. Fill the rolls with mixture. Wrap and chill.

Spicy Shellfish Stew

Yield: 6 servings

1 tablespoon curry
2 tablespoons oil
2 packages frozen crayfish or shrimp
2 green peppers, finely shredded
2 cloves garlic, crushed
2 tablespoons chili sauce
½ teaspoon salt
1 can crushed tomatoes
⅛ teaspoon cayenne pepper
1 container crème fraîche or ¾ cup sour cream

Sauté the curry in hot oil while stirring constantly. Sauté the crayfish or shrimp on all sides in the curry fat, but only for a short time so that the meat does not become tough; it should be just cooked through. Remove the fish from the pan and place on a plate.

Sauté the shredded peppers in the same oil. Add the garlic, chili sauce, salt, and crushed tomatoes. Stir and season with cayenne pepper, a few grains at a time, constantly testing the stew. Cover and allow the mixture to simmer until the green peppers feel soft. Then blend in the crayfish and the crème fraîche or sour cream. Bring the mixture to a slow boil and check the seasoning.

Serve with rice or freshly boiled noodles, salad, and warm, crisp bread.

Shellfish Kebab

Yield: 4 servings

12 large scampi in their shells (it is easiest to use frozen which have been thawed)
8 clams
About 8 slices leek
Freshly squeezed lime juice
Oil
Salt
Pepper

Curry Creamed Mussels

Push the scampi, clams, and leeks onto skewers. Brush each skewer with a small amount of oil and a few drops of lime juice. Add salt and pepper. Cook the skewers for 3 to 4 minutes on each side over a hot grill.

This kebab may also be fried in butter in a frying pan on top of the stove. In this case, the clams should first be dredged in a small amount of bread crumbs so that the fried surface comes out well.

Serve with Indonesian soy sauce and lime wedges.

Stuffed Clams

Yield: 3 to 4 servings

2 dozen clams (littleneck or rock)
¾ cup dry white wine
¼ cup water
½ teaspoon salt
3 tablespoons olive oil
½ cup onion, chopped
½ cup raw long-grain rice
¼ teaspoon pepper
½ teaspoon allspice
¼ teaspoon cinnamon
3 tablespoons currants
3 tablespoons pine nuts
2 tablespoons parsley, chopped

Scrub the clams; soak them in several changes of cold water to remove sand. Place them in a skillet with wine, water, and salt. Cover and steam 10 minutes, until the shells open. Discard any clams that do not open. Cool; remove the clams from their shells. Save the shells; strain the pan juices.

In a medium saucepan, heat the oil and sauté the onion until golden. Add the rice and 1 cup of pan juices. Bring to a boil. Cover, reduce heat to low. Cook 15 minutes. Add the pepper, spices, currants, pine nuts, and parsley. Cook 5 minutes. Cool.

Dice the clams; add them to the rice mixture. Stuff the shells with the rice mixture; chill.

Shellfish Rice Feast

Yield: 5 to 6 servings

1 to 1¼ cups long-grain rice
1 minced onion (optional)
1 tablespoon butter
About 2½ cups fish broth
⅓ cup snipped dill
1 teaspoon crushed tarragon (optional)

mushrooms

¼ to ½ pound fresh mushrooms
1 to 1½ tablespoons butter
About ½ tablespoon squeezed lemon juice
Salt
1 jar black caviar
½ cup crème fraîche or sour cream

curry shrimp

1¼ pounds shrimp
1 tablespoon butter
1 to 1½ teaspoons curry

garlic clams

1 8-ounce can clams in water
1 tablespoon butter
1 clove garlic, crushed

Sauté the rice and the onion, if desired, lightly in butter. Cover with the broth. Boil the rice for 20 to 25 minutes according to the directions on the rice package. Mix the dill and perhaps the tarragon with the rice. Transfer to a heated bowl.

While the rice is cooking, rub the mushrooms clean and sauté in butter over rather low heat for 5 to 8 minutes. Season with the salt and lemon. If you wish, you can place the mushrooms in a warm bowl and cover them with aluminum foil.

Place the caviar and the crème fraîche in separate bowls, or in a bowl together. Shell the shrimp. Drain the clams. Melt butter for the shrimp and the clams in separate pots right before serving. Add the curry for the shrimp and crush the garlic for the clams. Add the shrimp and clams to their individual pots. Sauté lightly and place them in warm bowls.

Place all the dishes on the table and let guests help themselves to whichever side dishes they want.

Deviled Clams

Yield: 2 servings

2 cups milk, scalded
2 tablespoons butter
1 egg, beaten
½ cup cracker crumbs
1 dozen large clams, minced
2 hard-cooked eggs, chopped
1 tablespoon onion, chopped
1 tablespoon parsley, minced
1 tablespoon Worcestershire sauce
Salt and pepper
Celery salt
4 tablespoons bread crumbs
2 tablespoons butter

Combine the milk, butter, egg, cracker crumbs, and clams. Add the eggs, onion, parsley, Worcestershire sauce, and seasonings. Pour into a greased baking dish. Brown the bread crumbs in 2 tablespoons of butter and sprinkle them over the top. Bake in a 400°F oven for ¾ hour.

French-Style Clams

Yield: 4 servings

2 cans clam meats in water
7 tablespoons butter, melted
1 3-ounce can sprats, herrings, or anchovies
⅓ cup parsley, finely chopped
⅔ cup sour cream
3 to 4 small cloves garlic, crushed
½ teaspoon salt
¼ teaspoon black pepper
⅓ cup fresh bread crumbs
⅓ cup grated cheese

Drain the clams. Spread them out in a deep ovenproof dish. Mix the melted butter with the drained, mashed sprats, parsley, sour cream, garlic, salt, and pepper. Divide the mixture up evenly over the clams.

Mix the grated bread and cheese together and sprinkle over the dish. Bake at 500°F for about 10 minutes, or until the top has become nicely brown. Serve with crisp warm bread and butter.

Crab Cakes

Yield: 4 servings

2 pounds backfin crabmeat
1 cup mayonnaise
½ cup bread crumbs
1 teaspoon yellow mustard
2 dashes Worcestershire sauce
1 tablespoon seafood seasoning
1 whole egg
1 teaspoon parsley, chopped
Juice of ½ lemon

Remove the cartilage from the crabmeat.

Combine the mayonnaise with all the other ingredients, except the crabmeat. Add the mayonnaise mixture to the crabmeat. Form into 8 5-ounce balls and bake at 500°F until golden.

Crab Imperial

Yield: 8 servings

1 green sweet pepper, minced
1 medium-sized onion, minced
2 teaspoons dry mustard
2 teaspoons prepared horseradish
2 teaspoons salt
½ teaspoon freshly ground white pepper
2 eggs, beaten
1 cup mayonnaise
3 pounds lump crabmeat
Paprika

Combine the green pepper, onion, mustard, horseradish, salt, white pepper, and eggs and mix well. Blend in the mayonnaise thoroughly, then fold in the crabmeat.

Spoon the crabmeat mixture into 8 large, cleaned crab shells or ramekins. Coat with additional mayonnaise and sprinkle generously with paprika. Arrange the crab shells in a shallow, oblong baking pan. Bake in a preheated 350°F oven for 15 to 20 minutes, or until heated through.

Crab Norfolk

Yield: 8 servings

2 tablespoons clarified butter
3 ounces country or prosciutto ham, cut into julienne strips
4 scallions, without tops, finely chopped
¾ cup Madeira
3 pounds backfin crabmeat, picked clean of shells
Chopped parsley
¼ pound butter
8 parsley sprigs

Heat a large sauté pan; season it with clear butter. Drop in the ham and scallions. Roll once. Add the Madeira. The pan temperature is right if the Madeira flames. If the alcohol is not burned off in flame, allow the Madeira to reduce for a minute. Add the crabmeat.

Bring the ham and scallions to the top of the pan. Sprinkle with chopped parsley; dot with cold butter. Place the pan in a 400°F oven for 2 minutes until the butter melts and the mixture is hot.

Spoon carefully into 8 ramekins. Garnish with parsley sprigs.

Herb-Marinated Mussels with Walnuts

Crab Casserole

Yield: 4 servings

1 pound crabmeat
2 tablespoons butter
1 green pepper, chopped
1 bunch scallions, chopped
1 tablespoon flour
1 cup milk
3 tablespoons Parmesan cheese

Carefully pick over the crabmeat to remove any shell pieces, then set aside. Melt the butter and sauté the pepper and scallions in it until softened. Sprinkle with flour and slowly stir in the milk. Stir over low flame until the mixture thickens slightly.

Stir in the crab and place in a 1-quart baking dish. Sprinkle with Parmesan cheese and brown quickly under the broiler.

Sautéed Crab Flakes

Yield: 6 to 8 servings

⅔ cup butter
¼ teaspoon salt
⅛ teaspoon pepper
¼ cup parsley, chopped
2 tablespoons brandy
2 pounds backfin crabmeat, picked over
Pinch nutmeg
Parsley and lemon wedges

Melt the butter in a 2½- to 3-quart saucepan or chafing dish. Add the salt, pepper, parsley, brandy, and nutmeg. Stir in the crabmeat, trying not to break up the lumps, and sauté slowly 5 to 8 minutes, or until the crabmeat is heated.

The dish is good served as is, on toast points, or on very thin slices of fried country ham. Garnish with parsley and lemon wedges.

Soft-Shelled Crabs

Yield: 4 to 6 servings

4 tablespoons butter
2 tablespoons lemon juice
6 to 8 soft-shelled crabs, cleaned
1 tablespoon cornstarch or flour
¼ cup water

Heat the butter and lemon juice in a medium-sized skillet. Cook the crabs over medium heat until browned, 5 minutes per side. Remove the crabs to a heated platter.

Mix the cornstarch and water; add to the pan juices, stirring until slightly thickened. Pour the sauce over the crabs. Serve at once.

Crayfish Timbales

Yield: 4 servings

2½ pounds frozen crayfish or small lobsters
2 tablespoons butter
¼ cup tomato paste
1 tablespoon brandy
⅓ cup water
⅔ cup heavy cream
⅓ cup dry white wine
1 envelope gelatin
Salt
Pepper
Sprigs of dill

Clean the thawed crayfish. Place the tails and the meat from the claws in a plastic bag in the refrigerator. Sauté the shells in a covered pot in butter and let simmer for a few minutes. Add the tomato paste and stir; pour in the brandy, remove from the heat, and ignite.

Put back on the stove; pour in the water, cream, and wine. Cover and simmer for another 10 minutes. Strain the heavy sauce.

Dissolve the gelatin in a little cold water, then dissolve the gelatin into the sauce while stirring constantly. Season with pepper and perhaps a little salt. If the sauce is too strong, add more cream.

Cut the crayfish meat into small pieces, but save some of the larger tails for garnishing; add the pieces to the sauce. Mix well and pour the mixture into 4 individual cups. Refrigerate for at least 6 hours and allow to become solid.

Before turning out from the dishes, dip for a second in hot water. Garnish with dill and crayfish tails.

Lobster Mousse in Avocado Sauce

Yield: 4 servings

1 boiled lobster, ¾ to 1 pound
1 envelope gelatin
¼ cup fish broth
1 tablespoon dry sherry
⅔ cup whipped cream
¼ teaspoon salt
⅛ teaspoon white pepper
Pinch of cayenne pepper
¾ teaspoon lemon juice

avocado sauce
1 large, well-ripened avocado
½ to 1 teaspoon lemon juice
⅓ cup sour cream
¼ cup water
¼ teaspoon salt
⅛ teaspoon white pepper

Marinated Mussels

Clean the lobster, saving the meat from the claws for garnish. Chop the rest of the meat.

Soak the gelatin in cold water for 5 minutes. Dissolve in boiling fish stock.

Using a blender or food processor, mix the lobster meat with the broth and sherry until it becomes a smooth purée. Refrigerate the purée. Whip the cream and fold it into the purée. Season with the spices.

Pack the mousse into a mold, cover with plastic wrap, and refrigerate until it is time to serve. Remove the mousse by using a spoon that has been dipped in cold water.

Scoop out the avocado meat and mix it with the other avocado sauce ingredients until smooth. Serve with the mousse.

Herb-Marinated Mussels with Walnuts

Yield: 4 servings

25 to 30 fresh mussels
8 cups water
1 tablespoon salt
½ tablespoon vinegar

marinade
1 large clove garlic, crushed
The white part of a small leek, chopped
2 tablespoons walnuts, chopped
4 to 5 tablespoons dill, finely chopped
½ lemon
1 teaspoon vinegar
Salt
Pepper
4 to 5 tablespoons oil

Clean and rinse the mussels. Place them in boiling water with salt and vinegar until they have all opened, about 5 to 7 minutes. Drain and allow to cool. Remove the upper part of the shell.

Combine the marinade ingredients. Drip the marinade over the mussels and refrigerate for several hours before serving so that the mussels soak in the taste of the marinade. The mussels will look most decorative if they are served on a plate that has been first covered with crushed ice or coarse rock salt.

Serve with warm French bread.

Lobster Boats

Yield: 4 servings

½ pound cooked lobster meat
24 fresh mushrooms, approximately 1½ inches in
    diameter
¼ cup condensed cream of mushroom soup
2 tablespoons fine soft bread crumbs
2 tablespoons mayonnaise or salad dressing
¼ teaspoon Worcestershire sauce
⅛ teaspoon liquid hot pepper sauce
Dash pepper
Grated Parmesan cheese

Drain the lobster meat; remove any remaining shell or cartilage. Chop the lobster meat. Rinse the mushrooms in cold water; dry them and remove their stems.

Combine the soup, crumbs, mayonnaise, seasonings, and lobster. Stuff each mushroom cap with a tablespoon of the lobster mixture. Sprinkle with cheese.

Place the mushrooms in a well-greased 15 × 10 × 1-inch baking pan. Bake in a 400°F oven 10 or 15 minutes, or until lightly browned.

Steamed Rock Lobster

Yield: 6 servings

3 8-ounce packages frozen rock lobster tails
6 large mushrooms, cut into slices
6 scallions, cut into long thin strips
1 cup celery, thinly sliced
1 bunch broccoli, trimmed and cut into flowerets
1 tablespoon soy sauce
1 envelope dehydrated chicken broth
¼ cup water

Remove the thin underside membrane from the lobster tails with scissors. Push a bamboo skewer lengthwise through the tail to prevent curling. Place the lobster tails in a steamer and place the vegetables on top and around the tails.

Combine the soy sauce, broth, and water, then brush over the tails and vegetables. Cover the pot and let it steam for 20 minutes, or until the vegetables are crisp-tender and the lobster meat loses its translucency and is opaque.

Crayfish-Perch

Yield: 10 servings

3 packages frozen crayfish or small lobsters
1 3-pound perch (1½ pounds perch fillet)

broth
Crayfish shells and trimmings from the fish
2 tablespoons butter
2 tablespoons brandy
2 small carrots
2 shallots
¼ pound celery root (celeriac)
4 sprigs parsley
1 bay leaf
½ teaspoon thyme
1 bottle dry white wine
4 cups water

fish pâté
3 egg whites
2⅓ cups heavy cream
1 teaspoon salt
¼ teaspoon white pepper
⅛ to ¼ teaspoon ground nutmeg

sauce
The broth
1⅔ cups heavy cream
⅛ to ¼ teaspoon cayenne pepper
Salt, if needed

Thaw and shell the crayfish carefully. Carefully remove the "stomach," which is situated right behind the eyes, and throw it away. The upper part of the shell and the tail meats should be in one piece. Try also to retain the long antennae. The claws, legs, and rest of the shell are to be saved for the broth. (See the picture. The upper shells/heads are pâté-filled.)

Rinse the upper shells well, and place them in the refrigerator, together with the tails.

Clean the perch and cut into fillets. Save the trimmings for the broth. Place the fillets in the refrigerator.

Crush or coarsely chop the crayfish shells, claws, etc., and the scrapings from the fish. Sauté these in butter in a large pan. Add the brandy and ignite.

Peel and finely chop the carrots, shallots, and celery root. Sauté them together with the shells for several minutes. Add the sprigs of parsley, the bay leaf, the thyme, white wine, and water. Cover and boil for about 20 minutes. Strain and then allow the broth to thicken, uncovered, until slightly more than half the original amount of liquid remains. You may prepare in advance up to this step.

Make the fish pâté. Run the fish fillets through a food processor or 3 times through a meat grinder. Then add the egg whites, one at a time, while beating constantly, and add the cream, a small amount at a time. Season with salt, white pepper, and nutmeg.

Spoon the pâté into the clean, cold upper crayfish shells, and place them closely together in a wide pan. Cover with the broth and let simmer for 5 to 7 minutes, until the pâté has become white. Then remove the shells from the pan, and keep them warm under a sheet of aluminum foil.

To make the sauce, add cream to the broth and let simmer until it becomes somewhat thick. Thicken with ½ tablespoon butter mixed with ½ tablespoon flour, if necessary. Season with cayenne pepper and salt, if needed.

Place the tails in the bottom of a copper pan or serving dish with sides. Place the filled upper shells on top, with the antennae sticking up. Carefully pour the hot sauce over the dish. Heat well on the stove or in the oven for about 5 minutes at 500°F.

Curry Creamed Mussels

Yield: 4 servings

2 onions
¾ cup dry white wine
¼ cup water
⅓ cup snipped parsley
Pinch thyme
5½ tablespoons butter
About 48 mussels, in their shells
1 teaspoon curry
Juice of ½ lemon
2 egg yolks
¾ cup heavy cream
1 carrot
½ fennel
1 leek
½ celeriac
Salt
Pepper

Mince 1 of the onions and place it in a thick-bottomed pot with the wine, water, parsley, thyme, and 2 tablespoons of the butter. Bring to a boil. Place the mussels in the pot and stir well. Cover the pot and shake well so that the mussels move around. Boil several minutes, until all the mussels have opened. Remove the mussels from their shells. Save the mussels for later, but discard the shells.

Strain the broth. Cut the carrots, fennel, leek, and celeriac into thin stalks and mince the remaining onion. Place the rest of the butter in a 2-quart skillet.

Add the vegetables and let simmer for a few minutes over low heat. Salt and pepper slightly. Pour over the mussel broth and simmer so that the vegetables become soft without becoming mushy. Remove the vegetables with a straining spoon and put them in a bowl.

Beat the egg yolks and the cream together in a bowl. Carefully beat in the hot broth. Then pour the mixture back into the pan. Place over medium heat and thicken, if you wish, with a little beurre manié (1 tablespoon butter mixed with 1 tablespoon

Shrimp Croquettes

flour). Season with curry, lemon, salt, and pepper. Adjust the seasoning if necessary with more wine or a fish bouillon cube. Fold in the mussels and the vegetables. The broth should be rather thick and creamy.

Spoon into large shell-like dishes or individual serving dishes. This may also be placed on toast with cheese on top and baked until golden brown.

Oyster Puffs

Yield: 3 servings

4 eggs, separated
¼ cup green onions, finely chopped
¼ teaspoon freshly ground white pepper
1 teaspoon salt
¼ cup flour, sifted
¼ cup ground almonds
1½ cups oysters, drained and chopped

Combine the beaten egg yolks, onions, pepper, salt, flour, and almonds in a medium-sized bowl. Beat the egg whites until stiff peaks form, then fold the egg whites and oysters into the egg yolk mixture. Drop the oyster mixture by tablespoonfuls into 370°F fat in a deep-fryer and fry until golden brown. Drain on paper towels.

Shrimp Omelet Sandwiches

Place the onion, wine, water, parsley, thyme, and butter in a thick-bottomed pot. Bring to a boil. Place the mussels in the pot and stir well. Cover the pot and shake well so the mussels move around. Boil for several minutes, until all the mussels have opened. Cool. Remove mussels from their shells.

Mix the marinade ingredients together. Add the mussels and mix well. Let stand for several hours.

Cut the tomatoes into 4 wedges, then slice into thin pieces. Cut the leek into thin rings; sprinkle with the snipped parsley. Sprinkle the rest of the marinade over the salad. Serve with marinated mussels.

Marinated Mussels

Yield: 4 servings

About 48 mussels (10 to 12 per person)
1 onion, minced
¾ cup dry white wine
¼ cup water
⅓ cup snipped parsley
Pinch thyme
2 tablespoons butter

marinade
4 tablespoons olive oil
2 tablespoons dry white vermouth or white wine
2 tablespoons shallot, finely minced
1 tablespoon snipped parsley
2 tablespoons mixed herbs: tarragon, thyme, basil, etc.
Salt
Pepper

salad
1 tomato per person
1 leek
Lettuce
Snipped parsley

Oysters Baltimore

Yield: 4 to 6 servings

4 slices bacon
18 oysters
3 tablespoons chili sauce
1 tablespoon Worcestershire sauce
6 tablespoons heavy cream
½ teaspoon tarragon
2 tablespoons lemon juice
1 teaspoon salt
¼ teaspoon pepper

In a medium-sized skillet, fry the bacon until crisp. Set the bacon aside to drain, then crumble it into bits.

Pour off all but 1 tablespoon of fat from the skillet. Add the oysters with their liquid. Cook, uncovered, over medium heat until most of the pan juices are absorbed.

Mix the remaining ingredients; add to the oysters. Simmer no more than 5 minutes to blend all flavors. Add extra seasonings if desired. These oysters are delicious served over hot buttered toast. Garnish with crumbled bacon.

Fried Oysters

Yield: 6 to 8 servings

50 prime oysters
3 or 4 beaten eggs
3 cups cracker crumbs
1 teaspoon salt

Take the oysters right out of their liquor without draining. Dip the oysters in the crumbs, then set them aside on a board in a cool place. (Don't pierce the oysters with a fork — lift them on a flat, slotted spoon.) Dip the oysters in the egg, then in the crumbs again, and set aside. Fry them quickly in deep, hot fat. Drain on brown paper. Serve at once.

Broiled Scallops

Yield: 6 servings

1½ pound fresh scallops
2 tablespoons honey
2 tablespoons prepared mustard
1 teaspoon curry powder
1 teaspoon lemon juice
Lemon slices

Rinse the scallops; pat them dry with paper towels. Combine the honey, mustard, curry and lemon juice.

Place the scallops on a broiler pan; brush with the honey mixture. Broil at 425°F 4 inches from the heat 8 to 10 minutes or until lightly browned. Turn the scallops; brush with the remaining sauce. Broil 8 to 10 minutes longer. Garnish with lemon slices.

Dill Scallops in Lemon Butter

Yield: 4 to 6 servings

1½ pounds scallops
½ cup dry bread crumbs
8 tablespoons butter or margarine
¼ teaspoon salt
Dash pepper
Dash paprika
1 tablespoon parsley, chopped
2 teaspoons dillweed
3 tablespoons lemon juice

Batter the scallops in bread crumbs until well coated.

Melt 4 tablespoons of butter in a skillet; add the salt, pepper, and paprika. Sauté the scallops slowly until evenly browned, about 8 minutes. Remove the scallops to a heated platter. Add the remaining butter to the skillet with the parsley, dill, and lemon juice. Stir until hot; pour over the scallops. Serve at once.

Shrimp Omelet Sandwiches

Yield: 4 servings

omelet batter
2 large eggs
2 tablespoons heavy cream
Salt
Pepper
Butter

filling
About 1 to 1½ pounds choice shelled shrimp
6 rounded teaspoons garlic butter

bread
6 slices white bread
Butter for the bread
Parmesan cheese for garnish
Dill for garnish

Deep-Fried Shrimp with Rhode Island Sauce

Beat the omelet batter ingredients together. If you want a light omelet, whip the cream before adding it to the batter. Make the omelet "pancakes" as thick as possible, frying them only on one side in a well-greased skillet. Place them so that they can cool separately.

Make round bread slices without crusts that are the same size. Spread butter on the slices and place the shrimp on top. Put a dab of garlic butter on each sandwich and cover with the omelet so that the baked side is facing upward. The omelet will then sink down around the shrimp.

Place the sandwiches in a small roasting pan at room temperature and wait for your guests to arrive. Sprinkle Parmesan cheese over the sandwiches and place them under the broiler for about 5 minutes, or until the cheese has become golden brown, the bread is thoroughly warm, and the garlic butter has begun to melt. Remove from the oven and garnish with dill before serving.

Shrimp Croquettes

Yield: 4 to 6 servings

½ pound shelled fresh shrimp, chopped
1 cup thick béchamel sauce (see below)
3 egg yolks
Pepper
Salt (optional)
Dash nutmeg
Flour
1 egg, beaten
Bread crumbs
Oil for deep-fat frying
Lemon
Parsley

Make a thick béchamel sauce and mix in the chopped shrimp. Let boil for just a second, and remove from the heat. Stir in the egg yolks, and season with pepper and perhaps a small amount of salt. Season with a dash of nutmeg.

Pour the mixture onto an oiled plate and let cool. It is best to allow the mixture to sit in the refrigerator overnight. The mixture should be really cold, or it will be difficult to form the croquettes.

Divide the mixture into small piles and shape them into croquettes the size of wine bottle corks. Roll them in flour. Then dip them in a beaten egg. Roll in bread crumbs. Fry them in smoking oil until they become golden brown in color. Remove with a spoon with holes in it, and let them drain on a piece of paper towel.

Serve the croquettes piled on top of each other in a pyramid shape on a plate, and serve with lemon and a bunch of deep-fat fried parsley.

Béchamel Sauce: Melt 3 tablespoons butter in top of a double boiler over boiling water; stir in 3 tablespoons flour with a wooden spoon until smooth. Add 2 cups milk gradually, stirring constantly; cook until sauce is thick. Stir in salt and pepper. Remove top of double boiler from water.

Strain sauce through a fine sieve; use as desired. Pour any remaining sauce into a small bowl. Cover top of sauce with a circle of wet waxed paper; refrigerate for future use. Makes 2 cups.

Deep-Fried Shrimp with Rhode Island Sauce

Yield: 4 servings

`batter`
¼ cup slightly warm beer
¼ cup slightly warm water
2 tablespoons oil
⅓ cup flour
1 teaspoon salt
1 egg white, stiffly beaten

shrimp
2½ pounds extra large, unshelled shrimp
3⅓ to 4 cups oil for deep-frying

Rhode Island sauce
⅔ cup mayonnaise
1 tablespoon tomato paste
1 tablespoon dry sherry
¼ teaspoon garlic powder
½ teaspoon salt
3 to 6 dashes Tabasco
⅓ cup sour cream
Parsley
Lemon wedges

Mix all but the egg white of the batter ingredients. Beat until smooth. Let stand and soak while you shell the shrimp. Beat the egg white into stiff peaks and fold it carefully into the batter. Stir only as much as is necessary. This is so the shrimp will be as crispy as possible.

Heat up the oil so that it is about 350°F, or until a little cube of white bread quickly becomes golden brown. Another sign that the oil is at the right temperature is if you can just see small smoke rings.

Mix the shrimp in the frying batter and put them carefully, one by one, into the oil. Do not put too many shrimp in the oil at one time. They easily bunch together and cause the oil to lose its heat. It is, therefore, best to deep-fry in several batches. Drain the shrimp by placing them on folded paper towels.

Make the Rhode Island sauce by mixing together the mayonnaise, tomato paste, sherry, garlic powder, salt, and Tabasco sauce. Mix until smooth, then add sour cream.

Finally, when everything else is done, deep-fry the parsley. The parsley should be dry and well drained, and all the stems should be removed. Carefully drop a fistful of parsley in the hot oil and fry it for several seconds until it becomes dark green in color. Serve the shrimp with the sauce, parsley, and lemon wedges.

Shrimp in Oriental Sauce

Yield: 5 to 6 servings

3 pounds shrimp
2 tablespoons oil
2 cups water
2 tablespoons butter
2 teaspoons curry
1 large onion, chopped
2 to 3 cloves garlic
1 tablespoon flour
1¼ cups shrimp juice
2 tablespoons tomato paste

Shrimp in Oriental Sauce

4 drops Tabasco
1 large green pepper
1 large red pepper
¾ cup crème fraîche or sour cream
1 tablespoon brandy (optional)

Shell the shrimp and place them in the refrigerator. Save the shrimp shells. Sauté the shrimp shells in a pan with oil until they start to look dry and turn white. Add the water and let the shells boil for 6 to 7 minutes. Strain the liquid.

Melt the butter in a pot, add the curry and then the onion. Sauté until the onion has become soft. Crush the garlic over the mixture.

Sprinkle with the flour and stir. Dilute with the shrimp liquid; let it come to a boil while stirring, then add the tomato paste and the Tabasco sauce. Simmer for 5 to 6 minutes.

Take the seeds out of the peppers and slice them into fine strips. Store them in a cool place in plastic wrap. Everything up to this point can be made in advance.

Bring the sauce to a boil and add the peppers. Stir in the crème fraîche and brandy, if desired. Simmer 4 to 5 minutes. The peppers should just have become soft. Season. Add the shrimp and heat until

they become warm. Note: the shrimp should not be boiled or they will become tough.

Serve with rice and a green salad.

Steamed Shrimp

Yield: 4 servings

¾ cup water
¼ cup vinegar
1 tablespoon seafood seasoning
1½ pounds jumbo shrimp, with shells
1 lemon

Wipe the shrimp dry with paper towels. Put the water, vinegar, and seafood seasoning into the saucepan and place over medium-high heat. After it boils, add the shrimp (with shells) to the pan. Cover the pan, leaving the lid about ½ inch open to let some steam escape. Cook the shrimp until they turn bright pink, 4 to 5 minutes. Then using the lid to hold the shrimp, drain the pan of the liquid.

Cut the lemon into 4 pieces. When the shrimp are cool enough to handle, peel and devein them and serve with the lemon quarters.

Shrimp with Tomatoes and Cheese

Shrimp Tarragon with Pimiento Rice

Yield: 4 servings

2 tablespoons butter, melted
3 tablespoons flour
1 can cream of shrimp soup
½ cup chicken broth
½ cup Sauterne
2 tablespoons lemon juice
½ teaspoon tarragon
½ teaspoon seasoned pepper
½ teaspoon salt
½ teaspoon onion powder
1¼ pound shrimp, shelled and deveined

pimiento rice
1 cup onion, chopped
2 tablespoons butter
2 to 3 cups boiled rice
¼ cup pimiento, diced

Blend the butter and flour in a saucepan until smooth, then stir in the soup, broth, Sauterne, lemon juice, tarragon, seasoned pepper, salt, and

onion powder. Cook over medium heat until thickened, stirring constantly. Add the shrimp and cook for 5 to 10 minutes longer or until the shrimp are pink. Turn into a heated serving dish.

Sauté the onion in the butter in a saucepan until tender, but not brown. Stir in the rice and pimiento and simmer, stirring frequently, until heated through.

Shrimp with Tomatoes and Cheese

Yield: 4 servings

1 can tomatoes (whole tomatoes)
2 tablespoons plus ⅓ cup olive oil
About ½ cup snipped parsley
15 large shrimp
½ pound soft whipped cheese, cream or soft Cheddar
3½ tablespoons butter
Black pepper
Tabasco sauce
Salt (optional)

Prepare the sauce at least 8 hours in advance so that it has time to pull together. Pour off the juice from the tomatoes. Chop the tomatoes into large pieces; mix the pieces with the juice and 2 tablespoons of the oil in a pot. Simmer, uncovered, for 15 minutes. Let cool.

Remove the shells from the shrimp but let the outer tip of the tail remain.

Grease a shallow, ovenproof dish, pour in the tomato sauce, and place the shrimp in the sauce with the tails facing upward. Cover with parsley, the soft cheese, and the butter in small dabs. Grind a fair amount of pepper over the dish and add a few drops of Tabasco sauce. No extra salt is needed if the cheese is salted. Drip the rest of the oil over the dish and place under the broiler until the shrimp are cooked and the dish has become golden brown. Serve with rice.

Vegetables

Asparagus Delight

Yield: 4 servings

1 9-ounce can asparagus or about 20 fresh asparagus, cooked and cooled
¾ cup crème fraîche or sour cream
1 jar red caviar

Place a pile of about 5-6 asparagus on each plate. Mix together the crème fraîche and red caviar. Dab it over the asparagus.

Baked Asparagus

Yield: 4 servings

16 stalks fat asparagus
Salt and freshly ground pepper
Sweet butter
1 lemon, cut into lengthwise wedges

Cut the asparagus just to fit a large, flat, ovenproof serving dish. With a vegetable peeler, lightly peel the heavy stalk to within 3 or 4 inches of the tip. Rinse the asparagus in cold water and arrange it in the dish, gently shaking off only the excess water. Sprinkle with salt and pepper and dot generously with butter. Cover the dish tightly with foil. Bake the asparagus at 350°F for 20 minutes or until it is tender-crisp. Serve with lemon wedges.

Asparagus with Dill

Yield: 4 servings

1½ pounds asparagus spears, about 28
Salt to taste, if desired
1 tablespoon butter, melted
1 tablespoon dill or parsley, finely chopped

Using a swivel-bladed paring knife, scrape the sides of the asparagus, leaving about 2 inches of the tops unscraped. Cut about 1 inch off the bottom of the asparagus stalks. Heat water in the bottom of a vegetable steamer; when it comes to a boil, place the asparagus in the top of the steamer. Cover and let steam 5 minutes.

Transfer the asparagus to a warm serving dish and sprinkle with salt, butter, and dill.

Home Baked Beans

Yield: 8 to 10 servings

2 cups dried pea beans
¾ pound lean salt pork
2 tablespoons molasses
5 tablespoons dark brown sugar
Boiling water
1 teaspoon dried English mustard
2 cups boiling water

Put the beans in a strainer and wash them under cold running water. Put them in a bowl and cover with cold water; soak overnight. Drain. Then cover with fresh water and heat slowly, keeping the water below boiling point. Cook until the skins burst open if a few beans are held on the end of a spoon and blown on.

Scald the pork by frying it briefly on all sides. Cut through the pork rind every ½ inch with 1-inch-deep cuts. Put the pork in a pot with the drained beans; cover.

Dissolve the sugar and molasses in boiling water. Add mustard to the cold water and stir into a paste. Add the paste to the molasses mixture and stir. Add the beans and pork. Add enough extra boiling water to cover the beans. Cover the bean pot and bake at 250°F for about 8 hours. Check every 2 hours to make sure the beans are covered with water.

Stuffed Avocado au Gratin

Yield: 4 servings

4 ripe avocados
1 package instant Hollandaise sauce
Milk and a little butter
4 to 6 ham slices, slivered
Grated Swiss cheese

Cut a "lid" off the avocados leaving the bottom part, which is to be filled. Remove the seed. Loosen the avocado meat and cut it into pieces.

Dilute the sauce powder with milk and a little butter. Add the ham and avocado pieces. Divide the mixture among the 4 larger avocado halves. Place them on aluminum foil or a cookie sheet on an oven rack. Cover them with a generous amount of cheese. Bake at 450°F about 15 minutes.

Banana Casserole

Yield: 4 to 6 servings

6 ripe bananas
½ cup orange sections
⅓ cup sugar
2 tablespoons orange juice
2 tablespoons lemon juice
Pinch salt

Peel the bananas; cut them lengthwise. Place them in a buttered dish.

Remove the membrane from the oranges; arrange the oranges on top of the bananas. Sprinkle sugar over the bananas. Add the orange and lemon juices, to which salt has been added.

Bake at 300° to 350°F for 30 to 45 minutes.

Baked Beans with Apples

Yield: 10 servings

2 pounds dried navy beans, soaked overnight
9 cups water
1 pound salt pork, diced
3 tart apples, peeled, cored, and coarsely cut
1 medium-sized onion, chopped
½ cup brown sugar, firmly packed
½ cup molasses
3 teaspoons dry mustard
3 tablespoons vinegar
¼ teaspoon pepper

Place the soaked beans and the salt pork in a kettle and cook until the beans are tender, about 1 hour.

Pour the bean mixture into a bean pot, add the remaining ingredients and bake, covered, 6 hours in a 300°F oven. Add more warm water during cooking if necessary.

Pinto Beans

Yield: 10 to 12 servings

3 quarts water
1 pound dried pinto beans, washed
1 1-pound can tomatoes
1 large onion, chopped
8 slices bacon, cut in 2-inch lengths
¾ cup celery, sliced
1½ teaspoons salt
¾ teaspoon ground cinnamon
6 tablespoons sugar
3 tablespoons vinegar

Put 3 quarts of water and the beans in a 6-quart kettle and simmer, covered, for 4 hours, or until the beans are tender. Add the rest of the ingredients.

Place the mixture in a 4-quart casserole; cover and bake in a 350°F oven 2 to 3 hours, or until done. Add water if necessary.

Butter Beans

Yield: 4 to 6 servings

2 pounds small butter beans
½ cup water
2 tablespoons bacon drippings
1 teaspoon seasoned salt
1 onion, cut in half
½ teaspoon pepper
1 clove garlic (optional)
1 teaspoon salt
2 teaspoons cornstarch
1 tablespoon butter

Put all the ingredients, except the cornstarch and butter, into a saucepan. Cook until the beans are tender, about 10 minutes. Remove the onion and garlic; drain the beans, reserving the liquid.

Slightly thicken the liquid with cornstarch. Add butter and mix well; pour over the beans. Serve at once.

Fresh Green Beans with Cherry Tomatoes

Yield: 6 servings

1 pound fresh green beans
1¼ teaspoons salt
3 tablespoons butter
½ teaspoon sugar
Pinch freshly ground pepper
1½ tablespoons fresh parsley, chopped
8 cherry tomatoes, halved

Wash the beans, remove the tips, and cut them into 1-inch pieces. Place the beans in a saucepan with 1-inch of boiling water and 1 teaspoon of salt.

Asparagus Delight

Cook 5 minutes; cover. Cook over medium heat 10 to 15 minutes, until just crisp-tender. Drain, if necessary. Add the butter, sugar, pepper, remaining salt, and parsley; toss lightly until the butter is melted and beans are coated. Place in a serving bowl and garnish with cherry tomatoes.

Ham-Seasoned Green Beans

Yield: 6 servings

1½ pounds green beans, broken into short pieces, or 2 10-ounce packages frozen cut green beans
2 small onions, quartered
½ stalk celery, sliced
About 2 ounces cooked ham, cut into bite-sized pieces
2 teaspoons salt
Pepper to taste
½ cup water
1 tablespoon butter or margarine

Place the beans in a 2-quart saucepan. Add the remaining ingredients; simmer until the beans are tender, 12 to 20 minutes.

Dilled Green Beans

Yield: 6 servings

⅔ cup onion, chopped
3 tablespoons butter or margarine
1 cup water
½ cup chili sauce
½ teaspoon dillweed
1½ tablespoons cornstarch
2 tablespoons water
3 cups cooked or canned green beans

Sauté the onion in melted butter in a saucepan until transparent. Stir in the water, chili sauce, and dillweed.

Mix the cornstarch and water together and add to the onion mixture. Cook, stirring, until thickened. Combine the sauce and beans.

Baked Limas in Cream

Yield: 4 to 6 servings

1 10-ounce package frozen lima beans
½ teaspoon seasoned salt
Freshly ground pepper to taste
¾ cup milk or cream

Allow the beans to thaw slightly so they can be put into a greased 1-quart casserole. Sprinkle the seasonings over the beans. Pour milk on top. Cover the casserole; bake at 350°F for 20 minutes; stir once. Reduce heat to 300°F; bake 20 minutes more. When the beans are tender, the dish is ready to be served.

Baked Broccoli

Yield: 8 servings

1 large egg
⅔ cup mayonnaise
10¾ ounce can cream of mushroom soup
20 ounces frozen chopped broccoli, cooked and drained well
1 medium onion, finely chopped
1 cup Swiss cheese, grated and packed loosely
½ cup fine dry bread crumbs, mixed with 2 tablespoons butter
Paprika

Stir the egg slightly with a whisk. Add the mayonnaise and soup and stir to blend. Stir in the cooked broccoli, onion, and cheese. Pour into a ½-quart baking dish. Sprinkle with the bread crumb mixture and top with paprika. Bake in a preheated 350°F oven until hot and the sides begin to bubble, about 35 minutes.

Fresh Lima Beans in Parsley Cream

Yield: 4 servings

3 pounds fresh lima beans
Salt and white pepper
2 tablespoons butter or margarine
½ cup cream
1 tablespoon parsley, chopped

Cut off the outer edge of each lima bean pod with scissors; open the shell. Shuck the beans into a small saucepan; cover with boiling water. Add 1 teaspoon of salt and cook until tender, 20 to 25 minutes unless the beans are very small.

Drain well and return to pan. Heat with butter and cream. Season to taste with salt and pepper. Serve in individual bowls; sprinkle with parsley.

Harvard Beets

Yield: 4 to 5 servings

1 1-pound can sliced beets
2 teaspoons cornstarch
¼ cup sugar
¼ cup cider vinegar

Drain the beets, saving ¼ cup liquid. In a 1-quart saucepan, stir together the cornstarch and sugar; gradually stir in the beet juice and vinegar. Cook over medium heat, stirring constantly, until thickened. Add the beets and heat gently.

Beets with Orange Sauce

Yield: 6 servings

¼ cup sugar
¾ teaspoon salt
2 tablespoons cornstarch
¾ cup orange juice
2 tablespoons lemon juice
1 tablespoon butter or margarine
3 cups beets, cooked or canned, sliced, drained

Mix the sugar, salt, and cornstarch well. Stir in the orange juice. Cook until thickened, stirring constantly. Remove from the heat; stir in the lemon juice and butter. Pour the sauce over the beets; stir carefully. Heat and serve.

Pickled Beets

Yield: 2 pints

4½ pounds beets
Water
1 piece horseradish

pickle juice
1⅔ cups vinegar
2⅓ cups water
½ tablespoon salt
1¼ cups sugar
10 white peppercorns
8 whole cloves
5 allspice corns

Brush and rinse the beets well without damaging the skins or root tips. Boil them in water until almost soft. Rinse the beets under cold running water. Pull off the skins.

Prepare the pickle juice by boiling together the vinegar, water, salt, sugar, and spices.

Place the beets in the juice and boil them until soft. Place the beets and juice in earthenware or glass jars. Put small pieces of horseradish on top. Close the lids tightly, and store in a cool place.

Variation: Boil large beets until partially soft. Peel them and cut into slices. Place in jars with the horseradish on top. Pour the hot juice over the beets.

Marinated Broccoli

Yield: 10 servings

3 pounds broccoli, cut in strips
1 cup cider vinegar
1 tablespoon sugar
1 tablespoon dillweed
1 tablespoon pepper
1 tablespoon salt
1 tablespoon garlic salt
1¼ cup vegetable oil

Combine all the ingredients and pour them over the broccoli. Marinate overnight in the refrigerator, shaking occasionally; serve cold. Before serving, pour off some marinade.

Broccoli-Potato Casserole

Yield: 4 servings

1 10-ounce package frozen chopped broccoli
¼ cup butter
1 small onion, finely chopped
2 medium-sized potatoes
Salt and pepper to taste

Cook the broccoli according to package directions; drain. In a small skillet, melt the butter; add the onion and cook gently until yellowed.

Pare the potatoes and steam or cook in boiling water until tender; drain and put through a food mill or ricer set over the top of a double boiler. With a fork or spoon, mix the broccoli, onion, and salt and pepper with the potatoes; cover and reheat over boiling water.

Sautéed Broccoli

Yield: 4 servings

1 pound fresh young broccoli
Boiling salted water
3 tablespoons olive oil
1 clove garlic, peeled, chopped
Salt and pepper

Cut off dry woody stems of the broccoli; trim all discolored parts and dead leaves. Separate into small spears; peel the stalks with a vegetable peeler. Cook 3 to 5 minutes in 1-inch of boiling salted water. Drain thoroughly. Heat the oil with the garlic and toss the broccoli in the oil for 1 minute. Season.

Brussels Sprouts

Yield: 6 servings

2 quarts Brussels sprouts
2 tablespoons butter
¼ cup lemon juice
1 cup sour cream
¼ cup fresh parsley, minced
½ teaspoon salt
⅛ teaspoon pepper
Sliced pimiento-stuffed olives (optional)

Stuffed Avocado au Gratin

Wash and trim the sprouts, removing any loose or yellow leaves. Cut an "X" in the stems so the sprouts will cook faster. Soak the sprouts in cool, salted water.

Melt the butter in a skillet over medium heat. Drain the sprouts, then add them to the skillet. Cover and steam about 10 minutes, shaking the skillet occasionally.

Add the lemon juice and steam 2 minutes more; then add the rest of the ingredients, except the olives. Heat, but do not boil. Serve topped with sliced olives, if desired.

Creamy Brussels Sprouts and Bell Peppers

Yield: 4 servings

1½ pounds Brussels sprouts
2 red bell peppers
¼ onion, chopped
1 bay leaf
2 tablespoons oil
1 potato, cubed
¼ cup stock
2 tablespoons butter
½ teaspoon salt

Clean and trim the Brussels sprouts; cut the large ones in half. Cut the peppers into ½-inch pieces. Sauté the onion in oil with a bay leaf until the onion is soft. Add the pepper pieces and stir briefly. Add Brussels sprouts and stir again. Add the stock and steam all the vegetables until just tender.

Steam or boil the potato cubes separately and purée them in a blender with butter, salt, and some of the juice from the vegetables. Stir together with the sprouts and peppers.

Pennsylvania Dutch Cabbage

Yield: 6 servings

5 cups cabbage, shredded
4 slices bacon, diced
½ teaspoon salt in 2 quarts boiling water
2 tablespoons brown sugar
2 tablespoons flour
⅓ cup cider vinegar
½ cup water
1 small onion, minced
Salt and pepper to taste

Cook the cabbage in 2 quarts of boiling, salted water for 7 minutes.

Meanwhile, fry the bacon pieces and set aside. Add the sugar and flour to the bacon fat; blend over low heat. Add the remaining ingredients and bacon pieces. Cook and stir until thickened and smooth. Pour over the drained, cooked cabbage in a casserole dish.

Fruity Red Cabbage

Yield: 6 to 8 servings

1 head of red cabbage
3½ tablespoons margarine
⅓ cup red wine
⅓ cup water
1 onion
4 whole cloves
2 teaspoons salt
½ teaspoon black pepper
8 to 10 plums without seeds, cut into pieces.
1 large tangy apple, peeled, cored, and cubed

Rinse the head of cabbage. Divide it into 4 parts. Remove the core. Shred the cabbage.

Heat the margarine in a pan.

Quickly stir the cabbage and heated margarine together in a large pot. Add the wine and water.

Peel the onion and divide it in half. Stick 2 cloves into each half. Place them in with the cabbage, adding the salt and black pepper. Let this come to a boil. Cover and let simmer about 15 minutes. Add the plums and apple. Let the cabbage boil, covered, for another 30 to 45 minutes, until it is soft. Remove the onion with cloves.

This can be frozen and kept for several months.

Sauerkraut

Yield: 4 servings

cabbage
6½ to 7 pounds cabbage
2 tangy apples
3 tablespoons coarse salt
2 teaspoons caraway seeds
10 dried juniper berries (optional)

sauerkraut
14 ounces sauerkraut
2 cups broth or pork drippings
1 onion with 1 clove inserted in it
1 teaspoon caraway seeds

To make sauerkraut:

Clean and rinse the cabbage. Put aside several whole leaves. Separate the head of cabbage and take away the core. Shred the cabbage into fine pieces.

Core the apples and cut them into thin slices.

In a large crock, layer the shredded cabbage with the salt, apple slices, caraway seeds, and, if desired, the juniper berries. Pound each layer hard so that the cabbage becomes juicy. Cover with the whole cabbage leaves. Place a plate with something heavy on it over the mixture. Let the cabbage stand for 3 to 4 days at room temperature and then in a cool place.

After about 14 days the cabbage is ready to be cooked. It will keep for several months if stored in a cool place, such as a refrigerator vegetable bin.

To cook sauerkraut, rinse it and let it drain. Place it in the broth with the onion and caraway seeds. Let simmer until soft, about 30 to 45 minutes. Season as desired.

Carrot Fritters

Yield: 6 to 8 servings

1 bunch carrots or 2 1-pound cans sliced carrots
1 egg
1 tablespoon sugar
3 tablespoons flour
Salt and pepper to taste
1 teaspoon baking powder
Deep fat for frying

If using raw carrots, cook them in a small amount of water until very tender. Mash the carrots; when pasty, add the egg and sugar. Next add the flour, salt, pepper, and baking powder; stir until well blended.

Drop by spoonfuls into deep fat (375°F). The fritters will brown quickly when the fat is the right temperature. Drain on paper towels; keep warm until all are finished. Serve at once.

Glazed Carrots

Yield: 4 to 6 servings

10 to 12 small young carrots, washed and trimmed
2 tablespoons margarine
1 tablespoon brown sugar
2 tablespoons honey
2 tablespoons fresh mint

Cook the carrots in a small amount of boiling, salted water for 10 minutes. When tender, drain; set aside.

Melt the margarine in a medium skillet. Add the sugar and honey; blend. Add the carrots and cook 3 or 4 minutes over low heat, stirring so each carrot is glazed. Sprinkle with mint.

Carrot Pudding

Yield: 6 to 8 servings

1 cup shortening
½ cup brown sugar
1 egg, beaten with 1 tablespoon water
2 cups carrots, grated
1½ cups flour
½ teaspoon baking soda
½ teaspoon nutmeg
1 teaspoon baking powder
½ teaspoon salt
½ teaspoon cinnamon

Vegetables

Cream the shortening and sugar. Add the rest of the ingredients and mix well. Pour the mixture into a greased ring mold or loaf pan. Refrigerate overnight. Remove ½ hour before baking. Bake at 350°F for 1 hour.

Carrots with Walnuts

Yield: 8 servings

5 cups carrot sticks
1½ cups water
½ teaspoon salt
½ cup butter or margarine, melted
2 teaspoons honey
½ teaspoon salt
¼ teaspoon coarse pepper
2 tablespoons lemon juice
¼ teaspoon lemon peel, grated
½ cup walnuts, coarsely broken

Cook the carrots in salted water until tender; drain.

In a saucepan, combine the remaining ingredients, except the walnuts, and heat. Pour this sauce over the carrots. Mix in the walnuts.

Cauliflower Chestnut Casserole

Yield: 6 servings

1 medium-sized cauliflower
Boiling water
1¼ teaspoons salt
2 tablespoons butter or margarine
1 pound chestnuts (see instructions below)
¼ teaspoon white pepper
2 tablespoons hot water

Break the cauliflower into florets. Place it in a saucepan with 1 inch of boiling water and 1 teaspoon of salt. Bring to a boil and cook uncovered 5 minutes. Cover and cook 5 minutes longer. Drain.

Put a layer of cauliflower in a buttered casserole, cover with a layer of prepared chestnuts, dot with butter or margarine, and sprinkle lightly with white pepper mixed with the remaining ¼ teaspoon salt.

Continue until all the ingredients are used. Add 2 tablespoons of hot water. Cover and bake in a preheated 350°F oven for 30 minutes.

To prepare the chestnuts: Prick them with a fork or split the top end in a cross slit.

Place in a saucepan, cover them with cold water, and bring to a boil. Boil 1 minute; drain and remove the outer shells. Return to the saucepan and cook in boiling, salted water until tender.

The brown coating of the chestnuts will come off during boiling. Chop the chestnuts semifine.

If chestnuts are not available, use ¾ cup sliced, blanched almonds.

Pickled Beets

Boiled Cauliflower

Yield: 8 servings

2 hard-cooked egg yolks
1 teaspoon dried parsley flakes
2 tablespoons sour cream
¼ teaspoon white pepper
1 head cauliflower
1 teaspoon salt
¼ cup butter
3 tablespoons bread crumbs

Mash the egg yolks in a small bowl. Add the parsley, sour cream, and white pepper; blend. Set aside.

Wash the cauliflower head; remove the outside leaves. Cover the bottom of a pan large enough to accommodate the cauliflower with 1 to 2 inches of water. Add salt and bring to a rapid boil. Add the cauliflower; cover. Boil 25 minutes or until fork-tender. Drain immediately.

Melt the butter; stir in the bread crumbs. Pour the buttered crumbs over the cauliflower; garnish with the egg-yolk mixture.

Cauliflower with Green Sauce

Yield: 4 servings

1 large cauliflower, or 2 small ones
4 tomatoes
1 tablespoon basil
½ teaspoon herb salt

green sauce
1 package frozen chopped spinach
1 teaspoon herb salt
1 or 2 cloves garlic
⅔ cup sour cream
¾ cup grated cheese
Black pepper

Cook the cauliflower in plenty of boiling, salted water for about 15 minutes. Halve the tomatoes, and sprinkle with basil and herb salt. Bake the tomatoes in a preheated 425°F oven for 10 minutes.

Let the spinach defrost and cook briefly over a gentle heat. Mix all sauce ingredients in a blender, then heat.

Combine the cauliflower and tomatoes and serve the sauce separately.

Creamed Celery with Pecans

Yield: 4 to 6 servings

4 cups celery, cut diagonally into ½-inch pieces
1 can cream of celery soup
1 teaspoon salt
¾ cup pecan halves
Buttered bread crumbs

Place the celery in a greased casserole. Add the undiluted soup and sprinkle with salt. Sprinkle with pecans; cover all with buttered bread crumbs. Bake at 400°F for 20 minutes.

Chick Pea Ratatouille

Yield: 4 servings

1 or 2 garlic cloves (optional)
1 onion
1 green pepper
2 tablespoons butter
2 cans chopped tomatoes
Juice of half a lemon
1 teaspoon herb salt
Black pepper
1 can chick peas
¾ cup sour cream
1 bunch parsley, finely chopped

Peel and finely chop the garlic and onion. Shred the pepper.

In a heavy saucepan fry the onion and garlic in butter until soft but not browned. Add the pepper, tomatoes, and lemon juice. Season with herb salt and black pepper. Simmer to reduce liquid for 7 or 8 minutes. Mix in the chick peas and bring to boil.

Serve sprinkled with parsley and a spoonful of sour cream. Black bread goes well with this dish.

Confetti Corn

Yield: 6 servings

6 ears corn
¼ cup butter
¼ cup green sweet pepper, chopped
¼ cup red sweet pepper, chopped
1 tablespoon fresh parsley, finely chopped

Remove the husks and silks from the corn. Cook in boiling water 8 to 10 minutes, until tender; drain. Cool until easily handled; cut the kernels from the cobs.

Melt the butter in a saucepan; add the peppers and parsley. Cook over low heat, stirring constantly, until the peppers are tender. Stir in the corn and heat through.

Cabbage and Sauerkraut

Southern Corn Fritters

Yield: 4 to 6 servings

1 1-pound can whole-kernel corn, drained
1 egg
½ teaspoon salt
¼ cup milk
1 cup flour
2 teaspoons baking powder
2 teaspoons butter, melted
½ teaspoon sugar
Deep fat for frying

While the corn is draining, mix the egg, salt, milk, flour, baking powder, melted butter, and sugar. Stir with a long-handled, wooden spoon. Add the drained corn. Allow the mixture to sit 5 minutes. Drop by teaspoonfuls into hot fat. Cook until puffy and golden brown. Drain on paper towels; transfer to a warmed platter.

Corn Alabama Style

Yield: Varies

Fresh ears of corn
Water
Salt
Butter, softened
Dill
Parsley
Chives
Leek
Tarragon

Rinse and shuck the corn. Save the best pieces of husk. Rinse the corn and husks again. Place the husks in the bottom of a shallow pan. Save a few husks to cover the corn. Add the corn. Cover with husks and boil in lightly salted water for 10 to 12 minutes. Serve with herb butter and salt.

To make the herb butter, season soft butter with dill, parsley, chives, leek, tarragon, or spices of your choice.

Corn Casserole with Ham and Cheese

Yield: 3 or 4 servings

6 ears of corn (cut the corn off the cob)
3 or 4 slices ham
1¼ cups milk
3 eggs
1⅔ to 2 cups grated sharp cheese
Pinch of nutmeg

Place the corn and ham in a greased ovenproof pan.

Beat together eggs and milk. Add cheese and nutmeg. Pour this mixture over the corn and ham. Bake at 400°F for 25 minutes.

Fresh Southern Corn Pudding

Yield: 6 servings

2 cups fresh corn, cut from the cob
2 teaspoons sugar
1½ teaspoons salt
⅛ teaspoon pepper
3 eggs, lightly beaten
2 tablespoons butter
2 cups milk

Combine the corn, sugar, salt, and pepper in a bowl. Add the eggs and mix well.

Place the butter and milk in a saucepan; heat until the butter is melted, then stir into the corn mixture. Turn into a greased, 1-quart casserole; place the casserole in a pan of hot water. Bake in a preheated 350°F oven 1 hour or until a knife inserted in the center comes out clean. Garnish with fresh parsley.

Cucumbers in Dill

Yield: 6 to 8 servings

4 cucumbers, peeled and thinly sliced
1 cup boiling water
¾ cup sour cream
¼ cup lemon juice
3 tablespoons dill, minced
1½ teaspoons salt
⅛ teaspoon pepper
1 teaspoon sugar

Pour boiling water over the cucumbers. Let them stand 5 minutes; drain. Plunge into ice water, then drain.

Mix the remaining ingredients together; pour them over the cucumbers, tossing until well mixed. Chill 30 minutes before serving.

Cucumbers in Sour Cream

Yield: 4 servings

4 cucumbers, garden-fresh
1 cup sour cream with chives
1 small bunch leaf lettuce, cleaned
1 tablespoon parsley

Wash cucumbers thoroughly; slice into small wedges.

Combine sour cream and cucumbers; mix to coat cucumbers.

Arrange lettuce leaves in salad bowls; pour ½ cup cucumber mixture on lettuce bed. Garnish with parsley.

Sour Pickled Cucumbers

Yield: 6 pints

4½ pounds small green cucumbers
Dill sprigs
Several bay leaves
2 tablespoons yellow mustard seeds
1 piece horseradish, cut into small cubes

pickle juice
3¼ cups water
1½ tablespoons white vinegar
1⅔ pounds sugar
⅓ cup fine salt

Brush the cucumbers extremely well in warm water, then cut them into rather thick slices. In jars, alternate the cucumber slices with sprigs of dill, bay leaves, mustard seeds, and horseradish cubes.

Bring all pickle-juice ingredients to a boil. Pour juice over the cucumbers. Let the mixture become cold. Seal jars and store in a cold place. After 2 weeks, they will have obtained their full taste.

Grandfather's Eggplant

Yield: 4 servings

1 medium-large eggplant, chopped
1 small onion, finely chopped
1 tablespoon butter
1 4-ounce can skinless and boneless herrings or anchovies
1 rounded teaspoon flour
1 cup crème fraîche or sour cream
¼ cup finely chopped parsley
About 3 ounces fine grated cheese, preferably aged Gruyère

Divide the eggplant lengthwise. Dig out the flesh from the skin, and finely chop the inside flesh.

Sauté the onion in the butter until soft but not brown. Drain and mash the herrings. Add to the onion.

Save the herring liquid. Whip it together with the flour. Add to the herring mixture. Let simmer a few minutes. Add the crème fraîche. Let simmer until it thickens. Blend in the eggplant and parsley. Remove from the heat.

Fill the eggplant skins with the mixture. Place them on an ovenproof plate. Sprinkle the grated cheese over the eggplants. Bake in 400°F oven for 30 to 35 minutes or until the top has browned. Let the dish cool before serving as an opening course, preferably with beer.

If this dish is served warm, it is rather gooey. When served cooled or cold, it is delicious.

Baked Hominy

Yield: 6 servings

2 cups milk
2 cups water
1 cup quick-cooking hominy grits
1 teaspoon salt
2 eggs
1 cup sharp Cheddar cheese, grated
2 tablespoons butter

Mix the milk, water, grits, and salt in a heavy saucepan and simmer until thick, about 5 minutes. Stir occasionally.

Beat the eggs; add a little of the grits mixture to warm them and then add the eggs to the saucepan. Mix in the cheese. Turn into a well-greased, 1-quart baking dish; dot with butter. Bake in a preheated 350°F oven for 35-45 minutes, or until lightly brown on top.

Creole Lentils

Yield: 4 servings

½ cup dried lentils
1 tablespoon butter
1 green pepper, finely chopped
1 small onion, finely chopped
1 cup tomatoes, chopped
½ teaspoon salt
⅛ teaspoon pepper
⅛ teaspoon file powder
2 cups cooked whole-grain rice

Cover the lentils with water and soak them overnight. Drain, cover with fresh water, and simmer for 50 minutes or until tender.

Melt the butter in a skillet; sauté the green pepper and onion until limp. Add the tomatoes, salt, pepper, and filé powder, if desired. Drain the lentils and add to the skillet; simmer until heated through. Serve hot over cooked rice.

Fried Okra

Yield: 4 to 6 servings

1 pound fresh young okra
Salt and pepper to taste
½ to 1 cup cornmeal
Fat for deep frying

Wash the okra and cut it into 1-inch pieces. Liberally sprinkle the pieces with salt and pepper.

Put the cornmeal into a brown paper bag; shake the okra in the bag until each piece is coated. Fry in deep fat (375°F) until golden brown and crisp; drain on paper towels.

Cauliflower with Green Sauce

Fried Eggplant

Yield: 6 to 8 servings

1 eggplant, peeled and thinly sliced
Salt
1 egg, beaten
Pepper
Bread crumbs
Oil

Generously salt each eggplant slice. Place the slices in a pile and top with a weighted plate. Drain for ½ hour.

Dip the eggplant in egg mixed with milk and pepper, then in bread crumbs. Fry quickly in hot oil until golden brown.

Stuffed Eggplant

Yield: 6 servings

3 small eggplants (about 2 pounds)
1 pound lean ground lamb or beef round
1 16-ounce can stewed tomatoes
1 cup tomato juice
½ teaspoon dried mint or marjoram
¼ teaspoon ground cinnamon
¼ teaspoon ground nutmeg
Salt and pepper, to taste
6 teaspoons Italian-seasoned bread crumbs
6 teaspoons sharp Romano cheese, grated
1 tablespoon lemon juice

Cut the eggplants in half lengthwise. Scoop out the centers and reserve the scooped-out eggplant pulp. Dice the pulp.

Spread the meat in a shallow layer in a nonstick skillet. Brown it with no fat added. Break it into chunks and turn it to brown evenly. Drain and discard any melted fat.

Add the diced eggplant pulp to the meat mixture. Stir in the tomatoes, juice, mint, cinnamon, nutmeg, salt, and pepper. Simmer, uncovered 15 to 20 minutes, until most of the liquid has evaporated.

Spoon the meat mixture into the eggplant shells and sprinkle it with bread crumbs, Romano cheese, and lemon juice. Arrange the stuffed eggplant halves on a shallow baking pan; bake uncovered, at 375°F, about 20 to 25 minutes, until the eggplant is tender.

Glazed Onions

Yield: 6 servings

3 tablespoons butter
2 tablespoons sugar
24 small white onions, peeled
½ cup chicken broth

Melt the butter in a large skillet; add the sugar,

then the onions. Sauté, stirring, until golden brown. Add the broth, cover, and cook down until syrupy and the onions are done. Baste frequently.

Onion Pie

Yield: 6 to 8 servings

Pie dough for a single-crust, 9-inch pie
3 tablespoons shortening
1 clove garlic, mashed to a pulp with 1 teaspoon salt
2 pounds onions, peeled and sliced (about 4 cups)
3 eggs
½ teaspoon freshly ground black pepper
8 to 12 black Greek olives, pitted and halved
4 to 6 anchovies (optional)

Prepare the pie dough according to package directions. Let it stand at room temperature to dry after you fit it into the pie pan.

Heat the shortening in a large skillet. When hot, add the mashed garlic. Add the onions at once. Stir with a large spoon; reduce the heat to low after 2 to 3 minutes and continue cooking, stirring frequently. Don't let the onions brown, but be sure at least half of them are golden in color and that all are fully cooked, translucent, and limp.

When onions are cooked, remove from heat.

Beat the eggs with a fork. Brush the surface of the pie dough generously with beaten egg. Place the pie shell in a preheated 375°F oven. Stir black pepper into the onions. After the pie shell has baked 2 to 3 minutes, remove it from the oven, spoon the onions into the shell and pour the remaining beaten egg over the onions. Bake 12 to 15 minutes. Remove from the oven, distribute olives evenly over the pie, and, if you use anchovies, chop them in small pieces and sprinkle them on top. Return to the oven for a minute or 2, cool, and serve as a first course for dinner or as a main course for luncheon.

Honey-Orange Glazed Parsnips

Yield: 6 servings

3 cups parsnips, diagonally sliced
¾ cup boiling water
½ teaspoon salt
2 teaspoons butter
1 tablespoon honey
¼ cup orange juice
1 teaspoon orange peel, grated

Place the parsnips in a saucepan with water and salt and cook until tender, about 10 minutes; drain, and combine the remaining ingredients and heat. Add the parsnips.

Chick Pea Ratatouille

Southern Peanut Loaf

Yield: 8 servings

1¼ cups crunchy peanut butter
1½ cups cooked baby lima beans
¼ cup onion, finely chopped
½ teaspoon basil
1 teaspoon salt
¼ teaspoon pepper
1¼ cups soft bread crumbs
1½ cups American cheese, grated
1½ cups milk
2 tablespoons parsley, chopped
4 eggs, well beaten
1½ cups well-seasoned tomato sauce

Combine all the ingredients except the tomato sauce, mixing well. Spoon the mixture into a greased 9×5×3 loaf pan. Bake in a 350°F oven 40 to 45 minutes. Serve hot with tomato sauce.

Peas and Cucumbers

Yield: 4 servings

1 medium-sized cucumber
2 pounds fresh green peas, shelled
¼ cup water

½ small head lettuce, shredded (about 2 cups)
2 tablespoons butter or margarine
1 teaspoon sugar
½ teaspoon salt
⅛ teaspoon pepper
¼ cup sour cream or plain yogurt
1 teaspoon lemon juice
Paprika

Cut the unpeeled cucumber lengthwise into fourths, then crosswise into 1-inch pieces. Heat the cucumber pieces, peas, and water to boiling; reduce the heat. Cover and simmer until the peas are tender, about 10 minutes; drain. Stir in the lettuce, butter, sugar, salt, and pepper; heat until the lettuce is hot. Mix the sour cream and lemon juice. Toss or serve with vegetables. Sprinkle with paprika.

Creamed Peas and Corn

Yield: 6 servings

1 10-ounce package frozen peas
1 10-ounce package frozen corn
2 tablespoons butter
2 tablespoons flour
1 cup milk
½ teaspoon salt
¼ teaspoon white pepper

Cook the peas and corn as directed on the packages. While the vegetables are cooking, melt the butter in a saucepan. Add the flour; cook 2 minutes, stirring constantly. Add the milk, salt, and pepper. Cook until thick, then remove from the heat.

Drain the cooked vegetables. Add the sauce and mix well. Serve immediately.

Corn Alabama Style

Black-Eyed Peas Supreme

Yield: 8 servings

2 1-pound cans black-eyed peas, drained
1 onion, sliced into thin rings
½ cup olive oil
¼ cup wine vinegar
1 medium-sized clove garlic, mashed
1 tablespoon Worcestershire sauce
1 teaspoon salt
Pepper to taste

Place the peas and onion in an ovenproof bowl. Combine the oil, vinegar, and seasonings in a small pan; bring to a boil. Immediately pour the mixture over the peas and onions; stir gently. Refrigerate several hours or overnight.

New Peas

Yield: 6 to 8 servings

4 cups peas, shelled
2 teaspoons sugar
2 teaspoons salt
6 pea pods
1 small green onion with top, chopped
Water
2 tablespoons butter
½ teaspoon pepper
1 cup light cream

Place the peas in a saucepan with the sugar, salt, pea pods, onion, and enough water to cover; cook for 10 to 15 minutes, or until the water has almost evaporated and the peas are tender. Add the butter and heat until melted. Add the pepper and cream and heat.

Sugar Peas

Yield: 4 servings

1 pound sugar peas
¾ pound slice of precooked ham
1 teaspoon sugar
1 very small onion
Salt
2 tablespoons butter, melted

String the peas. Cube the ham. Bring to a boil in unsalted water. Add the peas, sugar, and onion. Cook about 20 minutes, until the peas are tender. Drain. Salt to taste and coat with melted butter.

Corn Casserole with Ham and Cheese

Piquant Peppers

Yield: 4 servings

2 cloves garlic, minced
2 tablespoons olive oil
4 red bell peppers (or 2 red and 2 green), seeded and deveined, cut into thin strips
2 tablespoons red wine vinegar
Salt

In a large skillet, cook the garlic for 3 minutes in olive oil until golden.

Turn the heat up to high and add the peppers. Toss for 5 minutes until the peppers are hot and still crisp. Turn off the heat. Deglaze the pan with red wine vinegar. Taste and season with salt if desired.

Salt Pickles

Yield: About 6 pints

20 fine, firm green cucumbers
2 onions, peeled and sliced
20 whole allspice, crushed
Dill sprigs
Black currant leaves
A piece of horseradish cut into small pieces

pickle juice
4 quarts water
2 cups course salt
⅓ cup white wine vinegar

Brush the cucumbers extremely well in warm water. In jars, alternate the cucumbers with the onions, allspice, dill, currant, and horseradish.

Boil together the water, salt, and vinegar. Let cool. Pour the pickling juice over the cucumbers, seal, and store in a cold place. The pickles are done after 2 to 3 weeks.

Potatoes and Apples

Yield: 6 servings

4 medium-sized potatoes
2 medium-sized tart apples
Juice of 1 lemon
3 tablespoons butter
1 small onion, thinly sliced
¼ teaspoon salt
¼ teaspoon cinnamon
⅛ teaspoon cloves
3 slices bread, toasted and cubed
2 to 3 eggs
½ cup milk
½ cup half-and-half
½ teaspoon sugar

Put the potatoes in boiling, salted water. Cover and reduce the heat to simmer; cook 8 to 10 min-utes, or until tender. Drain. Refrigerate until chilled or overnight.

Peel the potatoes, then grate them coarsely. Peel and core the apples. Slice them thinly and toss with lemon juice.

Melt the butter in a large skillet. Add the potatoes, apples, onion, salt, cinnamon, and cloves; cook 5 minutes. Add the bread cubes to the potato mixture. Lightly beat the eggs, milk, and sugar; pour them over the potato-bread mixture and toss lightly.

Transfer the mixture to a buttered 12 × 8-inch baking dish. Bake at 375°F 10 to 15 minutes, or until the top is browned and crisp.

Stuffed Peppers

Yield: 6 servings

6 large green peppers, halved lengthwise and seeded
2½ teaspoons salt
1 pound ground beef
1 medium-sized onion, chopped medium-fine
1 medium-sized carrot, pared and grated medium-fine
2 cups cooked brown rice
½ to 1 teaspoon dried crushed oregano
1 15-ounce can tomato sauce

Cover the peppers with boiling water and add ¼ teaspoon of salt; boil 5 minutes, then drain. Place them in a single layer in a 13½ × 8¾ × 1¾-inch baking dish.

In a 10-inch skillet over moderate heat, cook the beef and onion, crumbling with a fork, until the meat loses its red color. Stir in the carrot, rice, 1½ teaspoons of salt, oregano, and ½ of the tomato sauce; fill the peppers with the mixture. Spread the remaining tomato sauce over the meat mixture. Bake in a preheated 350°F oven, basting every 15 minutes with pan juices until the peppers are tender and the meat mixture is hot—about 45 minutes.

Potato Balls

Yield: 4 servings

4 firm, large potatoes, peeled
Water
Butter

Scoop round balls out of the potatoes with the help of a melon baller (see the picture). Take out these balls as close to each other as possible. The easiest way to do this is to cut and scoop at the same time with the melon baller when going down into the potato.

Boil the potato balls for several minutes in water; then fry them in butter until they are golden brown.

Leftovers from the potatoes can be made into regular mashed potatoes.

Sour Pickled Cucumbers

Brown Potatoes

Yield: 8 servings

12 medium-sized potatoes, peeled and cut in half lengthwise
2 cups beef suet, chopped
Salt and pepper to taste

Place the potatoes in a pan of salted water and boil 8 minutes. Drain. Melt the beef suet in a shallow, ovenproof pan. Add the potatoes and bake in a 325°F oven about 1 hour, or until tender, turning occasionally. Season with salt and pepper.

Potatoes in Buttermilk

Yield: 4 servings

2 tablespoons butter or margarine
2 cups potatoes, peeled and chopped
½ teaspoon salt
⅛ teaspoon coarsely ground pepper
1 cup thick buttermilk

Melt the butter in a skillet. Cook the potatoes until browned. Add salt, pepper, and buttermilk; cook over low heat until the potatoes are tender and liquid thickened. Sprinkle with paprika.

New Potatoes With Herbed Cottage-Cheese Sauce

Yield: 6 to 8 servings

2 to 3 pounds small potatoes
Salt

herbed cottage-cheese sauce
½ cup plain yogurt
1½ cups cottage cheese, creamed in blender
1 onion, finely chopped
4 hard-cooked eggs
1 tablespoon lemon juice
Salt and pepper to taste
3 tablespoons chopped chives or scallions, thinly sliced

Scrub the potatoes with a soft brush; do not peel. Boil in salted water 20 to 30 minutes, until tender.

Stir the yogurt into the cottage cheese; add the onion. Strain the egg yolks through a sieve; chop the egg whites. Add to the cottage-cheese mixture. Season with lemon juice, salt, and pepper. Stir in the chives. Serve the sauce with the potatoes.

Baked Potatoes with Crab Stuffing

Yield: 4 to 6 servings

4 medium-large baking potatoes, baked
½ cup butter
¼ cup heavy cream
1 tablespoon onion, finely grated
1 cup sharp Cheddar cheese, grated
1 cup flaked crabmeat, picked over
¼ pound mushrooms, sliced and sautéed
⅛ teaspoon pepper
1 teaspoon salt

As soon as the potatoes are cooked, cut them in half lengthwise and scoop out the pulp, taking care not to tear the skins. Mash the potatoes thoroughly (or put through a ricer); heat the butter and cream over very low heat until the butter melts. Beat the butter-cream mixture into the potatoes. Stir in the grated onion, ⅔ of the cheese, crabmeat, and mushrooms and season with salt and pepper. Pile the mixture into the potato shells and sprinkle with the remaining cheese. Bake in a 350°F oven until the cheese melts and the potatoes are very hot, about 20 minutes. To brown the tops, run the potatoes under the broiler a few seconds.

Hashed Brown Potatoes

Yield: 6 servings

3 cups potatoes, cooked and cubed
¼ cup onion, minced
¼ cup parsley, minced
3 tablespoons flour
1½ teaspoons salt
½ teaspoon pepper
¼ cup light cream
3 tablespoons bacon drippings

Mix the potatoes, onion, parsley, flour, salt, and pepper together. Add the cream and stir.

Heat 2 tablespoons of the drippings in a heavy skillet. Spread the potatoes on the bottom of the skillet, packing them down with a spatula. Cook over medium heat, shaking the pan constantly, until the bottom is brown and crusty, 10 to 15 minutes. Place on a hot platter, browned side up. Wipe the pan with a paper towel.

Heat the remaining 1 tablespoon of drippings in the skillet. Slide the potatoes back into the skillet, browned side up. Cook 5 to 10 minutes more, shaking constantly and firming edges with a spatula. Turn onto a hot platter; cut into wedges.

Grandfather's Eggplant

Potato Cakes

Yield: 4 servings

3 large potatoes, grated
½ small onion, grated
2 eggs, lightly beaten
3 tablespoons cracker meal or 2 tablespoons flour
1 scant teaspoon salt
⅛ teaspoon pepper
Oil for frying

Press the liquid from the potatoes and mix with the onion, eggs, cracker meal or flour, and seasonings. Heat about ¼ inch of oil in a frying pan. Form the potato mixture into 8 patties and fry in hot oil until crisp and brown on both sides. Drain on absorbent paper. Serve topped with poached eggs and hot corn muffins.

Home Fried Potatoes

Yield: 4 to 6 servings

6 tablespoons oil
3 pounds potatoes, peeled and cubed
1 onion, cut in quarters
Onion salt
Garlic salt
Paprika

Heat the oil in a heavy skillet and add the potatoes and onion. Sprinkle with onion salt and garlic salt to taste. Then sprinkle with paprika. Fry for about 5 minutes, then lower the heat and simmer for about 10 minutes or until the potatoes are soft.

Oven-Fried Potatoes

Yield: 5 servings

4 medium-sized potatoes, peeled and sliced ⅜ inch thick
3 tablespoons fat, melted
1 teaspoon salt
⅜ teaspoon pepper
⅜ teaspoon paprika

Brush the potato slices with melted fat. Preheat the oven to 425°F and bake the potatoes, basting frequently with the fat, until they are tender and brown on both sides. Season.

Potato Pie

Yield: 4 servings

5 potatoes, chopped
¼ pound soy margarine
1 teaspoon salt
½ teaspoon pepper
2 cups onions, diced
1½ cups green peppers, chopped
5 tomatoes, or the equivalent in tomato sauce or crushed tomatoes
¼ cup honey
2 bay leaves
¼ teaspoon powdered cloves
Grated cheese
Oregano
Tarragon (optional)

Steam the potatoes and mash with soy margarine, a dash of salt, and pepper. Press into an oiled pan.

Sauté the onions and peppers for about 5 minutes. Then add the tomatoes, honey, salt, pepper, bay leaves, and cloves. Cook until the mixture resembles a sauce, but still retains a bit of its crispness. Pour it over the potatoes and bake about 30 minutes at 375°F. Sprinkle with grated cheese, oregano, and tarragon if desired.

Potato Twists

Yield: 10 servings

1 cup hot mashed potatoes
1 tablespoon lard, melted
2 tablespoons butter, melted
1 teaspoon salt
1½ tablespoons sugar
1 cup scalded milk
1 egg, lightly beaten
1½ yeast cakes, dissolved in ½ cup potato water
6 cups flour (approximately), sifted

Mix the mashed potatoes, lard, butter, salt, and sugar in a large mixing bowl. Add lukewarm scalded milk and let stand 5 minutes. Add the egg and the yeast in potato water. Gradually stir in the flour. Cover tightly and set aside in a warm place to rise, about 1 hour.

Turn the dough out on a floured board and knead vigorously, adding more flour to stiffen if needed. Return the dough to a greased bowl and let it rise again. Turn it out and knead some more, chopping through the dough with a knife. Return ⅓ of the dough to the bowl; divide the remaining dough into 2 parts. Roll one of these parts into 3 long strips; pinch the strips together at the ends and braid them to form a loaf. Repeat with the remaining part. Place the loaves in 3½ × 7½-inch bread pans. Brush the tops with a little milk. Repeat the process with the dough in the bowl, separating it to make 2 smaller braids. Place the small braids on top of the large braids, then brush with melted butter. Let them rise until the loaves have doubled in size.

Bake in a 450°F oven for a few minutes, until loaves have begun to brown. Lower the heat and bake 45-50 minutes.

Potatoes Scalloped with Ham

Yield: 6 servings

1 small slice ham, cut into small pieces
6 or 8 potatoes, thinly sliced
2 tablespoons flour
4 tablespoons butter
Onion salt
1½ cups milk
1 teaspoon parsley, minced
Bread crumbs

Cover the bottom of a greased baking dish with the ham. Place a layer of potatoes over the ham. Sprinkle with flour, dot with butter; season with onion salt and pepper and pour in milk to cover. Add another layer of ham and potatoes. Sprinkle again with flour and seasonings, then add milk. Add more layers of potatoes if needed to three-quarters fill the pan. The milk should just cover the potatoes.

Sprinkle the parsley and bread crumbs over the top; dot with butter. Place the baking dish in a large pan with a little water in the bottom. Bake in a 350°F oven until the potatoes are tender.

Stuffed Baked Potatoes

Yield: 6 servings

6 large, uniform russet potatoes
1 8-ounce package cream cheese, softened
½ cup mayonnaise or sour cream
1 teaspoon prepared yellow mustard
½ cup cream
1½ teaspoons salt
¼ teaspoon white pepper
¼ cup parsley, finely chopped
2 tablespoons chives

Scrub the potatoes clean and wrap each in foil. Bake in a preheated 400°F oven for 1¼-1½ hours, until fork-tender.

As the potatoes bake, combine the cream cheese, mayonnaise, mustard, cream, salt, and pepper in a small mixing bowl. Beat at medium speed with a hand mixer until smooth.

Unwrap the baked potatoes and cut off the tops of each lengthwise, about ½ inch thick. Carefully scoop out the potatoes, leaving the shells intact. Place the potato pulp in a large mixing bowl and mash it with a potato masher.

Add the cream-cheese mixture to the mashed potatoes and whip with an electric mixer until smooth and well mixed. Spoon it back into the potato shells. Sprinkle parsley and chives on top. Arrange the stuffed potatoes on a baking sheet. Heat in a 350°F oven for 15 minutes.

New Potatoes Vinaigrette

Yield: 4 servings

10 to 12 hot or warm potatoes, about 1⅓ pounds
1 small bunch chives
2 onions, thinly sliced

vinaigrette dressing
¼ cup vinegar
¼ cup water
⅓ cup oil, preferably olive oil
¼ teaspoon salt
½ teaspoon black pepper

Cut the potatoes into slices. Keep on the peels. The peels are thin and add a decorative touch. Place the potato slices into a bowl. Snip the chives into the bowl. Place onions on top of the potatoes.

Combine the dressing ingredients. Whisk or beat with a fork until smooth. Pour the dressing over the potatoes. Refrigerate for several hours before serving.

Creamed Spinach

Yield: 4 servings

½ cup water
¼ teaspoon salt
1 10-ounce package frozen chopped spinach
2 tablespoons butter or margarine
2 tablespoons flour
⅛ teaspoon garlic salt
White pepper to taste
¾ cup light cream
⅛ teaspoon ground nutmeg
Hard-cooked egg slices

Bring water and salt to a boil in a medium-sized saucepan. Add the spinach and return to a full boil. Break up the frozen spinach with a fork; cover. Reduce the heat to low and cook 4 minutes. Drain well; keep warm.

Melt the butter in a small saucepan. Add the flour, garlic salt, and pepper; stir well. Cook until bubbly. Add the cream and stir well. Cook over low heat until thickened. Season with nutmeg. Combine with spinach; mix thoroughly. Garnish with hard-cooked egg slices.

Acorn Squash with Sliced Apples

Yield: 6 servings

3 fresh acorn squash
Salt to taste
2 or 3 fresh tart apples
Butter
6 tablespoons brown sugar
Nutmeg to taste

Cut each squash in half; remove the seeds. Place cut side down, in a shallow, greased baking dish. Add ½ cup boiling water; cover. Bake in a preheated 350°F oven for 10 minutes. Remove from the oven. Take off the cover, turn the squash cut side up, and sprinkle with salt.

Peel and core the apples; cut them into wedges. Fill the squash cavities with apples; dot them generously with butter. Sprinkle each squash half with 1 tablespoon of brown sugar, then with a little nutmeg. Pour ½ cup of boiling water into the baking dish. Bake 30 minutes or until the squash and apples are tender.

Herbed Spinach Timbales

Yield: 6 servings

1⅓ cups milk, scalded
2 tablespoons butter or margarine
2 10-ounce packages frozen chopped spinach, thawed and well drained
3 eggs, beaten
¼ teaspoon dried tarragon leaves, crushed
¼ teaspoon onion salt
¼ teaspoon salt
⅛ teaspoon pepper

Combine the hot milk and butter in a bowl, stirring until the butter is melted. Stir in the spinach, eggs, tarragon, onion salt, salt, and pepper. Mix well. Spoon into 6 greased, glass custard cups. Set the custard cups in a 13 × 9 × 2-inch baking pan. Place on the oven rack. Pour very hot water into the pan to a depth of 1 inch. Bake in a 350°F oven 30 minutes or until a knife inserted in the center comes out clean. Loosen the edges with a spatula and invert onto a serving platter. Serve immediately.

Potato Balls

New Potatoes Vinaigrette

Crookneck Casserole

Yield: 6 servings

1 small yellow onion
2 tablespoons bacon fat
4 medium yellow summer squash
Salt and pepper
2 large eggs
⅓ cup cream
¼ cup soft bread crumbs

Sauté the onion in the bacon fat. Wash the squash carefully and cut it in chunks. Place them in a well-greased, 1-quart baking dish. Season with salt and pepper.

Beat the eggs with the cream and pour them over the casserole. Sprinkle with the bread crumbs and bake in a preheated 350°F oven, until the squash is tender, about 30 minutes.

Squash Sauté

Yield: 6 servings

3 tablespoons olive or salad oil
¾ pound zucchini squash, diced
¾ pound yellow squash, diced
½ cup onion, chopped
1 clove garlic, crushed
1 cup tomatoes, diced
1 tablespoon Worcestershire sauce
1 tablespoon tomato paste
1 tablespoon salt

In a large skillet, heat the oil. Add the squash, onion, and garlic; sauté 3 minutes, stirring carefully. Combine and add the remaining ingredients. Cover and simmer 8 to 10 minutes, until the vegetables are crisp-tender, stirring occasionally.

Blue-Veined Cheese Filled Squash

Yield: 6 servings

3 small zucchini squashes
⅓ pound blue-veined cheese
1 small cream cheese
¼ cup finely chopped radishes.

Rinse and dry the squashes. Divide them in half lengthwise. Dig them out slightly. Chop the removed squash meat.

Coarsely grate the blue-veined cheese. Stir until soft, together with the cream cheese. Add the squash meat and the radishes. Divide the cheese mixture among the squash halves. Do not serve them too chilled. Tastes good with hard rolls.

Curried Yogurt Spinach

Yield: 4 to 6 servings

2 tablespoons oil
½ medium-sized onion, thinly sliced
2 cloves garlic, minced
2 pounds fresh spinach, washed, trimmed, and
    coarsely chopped
1½ cups plain yogurt
1½ teaspoons curry powder
Salt and pepper
1 teaspoon dried mint

Heat the oil in a large skillet and sauté the onions and garlic over medium heat until well softened. Add the spinach and cook until the spinach is limp. Then blend the yogurt with the curry powder and combine with the spinach. When the mixture is heated, add salt and pepper to taste and sprinkle with dried mint.

Maple Butter Squash

Yield: 4 servings

2 fairly large acorn squash
Olive oil
4 tablespoons butter
4 tablespoons maple syrup
Salt
Freshly ground pepper

Preheat oven to 350°F. Rub the skins of each acorn squash with olive oil, which will keep the skins crisp and help maintain their shape. Place the squash in the center of the oven on a sheet of foil and cook for 60-75 minutes, depending on the size of the squash.

When cooked, remove the squash from the oven and cut in half. Scoop out the seeds and fibers. Remove the flesh and mash with a fork, blending in the butter, maple syrup, salt, and pepper.

Place equal amounts of the mixture in each of the 4 halves of the skin, fluffing up the mixture. Put them back in the oven and reheat for about 5 minutes. Serve hot.

Sweet Potatoes, Apples, and Sausage

Yield: 6 servings

4 cups unpeeled tart apples, thinly sliced
4 cups uncooked sweet potatoes, thinly sliced
2 teaspoons instant minced onion
2 teaspoons salt
½ cup maple syrup
½ cup apple juice
¼ cup butter, melted
1 pound bulk pork sausage
⅓ cup dry bread crumbs

Place first a layer of apple, then a layer of sweet potato slices in a greased, 2-quart casserole, sprinkle each layer with onion and salt. Mix the syrup, apple juice, and butter together; pour the sauce over the apples and potatoes. Cover and bake in a 350°F oven 1 hour.

While the potatoes are cooking, crumble the sausage into a skillet and brown. Drain the sausage and combine with bread crumbs. After the potatoes have cooked, uncover the dish and spread with the sausage mixture. Bake uncovered 20 minutes.

Sweet-Potato Balls

Yield: 4 to 6 servings

½ teaspoon salt
Dash pepper
2 cups sweet potatoes, mashed
4 marshmallows
1 cup bread or cracker crumbs
1 egg, beaten
2 tablespoons water
Shortening for deep frying

Mix the salt and pepper with the sweet potatoes; roll into 8 balls. Put 1 marshmallow into the center of each ball; roll each ball in crumbs.

Combine the egg and water; dip the balls into this mixture. Roll again in crumbs. Fry in heated, deep shortening about 4 minutes, until golden brown and crispy; drain.

Sweet Potato and Banana Casserole

Yield: 6 servings

4 medium-sized sweet potatoes
4 tablespoons butter
1½ teaspoons salt
4 bananas, sliced
¾ cup brown sugar
¾ cup orange juice

Cook the sweet potatoes in boiling water until tender but still firm; cool. Peel and slice ¼ inch thick. Place in a buttered casserole in alternate layers of potatoes dotted with butter and sprinkled with salt, and bananas sprinkled with brown sugar. End the top layer with bananas dotted with butter. Add the orange juice. Bake in a 350°F oven about 30 minutes or until the top is browned.

Sweet Potato French Fries

Yield: 4 servings

2 medium or large sweet potatoes, peeled
1 48-ounce bottle vegetable oil
3 tablespoons raspberry vinegar (available at spe-
    cialty stores)
Salt to taste

Wash the potatoes and cut them into shoestrings. Pat them dry with paper towels. Heat the oil to 260° to 275°F. Drop in half of the potatoes and cook for 5 minutes. Drain well on paper towels. Repeat with the remaining potatoes. (This may be done an hour or 2 in advance.)

Reheat the oil to 375°F and fry the potatoes in batches for 30 seconds to 1 minute, or until they are lightly browned. Drain, sprinkle with vinegar, and salt very lightly.

Sweet Potatoes with Maple Syrup

Yield: 4 servings

½ cup maple syrup
¼ cup butter or margarine
1 pound sweet potatoes, cooked and sliced, or 1 17-ounce can sweet potatoes, drained

Place the syrup and butter in a saucepan; bring to a boil and cook until thickened.

Add the sweet potatoes and cook over low heat until the potatoes are hot and glazed.

Sweet Potato Pudding with Raisins and Nuts

Yield: 8 servings

½ cup butter
4 cups sweet potatoes, grated
½ cup sugar
½ teaspoon cloves
1 teaspoon cinnamon
1 cup milk
1 cup dark cane syrup
½ cup nuts, chopped
1 teaspoon allspice
1 cup raisins
3 eggs, beaten

Melt the butter in a heavy iron skillet in the oven. In a bowl, mix all the ingredients together, adding the eggs last. Pour the mixture into the hot pan of butter and mix well. Bake in a 350°F oven for 45 minutes, stirring twice.

Blue-Veined Cheese Filled Squash

Spicy Sweet-Potato Pie

Yield: 6 to 8 servings

1½ cups sweet potatoes, cooked and mashed
½ cup sugar
1 teaspoon cinnamon
1 teaspoon allspice
½ teaspoon salt
3 eggs, well beaten
1 cup milk
2 tablespoons butter, melted
1 9-inch unbaked pie shell

Combine the mashed sweet potatoes, sugar, cinnamon, allspice, and salt. Add the eggs.

Mix the milk and butter; stir into the potato mixture. The mixture will be fairly liquid. Pour it into an unbaked pastry shell. Bake at 350°F for 40 to 45 minutes.

Sweet Potato Puff

Yield: 2 to 4 servings

2 cups sweet potatoes, mashed
2 tablespoons butter or margarine
Salt and pepper to taste
¼ cup milk or cream
1 egg, separated

Combine the mashed potatoes, melted butter, seasonings, and milk. Add a beaten egg yolk and beat until light and fluffy. Fold in a stiffly beaten egg white.

Place in a greased casserole and bake in a 350°F oven 30 minutes, or until puffy and browned. If desired, ¼ cup of walnuts may be added.

Dilled Tomato Cups with Peas

Yield: 4 servings

4 medium-sized tomatoes
2 tablespoons butter, melted
½ teaspoon salt
¼ teaspoon white pepper
½ teaspoon dried dillweed
½ cup water
1 cup peas, frozen

Slice the tops from the tomatoes; spoon out the centers carefully.

Melt the butter. Add salt, white pepper, and dillweed. Brush the insides of the tomatoes with this mixture. Bake in a preheated 400°F oven 15 minutes or until tender.

While the tomatoes are baking, bring ½ cup of water to a rapid boil. Add the peas; cook 8 to 10 minutes, until tender. Fill the tomato halves with hot peas. Serve immediately.

Corn-Stuffed Tomatoes

Yield: 10 servings

10 medium-sized tomatoes
4 cups cooked corn, or 2 1-pound cans whole kernel corn, drained
1 teaspoon salt
¼ teaspoon pepper
¼ cup butter or margarine, melted

Slice off the tops of the tomatoes, then scoop out the pulp. Mix the pulp with the corn, salt, pepper, and butter.

Stuff the tomatoes with the mixture. Place in a greased muffin pan and bake in a preheated 375°F oven about 20 minutes.

Country-Style Tomatoes

Yield: 4 servings

2 slices bacon, cooked and crumbled
1 small onion, sliced into rings
1 1-pound can tomatoes
¼ teaspoon celery seeds
Salt and pepper to taste

Cook the onion rings in bacon fat until tender, but not brown. Add the tomatoes, celery seeds, salt and pepper. Cook until the tomatoes are heated through. Sprinkle the bacon on top.

Herbed Stuffed Tomatoes

Yield: 4 servings

2 tablespoons butter or margarine
⅓ cup onion, chopped
3 tablespoons scallion tops, chopped
4 large tomatoes
½ teaspoon dried parsley
Dash dried leaf thyme
Dash cayenne pepper
½ cup plus 3 tablespoons soft fresh bread crumbs

In a skillet over medium heat, melt 1 tablespoon of butter or margarine. Add the onion and scallion; cook until tender.

Meanwhile, cut a ¼-inch slice off the tops of each tomato; scoop out the pulp to make a shell ¼-inch thick. Chop the pulp coarsely and add it to the onion in the skillet. Stir in the parsley, thyme, and pepper. Simmer 10 minutes, until the liquid has cooked off. Stir in ½ cup of bread crumbs. Spoon the mixture into the tomato shells.

In a small bowl, mix the remaining butter and bread crumbs together; sprinkle onto the filled tomatoes. Cook on a baking tray in a 350°F oven for 25 to 30 minutes.

Assorted Vegetable Fritters

Yield: 6 to 8 servings

1½ cups flour
1 teaspoon salt
2 tablespoons oil
1 egg
1 cup water
1 zucchini, sliced
1 eggplant, sliced
Cauliflower flowerets
1 tablespoon corn kernels

In a bowl, combine the flour and salt. Add the oil, egg, and cold water; mix until thick. If the batter does not adhere to the vegetables, add more water. Dip the vegetables into the batter 1 slice or piece at a time. For the corn, stir in just enough to hold the corn together. Deep-fry in hot oil until brown. Keep warm in a low oven until ready to serve.

Zucchini and Cottage-Cheese Casserole

Yield: 6 servings

3 medium-sized zucchini, sliced
¼ cup onion, chopped
2 tablespoons vegetable oil
1 pound cottage cheese
1 teaspoon basil
⅓ cup Parmesan cheese

Sauté the zucchini and onion in oil.

Whip the cottage cheese with basil in a blender. Place alternating layers of zucchini and cheese in a 1½-quart casserole; top with Parmesan. Bake, uncovered, in a preheated 350°F oven for 25 to 30 minutes.

Fried Zucchini

Yield: 4 to 6 servings

3 to 4 medium-sized zucchini, sliced into rounds
1 egg
1 tablespoon milk
3 tablespoons flour
1 teaspoon salt
1 teaspoon garlic salt
Deep fat for frying

Wash the zucchini; slice it into rounds about ¼ inch thick. Set aside.

Combine the egg, milk, flour, salt, and garlic salt in a bowl; mix well to form a batter. Dip each zucchini round into the batter; fry in deep fat until crisp and golden brown. Drain on paper towels.

Mixed Vegetables

Yield: 4 servings

½ pound mushrooms
4 or 5 small carrots, about ¾ pound, trimmed and scraped
1 tablespoon butter
1 cup celery, chopped
¼ cup water
Salt to taste, if desired
Freshly ground pepper to taste
¼ cup heavy cream
1 tablespoon parsley, finely chopped

If the mushrooms are small, leave them whole. If they are large, cut them lengthwise in half. There should be about 2½ cups. Cut the carrots into thin, ¼-inch rounds. There should be about 1¼ cups.

Heat the butter in a saucepan and add the mushrooms, shaking the skillet and tossing them so that they cook evenly, about 2 minutes. Add the carrots, celery, salt, and pepper and cover tightly. Cook 8 to 10 minutes.

Add the cream and cook down over high heat about 2 minutes. Sprinkle with chopped parsley and serve hot.

Oven-Baked Root Vegetables

Spanish Vegetables

Fresh Vegetable Bake

Yield: 6 servings

6 carrots, cut in strips
3 small zucchini, cut in ¼-inch diagonal slices
1 cup cherry tomatoes
1 cup herb-seasoned croutons
2 tablespoons cornstarch
1½ cups milk
¼ cup butter or margarine
1 teaspoon salt
¼ teaspoon pepper
1 teaspoon dried basil leaves

Cook the carrots in boiling, salted water about 5 minutes or until tender-crisp; drain. In a 1-quart shallow baking dish, toss the vegetables and croutons.

In a saucepan, stir the cornstarch and milk together until smooth; add the butter, salt, and pepper. Bring to a boil over medium heat, stirring constantly, and boil 1 minute; pour over the vegetables. Sprinkle with basil. Bake in a 350°F oven 25 minutes, or until the vegetables are tender.

Oven-Baked Root Vegetables

Yield: 4 servings

1 pound carrots
1 pound beets
⅔ pound parsnips
¼ pound celery sticks
3 tablespoons oil
½ teaspoon salt

Peel the carrots, beets, parsnips, and celery. Cut them into ¼-inch-wide strips. Place the vegetables in a baking pan. Pour the oil over them and sprinkle with a little salt. Bake in a preheated 425°F oven for 25 to 30 minutes, until done as desired. Turn them over several times while baking.

Spanish Vegetables

Yield: 4 servings

¾ cup split peas, plus water (1 teaspoon salt to 2 cups water) or 1 can (about 14 ounces) garbanzo beans
1 small eggplant (about 10 ounces) or an equal amount of squash
1 green pepper
1 red pepper
2 onions
1 tablespoon margarine or oil
1¼ cups chicken or beef broth
2 cloves garlic, crushed
1 teaspoon salt
1 teaspoon thyme
Pinch of ground saffron (optional)
4 hard-boiled eggs, halved
Coarse bread

Soak the split peas in salted water 10 to 12 hours. Pour off the water and boil in new lightly salted water 1 to 1½ hours. Drain.

Slice the eggplant or squash. Halve the peppers, take out the seeds and membranes, and cut them into strips.

Peel the onions and chop into large pieces. Sauté the onion in a little margarine. Add the eggplant or squash and the peppers. Add the broth, the garlic, salt, thyme, and saffron. Boil the vegetables approximately 15 minutes until they become soft. Add more water if necessary. Stir in the split peas. Season to taste. Serve with the hard-boiled egg halves and bread.

Stuffings, Rice and Noodles

Apple Stuffing

Yield: 4 cups

3 cups bread, diced
¾ cup butter
1 tablespoon lemon juice
1 teaspoon salt
1 cup sour apples, chopped
1 teaspoon mint, chopped

Mix the bread, butter, lemon juice, moistening with a little water if needed. Add the salt, apples, and mint. Stuff loosely.

Bread Stuffing

Yield: 4 cups

⅓ cup butter or margarine
3 tablespoons onion, chopped
4 cups dry bread crumbs
1 teaspoon salt
¼ teaspoon pepper
¼ teaspoon poultry seasoning
Sage to taste
Hot chicken broth or water

Melt the butter in a saucepan and cook the onion until it is soft but not brown. Add the bread crumbs and seasonings. Mix in the remaining butter and enough broth to moisten the stuffing.

Oyster Filling

Yield: 10 cups

Liquor from 1 quart oysters
1 loaf stale bread, crumbled
1 cup melted butter
1 teaspoon salt
¼ teaspoon pepper
1 egg, beaten
¼ cup milk (optional)
1 quart oysters

Heat the oyster liquor; skim it, then pour the liquor over the bread. Add butter, seasonings, and the egg. If the stuffing is too dry, pour in a little milk. Add the oysters carefully, so you don't break them.

Apple Rice

227

Roanoke Pecan Stuffing

Yield: 12 cups

1 cup wild rice
3 cups chicken stock
1 carrot, quartered
2 bay leaves
Salt
1 large onion, chopped
½ cup butter or margarine
4 cups mushrooms, sliced
4 ribs celery, sliced
¼ cup parsley, chopped
2 teaspoons sage
1 cup chicken stock, approximate
4 cups corn bread or corn-bread stuffing mix
2 cups whole wheat bread, cubed
2 cups pecans, halved or chopped

Cook the wild rice in 3 cups of chicken stock with the carrot, bay leaves, and a pinch of salt for 40 minutes. Remove the carrot quarters and bay leaves. Sauté the onion in butter with the mushrooms and celery, until soft. Add the parsley, sage, and 1 cup chicken stock to the mushroom mixture and simmer 8 to 10 minutes. Toss with corn bread, whole wheat bread, pecans, and cooked rice.

Season with salt and pepper, to taste. For a moister dressing, add more chicken stock, as desired. Use as filling or bake in a casserole at 325°F for about 30 minutes.

Rice Dressing

Yield: 6 cups

2 tablespoons flour
2 tablespoons vegetable oil
1 cup onions, chopped
1 cup celery, chopped
½ cup green pepper, chopped
2 cloves garlic, minced
½ pound lean ground beef
½ pound pork
½ pound chicken giblets, chopped
2 teaspoons salt
¼ teaspoon black pepper
¼ teaspoon red pepper
1 cup chicken broth
3 cups hot cooked rice
1 cup green onion tops, sliced

Brown the flour in oil until it is a deep red brown, stirring constantly to prevent burning. Add onions, celery, green pepper, and garlic. Cook until the vegetables are tender. Stir in beef, pork, giblets, and seasonings. Continue cooking until the meat loses its color. Blend in the broth; cover, and simmer 25 minutes. Stir in the onion tops. Cook 5 minutes longer.

Wild Rice Stuffing

Yield: 7 cups

4 cups cooked wild rice
1 turkey liver, optional
1½ cups pecans, coarsely chopped
8 tablespoons butter
1 cup onion, finely chopped
1 cup celery, finely chopped
¼ pound mushrooms cut into ½-inch cubes (about 2 cups)
Salt to taste, if desired
Freshly ground pepper to taste

Prepare the wild rice and set it aside. Finely chop the liver and set it aside. Toast the chopped pecans lightly in a skillet.

Heat the butter in a heavy skillet and add the onion and celery. Cook, stirring, until wilted. Add the mushrooms and chopped liver. Add salt and pepper. Cook, stirring, about 5 minutes. Add the wild rice and pecans and blend thoroughly. Let cool.

Striped Rice

Bread and Chestnut Dressing

Yield: 6 cups

⅓ pound fresh chestnuts
¼ cup margarine or butter
¼ cup onions, diced
5 cups day-old bread, diced
1 egg, beaten
⅛ teaspoon white pepper
¼ teaspoon celery seed
¾ teaspoon sage
¼ teaspoon salt
1¼-1¾ cups chicken or turkey stock
Margarine or butter (for greasing casserole dish)

Score the chestnuts with an X. Cover with water and simmer about 15 minutes. Drain and peel the chestnuts while warm. Chop in ¼-inch pieces.

Melt the margarine or butter. Sauté the onions and chestnuts until the onions are tender. Combine the diced bread, egg and seasonings. Add the onions and chestnuts and mix until the chestnuts are evenly distributed.

Add the stock slowly until the bread mixture is evenly moistened. Mix thoroughly and place in a greased casserole dish to a depth of 2 inches. Bake uncovered at 375°F for 35 to 40 minutes.

Sweet Corn Bread Stuffing

Yield: 9 cups

½ cup butter or margarine
½ cup onion, chopped
½ cup green pepper, chopped
½ cup celery, chopped
2½ teaspoons salt
2 teaspoons sage
½ teaspoon pepper
6 slices dry wheat bread, cubed
4 cups sweetened corn bread, coarsely crumbled
1½ cups turkey broth or water

Melt the butter in a skillet and sauté the vegetables in butter until just tender. Stir in seasonings. Place the breads and the vegetable mixture in a large bowl. Stir in the broth.

Apple Rice

Yield: 4 servings

⅓ cup round-grained rice
¾ to 1¼ cups water
½ teaspoon salt
3 sour apples
2 tablespoons sugar
⅓ cup whipped cream (can be omitted if the rice is to be eaten warm)
1 ounce roasted sliced almonds

Rice Pilaff

Boil the rice in the water, into which the salt has been added, for about 10 minutes.

Peel the apples, if you wish, and carefully remove all of the core. Cut the apples into small cubes. Stir the fruit into the rice together with the sugar. Boil for 5 minutes, then let stand for 5 minutes. Let the rice cool.

Whip the cream and stir it into the apple rice. Add the roasted almonds or sprinkle them on top of the rice. Serve with cinnamon or ginger, or with milk if the rice is warm.

Peanut-Rice Roast

Yield: 4 servings

1 cup peanut butter
1 cup (or more) water
1 medium-sized onion
1 teaspoon sage or poultry seasoning
1 teaspoon salt
2 cups cooked rice

Mix the peanut butter with water until it is the consistency of thick cream. Add the remaining ingredients and mix well. Bake at 350°F for 45 minutes to 1 hour, or until firm.

Green Chilies and Rice Frittata

Yield: 4 servings

½ cup onions, finely chopped
1 tablespoon butter or margarine
8 eggs
½ cup milk
1 teaspoon salt
1 teaspoon Worcestershire sauce
4 to 5 drops Tabasco sauce (optional)
2 cups cooked rice
1 4-ounce can chopped green chilies, undrained
1 medium-sized tomato, chopped
½ cup Cheddar cheese, shredded

In a 10-inch skillet, cook the onion in butter until tender. Beat the eggs with milk and seasonings. Stir in the rice, chilies, and tomato. Pour the rice mixture into a skillet. Reduce the heat to medium-low. Cover; cook until the top is almost set, 12 to 15 minutes. Sprinkle with cheese. cover the skillet, then remove it from the heat; let stand about 10 minutes.

Savory Chicken Rice with Oranges

Yield: 6 servings

2 cups mushrooms, diced
1 cup onions, chopped
¾ cup green sweet pepper, finely chopped
1 cup celery, finely chopped
1 large carrot, grated
6 tablespoons olive oil
3 cups cooked chicken, diced
½ cucumber, peeled and diced
1 10½-ounce can tomato purée
Salt and pepper to taste
3¾ cup chicken stock
1¼ cup long-grain rice
Orange slices

Sauté the mushrooms, onions, green pepper, celery, and carrot in 4 tablespoons olive oil in a Dutch oven until tender, stirring frequently. Add the chicken, cucumber, tomato purée, salt and pepper, and ¾ cup chicken stock, stirring to combine. Cover; simmer for 5 minutes, stirring occasionally.

Sauté the rice in a frying pan in the remaining olive oil until golden, stirring constantly. Add rice to the tomato mixture. Stir in the remaining chicken

Gratin Vegetables and Noodles

Noodles with Ham

stock; cover. Cook for about 30 minutes or until the rice is tender and the liquid absorbed, stirring frequently. Turn into a serving bowl; garnish the edge with fresh orange slices.

Rice with Mushrooms

Yield: 6 servings

1 10½-ounce can beef consommé
1 cup rice
½ pound fresh mushrooms
1 tablespoon lemon juice
¼ cup butter
¼ cup onion, chopped
¼ cup fresh parsley, chopped

Combine the consommé and 1¾ cup of water in a 1½-quart saucepan and bring to a boil. Add the rice and stir well. Reduce the heat and cover. Simmer for about 15 minutes or until the rice is tender and all the liquid is absorbed.

Meanwhile, wash the mushrooms briefly under cold water and wipe them dry. Thinly slice the mushrooms, then toss with the lemon juice. Melt the butter in a small saucepan, then add the mushrooms and onions and sauté for 5 minutes.

Add the mushroom mixture and the parsley to the hot rice and toss well.

Rice and Peas

Yield: 6 to 8 servings

1 tablespoon olive oil
2 tablespoons butter
¼ cup onion, finely chopped
1 slice bacon, diced
2 cups fresh green peas
1 cup long-grain rice
2 cups chicken stock
Salt and freshly ground pepper to taste
1 tablespoon Parmesan cheese, grated

Heat the oil and butter in a heavy skillet, then add the onion and bacon and cook over low heat for 3 minutes, stirring constantly. Add the peas and cook, stirring for 5 minutes. Add the rice and stir until coated with the oil mixture. Stir in the chicken stock, salt, and pepper and cover.

Cook over low heat, stirring occasionally, for 15 to 20 minutes or until the rice is tender and all the liquid is absorbed.

Add the cheese just before serving and toss to mix well.

Noodles with Mushroom Sauce

Add the rice to the pan and pour in the water. Increase the heat to high and bring the liquid to a boil. Cover the pan, reduce the heat to low and simmer, stirring occasionally for 20 to 25 minutes or until the rice is tender and all the water has been absorbed.

Remove the pan from the heat and transfer the mixture to a warmed serving dish. Arrange the onion rings on top and serve.

Striped Rice with Ground Meat

Yield: 4 servings

1⅔ cups rice
1 bouillon cube
1 onion
Butter
1 pound ground beef
1 can crushed tomatoes
Salt
Pepper
1 red pepper
1 green pepper
1 can strained tomatoes
Vegetable broth

Boil the rice according to the directions on the package. Use a bouillon cube instead of salt when preparing the rice.

Chop the onion and brown it in a little butter. Stir in the ground meat with a fork so that it crumbles while browning. Add the crushed tomatoes and allow to boil for about 20 minutes. Season with salt and pepper.

Chop each of the peppers separately. Preheat oven to 475°F. Alternate the rice and the ground meat in an ovenproof dish. Place the green and red chopped peppers on top. Dot with a little butter and bake in the oven for 15 minutes.

Make the sauce using strained tomatoes from a can or fresh tomatoes which are first boiled and then strained. Stir a small amount of vegetable broth into the tomatoes, and season with salt and pepper.

Rice with Fruit and Nuts

Yield: 4 to 6 servings

¼ cup corn oil
⅔ cup dried apricots, soaked overnight, drained, and chopped
⅓ cup dried prunes, soaked overnight, drained, and chopped
½ cup seedless raisins, soaked in cold water for 30 minutes and drained.
2 carrots, scraped and thinly sliced
2 large bananas, thinly sliced
½ cup walnuts, chopped
2 tablespoons pine nuts
1 tablespoon clear honey
1⅓ cup long-grain rice, washed, soaked in cold water for 30 minutes and drained
2 cups water
1 small onion, sliced and pushed out into rings

In a large saucepan, heat the oil over moderate heat. When the oil is hot, add the apricots, prunes, raisins, carrots, and orange juice. Cook, stirring occasionally, for 5 minutes. Reduce the heat to low and add the bananas, walnuts, pine nuts, and honey and stir well to blend.

Pasta with Cold Sauce

Rice Pilaf

Yield: 4 servings

1¼ cups long-grained rice
4 whole cloves
1 piece of cinnamon, about 2 inches long
1 onion, sliced
8 cardamom seeds
2 bay leaves
30 almonds
⅓ cup raisins

Boil the rice with water and salt according to the directions on the package. Add the cloves, cinnamon, onion, cardamom, and bay leaves while the rice is cooking. Boil as long as the directions on the package specify.

Scald and peel the almonds. Cut them in half lengthwise.

Remove the bay leaves and the piece of cinnamon from the prepared rice and mix in the almonds and raisins.

Thanksgiving Rice

Yield: About 14 servings

3 cups uncooked rice
1 pound country sausage
1 cup celery, chopped
2 medium-sized onions, chopped
1 green pepper, diced
1 egg, beaten
Salt and pepper to taste

Boil the rice; set it aside in a colander.

Use a large skillet to cook the sausage thoroughly. Then sauté the celery, onions, and green peppers in some of the sausage fat. When the vegetables are very lightly browned, add the rice. Stir well about 3 minutes. Remove to a large bowl. Add the egg and seasonings; mix well.

Put the rice in well-greased casseroles for serving or freezing. Reheat in oven just until rice is hot.

Epicurean Wild Rice

Yield: 6 servings

⅓ cup butter
½ cup fresh parsley, minced
½ cup green onions or scallions, chopped
1 cup celery, diagonally sliced
1¼ cups wild rice
1 can chicken consommé
1½ cups boiling water
1 teaspoon salt
½ teaspoon dried marjoram
½ cup sherry

Melt the butter in a large saucepan, then add the parsley, onions, and celery and sauté until soft but not brown. Add the rice, consommé, water, salt, and marjoram and cover. Bake in a preheated 350°F oven for about 45 minutes or until the rice is tender, stirring occasionally and adding boiling water if needed.

Remove the cover and stir in the sherry. Bake for about 5 minutes longer or until the sherry is absorbed.

Green Ribbon Noodles with Tomato

Yield: 8 servings

1 12-ounce package green noodles
½ cup olive oil
4 cups tomatoes, chopped, skinned, and seeded
1 teaspoon salt
⅛ teaspoon sugar
⅛ teaspoon freshly ground black pepper
1 teaspoon basil

Cook the noodles according to the package directions. Prepare the sauce while the noodles cook. Heat the oil in a skillet until sizzling, then stir in the tomatoes and seasonings. Cook for about 5 minutes or until the tomatoes are tender, stirring occasionally with a wooden spoon.

Drain the noodles and arrange in a serving dish, then spoon the sauce over the noodles. Serve immediately with freshly grated Parmesan cheese.

Noodle Kugel

Yield: 10 servings

1 pound wide noodles
¼ pound butter
4 eggs
1½ pounds applesauce
1 pint sour cream
1 pound cottage cheese
½ cup raisins (optional)
1 cup sugar
2 tablespoons brown sugar
1 tablespoon cinnamon

Boil and drain the noodles. In a large bowl, add the butter, eggs, applesauce, sour cream, cottage cheese, and raisins. Mix well; fold in the sugar. Place the mixture in a greased 9×13-inch casserole. Sprinkle the top with brown sugar and cinnamon, mixed together. Bake in a 350°F oven for 40 to 60 minutes.

Pasta with Luxurious Sauce

Gratin Vegetables and Noodles

Yield: 4 to 6 servings

2 onions
2 green peppers
1 pound eggplant or squash
5 or 6 tomatoes
2 tablespoons margarine or oil
2 cloves garlic, crushed
2 to 3 tablespoons chili sauce or tomato paste
1 teaspoon salt
1 to 2 teaspoons thyme or oregano
7 to 8 ounces noodles
¾ to 1¼ cups coarsely grated cheese

Slice the onions.

Remove seeds and membranes from the peppers, and dice.

Slice the eggplant or squash.

Dip the tomatoes in hot water. Peel off the skins. Cut the tomatoes into pieces.

Heat margarine or oil in a large pot. Sauté the onion. It should not become brown, only a golden yellow. Add the vegetables. Stir, and season with garlic, chili sauce, salt, and thyme or oregano. Cover and simmer over low heat for 10 to 15 minutes.

Uncover and simmer 15 minutes, until the mixture thickens. Should it become too thick, thin with water.

Meanwhile boil the noodles according to the package directions.

Grease a baking dish. Place half of the noodles in the bottom of the dish. Cover with the vegetable mixture. End with the noodles and a large amount of grated cheese on top. Bake in a preheated 425°F oven about 10 minutes.

This is ideal for freezing.

Stilton Noodles

Yield: 4 servings

¼ pound, noodles, cooked
1 cup Stilton cheese, crumbled
1 cup sour cream
1 egg, lightly beaten
½ teaspoon salt
Dash pepper
4 tablespoons butter, melted

Toss the cooked noodles with the rest of the ingredients. Place in a well-buttered 1½ quart casserole. Bake in a preheated 350°F oven for about 1 hour or until bubbling and set.

Pasta with Mediterranean Sauce

Noodles with Ham

Yield: About 4 servings

7 ounces smoked ham
1 7-ounce can whole or sliced mushrooms
1 leek
Butter or margarine
1 container (1 cup) crème fraîche or sour cream
1 tablespoon light French mustard
Salt
Pepper
A little milk, if necessary
½ pound noodles or pasta of your choice

Cut the ham into strips. Drain the mushrooms. Shred the leek. Sauté the ham, mushrooms, and leek in a little butter. Add the crème fraîche or sour cream and mustard. Blend well. Heat mixture and season with salt and pepper. Add a little milk if the sauce becomes too thick.

Cook the noodles or pasta according to package directions. Serve ham sauce over the noodles.

Noodles with Mushroom Sauce

Yield: 4 servings

8 ounces noodles or tagliatelle
1 14-ounce can chopped tomatoes
1 can cream of mushroom soup, concentrated
2 tablespoons tomato purée
Salt
Black pepper
2 tablespoons finely chopped parsley
1 tablespoon finely chopped dill
Crumbled tarragon
1 to 2 tablespoons plain flour
⅓ cup water, milk, or cream
4 thin slices of lemon
½ pound fresh mushrooms
Parsley for garnish

Bring water for the pasta to a boil. Cook pasta according to package instructions.

Pour the chopped tomatoes, undiluted soup, and tomato purée into a saucepan. Season with salt and pepper. Add parsley, dill, and tarragon. Mix well. Bring to a boil.

Blend the flour and liquid and add to the sauce. Bring to a boil, stirring all the time. (If you think the sauce is thick enough, omit the extra thickening.) Add the lemon slices. Simmer the sauce for 5 minutes.

Meanwhile clean the mushrooms and brown them well in a little butter.

Serve the noodles topped with the sauce and mushrooms and sprinkled with a little parsley. Accompany with grated cheese and a green salad.

Pasta with Salmon Sauce

Fettuccine with Peaches

Yield: 4 servings

8 ounces fettuccine
3 quarts boiling water
1 tablespoon salt
1 tablespoon oil
2 firm-ripe fresh peaches
½ cup ham, cut into julienne strips (optional)
Butter
½ cup heavy or light cream
1 egg yolk
½ cup Romano cheese, grated
1 tablespoon parsley, finely chopped
Nutmeg

Cook the fettuccine in boiling water with salt and oil until tender but firm, about 9 minutes. Dip the peaches in boiling water a few seconds and slip off the skins.

Cut the fruit in wedges. Sauté the ham in butter 1 minute. Add the peaches. Add the cream, lightly beaten with a egg yolk. Heat gently and stir in the cheese. Drain the fettuccine well. Sprinkle with parsley, add the peach mixture, and toss gently. Serve lightly sprinkled with nutmeg, if desired.

Pasta with Saucy Sauce

Zucchini and Fettucine with Garlic-Basil Sauce

Yield: 4 to 6 servings

2 medium-sized zucchini, cut into 1½-inch julienne strips
¼ cup olive oil
1 tablespoon butter
3 large cloves garlic, minced
3 tablespoons fresh basil, chopped
¾ pound fettucine noodles
½ cup Parmesan cheese, grated
Salt

Steam the zucchini for 3 minutes; set aside. Combine the oil, butter, garlic, and basil in a small saucepan and simmer gently, covered, for 15 minutes (garlic should not be allowed to brown).

Cook the fettucine in boiling, salted water until just tender; drain and toss with the zucchini, garlic-basil sauce, and cheese. Salt to taste.

Pasta with Cold Sauce

Yield: 4 to 6 servings

⅔ pound farfel or tagliatelle
2 tablespoons chopped parsley
⅓ ounce grated Parmesan cheese
1 clove garlic
⅔ cup olive oil
1 tablespoon dried basil
3 tablespoons finely chopped blanched almonds
Salt
Pepper

Boil the pasta according to the directions on the package.

Grind the parsley, cheese, and garlic in a mortar with a little olive oil. Add basil, almonds, salt, and pepper. Add remaining olive oil in a fine thin trickle.

Serve the cold sauce with pasta, preferably prepared "al dente," so that the elasticity is retained.

Pasta with Smart Sauce

Pasta with Luxurious Sauce

Yield: 4 to 6 servings

⅔ pound noodles, preferably both yellow and green
Water
Salt
2 tablespoons butter
1 jar black caviar
1 jar red caviar
1 container (1 cup) crème fraîche or sour cream

Boil the pasta as usual in salted water. Let drain in a colander. Pour back into the pot and stir with a dab of butter until the butter melts. Serve with the crème fraîche or sour cream and the black and red caviar. A fresh salad goes nicely with this dish.

Pasta with Mediterranean Sauce

Yield: 4 to 6 servings

⅔ pound pasta
1 large red onion, chopped
1 green pepper, cubed
1 small eggplant, sliced
Olive oil for frying
2 cloves garlic, crushed
Salt
Black pepper
2 teaspoons thyme
½ teaspoon curry
1 teaspoon cayenne pepper
1 can crushed tomatoes
⅔ to 1 pound shelled shrimp

Boil the pasta in the usual manner.

Brown the onion, green pepper, and eggplant separately, in olive oil, then place in a pot. Add the crushed garlic, salt and pepper. Add the thyme, curry, and a few grains of the cayenne pepper. Pour in the tomatoes. Let the sauce simmer until it thickens, about 15 minutes.

Warm the shrimp in the sauce.

Sprinkle with a little parsley if desired. Serve with the pasta.

Pasta with Salmon Sauce

Yield: 4 to 6 servings

⅔ pound tagliatelle, farfalle, or another variety of spaghetti
2 tablespoons white wine
1½ to 2 tablespoons lemon juice
1 cup heavy cream
3 tablespoons finely chopped dill
Salt
Pepper
3½ ounces smoked or raw spiced salmon (graulax), cut in thin strips

Spaghetti with Shrimp

Boil the pasta according to the directions on the package.

Warm the wine and the lemon juice in a pot. Let it evaporate some. Add the cream. Let simmer, while stirring constantly, over low heat for about 10 minutes, until the sauce thickens and becomes very creamy. Season with dill and perhaps a few more drops of the lemon juice, plus the salt and pepper.

Pour the sauce over the pasta or serve separately along with the salmon strips.

Pasta with Smart Sauce

Yield: 4 to 6 servings

⅔ pound noodles (or another variety of pasta)
1¼ cups heavy cream
⅓ to ½ cup blue-veined cheese, crumbled
½ to ⅔ cup Parmesan cheese, grated
About 15 walnuts, divided into smaller pieces

Boil the pasta in salted water according to the directions on the package.

Warm the cream together with the blue-veined and Parmesan cheeses in a pot over low heat. Stir the sauce slowly until it thickens. Pour it over the pasta. Garnish with the walnuts.

Pasta with Saucy Sauce

Yield: 4 to 6 servings

⅔ pound shell macaroni
Butter
¼ pound smoked ham, finely cubed
1 large clove garlic, crushed
⅓ pound fresh mushrooms, sliced
⅓ cup green peas
2 to 3 tablespoons white wine
⅓ cup light cream
1½ to 2 ounces grated Parmesan cheese
Parsley, finely chopped
Black pepper

Boil the pasta according to the directions on the package.

Melt a little butter. Add the ham cubes, crushed garlic, and mushrooms. Add the peas and the wine. Let simmer.

Pour the cream and add a dab of butter into the pasta. Mix well. Stir in the ham mixture, then the cheese. Sprinkle with parsley. Turn the pepper grinder several times over the dish.

Pasta with Vegetable Sauce

Yield: 4 servings

1 leek (or 1 large onion)
2 peppers
1 clove garlic (optional)
1½ to 2 tablespoons butter
1 piece of cucumber, about 7 ounces
5 or 6 tomatoes
½ teaspoon salt
¼ teaspoon black pepper
1 small bay leaf
1 small can fillets sprats, herrings, or anchovies
About 15 black olives
½ to ¾ pound spaghetti

Rinse and slice the leek, or peel and chop the onion. Take out seeds and membranes and slice the peppers. Sauté the leek or onion, the peppers, and the crushed garlic clove for a few minutes in butter.

Cut the cucumber into cubes. You may wish to peel the tomatoes by dipping them in boiling water and pulling off the skins. Cut the tomatoes into pieces. Add the cucumber and then the tomatoes to the peppers. Simmer the mixture for a few minutes, uncovered. Then add the salt, pepper, and bay leaf. Cover and simmer over low heat about 15 minutes.

Drain the sprats, herrings, or anchovies. Cut them into pieces. Add them to the vegetable mixture. Simmer for a few minutes. Season to taste. Add the olives.

Spaghetti with Spinach

Cook the spaghetti according to package directions. Serve the sauce with the spaghetti, a green salad, and grated cheese.

Spaghetti with Tuna Fish Sauce

Yield: 4 servings

1 7-ounce can tuna fish in water
1 onion, peeled and chopped
1 clove garlic, crushed
Butter or margarine
¾ cup cream
1 tablespoon lemon juice
2 to 3 tablespoons snipped dill
Salt
Pepper
¾ pound spaghetti

Drain the tuna fish. Sauté the onion and garlic in butter in a frying pan. Pour in the cream and add the pieces of tuna fish. Carefully warm and season with lemon, dill, salt, and pepper.

Boil the spaghetti according to package directions. Serve the sauce with the newly boiled spaghetti.

Spaghetti with Spinach and Mussels

Yield: 4 servings

3 quarts water
1½ tablespoons salt
1 package creamed, frozen spinach
2 cans (about 4 ounces each) mussels in water
½ to ¾ pound spaghetti
Parmesan cheese
1 clove garlic, crushed
Black pepper

Put the water and salt in a pot and bring to a boil. Place the spinach block and the liquid from the cans of mussels in a pan and allow the spinach to melt slowly, about 10 minutes. Meanwhile, chop the contents of 1½ cans of mussels, reserving the rest for garnish.

When the water boils cook the spaghetti. Mix the chopped mussels with the spinach and cheese, garlic, salt, and pepper. Bring the sauce to a boil.

Drain the spaghetti and serve with the sauce, garnished with the whole mussels. Serve more cheese separately.

Spaghetti with Shrimp

Yield: 4 servings

4 tablespoons shallots, minced
1 clove garlic, crushed
Butter or margarine
1¼ cups heavy cream
About 1 tablespoon chili sauce
¼ cup snipped parsley
Salt
Pepper
1 to 1½ pounds shrimp with shells
¾ pound spaghetti

Sauté the onion and the garlic in the butter until they become soft and glossy but not brown. Stir in the cream, chili sauce, and parsley. Add the shelled shrimp and warm up the sauce. Season with salt and pepper.

Boil the spaghetti according to package directions. Serve the sauce with the freshly made spaghetti.

Pasta with Vegetable Sauce

Lasagne

Spaghetti with Bourguignonne Meat Sauce

Yield: 4 servings

½ onion
1 small piece celeriac (optional)
1 tablespoon margarine
⅔ pound ground meat
3 slices of bacon
¼ pound mushrooms
⅛ teaspoon black pepper
1 tablespoon tomato paste
1 tablespoon flour
⅓ cup red wine plus 1 cup water
½ to 1 teaspoon salt
½ to ¾ pound spaghetti

Mince the onion and finely chop the celeriac. Sauté both ingredients in margarine until they become glossy. Increase the heat and add the ground meat. Stir with a fork so that it crumbles and becomes brown.

Cut the bacon into pieces and add to the meat. Continue to brown. Also add the mushrooms.

Mix in the pepper, tomato paste, and the flour. Add the wine and water, and let the sauce simmer for several minutes. Dilute with more water if the mixture becomes too dry. Season to taste with salt.

Serve with spaghetti or your favorite pasta.

Lasagne

Yield: 4 servings

9 lasagna noodles
2 onions, peeled and chopped
¾ pound ground meat
1 14-ounce can crushed tomatoes
1 tablespoon tomato paste
1 bouillon cube
½ teaspoon salt
¼ teaspoon white or black pepper
About 1 teaspoon crushed oregano or basil

cheese sauce
3 tablespoons butter or margarine
5 tablespoons flour
3⅓ cups milk
½ to 1 teaspoon salt
Black pepper
Ground nutmeg
1¼ cups grated cheese

Boil the lasagna noodles.

Make the meat sauce. Brown the onions and meat in a frying pan, while stirring, so that it becomes a crumbled mixture. Add the tomatoes, tomato paste, bouillon cube, and salt and pepper. Cover and simmer for 20 to 30 minutes. Season with oregano or basil toward the end of the simmering time.

Make the cheese sauce. Melt the butter and stir in the flour. Add the milk and bring to a boil while stirring constantly. Let the sauce boil for 3 to 5 minutes. Stir in the cheese and season with salt, pepper, and the ground nutmeg.

Alternate the lasagna noodles with the meat sauce and the cheese sauce in a greased, ovenproof dish. Start and finish with the cheese sauce. Three layers of the pasta is usually about right. Finally sprinkle plenty of grated cheese on top.

Bake for 15 to 20 minutes at 425°F if the dish has just been prepared and the sauces are still warm. Bake it for 30 to 40 minutes at 400°F if the lasagne is cold.

Bourguignonne Meat Sauce

Spaghetti with Tuna Fish Sauce

Breads, Pancakes, and Waffles

Apple Bread

Yield: 1 loaf

2 tablespoons butter
¾ cup sugar
1 teaspoon cinnamon
1 apple, peeled and thinly sliced
A few raisins
1 package active dry yeast
¾ cup warm water
1 teaspoon salt
2¼ cups flour, sifted
1 egg
¼ cup shortening

Melt the butter in a 9 × 9-inch baking pan. Mix ½ cup of the sugar and the cinnamon in a small bowl. Sprinkle the sugar mixture on the melted butter. Arrange the apple slices in rows on the sugar mixture in the pan. Sprinkle with a few raisins.

Stir the yeast and water together in a large bowl. Add the remaining ¼ cup of sugar, salt, and 1 cup of flour. Beat 2 minutes or until the batter drops in sheets from the beater or spoon. Add the egg, shortening, and remaining 1¼ cup of flour; beat until smooth.

Drop the batter by small spoonfuls over the apples and raisins in the pan. Cover the pan and let rise 50-60 minutes or until double in size. Bake at 375°F for 30-35 minutes or until brown. Immediately remove the bread from the pan by inverting it onto a serving plate.

Beer-Herb Bread

Yield: 2 loaves

2 packages dry yeast
½ cup lukewarm water
1 12-ounce can beer, heated to lukewarm
¼ cup sugar
1 tablespoon salt
¼ cup butter, melted
2 eggs, lightly beaten
1 teaspoon sage
2 teaspoons thyme
3 teaspoons savory
1 small onion, grated
6½ to 7 cups flour

Sprinkle the yeast over the water and stir until dissolved. Add the beer, sugar, salt, and melted butter to the yeast mixture. Add the eggs, herbs, grated onion, and 4 cups of the flour and beat until smooth. Add enough of the remaining flour until the mixture becomes difficult to beat.

Turn the dough out onto a lightly floured board and begin kneading, adding enough flour so that the dough does not stick to your hands or the board. Knead until the dough is smooth and elastic. Place the dough in a lightly oiled bowl, cover it with a damp cloth, and let it rise in a warm place until doubled in bulk, about 1½ hours.

Punch the dough down and let stand for 10 to 15 minutes. Divide the dough into 2 pieces and shape each into a round loaf. Place each in a round pie plate, cover, and let rise again until doubled in size. Bake the loaves in a preheated 400°F oven for 35 minutes. Remove the loaves immediately from the pie plates and let cool on wire racks.

Serve the bread slightly warm.

Overnight Bread

Apricot Nut Bread

Yield: 1 loaf

1 cup boiling water
1 cup dried apricots, chopped
3 cups unsifted flour
1 tablespoon baking powder
½ teaspoon salt
⅓ cup butter or margarine
1 cup sugar
2 eggs
½ cup light corn syrup
1 cup nuts, chopped

Grease and lightly flour a 9 × 5 × 3-inch loaf pan. Pour water over the apricots and let stand 15 minutes. stir the flour, baking powder, and salt together.

In a large bowl, mix the butter, sugar, eggs, and corn syrup until smooth and well blended. Mix in the apricot mixture and nuts. Gradually mix in the dry ingredients.

Pour the mixture into the pan. Bake in a 350°F oven about 1¼ hours or until a cake tester inserted in the center of the loaf comes out clean. Cool in the pan 10 minutes. Remove from the pan and cool on a rack. Serve with jam or jelly, if desired.

Batter Bread

Yield: 2 loaves

1 cup milk
3 tablespoons sugar
2 teaspoons salt
1½ tablespoons butter
1 cup warm water
2 packages dry yeast
4½ cups flour

Heat the milk, sugar, salt, and butter on low heat until the butter has melted and the sugar and salt dissolved. Do not boil. Set aside to cool slightly.

Add the yeast to the warm water; stir until dissolved. Add the cooled mixture. Gradually add in the flour; stir until all is well blended. Cover with a towel; store in a warm place to rise about 40 minutes.

Stir the batter; beat a few vigorous strokes. Divide into 2 parts; place each in a well-greased, round casserole. Bake at 375°F ½ hour to 45 minutes, until nicely crusted on top. Cool on a rack.

Banana Bread

Yield: 1 loaf

1¾ cups unsifted flour
1 tablespoon baking powder
½ teaspoon salt

¾ cup sugar
½ cup shortening
2 eggs
1 cup bananas, mashed
½ cup walnuts, chopped (optional)

Grease a 9 × 5-inch pan.

Mix the flour, baking powder, and salt thoroughly. Beat the sugar, shortening, and eggs together until light and fluffy. Mix in the bananas. Add the dry ingredients; stir just until smooth. Pour into the prepared pan. Bake in a preheated 350°F oven until firmly set when lightly touched in the center, 50 to 60 minutes. (Bread may crack across the top.) Cool on a rack. Remove from the pan after 10 minutes.

Black Bread

Yield: 2 loaves

4 cups rye flour
4 cups white flour
2 packages active dry yeast
½ cup warm water
½ cup unsweetened cocoa
2 tablespoons caraway seeds
2 teaspoons salt
2 teaspoons instant coffee
¾ cup honey
¼ cup vinegar
¼ cup butter

Combine the flours in a large bowl; set aside 3 cups. Sprinkle the yeast over the warm water and stir until blended; set aside. In a large bowl, stir the reserved flour mixture, cocoa, caraway seeds, salt, and instant coffee together.

Heat 2 cups of water, honey, vinegar, and butter in a saucepan just until warm. The butter does not need to be completely melted. Blend well with the cocoa mixture. Add the yeast; stir until thoroughly combined. Stir in enough additional flour, 1 cup at a time, until the dough no longer clings to the sides of the bowl.

Turn out on a lightly floured board; cover and let rest 10 minutes. Knead until smooth and elastic, about 15 minutes. Place in a greased bowl; turn greased side up. Cover; let rise in a warm place about 1 hour, or until doubled. Punch down; turn onto a lightly floured board. Divide in half; shape each half into a smooth ball. Place each ball in the center of a greased, 8-inch round cake pan. Cover; let rise in a warm place about 1 hour, or until doubled.

Bake at 350°F 45 to 50 minutes, or until the loaves sound hollow when tapped lightly. Remove from the pan; put on wire racks. Brush with a little milk for a soft crust, if you wish.

Blueberry Nut Bread

Yield: 1 loaf

¼ cup butter
1 cup sugar
2 eggs
3 cups flour, sifted
4 teaspoons baking powder
1 teaspoon salt
1 cup milk
1 cup fresh blueberries
½ cup pecans, chopped

In a mixing bowl, cream the butter; gradually add the sugar and beat until light and fluffy. Beat in the eggs, one at a time. Sift the flour, baking powder, and salt together. Reserve 2 to 3 tablespoons of the flour mixture.

Add the remaining mixture to the creamed mixture alternately with the milk, beginning and ending with the dry ingredients. Toss the reserved flour with blueberries and nuts; stir into the batter. Turn into a buttered 9 × 5 × 2¾-inch loaf pan. Bake in a preheated 350°F oven for 60 to 70 minutes.

Christmas Breads: Wort Buns, Breakfast Buns, Rye Bread and, in front, Wort Bread, Scalded Rye Loaf, Old-Fashioned Christmas Bread

Wort Bread

Yield: 4 large loaves

4 cakes compressed yeast
7 tablespoons butter or margarine
1 package porter wort plus water so that together they measure 4 cups, or Pilsener beer or stout
⅓ cup dark corn syrup
1 tablespoon salt
1½ tablespoons ground ginger
1 tablespoon ground bitter orange peel
1 tablespoon aniseed and fennel (mixed)
¾ cup raisins (optional)
About 12 cups graham flour or rye flour, sifted

Crumble the yeast into a dough bowl. Melt the butter in a pot, pour in the porter wort or beer, and the syrup. Bring the liquid to finger temperature (98.6°F). Dissolve the yeast in a small amount of the liquid. Add the rest of the liquid, the spices, the raisins if desired, and most of the flour. Make into a workable dough, and let rise for 30 to 45 minutes.

Knead the dough on a baking board until smooth and elastic (10 to 15 minutes) and shape into loaves or buns. Place on a greased cookie sheet. Let the bread rise, covered, for 20 to 30 minutes. Bake the loaves at 400°F for 30 to 40 minutes. (Bake buns at 425°F.)

Brioche

Yield: 2 loaves

2 packages dry yeast
¼ cup lukewarm water
½ cup lukewarm milk
2 tablespoons sugar
1½ teaspoons salt
4½ cups flour, sifted
1 cup butter, cut into small pieces and softened
4 eggs
1 additional egg yolk

glaze
1 egg yolk
1 tablespoon milk

Combine the lukewarm water and yeast; stir to dissolve. Add the milk, sugar, and salt. With an electric mixer, beat in 2 cups of the flour and the butter until the mixture is well mixed. Add the eggs and egg yolk alternately with the remaining flour and continue to beat until the dough is smooth and does not feel sticky.

Place the dough in a buttered bowl. Cover with a damp towel and let it rise until doubled in bulk, 3 hours. Punch the dough down and form into 2 loaves. Place them in buttered loaf pans and let them rise until they reach the top of the pans.

Combine the egg yolk and milk for the glaze and brush the tops of the loaves with the mixture. Bake in a preheated 400°F oven for 15 minutes. Reduce the heat to 350°F and bake for 30 more minutes. Cool the loaves in the pans for 15 minutes before turning out on a wire rack.

Boston Brown Bread

Yield: 1 loaf

½ cup yellow cornmeal
½ cup rye flour
½ graham flour
1⅛ teaspoons baking soda
½ teaspoon salt
¾ cup milk
3 tablespoons butter, melted
6 tablespoons molasses
½ cup currants

Mix the dry ingredients together in a large bowl. Mix the milk, butter, molasses, and currants together in a separate bowl. Add the milk mixture to the dry ingredients and mix well.

Pour the batter into a buttered one-quart mold that can be fitted into a steamer. Steam for 1½-2 hours or until a cake tester inserted in the center comes out clean.

Coarse Bread in a Roasting Pan

Cheddar Cheese Bread

Yield: 2 loaves

½ cup warm water
2 ¼ ounce packages dry yeast, or 2 0.6-ounce cakes compressed yeast
2 tablespoons sugar
1 cup milk, scalded, or ½ cup evaporated milk and ½ cup hot water
2 tablespoons shortening
2 teaspoons salt
5 cups unbleached flour, divided
2 cups natural sharp Cheddar cheese spread
Melted butter

Dissolve the yeast and 1 teaspoon of sugar in water in a small bowl. Let stand for 5 to 10 minutes, or until the mixture expands and becomes bubbly. Set it aside.

Combine the shortening, remaining sugar, and salt with milk in a large bowl. Stir until the shortening melts.

Stir in 1 cup of flour. Add the cheese. Add the reserved yeast mixture. Gradually stir in enough of the remaining flour to make a stiff dough.

Turn out onto a lightly floured board. Knead 8 to 10 minutes, or until the dough is smooth and elastic. Dust the board and dough with more flour if necessary to prevent sticking.

Shape into a ball. Place in a large greased bowl. Turn to grease the ball on all sides. Cover and let it rise in a warm draft-free place for 1 hour, or until doubled in bulk.

Punch down the dough. Turn out on a lightly floured board. Cover and let it rise for 10 minutes. Cut the dough in half and shape into 2 loaves. Grease 2 8½ × 4½ × 2⅝-inch loaf pans.

Place the dough in the pans. Cover and let rise in a warm, draft-free place for 30 minutes, or until the dough has risen to the rim of the pans.

Bake at 375°F for 35 minutes, or until the crust is brown and the top sounds hollow when tapped. Remove from the pans. Cool on racks. Brush the tops lightly with melted butter.

Breakfast Buns

Yield: About 30 buns

1 ounce yeast
2⅓ cups lukewarm water
2 tablespoons oil
2 teaspoons salt
6 to 6⅓ cups flour
Egg white

Crumble the yeast into a dough bowl. Add the water and stir so that the yeast dissolves. Add the oil, salt, and most of the flour. Knead 10 minutes or until smooth and elastic. Cover and let rise for about 40 minutes.

Knead the dough and shape into round buns. Cover and let rise on a greased baking sheet for 40 to 50 minutes.

Brush with a slightly beaten egg white and bake at 475°F to 500°F for about 10 minutes.

Rye Bread

Yield: 4 loaves or 25 buns

3½ cakes compressed yeast
2 cups lukewarm water
Almost 1 tablespoon salt
2⅓ cups rye flour, sifted
2⅓ cups all-purpose flour
Coarse rye flour

Dissolve the yeast in the water. Add the salt, sifted rye flour, and most of the all-purpose flour. Make into a workable dough and let rise, covered, for 30 mintues.

Knead the dough and work in coarse rye flour. Form into about 25 round buns or 4 French bread loaves. Place on a greased baking sheet and cover. Let rise for 40 to 50 minutes in a slightly cool place. French bread loaves should be slashed with a knife right after being shaped. Bake the buns and loaves at 475°-525°F for 12 to 15 minutes.

Old-Fashioned Christmas Bread

Yield: 4 loaves

the first day
4 cups boiling water
10 cups sifted rye flour
3½ cakes compressed yeast dissolved in a little lukewarm water

the next day
1.7 ounces yeast dissolved in a little lukewarm water
⅓ cup corn syrup
1 tablespoon salt
⅓ cup melted butter or grease
5¾ cups rye flour, sifted

The first day, pour the boiling water over the flour and work into an even, firm dough. Cover with a baking cloth and let cool. Add the dissolved yeast, cover well, and let the dough rise overnight.

The next day, add the dissolved yeast, corn syrup, salt, melted and cooled butter or grease, and the flour. Work into a rather firm dough. Knead the dough well and let rise for ½ to 1 hour.

Shape the dough into 4 loaves of bread that should not have any cracks in them. Place on a greased baking sheet. Cover and let rise until almost double in size. Prick the loaves with a fork before they have finished rising. Bake at 425°F for about 15 minutes. Decrease the heat to 350°F to 400°F and bake for another 30 minutes. Brush the loaves with syrup and let them become cold while well wrapped in baking cloths.

Cherry Nut Bread

Yield: 1 loaf

¼ cup shortening
1 cup sugar
1 teaspoon salt
2 eggs
1½ cups flour
1½ teaspoons baking powder
8-ounce can pitted cherries
½ cup pecans, chopped

Combine the shortening, sugar, salt, and eggs in a medium-sized mixing bowl. Beat well, set it aside. Combine the flour and baking powder; mix well. Drain the cherries, reserving the liquid. Add the flour mixture to the egg mixture alternately with the reserved cherry liquid, mixing after each addition. Stir in the cherries and pecans.

Spoon the batter into a floured, greased 9 × 5 × 3 inch loaf pan. Bake at 350°F for 1 hour. Cool in the pan 10 minutes. Remove to a rack and cool completely.

Scalded Rye Loaf

Yield: 1 round loaf

2¾ cups water
½ tablespoon salt
½ tablespoon vinegar
2⅓ cups coarse rye flour
3½ cakes compressed yeast
2 teaspoons ground fennel
¼ cup corn syrup
4 to 4¾ cups flour

Bring the water to a boil, add the salt and vinegar and pour the boiling mixture over the coarse rye flour. Work the dough, cover, and let stand at room temperature overnight.

Crumble the yeast and dissolve it in several tablespoons of lukewarm water. Add the yeast to the dough together with the fennel, syrup, and most of the flour. Make into a workable dough, cover, and let rise for 30 to 40 minutes.

Knead the dough with a little more flour and shape into a smooth, round loaf. Place on a greased baking sheet. Prick with a fork and let rise under a damp baking cloth for about 45 minutes.

Bake at 400°F for about 20 minutes. Decrease the temperature to 350°F and bake for another 30 to 40 minutes. Let the loaf cool, well wrapped in baking cloths.

Cinnamon Bread

Yield: 2 loaves

1 cup milk, scalded
¼ cup shortening
1 cup sugar
2 teaspoons salt
2 packages active dry yeast
½ cup warm water
6 cups flour, sifted
2 eggs, slightly beaten
½ cup sugar
1 tablespoon ground cinnamon
1 tablespoon soft butter

Mix the milk, shortening, ½ cup of the sugar, and salt together. Cool to lukewarm. Sprinkle the yeast on warm water in a large bowl and stir until it is dissolved. Stir in 3 cups of the flour, eggs, and the milk mixture. Beat 2 minutes with an electric mixer at medium speed, scraping the bowl occasionally. Stir in enough additional flour with your hands to make a soft dough that leaves the sides of the bowl. Turn out onto a lightly floured board; knead until smooth, about 10 minutes.

Place the dough in a lightly greased bowl; turn the dough over to grease the top. Cover and let rise in a warm place until doubled in bulk, about 1½

hours. Punch it down; cover and let it rise again until almost doubled, about 30 minutes. Turn onto the board; divide in half. Make a ball out of each half. Cover and let rest 10 minutes.

Roll each half into a 12 × 7-inch rectangle. Combine the remaining ½ cup of sugar and the cinnamon; put aside 1 tablespoon for the topping. Sprinkle the dough rectangles evenly with the sugar-cinnamon mixture, then sprinkle 1 teaspoon of cold water over each rectangle. Spread smooth with a spatula. Roll as for a jelly roll, starting at the narrow end. Seal the long edge; tuck under the ends. Place, sealed edge down, in 2 greased 9 × 5 × 3-inch loaf pans. Cover and let it rise until almost doubled in bulk, 45 to 60 minutes.

Brush the tops of the loaves with soft butter and sprinkle with the reserved sugar-cinnamon mixture. Bake in a 375°F oven 35 to 40 minutes. If necessary, cover the tops of the loaves with aluminum foil the last 15 minutes of baking to prevent excessive browning. Remove the bread from the pans and cool on wire racks.

Cornbread

Yield: 6 servings

1 cup cornmeal
1 cup flour
1 tablespoon baking powder
½ teaspoon salt
2 to 4 tablespoons sugar (optional)
1 egg
1 cup milk
¼ cup fat or oil, melted

Mix the cornmeal, flour, baking powder, salt, and sugar. Set aside.

Beat the egg. Add the milk and fat. Add to the cornmeal mixture, stir just enough to mix. Fill a greased pan half full.

Bake at 425°F 20 to 25 minutes, until lightly browned.

Coarse Bread in a Roasting Pan

Yield: 12 pieces

3½ cakes compressed yeast
2⅓ cups water
2 teaspoons salt
5¼ cups coarse bread flour made from wheat and
    rye
Margarine

Crumble the yeast in a bowl. Warm the water to 98.6°F and dissolve the yeast in a little of the water. Then add the rest of the water. Add the salt and all the flour, and work the dough, which should be rather loose. Let the dough rise for 1 hour.

Knead the dough in the bowl and let it rise for another hour in the bowl.

Grease the roasting pan, about 12 × 16 inches, with margarine. Pour the dough into the roasting pan and flatten it with a floured hand. Cut the dough into 12 pieces. Cover with a baking cloth. Place the roasting pan on top of the stove, and preheat the oven to 525°F.

When the oven has become warm, bake the bread on the bottom rack of the oven for 15 minutes. Then decrease the heat to 225°F and let the bread bake for 60 more minutes. Wrap the bread in a baking cloth. Eat it while it still is warm (it also may be heated up).

Cranberry-Nut Bread

Yield: 1 loaf

2 cups flour, sifted
1 cup sugar
1½ teaspoons baking powder
½ teaspoon baking soda
1 teaspoon salt
¼ cup shortening
¾ cup orange juice
1 tablespoon orange rind, grated

Light Dinner Bread

1 egg, well beaten
½ cup nuts, chopped
1 or 2 cups cranberries, chopped and sprinkled with sugar

Sift the flour with all the dry ingredients; cut in the shortening. Combine the orange juice and grated rind with the egg. Pour the mixture over the dry ingredients. Mix enough to dampen. Fold in the chopped nuts and cranberries.

Bake at 350°F for 1 hour in a loaf pan.

Dark Date Nut Bread

Yield: 1 loaf

½ cup boiling water
½ cup mixed light and dark raisins
½ cup dates, chopped
1½ tablespoons butter
¾ teaspoon baking soda
¾ cup plus 2 tablespoons flour, sifted
½ cup sugar
¼ teaspoon salt
1 egg
½ teaspoon vanilla
¼ cup nuts, chopped

Pour boiling water over the raisins, dates, butter, and baking soda. Let stand. Mix the flour, sugar, and salt. Add the fruit mixture, including the water, and the remaining ingredients. Beat well.

Pour the batter into a greased and flour 1-pound coffee can. Bake 60-70 minutes, until done.

Dilly Bread

Yield: 1 loaf

1 package dry yeast
¼ cup warm water
1 cup cottage cheese, room temperature
2 tablespoons sugar
1 tablespoon instant onion
1 tablespoon butter
2 teaspoons dillseed
1 teaspoon salt
¼ teaspoon soda
1 unbeaten egg
2¼ cups flour

Soften the yeast in warm water. Add the lukewarm cottage cheese, sugar, onion, butter, dillseed, salt, soda, and egg. Stir well. Add the flour to form a stiff dough. Finish kneading the bread with your hands. When the dough is well kneaded, cover; let it rise in a warm place at least 60 minutes.

Beat down the batter; place in a greased 1½-quart round casserole. Allow it to rise 40 minutes more. Bake at 350°F 45 minutes. Turn out the bread onto a rack. While still hot, brush the top with melted butter and sprinkle with salt.

Light Dinner Bread (Food Processor Method)

Yield: 1 loaf

4 to 4⅓ cups flour
1 teaspoon salt
1½ teaspoons ground caraway
1¾ tablespoons margarine
1⅔ cups milk
3½ envelopes dry yeast

Place the flour, salt, and caraway in your food processor. Melt the margarine in a pan. Add the milk and heat to 98.6°F. Dissolve the yeast in the liquid mixture.

Using the plastic mixing attachment, start the food processor. Pour in the liquid mixture through the feeder funnel. Run the machine for 20 to 30 seconds. Take off the top and let the dough rise, covered with a baking cloth, for about 30 minutes.

Work the dough on a floured baking board. Shape it in an oval loaf and place it on a buttered baking sheet. Cut slits in the top of the bread with a sharp knife. Let the bread rise, covered, for about 30 minutes. Meanwhile, preheat the oven to 400°F.

Bake in the lower part of the oven for 30 to 35 minutes. Let the bread cool under a baking cloth.

The dough can also be rolled out into 24 buns. Bake them in the middle of the oven at 425°F for about 10 minutes.

Easy Bread

Yield: 2 loaves

3½ cakes fresh yeast
3½ tablespoons margarine or butter
4 cups milk
1 tablespoon salt
1 tablespoon ground caraway (optional)
2¾ cups whole-wheat flour
4 cups white flour

Preheat oven to 400°F. Grease and dust with whole-wheat flour 2 1½-quart loaf pans.

Crumble yeast in a large bowl. Melt the margarine and add the milk. Heat until lukewarm (98.6°F). Pour the mixture over the yeast and stir the salt, caraway (if desired), and all the whole-wheat and white flour. Measure the flour by lightly pouring it from the bag directly into a large measuring cup. Work together into a loose dough.

Place the dough in the loaf pans. Sprinkle with a little whole-wheat flour. Let rise for 25 to 30 minutes.

Bake for 35 to 40 minutes at 400°F. Turn out onto a rack and let cool under a cloth.

Buns

Yield: 36 buns

3½ cakes fresh yeast
3½ tablespoons margarine or butter
2⅓ cups water
2 teaspoons salt
½ teaspoon ground aniseed or caraway (optional)
6 to 6¾ cups flour

Grease 2 baking sheets or place baking paper on them.

Crumble the yeast into a large bowl. Melt the margarine and add the water. Heat until lukewarm (98.6°F). Pour the mixture over the yeast and stir. Add the salt, aniseed or caraway, and 5⅔ cups of the flour. Measure the flour by lightly pouring it directly from the bag into the measuring cup. Vigorously work the dough. Add and work in more of the flour. The dough should be rather firm. Let the dough stand in the bowl for 10 minutes (even better, let the dough rise under a cloth for 30 minutes).

Turn the dough out onto a floured baking board and work again until smooth. Divide the dough into 2 parts. Form each part into a long roll about 20 inches long. Divide each of the rolls into smaller pieces with a knife or a dough scraper. Dip one of the cut edges in flour. Place the buns on the baking sheets. The buns can be made even more attractive by cutting 5 slits in each piece—just don't slice all the way through. Let rise 30 to 40 minutes. Preheat oven to 475°F.

Bake in the middle of the oven for about 6 minutes. The buns taste best when served warm and fresh from the oven.

Square-Decorated Country Bread

Yield: 1 round loaf

3½ cakes fresh yeast
2 cups water, at 98.6°F
2 tablespoons oil
2 teaspoons salt
4¾ to 5½ cups flour

Grease and dust a 9-inch round cake pan.

Crumble the yeast into a large bowl. Add the warm water and the oil. Stir so that the yeast dissolves. Add the salt and 4¾ cups of the flour. Measure the flour by lightly pouring it directly from the bag into the measuring cup. Work the dough vigorously. Add ⅓ or ¾ cup more of the flour and work the dough again. It should be rather loose. Sprinkle a little flour over the dough and let it rise under a cloth for about 30 minutes.

Work the dough again in the bowl until it is smooth. Pour or dab it into the prepared pan. Even out the surface with a floured hand. Preheat oven to 475°F. Let dough rise for 30 minutes.

Cut the bread with a sharp knife or a razor blade just before baking. Brush the surface with water or spray on water with a flower sprayer. Bake on the bottom rack for 10 minutes at 475°F. Decrease heat to 400°F and bake for another 30 minutes. If the bread starts to get too dark, place the baking sheet on the highest rack of the oven, toward the end of the baking time.

Turn out the bread and let it cool on a rack under a cloth.

Honey Spice Bread

Yield: 2 loaves

1 package dry yeast
¼ cup lukewarm water
1 egg
½ cup honey
1 tablespoon ground coriander
½ teaspoon ground cinnamon
¼ teaspoon ground cloves
1½ teaspoons salt
1 cup lukewarm milk
6 tablespoons butter, melted
4 to 4½ cups flour

Sprinkle the yeast over the lukewarm water, stirring until dissolved.

Combine the egg, honey, spices, and salt in a large bowl and beat with a whisk until well mixed. Add the yeast mixture, milk, and 4 tablespoons of melted butter and beat again. Stir in the flour, ½ cup at a time, until the dough can be gathered into a soft ball. Blend in the remaining flour with your fingers.

Turn the dough out onto a lightly floured surface and knead until it is smooth and elastic. Do not add any additional flour. The dough should be rather soft. To prevent sticking, rub your hands occasionally with some of the remaining melted butter.

Form the dough into a ball and place in a lightly oiled bowl, turning to cover all surfaces. Place a damp towel over the bowl and let the dough rise until doubled in bulk.

When dough has risen, punch it down a few times and knead again for a few minutes. You may divide the dough in half and shape into two loaves or form the dough into a round and place in a 3-quart buttered casserole. Let the dough rise in the pans or in the casserole until it almost reaches the top.

Bake in a preheated 300°F oven, 1 hour for the loaves or 1 hour 10 minutes for the round, until the top is crusty and golden brown. Cool on a wire rack.

Easy Bread, Buns, and Square-Decorated Country Bread, Lemon Muffins, Raisin Muffins, Almond Muffins, Apple Muffins, Chocolate Muffins, Orange Muffins, Nut-Frosted Muffins

Fruit Loaf

Yield: 1 loaf

2 cups mixed dried fruits, finely chopped
1½ cups flour, sifted
3 teaspoons baking powder
½ teaspoon salt
¾ cup sugar
¾ cup butter
2 eggs, beaten
1 tablespoon milk
¼ teaspoon almond extract

Soak the dried fruits in enough boiling water to cover for 10 minutes, then drain well. Sift the flour, baking powder, salt, and sugar together into a mixing bowl. Cut in the butter with a pastry blender until the mixture is the consistency of fine bread crumbs. Stir in the dried fruits until evenly distributed. Add the eggs, milk, and almond extract and beat thoroughly. The batter will be very stiff.

Spread the batter in a well-greased loaf pan. Bake in a preheated 350°F oven for 1 hour or until the bread tests done. Cool slightly, then remove from the pan. Serve warm with butter, if desired.

Gingerbread

Yield: 16 to 20 squares

3 cups flour
¼ teaspoon salt
2 tablespoons ground ginger
2 teaspoons mixed spice
2 teaspoons ground cinnamon
½ cup brown sugar, tightly packed
4 tablespoons milk
½ cup light molasses
2 tablespoons dark molasses
½ cup butter or margarine
3 eggs
2 teaspoons baking soda

Grease and line a 10 × 7 × 2½-inch baking pan. Sift the flour, salt, and spices together. Add the sugar.

Put 3 tablespoons of milk into a small pan with the molasses and butter or margarine and melt over low heat. Add the beaten egg and stir all into the flour mixture. Beat well.

Dissolve the soda in the remaining 1 tablespoon of warm milk and beat into the mixture.

Spread evenly in the prepared pan, and bake in a preheated 375°F oven about 50 minutes. Cool in the pan; cut into squares.

Molasses Pumpkin Bread

Yield: 1 loaf

⅓ cup shortening
1 cup sugar
2 eggs
½ cup light or dark molasses
1 cup pumpkin, mashed
2 cups flour
¼ teaspoon baking powder
1 teaspoon baking soda
½ teaspoon salt
2 teaspoons pumpkin spice
1 cup walnuts, coarsely chopped

Cream the shortening; stir in the sugar and eggs. Stir in the molasses and pumpkin. Stir in the remaining ingredients and beat well.

Bake in a greased loaf pan for 1 hour or more at 350°F. Turn out and cool on a rack. Slice thinly; spread with butter or whipped cream cheese.

Onion Bread

Yield: 2 loaves

1 cup milk, scalded
3 tablespoons sugar
1 tablespoon salt
1½ tablespoons vegetable oil
2 envelopes dry yeast
¾ cup warm water
½ cup onion, minced
6 cups flour

Pour the milk into a large mixing bowl. Add the sugar, salt, and oil and mix until the sugar is dissolved. Cool until lukewarm. Dissolve the yeast in the warm water, then stir into the milk mixture. Add the onion and 4 cups of the flour and mix until blended. Add enough of the remaining flour, a small amount at a time, to make a stiff dough. Knead well. Cover and let rise for 45 minutes.

Punch the dough down, then place it in 2 greased loaf pans. Let it rise until doubled in bulk. Bake in a preheated 350°F oven for 1 hour, or until the bread sounds hollow when tapped with your fingers. Remove from the pans and place on wire racks to cool.

Orange Bread

Yield: 1 loaf

3 cups flour
3 tablespoons baking powder
⅔ cup sugar
1 teaspoon salt
1¼ cups milk
2 tablespoons butter, melted
1 egg, beaten

Peel of 1 orange, finely chopped

Measure the dry ingredients into a 4-cup measure. Sift them into a mixing bowl. Add the milk, butter, and egg; mix with a wooden spoon. Add the orange peel. Place the mixture in a greased 9×5×2-inch loaf pan. Let rise 15 minutes.

Bake the bread in a 350°F oven 50 minutes.

Honey Tea Bread

Yield: 1 loaf

1 cup milk
1 cup honey
4 tablespoons butter, cut into small pieces
2 eggs, lightly beaten
1¼ cups whole-wheat flour
1¼ cups white flour
1 teaspoon salt
3 teaspoons baking powder
½ cup walnuts

Place the milk and honey in a heavy saucepan and heat, stirring until well blended. Add the butter to the milk mixture; stir until the butter is dissolved. Beat in the eggs. Stir in the flours, salt, and baking powder. Fold in the nuts.

Pour the batter into a well-buttered and floured loaf pan. Bake in a preheated 325°F oven 1 hour to 1 hour 20 minutes, or until a cake tester comes out clean. Cool 15 minutes before removing from the pan. Cool further before slicing.

Lemon Bread

Yield: 1 loaf

⅓ cup butter, melted
1¼ cups sugar
2 eggs
¼ teaspoon almond extract
1½ cups flour, sifted
1 teaspoon baking powder
1 teaspoon salt
½ cup milk
1 tablespoon lemon peel, grated
½ cup nuts, chopped
3 tablespoons fresh lemon juice

Mix the butter and 1 cup of sugar together; beat in the eggs, 1 at a time. Add the almond extract. Sift the dry ingredients together; add them to the egg mixture alternately with the milk. Stir until just mixed. Fold in the lemon peel and nuts.

Turn the batter into a greased, 8½×4½×2½-inch loaf pan. Bake at 350°F about 70 minutes, or until the loaf tests done in the center.

Mix the lemon juice and remaining ¼ cup of sugar; immediately spoon the glaze over the hot loaf. Cool 10 minutes. Remove the bread from the pan; cool on a rack. Do not cut for 24 hours.

Potato Bread

Parmesan Casserole Bread

Yield: 1 round loaf

1 package dry yeast
¼ cup lukewarm water
1½ cups flour, sifted
1 tablespoon sugar
½ teaspoon salt
⅓ cup butter
1 egg, lightly beaten
¼ cup lukewarm milk
½ cup Parmesan cheese, grated
2 tablespoons parsley, chopped

Sprinkle the yeast over the water, stirring until dissolved. Sift the dry ingredients into a mixing bowl. With a pastry blender, cut the butter into the flour mixture until it resembles coarse meal. Add the egg, yeast mixture, and milk and beat the mixture well. Stir in the cheese and parsley.

Turn into an oiled, 8-inch round cake tin, cover with a damp cloth, and let rise until doubled in bulk. Dot the loaf with butter and bake in a preheated 375°F oven for 20 to 25 minutes. Let the bread cool a little, then cut into pie-shaped wedges.

Roasting Pan Bread

Glazed Orange-Raisin Bread

Yield: 2 loaves

1 cup milk, scalded
1½ teaspoons salt
½ cup sugar
½ cup butter or shortening, softened
2 packages active dry yeast
¼ cup warm water
5¼-5¾ cups flour, sifted
2 eggs
1 teaspoon orange peel, grated
1 teaspoon ground ginger
1½ cups raisins

orange-nut glaze
1 cup confectioners' sugar, sifted
2 teaspoons butter, softened
½ cup walnuts, finely chopped
2-4 tablespoons orange juice

Pour the milk over the salt, sugar, and butter in a large bowl. Mix well and cool to lukewarm.

Sprinkle the yeast on warm water; stirring until dissolved. Add the yeast mixture and 2½ cups of flour to the milk mixture. Beat 2 minutes with an electric mixer at medium speed, scraping the bowl occasionally.

Beat in the eggs, orange peel, ginger, raisins, and ½ cup of flour. Then mix in enough remaining flour, a little at a time, first with a spoon and then with your hands, to make a soft dough that leaves the sides of the bowl.

Turn the dough onto a lightly floured board. Knead just until smooth, about 50 strokes. Roll it into a ball; place in a lightly greased bowl; turning the ball over to grease its top. Cover and let rise in a warm place until doubled in bulk, 1-1½ hours. Punch it down and let it rest 15 minutes. Divide the dough in half. Shape each half into a loaf and place in 2 greased 8½ × 4½ × 2½-inch or 9 × 5 × 3-inch loaf pans. Make 3 diagonal, ¼-inch deep slashes deep across the top of each loaf. Cover and let rise in a warm place only until doubled, about 1 hour.

Bake in a 375°F oven 40 to 50 minutes. Cover with a sheet of aluminum foil after the first 20 minutes of baking if the loaves are browning too fast. Remove the loaves from the pans; place on wire racks.

Blend all the ingredients for the orange-nut glaze together until the glaze is of spreading consistency. Spread the glaze on top of the warm loaves, then cool.

Swedish Overnight Bread

Yield: 4 loaves

1⅔ cups bran
6⅓ cups water
6 cakes compressed yeast
2 to 2½ tablespoons salt
2 tablespoons oil
12 cups flour

Bring to a boil the crushed wheat in 2 cups water and then let it carefully simmer for 10 minutes. Pour into a dough bowl and add the remaining 4⅓ cups cold water. Let stand until cold.

Grease 4 bread tins.

Crumble the yeast into the dough liquid, add the salt and oil, and work in the flour. Pour the dough out onto a baking board and knead well. Divide the dough into 4 parts and make loaves of each. Place in the refrigerator, covered with a baking cloth, and allow to stand until the next morning.

Preheat the oven to 400°F and place the baking tins directly from the refrigerator into the warm oven for 45 minutes. Bake in 2 batches, allowing 2 of the tins to remain in the refrigerator while the other 2 are in the oven.

Cool the loaves on a rack, covered with a baking cloth.

Potato Bread

Yield: 2 loaves

8 medium-large potatoes
1 teaspoon salt
2⅓ cups skim milk
2 tablespoons oil
3 cakes compressed yeast
6⅓ to 7¼ cups unbleached flour
¾ cup coarse rye flour
1 tablespoon ground fennel

Peel the potatoes, boil them until soft, and mash them with the salt, a small amount of the skim milk, and the oil. Add the rest of the milk, warm to finger temperature (98.6°F). Stir the yeast into a small amount of the mixture, and pour into the dough.

Add most of the country flour, the rye flour, plus the fennel, and knead into a workable dough. Let rise until doubled in size (about 45 minutes), covered under a cloth.

Knead the dough on a baking board and divide it into 2 parts. Form each part into 2 round rolls. Let rise until doubled in size, about 40 minutes. Cut a diamond pattern on the top of the loaves, using a sharp knife or a razor blade. Bake at 400°F for about 40 minutes. Test for doneness, using a toothpick.

Pumpkin Bread

Yield: 2 loaves

4 cups flour, unsifted
3 cups sugar
2 teaspoons baking soda
1½ teaspoons salt
1 teaspoon baking powder
1 teaspoon cinnamon
1 teaspoon nutmeg
½ teaspoon cloves
¼ teaspoon ginger
1 16-ounce can pumpkin
1 cup oil
4 eggs
⅔ cup water

Grease 2, 9 × 5 × 3-inch loaf pans. Mix the dry ingredients thoroughly in a large bowl. Beat the pumpkin, oil, eggs and water together. Add the dry ingredients. Stir just until the dry ingredients are moistened. Do not overmix.

Pour half of the batter into each loaf pan. Bake at 350°F for 1-1¼ hours, or until a toothpick inserted in the center of the loaf comes out clean. Cool on a rack. Remove the bread from the pans after 10 minutes.

Roasting Pan Bread

Yield: 4 loaves

¼ pound yeast
7 tablespoons butter or margarine
4 cups water
1 bottle light beer
4 teaspoons salt
2 tablespoons corn syrup
1 4¼ pound bag whole-wheat flour

Crumble the yeast into a large bread bowl. Melt the butter and pour in the water and the beer. Dissolve the yeast in a little of the lukewarm liquid mixture. Add the rest of the liquid, plus the salt, syrup, and most of the flour. Make into a workable dough.

Place the entire dough in a greased roasting pan, about 12 × 16 inches, and flatten it with a floured hand. Prick the surface with a fork. Let the dough rise, covered with a damp baking cloth, for about 1 hour.

Bake at 475°F for about 15 minutes, until the bread has become a golden brown. Decrease the heat to 400°F and bake for another 30 minutes.

Cut the bread into 4 loaves when it has become cold.

Pumpernickel Bread

Yield: 3 round loaves

9 cups white flour
3 cups rye flour
2 tablespoons salt
1 cup all bran cereal
¾ cup yellow cornmeal
2 packages dry yeast
3½ cups water
¼ cup dark molasses
2 squares unsweetened chocolate
1 tablespoon butter
2 cups mashed potatoes, at room temperature
1 tablespoon caraway seeds

Combine the flours. Place 2 cups of the flour mixture, the salt, cereal, cornmeal, and dry yeast in a bowl. Combine the water, molasses, chocolate, and butter in a saucepan and heat over low heat until the chocolate and butter melt. Gradually add the liquids to the flour mixture and beat 2 minutes with an electric mixer at medium speed. Add the potatoes and another cup of the flour mixture, or enough to make a thick batter. Beat at high speed 2 minutes. Stir in additional flour and the caraway seeds. When the dough begins to pull away from the sides of the bowl, turn it out onto a floured board. Cover and let rest 15 minutes.

Knead, using more flour as necessary, until the dough is smooth and elastic, about 15 minutes. Place in an oiled bowl. Cover with a damp towel and set in a warm place to rise until doubled in bulk. Punch the dough down with your fist a few times. Cover and let rise again about 45 minutes.

Punch the dough down and turn out onto the board. Divide it into 3 equal pieces and shape each into a round ball. Oil 3 8 × 9-inch cake tins and place the dough in these. Cover and let rise until doubled in bulk. Bake in a preheated 350°F oven for about 50 minutes. Immediately remove from the pans and cool the loaves on wire racks.

Saffron Breads and Rolls

Yield: Depends on shapes used

3 packages compressed yeast
14 tablespoons butter or margarine
2 cups milk
½ teaspoons saffron
¾ cup sugar
½ teaspoon salt
1 egg
About 7 cups flour
Egg
Decorate with: raisins, chopped almonds, pearl
sugar

Crumble the yeast into a dough bowl. Melt the butter in a pan, pour in the milk, and heat to finger temperature (98.6°F). Dissolve the yeast in a little of the liquid. Then add the rest of the liquid, in which finely ground saffron has been mixed. Add the sugar, salt, egg, and most of the flour. Make into a workable dough and let rise in a draft-free spot, covered, for about 40 minutes.

Knead the dough on a baking table, and make into the various traditional shapes:

Small Rolls are placed on a greased cookie sheet. Cover and let the rolls rise until about doubled in size. Brush with a beaten egg and bake at 475°F.

Large Rolls and Coffee Cakes such as cut wreaths and braided cakes are baked at 400°-425°F.

Baking Tips: Mixing the saffron with a little brandy is an old-fashioned trick for getting the most flavor out of the spice. Grind the saffron in a mortar with a sugar cube. Then stir it into a little brandy or milk.

Hard Rye Bread

Saffron Breads and Rolls

Hard Rye Bread Wafers

Yield: About 25 slices of bread

1½ cakes compressed yeast
2 cups water, at 98.6°F
3 cups coarse rye flour
2 cups flour
2½ teaspoons salt
1 teaspoon sugar for the rising process
2 teaspoons caraway

Crumble the yeast into a large bowl and dissolve it in the 98.6°F water. Add the remaining ingredients and work together into a smooth dough. Sprinkle with a little flour, cover with a baking cloth, and let rise for about 30 minutes.

Knead the dough and roll it out so that it is very, very thin (less than ⅟16 inch thick). Cut out large, round "cookies" with the help of a plate that is about 7 inches in diameter. Prick the dough with a fork, place the rounds on a baking sheet, spread a baking cloth over them, and let rise for about 20 minutes.

Preheat the oven to 400°F while the dough is rising. Bake for 5 minutes. Turn the slices over and bake for another 5 minutes.

Zucchini Bread

Yield: 2 loaves

3 eggs, beaten until frothy
2 cups sugar
1 cup oil
1 tablespoon vanilla
2 cups loosely packed zucchini, coarsely grated
1 cup nuts, chopped
2 cups flour (white or whole-wheat)
1 tablespoon cinnamon
2 teaspoons baking soda
2 teaspoons salt
¼ teaspoon baking powder
1 cup raisins

Beat the eggs until frothy. Gradually beat the sugar, oil, and vanilla into the eggs until thick and creamy. Stir in the remaining ingredients.

Pour into 2 greased and floured, 8 × 3 × 4-inch loaf pans. Bake at 350°F for 1 hour. The bread keeps for a long time and becomes more moist with age.

Tea Bread

Yield: 16 small buns

⅔ cup milk
1 cake compressed yeast
1 egg
1 tablespoon sugar
½ teaspoon salt
About 2 cups flour
5¼ tablespoons butter
Egg
Poppy seeds

Heat the milk so that it is lukewarm (98.6°F). Dissolve the yeast in the milk. Add the egg, sugar, salt, and flour, and knead well. Let stand and rise in a warm place for about 20 minutes.

Preheat oven to 400°F.

Punch down the dough and knead again. Roll it out into a rectangle about 10x16 inches. Slice the butter with a cheese cutter and lay the slices out over half the dough. Fold the other half over the buttered half. Roll the dough and fold it together into 3 layers. Roll again and fold it again in the same way. Repeat 1 or 2 more times.

Finally, roll out the dough so that it is about 12 × 30 inches and fold it lengthwise into 3 layers. Cut the dough into 2-inch wide pieces and let it rise on a baking sheet for about 15 minutes. Brush with the egg and sprinkle with poppy seeds. Bake for about 15 minutes at 400°F.

Shortbread

Yield: 20 to 24 pieces

¾ cup unsalted butter
⅔ cup confectioners' sugar
1¾ cups flour
½ teaspoon salt

Cream the butter, add the sugar gradually, and beat until very light and fluffy. Sift the flour and salt over the butter mixture and work it with your hand until thoroughly blended.

Pat the batter into the bottom of an 11-inch pie plate and flute the edges. Using a sharp knife, mark through the dough into about 24 wedges, then prick all over with a fork.

Bake in the center of a preheated 325°F oven for about 45 minutes or until the shortbread is firm to the touch in the center and a pale yellow color. It should not be allowed to brown. Cool on a cooling rack, then turn out, right side up, and cut into wedges to serve.

South Carolina Spoon Bread

Yield: 1 loaf

1 pint milk
¼ cup cornmeal
3 tablespoons butter
1 teaspoon salt
3 eggs, separated

Heat the milk in a double boiler, stir in the cornmeal and cook slowly until thick and smooth. Remove from the heat and add the butter and salt. Let the mixture cool while you beat the egg whites stiff.

Beat the egg yolks and add to the cornmeal mixture, then fold in egg whites and bake for 30 minutes in a buttered pan in a 325°F to 375°F oven.

Spice Bread

Yield: 2 loaves

2 packages dry yeast
¼ cup lukewarm water
¼ teaspoon sugar
2 cups milk, scalded
⅓ cup butter

Tea Bread

¼ cup brown sugar
¼ cup honey
2 teaspoons salt
⅓ cup orange juice
1 egg, lightly beaten
1 tablespoon cumin
4 cups whole-wheat flour
3½ cups white flour
2 tablespoons softened butter
2 tablespoons honey

Sprinkle the yeast over the warm water. Add the sugar and stir to dissolve. Add the butter, brown sugar, honey, salt, and orange juice to the scalded milk. Cool the mixture to lukewarm. Add the yeast mixture, the egg, cumin, and the whole-wheat flour; beat until smooth. Add enough of the white flour to produce a stiff dough. When the dough begins to pull away from the sides of the bowl, turn it onto a floured board and begin kneading, using as much white flour as is necessary to prevent sticking. Knead until the dough is smooth and elastic.

Place the dough in an oiled bowl, cover it with a damp cloth, and allow it to rise until doubled in bulk. Punch the dough down and knead it for 1 minute. Return the dough to the bowl and let it rise again until doubled in bulk. Punch the dough down again, shape it into a ball, and divide it in half. Place each half in a buttered loaf tin, cover, and let the loaves rise until doubled in bulk. Bake the loaves in a preheated 425°F oven for 10 minutes. Reduce the heat to 350°F and continue baking for 25 to 30 minutes or until the loaves test done.

Let the loaves cool in the tins on a wire rack for 5 minutes. Combine the 2 tablespoons of softened butter and honey. Turn the loaves out of the pans and brush the tops with this mixture. Allow the bread to cool further on the racks.

Skillet Bread

Yield: 1 loaf

2 cups flour
4 teaspoons baking powder
2 teaspoons salt
1¼ cups milk
2 tablespoons butter

Mix the dry ingredients in a bowl. Add the milk; blend with a wooden spoon. It will have a biscuit-like spongy texture.

Heat the butter in a medium-sized skillet. Keep the heat low. Spread the butter around evenly. Pour in the batter. Cook 15 minutes or until the underside is golden brown. Lift with a large spatula; turn to cook the other side 15 minutes.

Turn the bread out onto a round plate; serve at once.

Walnut Bread

Yield: 3 small loaves

2 cups water
2 tablespoons oil
.9 ounce yeast
2 teaspoons salt
⅓ cup wheat bran
3¼ cups flour
2¾ cups light rye flour
½ cup walnuts, chopped into large pieces

Warm the water and the oil to 96.8°F. Dissolve the yeast in a little of the liquid, then add the rest of the liquid. Blend in the salt, wheat bran, flours, and nuts. Pour in the liquid and make into a workable dough; let the dough rise under a cloth for about 45 minutes.

Knead the dough and shape it into three small loaves or two larger loaves. Slash the top with a razor blade, brush with water, and sprinkle with a little of the rye flour. Let rise until doubled in bulk.

Bake in the oven at 400°F for 30 to 40 minutes. Test with a toothpick to make sure the bread is done.

Whole-Wheat Bread in a Roasting Pan

Yield: 15 pieces

2¾ cups whole-wheat flour
1⅔ cups flour, bleached or coarser variety
1 teaspoon salt
2 teaspoons ground bitter orange peel
1¾ tablespoons margarine
1⅔ cups water
¼ cup corn syrup
3 cakes compressed yeast
Brush with 1 egg

Place the flour, salt and the bitter orange peel in your food processor. Melt the margarine in a pan and pour in the water and corn syrup. Heat to 98.6°F. Dissolve the yeast in the liquid mixture.

Using the plastic mixer attachment, start the machine; pour in the liquid through the feeder funnel. Knead the dough quickly 20 to 30 seconds. Take off the lid and let the dough rise under a cloth for 30 minutes. Preheat the oven to 425°F.

Turn the dough out onto a baking board and work it lightly. Flatten the dough into a greased roasting pan. Cut the dough into 15 pieces with a floured dough cutter or knife. Cover and let the bread rise for about 30 minutes.

Brush the bread with the whipped egg. Bake in the middle of the oven for about 15 minutes. Break the bread into pieces when it has cooled.

Hush Puppies

Yield: 2 dozen

½ cup flour
2 teaspoons baking powder
½ teaspoon salt
1½ cups cornmeal
1 small onion, finely chopped
¾ cup milk
1 egg, beaten
Deep fat for frying

Put the dry ingredients into a large bowl in the order listed. Add the onion, then the milk and egg. Stir until all the ingredients are well blended.

Heat the fat to 375°F in a deep skillet. Drop the batter by teaspoonfuls into the hot fat; fry until golden brown all over. Remove; drain the hush puppies on paper towels. Keep warm until ready to serve.

To vary the hush puppies, use the above recipe, substituting ½ cup chopped apple or ½ cup cooked corn in place of the onion.

Fried Mush

Yield: 1 loaf

5 cups boiling water
1½ cups cornmeal
1½ cups water
1 teaspoon salt
1 egg yolk
2 tablespoons milk
1 cup crumbs
Butter or bacon fat
Maple syrup

Place boiling water in the top of a double boiler; combine the cornmeal, water, and salt and add the mixture to the boiling water a little at a time, stirring. Cook over high heat for 3 minutes; cover and steam for 15 minutes longer. Pour into a greased bread pan. Cool, then cut into ¾-inch slices.

Combine the egg yolk and milk. Dip the slices into the egg yolk mixture, then in the crumbs. Let stand a few minutes; then fry in butter or bacon fat in a hot pan. Turn carefully, fry the other side. Serve with maple syrup.

Country Biscuits

Yield: 20 biscuits

2 cups flour
4 teaspoons baking powder
1 stick unsalted butter
Dash salt
Milk

Whole-Wheat Bread in a Roasting Pan

Grease a large mixing bowl. Sift the flour, baking powder, and salt into a bowl; add cold butter cut into pieces. With a pastry blender, work the dough until mealy. Add just enough cold milk to hold the dough together; form a ball and press onto a floured surface, patting down until about ½-inch thick.

Flour a biscuit cutter. Cut the dough into biscuits and place 2 inches apart on a greased cookie sheet. Chill for 1 hour.

Preheat the oven to 450°F. Prick the tops of the biscuits with the times of a fork. Bake for 10-12 minutes.

Cottage Cheese Biscuits

Yield: 24 biscuits

1 cup flour
1⅛ teaspoons baking powder
¼ teaspoon baking soda
⅛ teaspoon salt
2 teaspoons sugar
2 tablespoons butter
½ cup small-curd, tangy cottage cheese
1 large egg
3 tablespoons milk

Walnut Bread

In a medium bowl, stir the flour, baking powder, baking soda, salt, and sugar together; cut in the butter. In a small bowl, with an electric beater at high speed, beat the cheese until it is as smooth as ricotta, at least 2 minutes; add the egg and milk; beat until blended. Add the cheese mixture to the flour mixture and stir with a fork until flour mixture is moistened and rather sticky.

Turn the dough, by level tablespoons, into buttered, 1¾-by-¾-inch muffin-pan cups. Bake in a preheated 450°F oven until a cake tester inserted in the center comes out clean, about 15 minutes. Serve hot.

Popovers

Yield: 8 large popovers

1 cup flour
¼ teaspoon salt
2 eggs, beaten
1 cup milk (scant measure)
1 tablespoon shortening, melted

Sift the flour and salt together. Mix the eggs, milk, and shortening; add gradually to the flour. Beat until smooth, with a whisk or electric mixer, about 1 minute. Fill greased popover tins, Pyrex cups, or muffin pans to ⅓ full.

Bake 20 minutes in a preheated 450°F oven. Reduce the heat to 350°F; bake 15 minutes, until the popovers are firm.

Sweet Cream Biscuits

Yield: 36 small biscuits

4 cups flour, sifted
1 teaspoon salt
2 tablespoons baking powder
1½ cups heavy cream
4 tablespoons water (optional)

Sift the flour, salt, and baking powder together. Stir in the heavy cream with a fork, just until all the flour is moistened; add water if necessary to get the proper consistency.

Knead on a lightly floured surface, about 10 times. Roll ¾ inch thick; cut with a small floured cutter. Bake on an ungreased baking sheet in a 450°F oven 12 minutes, or until golden brown.

Jam Slices

Yield: About 60 slices

1⅔ cups flour
¼ cup sugar
14 tablespoons margarine or butter, at room temperature
⅓ cup jam or applesauce
⅔ cup confectioners' sugar
½ tablespoon water

Preheat oven to 400°F.

Place the flour and sugar in your food processor. Divide the margarine or butter into 6 to 8 pieces and add to the flour and sugar. Using the plastic mixer attachment, start the machine; let the mixture blend for 20 to 30 seconds. Let the dough stand in a cold place for about an hour.

Roll the dough out into 4, flat, long-shaped buns and place them on a baking sheet lined with baking paper. Make a depression down the middle of the buns. Fill with jam or applesauce. Bake in the middle of the oven for about 10 minutes. Let the buns cool on the baking sheet.

Mix the confectioners' sugar and water together. Brush it over the buns and cut them into slanted slices.

Cinnamon-Nut Rolls

Yield: 36 rolls

1 package active dry yeast
1 cup milk, scalded and cooled to warm (110 to 115°F)
6 tablespoons shortening
6 tablespoons butter or margarine
¾ cup sugar
1 teaspoon salt
2 egg yolks or 1 egg, beaten
About 3 cups flour, sifted
Melted butter or margarine
½ cup brown sugar, firmly packed
2 teaspoons ground cinnamon
1 cup corn syrup
1 cup brown sugar, firmly packed
¼ cup butter
1½ cups pecans

Sprinkle the yeast on warm milk, stirring until dissolved. Cream the shortening and 2 tablespoons of the butter; add ¼ cup of sugar and salt. Beat until light and fluffy. Add the egg yolks, yeast, and enough flour to make a soft dough that leaves the sides of the bowl. Turn out onto a lightly floured cloth or board; knead until smooth and elastic.

Place in a greased bowl; turn the greased side of the dough up. Cover; let it rise until doubled in bulk. Divide the dough in half; roll into 2 18 × 9-inch rectangles, about ¼-inch thick. Brush with melted butter.

Mix the remaining sugar, ½ cup of brown sugar, and cinnamon together; sprinkle each piece of dough with half of the sugar mixture. Roll like a jelly roll, cut into 1-inch slices.

Mix the corn syrup, 1 cup of brown sugar, and ¼ cup butter together; heat slowly or in top of a double boiler. Place 1 tablespoon of syrup and 4 to 5 pecans, rounded side down, in greased muffin-pan cups. Drop the dough slices, cut side down, in syrup; cover and let rise until doubled in bulk.

Bake in a 400°F oven 12 to 15 minutes. Remove from the oven, flip over the pans at once. Remove the rolls, pecan side up, onto a large tray. Let the pans stand over the rolls a minute, so the syrup drains onto them.

Sour Milk Biscuits

Yield: 24 biscuits

2 teaspoons white vinegar
⅔ cup milk
1¾ cups flour, sifted
2 teaspoons baking powder
½ teaspoon baking soda
1 teaspoon salt
5 tablespoons butter
Melted butter

"Sour" pasteurized milk by mixing it with the vinegar and letting it stand at room temperature for 10 or 15 minutes until it looks curdled.

Sift the dry ingredients together. Cut in the 5 tablespoons butter. Add the sour milk all at once; stir quickly with a fork until a soft dough forms.

Turn onto a floured board and knead the dough gently and quickly for 30 seconds. Roll the dough lightly ½ inch thick. Cut with a floured, 1½-inch biscuit cutter. Prick the tops with a fork and brush with melted butter. Bake on an ungreased baking sheet in a preheated 425°F oven 12-15 minutes.

Parker House Rolls

Yield: 36 rolls

1 cup milk, scalded
2 tablespoons shortening
2 tablespoons sugar
1 teaspoon salt
1 fresh cake or 1 package granular yeast
¼ cup lukewarm water
1 egg, well beaten
3½ cups enriched flour

Combine the milk, shortening, sugar, and salt; cool to lukewarm. Add yeast softened in lukewarm water; add the egg. Gradually stir in the flour to form a soft dough. Beat vigorously. Cover and let it rise in a warm place (82°F) until doubled in bulk, about 2 hours.

Turn out onto a lightly floured surface. Roll the dough ¼ inch thick. Cut with a biscuit cutter. Brush with melted butter. Make a crease across each. Fold so the top half slightly overlaps. Press the edges together at the crease. Place close together on a lightly greased pan. Bake at 400°F about 15 minutes. Serve hot.

Refrigerator Rolls

Yield: 36 rolls

2 packages active dry yeast
1¾ cup warm water (110° to 115°F)
½ cup sugar
1 tablespoon salt
5½ to 6 cups flour
1 egg
¼ cup soft shortening, butter, or margarine

Sprinkle the yeast over warm water, stirring until dissolved. Stir in the sugar, salt, and ½ the flour with an electric mixer on medium speed for 2 minutes, or by hand until the mixture is smooth. Beat in the egg and shortening; mix in the remaining flour with your hands or a spoon until the dough is easy to handle. Shape the dough into a ball and place it in a lightly greased bowl; turn the greased side of the dough up. Cover tightly with aluminum foil, or place the bowl in a plastic bag.

Put the dough in the refrigerator and let rise at least 2 hours, or until doubled in bulk. Punch down the dough and shape into individual rolls. Brush the tops with melted butter; cover and let rise in a warm place until nearly doubled, about 1½ hours. Bake in a 400°F oven 12 to 15 minutes.

The dough may be kept up to 5 days in the refrigerator with 45°F or lower temperature. Punch down the dough everyday until you use it.

Corn Muffins

Yield: 12 muffins

1 cup cornmeal
1 cup flour
1 teaspoon salt
2½ teaspoons baking powder
1 cup milk
2 eggs, well beaten
2 tablespoons shortening, melted

Place the dry ingredients in a large mixing bowl. Combine the milk and eggs in a smaller bowl; add to the dry ingredients. Stir in the shortening until all ingredients are well blended. Drop by spoonfuls into 2-inch, greased muffin tins, filling the tins about ½ full. Bake at 400°F about 20 minutes.

Serve the muffins with hot butter and your favorite jam or jelly, or break the muffins in half, cover with syrup, and eat with a fork.

Cottage Cheese Muffins

Yield: 12 to 15 muffins

1 pound small curd cottage cheese
2 tablespoons sour cream
¼ cup sugar
4 eggs
½ cup biscuit mix
1 teaspoon vanilla

Beat all the ingredients except the eggs until smooth, either in a blender or a food processor. Add the eggs one at a time and continue beating until smooth.

Pour the batter into well-greased muffin tins until the cups are ¾ full. Bake at 350°F for 45-50 minutes.

Jam Slices

Blueberry Muffins

Yield: 12 muffins

½ cup butter
1 cup plus 2 teaspoons sugar
2 eggs
2 cups flour
2 teaspoons baking powder
½ teaspoon salt
½ cup milk
2 cups fresh or frozen blueberries
1 teaspoon vanilla

On the low speed of an electric mixer, cream the butter and 1 cup of the sugar until fluffy. Add the eggs, one at a time, and mix until blended. Sift the flour, baking powder, and salt together. Mix the dry ingredients with the butter mixture alternately with the milk. Add the blueberries and vanilla.

Grease a muffin tin, including the top of the muffin tin, or you can use paper-cup cake liners. Pile the batter high in the tins and sprinkle with the remaining 2 teaspoons of sugar. Bake at 375°F for 30 minutes.

French Buns

Yield: 32 buns

5¼ tablespoons margarine or butter
2 cups milk
2 cakes compressed yeast
2 teaspoons salt
5⅔ to 6 cups flour

Melt the butter in a pot. Add the milk and allow the mixture to become finger temperature (98.6°F). Mix the yeast in a small amount of the milk mixture, and then pour over the rest of the milk. Add most of the flour and the salt. Work into a smooth dough and let rise in a draft-free place for about 40 minutes.

Knead the dough on a baking table. Divide the dough into 4 parts. Roll each dough piece out into a long roll and cut each roll into 8 pieces. Dip the pieces in the rest of the flour. Place them on a greased baking sheet. Let rise for about 30 minutes.

Bake in a hot oven, 425° to 450°F, for about 8 to 10 minutes. Serve with marmalade.

Almond Muffins

Yield: About 12 muffins

2 boiled, cold potatoes
⅓ cup almonds
5½ tablespoons soft butter or margarine
⅔ cup sugar
2 eggs
Grated peel of ½ lemon

⅓ cup flour
1½ teaspoons baking powder

Grate the potatoes; grind the almonds (they do not need to be scalded and peeled). Mix the butter and sugar together until light. Add the eggs, one at a time, and beat vigorously. Carefully stir in the potatoes, the almonds, the lemon peel, and the flour which has been mixed with the baking powder.

Fill paper muffin cups until about ½ full and bake at 400°F until they feel dry, about 15 minutes.

You can even brush melted cooking chocolate on top of the muffins and place a piece of almond in the chocolate. Do this shortly before serving.

Pecan Whole-Wheat Muffins

Yield: 12 muffins

1 cup flour
3 teaspoons baking powder
4 tablespoons sugar
1 teaspoon salt
1 cup whole-wheat flour
1 cup pecans, chopped
4 tablespoons butter, melted
1 cup milk
2 eggs

Mix the flour, baking powder, sugar, and salt together in a medium-sized bowl. Stir in the whole-wheat flour and nuts. Add the butter, milk, and eggs to the dry ingredients; blend until thoroughly moistened. Spoon the batter into well-greased muffin tins. Bake at 375 °F 15 to 18 minutes.

Drop Doughnuts

Yield: 36 doughnuts

¼ cup soft butter
1 cup sugar
2 egg yolks, beaten
1 whole egg, beaten
4 cups flour
2 teaspoons baking powder
¼ teaspoon nutmeg
½ teaspoon soda
¾ cup buttermilk
Powdered sugar

Cream the butter and sugar. Stir in the egg yolks and whole egg; blend. In a separate bowl, sift all the dry ingredients together except powdered sugar; add to the creamed mixture, alternating with buttermilk. Stir to mix all ingredients.

Cook by dropping spoonfuls of dough into 375°F deep fat. Fry a few at a time, to keep the fat temperature constant. Turn to brown on all sides. Drain on paper towels; sprinkle with powdered sugar.

French Buns

Cranberry Muffins

Yield: 10 muffins

1¾ cups flour
5 tablespoons sugar
2½ teaspoons baking powder
¾ teaspoon salt
1 egg, well beaten
¾ cup milk
⅓ cup liquid shortening
1 cup cranberries, chopped
3 tablespoons sugar

Mix the flour with 2 tablespoons of the sugar, the baking powder, and salt. Combine the egg and milk and add all at once to the flour mixture. Add the shortening and stir only until the dry ingredients are dampened. (Batter will be lumpy.)

Sprinkle the cranberries with the remaining 3 tablespoons of sugar and stir into the batter. Spoon into greased muffin pans, filling each about ⅔ full. Bake at 400°F for 25 to 30 minutes, or until done.

Lemon Muffins

Yield: About 15 muffins

2 eggs
¾ cup sugar
⅓ cup light cream
3½ tablespoons melted butter or margarine, cooled
Grated peel and juice of ½ lemon
1¼ cups flour
1½ teaspoons baking powder

Beat the eggs and sugar together until light. Add the cream, the cooled, melted butter, and the peel and juice of the lemon. Mix the flour with the baking powder and add it to the other ingredients.

Spoon the batter into paper muffin cups. Fill them about ¾ full, since they rise during baking. Bake at 400°F to 425°F for about 10 minutes. When serving the muffins, confectioners' sugar may be sprinkled on top.

Raisin Muffins with Cardamom: Instead of lemon, use ⅔ cup raisins and ½ teaspoon ground cardamom, which is mixed with the flour before it is added to the batter.

Apple Muffins: 2 peeled, grated apples are mixed into the batter instead of the lemon.

Chocolate Muffins: ¼ pound dark cooking chocolate adds a tasty flavor when used instead of the lemon.

Orange Muffins with Whole-Wheat Flour: Instead of the lemon, use the grated peel of 1 orange. Substitute half the cream with orange juice and half the flour with whole-wheat flour. For an added touch, ice the muffins with confectioners'

sugar mixed with a little orange juice and sprinkle candied orange peel on top.

Nut Frosted Muffins: Flavor the batter with only the lemon peel (that is, leave out the lemon juice). Fill the muffin cup until only ½ full and bake them until they are almost done, about 8 minutes.

Mix ⅓ cup chopped hazel nuts, ⅓ cup sugar, 3½ tablespoons butter or margarine, 2 tablespoons candied chopped orange peels, ¼ teaspoon ginger, 1 tablespoon milk, and 1 tablespoon flour together in a saucepan. Bring just to a boil but do not let the mixture continue to boil. Place a spoonful of the icing on each muffin and bake for another 5 minutes in the oven, or until the icing has become a golden brown.

Sweet Milk Doughnuts

Yield: 48 doughnuts

4¼ cups flour, sifted
3½ teaspoons baking powder
1 teaspoon salt
½ teaspoon ground nutmeg
¼ teaspoon ground cinnamon
3 eggs, beaten
1 teaspoon vanilla
¾ cup sugar
3 tablespoons soft butter or margarine
¾ cup milk
Fat for frying

Sift the dry ingredients together. Beat the eggs, vanilla, and sugar. Mix in the butter. Add the milk and sifted dry ingredients alternately. Mix into a soft dough.

Turn the dough onto a lightly floured board. Knead lightly for 30 seconds, then roll out ⅓-inch thick. Cut with a floured doughnut cutter. Remove the trimmings.

Lift each doughnut on a spatula and carefully place into deep, hot fat (375°F). Put as many into the fat at a time as can be turned easily. Cook until browned; drain on paper towels.

Flannel Cakes

Yield: 35 to 40 cakes

1 cup milk, scalded
1 heaping tablespoon butter
1 cup cold milk
2 egg yolks, beaten
1 yeast cake, dissolved in lukewarm water
½ teaspoon salt
4 cups flour
2 egg whites, beaten

Melt the butter in the scalded milk, then add the cold milk. Add the egg yolks and the yeast in lukewarm water. Sift the salt with the flour and add enough to the milk mixture to make a stiff batter. Let it rise, covered, in a warm place overnight.

In the morning, add the egg whites. If additional flour is needed, add and set the bowl aside to rise a second time. Fry on a hot griddle until browned.

Apple Griddlecakes

Yield: 30 small cakes

2 cups flour, sifted
5 teaspoons baking powder
2 teaspoons salt
3 tablespoons sugar
1 teaspoon ground cinnamon
2 cups milk
6 tablespoons melted shortening or salad oil
2 eggs, beaten
1 cup unpeeled apples, finely chopped

Sift the dry ingredients together. Add the milk, shortening, and flour mixture to the eggs; beat until smooth. Fold in the apples.

Heat a lightly greased or heavy frying pan slowly until moderately hot. Test the temperature by sprinkling a few drops of water on it — if they "dance", the temperature is right.

Pour on about ¼ cup of batter for each cake. Bake until the top is bubbly and edges dry; turn and brown on the other side.

Blueberry-Sour Cream Pancakes

Yield: 12 pancakes

1 cup flour, sifted
3 teaspoons baking powder
¼ teaspoon salt
1 tablespoon sugar
1 egg
1 cup milk
¼ cup sour cream
2 tablespoons butter, melted
½ cup blueberries

Sift the dry ingredients together. Beat the egg, milk, and sour cream together. Pour the milk mixture over the dry ingredients and blend with a rotary beater until the batter is just smooth. Stir in the butter. Fold in the blueberries.

Pour 2 tablespoons of batter onto a hot griddle for each cake. Brown on 1 side until golden. Turn and brown on the other side. If the cakes brown too fast, lower the heat. Serve them hot with butter and maple syrup.

Raspberry-Sour Cream Waffles

Yield: 4 waffles

1 cup fresh raspberries
2 cups sweetened whipped cream
¾ cup strong brewed coffee
¾ cup milk
1 cup sour cream
1 egg
¼ cup vegetable oil
1½ cups pancake mix

Fold the raspberries into the whipped cream; chill.

Combine the coffee, milk, sour cream, egg, and oil in a bowl; blend well. Add the pancake mix; beat with an electric mixer until smooth. Pour onto a hot waffle iron; bake until the steaming stops. Repeat with the remaining batter. Serve immediately with the whipped-cream mixture.

One-half cup of raspberry jam can be substituted for fresh raspberries, if desired.

Seven Kinds of Muffins

Filled Pancakes

Yield: 12 6-inch pancakes

2 eggs
1 cup flour
2 cups milk
¼ teaspoon salt
1 tablespoon margarine

filling

½ pound fresh mushrooms
¾ pound smoked ham
1 leek
⅓ cup parsley, finely chopped
1¼ cups sour cream
½ teaspoon salt
¼ teaspoon lemon pepper
¼ teaspoon Italian salad spice
1 teaspoon French mustard
¼ pound freshly grated cheese

Make a smooth pancake batter by beating together the eggs, flour, and ⅔ cup of the milk. Then add the rest of the milk and the salt.

Make the pancakes, allowing 3 pancakes per person. As the pancakes are done, place one on top of the other. Preheat oven to 475°F.

Rinse and slice the mushrooms. Cut the ham into small, fine cubes and the leek into thin slices, and chop the parsley. Mix together the sour cream and the spices. Blend carefully as sour cream will become thin if it is stirred too vigorously. Fill the pancakes with the chopped ingredients and the sour cream, roll them up, and place them on an ovenproof plate.

Cover with the grated cheese and bake on the top rack of a 475°F oven for 10 to 12 minutes. The pancakes can be made several hours before dinner if you wish to prepare the food in advance.

Pecan Waffles

Yield: 5 to 6 waffles

1½ cups flour
1½ tablespoons sugar
2½ teaspoons baking powder
½ teaspoon salt
3 eggs, separated, whites beaten stiff
1½ cups milk
5 tablespoons butter, melted
¼ cup pecans, chopped

Measure the dry ingredients into a 4-cup measure; set aside.

Beat the egg yolks until thick; combine with the milk and butter. Add the dry ingredients. When the batter is well mixed, gently add the pecans. Fold in the egg whites. Bake in a hot waffle iron. Serve with syrup or cinnamon-sugar mixture.

Filled Pancakes

Baked French Toast

Yield: 12 pieces

¾ cup cornflake crumbs
2 eggs
¾ cup milk
½ teaspoon vanilla
6 slices day-old bread, cut into halves diagonally
¼ cup margarine or butter, melted
Jelly, maple syrup, or honey

Measure the cornflake crumbs into a shallow dish or pan. Set aside.

In a second shallow dish or pan, beat the eggs until foamy. Stir in the milk and vanilla. Dip the bread into the egg mixture, turning once and allowing time for both sides to take up the liquid. Coat evenly with the crumbs. Place in a single layer on a well-greased baking sheet. Drizzle with melted margarine.

Bake in a 450°F oven about 10 minutes or until lightly browned. Serve with jelly, warm maple syrup, or honey.

Desserts

Apple Cobbler

Yield: 6 to 8 servings

4 cups peeled, sliced baking apples
1⅓ cups sugar
⅛ teaspoon cinnamon
½ teaspoon almond extract (optional)
2 tablespoons butter
1½ cups sifted flour
2 teaspoons baking powder
½ teaspoon salt
¼ cup butter
1 egg, beaten
⅔ cup milk

Place the apples in a 1½-quart baking dish. Sprinkle with 1 cup sugar, the cinnamon, and the almond extract. Dot with 2 tablespoons of butter.

Sift the flour, baking powder, ⅓ cup sugar, and salt into mixing bowl. Cut in ¼ cup butter until mixture is slightly coarser than cornmeal.

Combine the egg and milk; pour into dry ingredients. Stir just enough to combine, and spoon over apples in baking dish.

Bake in 425°F oven about 30 minutes, until browned. Serve with fresh cream, sour cream, or ice cream, if desired.

Apple Compote

Yield: 4 servings

8 apples, about 2 to 2½ pounds
1⅔ cups water
⅔ cup sugar
Juice from ½ lemon or ¼ teaspoon ascorbic acid

Peel the apples and cut into wedges. Remove the cores. Place the apples in the water immediately after they have been peeled so that they do not turn brown. Bring the water to a boil. Add the sugar and lemon juice. Simmer the apples until soft but not falling apart.

Remove the apples. Place them in a bowl. Let the syrup boil for several more minutes. Pour the syrup over the compote and let it become cold. Serve the compote cold.

Baked Nut Apples

271

Baked Apple with Almond Hat

Baked Apple with Almond Hat

Yield: 4 servings

pastry
1¾ cups flour
1 tablespoon sugar
⅔ cup margarine
1 egg
1 tablespoon cold water

filling
4 tasty smallish apples
¼ to ⅓ cup almond paste

when serving
2 cups ice cream
¾ cup whipped cream

Quickly cut and knead together all the dough ingredients or spin in a food processor. Refrigerate.

Peel and core the apples.

Press the apple-corer into the almond paste to make an almond-paste core with which to fill the apples. Roll out a bit of the almond paste and cut out 4 little cookies for the hats.

Divide the dough into 4 parts. Roll out each on

Apple Compote

Baked Nut Apples

Yield: 6 servings

6 fine apples
3½ tablespoons butter or margarine
1½ to 2 ounces chopped nut meats
2 tablespoons sugar

Core the apples. Cut off a piece of the core and place it back in the bottom. This is so the filling does not run out as easily. Place the apples in a greased, ovenproof dish.

Mix the butter, nuts, and sugar together. Fill the holes in the apples with the mixture. Bake at 425°F until the apples are soft, about 20 minutes.

Serve with lightly whipped cream, vanilla custard sauce, or ice cream.

Variation: To make Port-Wine Apples, beat together 1½ to 2 ounces grated marzipan and 3½ tablespoons butter or margarine. Fill the holes from the apple cores with this mixture. Drip 2 to 3 tablespoons syrup over apples. Pour ⅓ to ¼ cup port wine into the bottom of the dish. Bake the apples as described above. While baking, baste the apples several times with the port-wine syrup.

Serve the apples hot with ice-cold lightly whipped cream or with ice cream that has been stirred until it is soft.

Apple-Filled Puff Pastries

waxed paper, with a flour-sprinkled rolling pin. Cut the dough around a plate. Put the apples in the middle of the 4 dough "cookies." Turn them upside down so that the dough hangs down and folds gracefully around the apples. Press the cookie hats on the tops.

The preceding can be prepared in advance.

Bake the apples at 400°F on the lowest rack. The almond-paste pastry can be protected with aluminum foil during the first 25 minutes.

Whip the cream. Cut the ice cream into cubes. Mix together and serve.

Apple-Filled Puff Pastries

Yield: 10 pastries

1 package (17¼ ounces) frozen puff pastry
5 tablespoons sugar
1 to 2 teaspoons cinnamon
4 cups frozen apple slices, or 4 to 6 apples, depending on size
1 egg, beaten
Baking paper for 2 baking sheets

Take the puff pastry out of the freezer and let the pieces defrost for about 15 minutes. They can defrost longer.

Mix together the sugar and cinnamon. Sprinkle ½ tablespoon of the mixture evenly over each piece of puff pastry. Press in the mixture when the pieces are rolled out into about 4-inch-long rectangles. Turn over the rectangles so that the sugar-cinnamon mixture is on the bottom. Place the apple slices (close together) in two rows across, with a slight space between the two rows, on half of the rectangle. Sprinkle ½ tablespoon sugar-cinnamon on each. Brush with the beaten egg along the edges and between the two apple rows. Fold half of the pastry over the apple-covered half. Cut between the rows of apples. Press the edges together with a fork. Two pastries are made from each pastry rectangle. Place them on baking sheets that have been covered with baking paper. They can stay like this until it is time to bake them.

Brush with egg. Bake in the center of a preheated 400°F oven for 15 to 20 minutes.

These taste best when just made, but they are also good when reheated.

Silver Apples

Yield: 4 servings

4 ripe, sour-type apples
½ lemon
⅔ cup apricot purée (baby-food jar)
4 tablespoons water
2 tablespoons sugar
⅛ teaspoon vanilla extract
4 drops bitter almond oil
4 pieces aluminum foil

Peel the apples. Rub them with the lemon so the fruit will not darken.

Boil the apricot purée together with the water and sugar until thickened. Add the vanilla extract and the bitter almond oil.

Shape the pieces of aluminum foil into deep bowls. Place one apple in each, and divide the sauce over the apples. Fold and close the aluminum bowls well. Bake in a 425°F oven for about 25 minutes.

Serve with vanilla ice cream, if desired.

Variation: Pears can be baked in the same way.

Tosca Apples

Yield: 4 servings

4 medium apples or 6 to 8 small apples
4 cups water
⅓ to ¾ cup sugar
Shreds of lemon peel

tosca batter
7 tablespoons margarine
½ cup sugar
2 tablespoons flour
2 tablespoons milk
2 bags sliced almonds, 1½ ounces each

If the apples are soft and mealy, they do not need to be boiled first. Otherwise, boil the apples in a syrup made from the water, sugar, and shreds of lemon peel.

Peel, core, and cut the apples in half. Place the apples in batches in the syrup and let them simmer until partially soft, 5 to 10 minutes. Remove the apple halves with a spoon with holes in it, and let them drain.

Melt the margarine for the tosca. Stir in the sugar, flour, and milk. Let the batter come just to a simmering point; do not let it boil. Mix in the almonds.

Place the apples close together on a baking plate. Divide the tosca on the tops. Bake at 425°F for 10 to 15 minutes, until the tosca has become a pretty, golden brown.

Serve the apples warm with cold whipped cream, preferably flavored with a dash of rum with finely grated lemon peel.

Silver Apples

Apple Yummy

Yield: 2 or 3 servings

3 bitter apples
⅓ cup raisins
1¼ cups sour cream or yogurt, cold
3 to 4 tablespoons frozen orange juice, partially thawed
2 tablespoons roasted oatmeal flakes
Brown sugar

Peel and finely grate the apples. Mix the grated apples and the raisins with the cold sour cream. Quickly fold in the partially thawed orange juice (it should still be slightly icy) with the sour cream mixture. Spoon into tall glasses. Sprinkle with roasted oatmeal flakes and brown sugar. Serve immediately.

Fried Bananas

Yield: 4 to 6 servings

¼ cup flour
1 teaspoon cinnamon
6 bananas, sliced lengthwise
2 or more tablespoons shortening

Mix the flour and cinnamon together; thoroughly coat each piece of banana with the mixture. If bananas are very long, you may prefer to quarter them.

Heat the shortening in a medium skillet. Brown the floured bananas; slowly turn them once. Remove them to a heated platter; sprinkle with sugar.

Rum Bananas

Yield: 4 servings

4 firm ripe bananas
¼ cup butter
¼ cup brown sugar
Lemon juice
½ cup rum

Peel the bananas and cut them into halves lengthwise.

Melt the butter in an ovenproof baking dish and add the banana halves. Sprinkle with the sugar and bake in a preheated 450°F oven about 10 minutes, until the bananas are thoroughly hot and the sugar is melted. Sprinkle with lemon juice and baste briefly. Return to the oven for 2 minutes.

Warm the rum and pour it over the bananas. Ignite the rum and, when the flame dies, serve immediately.

Cherry Cobbler

Yield: 8 servings

½ cup butter or margarine
¾ cup sugar
1 egg, beaten
⅓ cup milk
2 cups all-purpose flour
2 teaspoons baking powder
½ teaspoon salt
1 No. 2 can cherry pie filling

Cream butter and sugar. Add egg; mix well. Blend in milk.

Combine the dry ingredients; add to the butter mixture. Spread half of batter in a greased 8-inch-round container; cover with ¾ can pie filling. Spread with remaining batter; top with remaining filling. Bake in a 375°F oven 30 minutes or until done. Serve warm with plain or whipped heavy cream or with vanilla ice cream.

Tosca Apples

Cranberry Apple Crisp

Yield: 6 to 8 servings

3 cups apple slices (5 to 6 medium apples, peeled, cored, sliced)
2 cups whole fresh or frozen cranberries
2 tablespoons honey
½ cup butter or margarine
1 cup rolled oats
½ cup whole-wheat flour
¾ cup firmly packed brown sugar
½ cup chopped nuts
½ teaspoon vanilla

Combine the apple slices and cranberries. Drizzle with honey and toss lightly to coat.

With pastry blender cut the butter into the oats, flour, and brown sugar. Mix until crumbly. Stir in the nuts and vanilla.

Place the apples and cranberries into a greased 11¾ × 7½-inch baking dish. Top with the oat mixture. Bake at 350°F about 50 minutes or until browned and bubbly.

Serve dish warm, with whipped cream if desired.

Berry-Filled Melon

Swimming Grapes

Yield: 4 servings

1⅓ to 1½ pounds large green grapes
¾ cup water
⅓ to ½ cup sugar
1 tablespoon aromatic honey, such as heather honey
Grated peel of at least ½ lemon
⅔ cup brandy
⅓ cup Cointreau or similar orange liqueur

Prepare this dessert at least 24 hours in advance.

Cut the grapes in half and remove the seeds, using a little pointed knife. Divide the grapes among 4 tall glasses.

Boil a syrup of water and sugar. Let cool. Add honey, lemon peel, brandy and liqueur. Stir, and pour over the grapes in the glasses so that they are almost totally covered. Place the glasses in the refrigerator until it is time to serve them the following day.

Serve with chilled whipped cream and slivers of almonds.

Fresh Blueberry Cobbler

Yield: 6 servings

½ cup sugar
1 tablespoon cornstarch
4 cups blueberries
1 teaspoon lemon juice
1 cup flour
1 tablespoon sugar
1½ teaspoons baking powder
½ teaspoon salt
3 tablespoons shortening
½ cup milk

Blend ½ cup sugar and the cornstarch in a medium saucepan. Stir in the blueberries and lemon juice. Cook, stirring constantly, until mixture thickens and boils. Boil and stir 1 minute. Pour into ungreased 2-quart casserole; place in oven while preparing bisquit topping.

Measure flour, 1 tablespoon sugar, baking powder, and salt in bowl. Add shortening and milk. Cut through shortening 6 times; mix until dough forms a ball. Drop dough by 6 spoonfuls onto hot fruit. Bake, uncovered, in a preheated 400°F oven 25 to 30 minutes or until done. Serve warm.

Apple Yummy

Berry-Filled Melon

Yield: 1 serving

½ small honeydew melon
3 to 4 tablespoons red berries, for example wild
   strawberries and currants (preferably 2 kinds)
1 teaspoon sugar
Several drops calvados

Cut the melon in half and fill with the berries. Sprinkle the sugar on top. Moisten with a few drops of calvados.

Melon Basket with Fruit Salad

Yield: Varies

1 watermelon
Mixed fresh fruit
Nuts (optional)
Port wine

Make a melon basket by cutting out a watermelon. Spoon out the fruit, removing as many of the seeds as possible. Cut the melon fruit into cubes.

Make a fruit salad with fresh fruit; for example, oranges, apples, pears, pineapple, kiwi, bananas, strawberries, and mango. Even nuts can be added.

Dash a little port wine over the salad before serving. This tastes good with ice cream.

Fruit or Sherbet with Honeydew Sauce

Yield: Varies

1 honeydew melon
Strawberries
Pears
Bananas
Sherbet (optional)

Cut a lid off the melon. Dig out all the seeds, then the melon fruit, with a spoon. Press the melon fruit through a fine strainer. Use the melon shell as a bowl from which to serve the fruit salad or ice cream.

Fill the melon shell with strawberries, pears, and bananas. Serve with the melon sauce.

Variation: Spoon sherbet into the dug-out melon boat. Pour the melon sauce over the sherbet.

Fruit or Sherbet with Honeydew Sauce

Swimming Grapes

Orange Compote with Crème Fraiche

Yield: 4 to 6 servings

6 oranges
Juice from 3 oranges
¼ cup Cuarenta y tres (Spanish herb liqueur with vanilla flavor)
Sugar
1 to 2 tablespoons corn flour
Water
Crème Fraîche or sour cream

Peel the six oranges with a knife so that all the white membranes are removed. Cut out the wedges. Place them in a bowl. Pour the juice from three of the oranges into a pan. Pour in the liqueur, and a little sugar, if necessary.

Mix the corn flour with a little water.

Bring the orange juice to a boil. Thicken with a little corn flour until the juice has the right consistency. Adjust the flavor, if desired, with a little more liqueur. Mix with the orange wedges.

Serve the compote warm or cold with a dab of crème fraîche.

Orange Compote with Crème Fraîche

Mango Purée

Yield: 1 serving

1 well-ripened mango fruit
2 tablespoons cottage cheese

Peel the fruit and take out the fruit with a small sharp knife. Mix the fruit and cottage cheese into a smooth purée. Use an electric blender or press it through a sieve.

Ice-Cream-Filled Oranges

Yield: 4 servings

4 oranges
Vanilla ice cream
2 to 3 tablespoons frozen orange juice
2 egg whites
¼ cup sugar
Several drops of rum, brandy, or orange liqueur

Cut a lid off the oranges. Spoon out the fruit. (Save the juice to drink.)

Beat the ice cream until soft. Flavor with the frozen orange juice. Fill the orange peels with the ice cream. Place in the freezer for several hours so that the ice cream becomes frozen again.

Beat the egg whites until stiff. Stir in the sugar and liqueur. Top the oranges with the meringue batter. Bake for about 4 minutes in a very hot oven until the meringue has become a golden brown. Serve immediately.

Orange Parfait

Yield: 4 to 8 servings

4 oranges
4 egg yolks
6 tablespoons sugar
1¼ cups heavy cream
2 to 3 egg whites

Cut a lid off the oranges, or cut them in half. Dig out the inside with a teaspoon and strain the fruit.

Beat the egg yolks until light and fluffy with 4 tablespoons of the sugar. Whip the cream until firm; then fold it into the egg yolk mixture together with about ⅓ cup of the orange juice.

Fill the oranges and freeze them.

When it's time to serve, make the meringue "hats." Preheat the oven to 475°F to 525°F. Remove the oranges from the freezer about 40 minutes in advance so that they are not completely frozen.

Beat the egg whites in a clean bowl with a clean beater. Add 1 tablespoon sugar per egg white and continue to beat until the whites become stiff peaks.

Squirt out the meringue with a pastry bag or spoon it into the oranges and place them in the middle of the oven for 1 to 2 minutes, until the meringue has become a pretty golden brown.

Melon Basket with Fruit Salad

Sherbet-Filled Pears in Caramel Sauce

Baked Ginger Peaches

Yield: 6 servings

3½ cups preserved peach halves
¼ cup brown sugar
2 teaspoons diced preserved ginger
2 tablespoons butter

Put the peaches, cut side up, into a shallow baking dish. Add peach syrup. Sprinkle with sugar and ginger. Dot with butter. Bake in a 350°F oven until brown, 15 to 20 minutes.

Fresh Peach Crisp

Yield: 6 servings

8 or 9 fresh ripe peaches
1 cup flour
½ teaspoon cinnamon
1 cup sugar
½ cup soft butter
Light cream

Peel and slice the peaches. Place into a lightly buttered 8-inch-square baking dish.

Orange Parfait

Sift together the flour, cinnamon, and sugar in a bowl. Cut in the butter with a pastry blender or 2 knives until the mixture resembles coarse corn-meal. Sprinkle mixture evenly over peaches. Bake 45 to 50 minutes in a 375°F oven or until the topping is golden brown. Serve warm with cream, if desired.

Baked Pears

Yield: 6 servings

6 medium Bartlett pears
6 whole cloves
1½ cups wine
¾ cup sugar
¾ cup water

Pierce each blossom end of pear with a clove. Place unpeeled pears into a deep casserole.

Combine the remaining ingredients and pour over the pears. Cover and bake at 400°F for about 30 minutes or until done. Baste occasionally.

Ice-Cream-Filled Oranges

Sherbet-Filled Pears in Caramel Sauce

Yield: 4 servings

2⅓ to 2¾ cups water
⅔ cup sugar
2 or 3 thin slices of lemon
4 ripe pears (not too soft, however)
1½ cups unsweetened whipped cream
⅓ to ⅔ cup orange sherbet
1½ cups unsweetened whipped cream

caramel sauce
¾ cup heavy cream or ⅓ cup heavy cream plus ⅓ cup crème fraîche or sour cream
⅓ cup sugar
3 tablespoons corn syrup
1½ teaspoons cocoa (unsweetened)
½ teaspoon vanilla extract

Make a syrup by boiling the water with the sugar and lemon slices.

Peel the pears. Remove the core with a corer so that a hole is left down the middle of the fruit. Drip a little lemon juice over the pears. Place the pears in the boiling syrup, and cover. Boil the fruit until

done. Cooking time can vary between 5 to 15 minutes, depending on how ripe the pears are and the kind used. Test with a needle or toothpick. The pears should still be slightly firm without being hard on the inside. Refrigerate the pears in the syrup and let them become cold.

Make the caramel sauce while the pears are cooling. Mix all the sauce ingredients together in a pan. Bring to a boil, beating constantly. Boil for 3 to 4 minutes. Cool the sauce, continuing to beat, by setting the pot in a pan of cold water.

When it is time to serve the pears, whip the cream. Dab it into 4 individual dessert bowls. Set a pear on each dab of cream.

Stir the sherbet until soft. Place it in a heavy pastry bag. Press the sherbet out into the hole of the pears so that they are well filled. Spoon the caramel sauce over the pears and around the cream. Serve immediately. Serve any remaining sauce in a separate dish. A white port wine goes well with this dessert.

Ice-Cream-Filled Pineapple

Yield: 4 servings

2 small pineapples, divided lengthwise
2 tablespoons Grand Marnier or other liqueur
1⅓ cups vanilla ice cream
¾ cup whipped cream
8 to 10 crushed walnuts

Spoon out the pineapple-fruit meat. Cut it into cubes. Place the cubes into the pineapple shell. Drip Grand Marnier over the cubes. Fill with vanilla ice cream. Garnish with whipped cream and walnuts.

Pineapple Dessert

Yield: 8 servings

5 or 6 egg yolks
⅔ cup sugar
4 oranges
Ice cream, thawed
1 pineapple
Chocolate shavings

Beat the egg yolks and sugar until fluffy.

Carve out the oranges with a knife. Add the orange meat and juices to the egg batter. Fold in thawed ice cream. Stir until smooth. Pour the batter into a tube cake pan. Freeze for 8 to 10 hours.

Turn the dessert out onto a serving tray. Garnish with peeled and sliced fresh pineapple. Decorate with chocolate shavings. Cover the hole with the top of the pineapple.

Pears on Almond Crusts with Caramel Sauce

Pineapple Dessert

Ice-Cream-Filled Pineapple

Combine the water, sugar, and cinnamon. Bring to a boil. Simmer the pears in the syrup until they have become soft. Let them thoroughly cool in the syrup.

Mix the almond-crust ingredients together. Spread the batter into thin cookies on a greased and floured baking sheet, so that they are about 6 inches in diameter. If you use baking sheet paper, you can draw rings on the paper, and fill these rings. Bake in a hot 425°F oven, until the crusts are brown but not burned. While they still are warm, carefully loosen them from the baking sheet, using a sharp knife. Shape them into bowls by placing them over a bowl, or similarly shaped object, so that they can cool.

Boil all the caramel-sauce ingredients together. Do not boil too long or the sauce will be too thick when it cools. Beat until it becomes cold.

Place a little vanilla ice cream on each almond crust. Push a pear down into the ice cream, and pour a little sauce over them. Pour the rest of the sauce into a serving dish, and serve separately.

Limed Strawberries with Rum Cream

Yield: 8 servings

3 pints fresh strawberries
5 tablespoons limeade concentrate, thawed
5 tablespoons rum
5 tablespoons sugar
8 ounces heavy whipped cream
2 tablespoons sugar
2 tablespoons rum

Wash, hull, and slice the strawberries.

Mix the limeade, 5 tablespoons rum, and 5 tablespoons sugar. Pour over the strawberries. Mix gently. Cover and marinate in refrigerator 3 to 4 hours.

Whip the cram with 2 tablespoons sugar and 2 tablespoons rum until thick and creamy but not stiff. Pass the berries and cream and let guests help themselves.

Strawberry-Shortcake Bowl

Yield: 6 to 8 servings

2 pints strawberries, sliced, sweetened to taste
¼ cup melted butter or margarine
1 10-ounce container refrigerated flaky biscuits
¼ cup sugar mixed with 1½ teaspoons ground cinnamon
½ cup pecans, chopped
1 cup whipping cream, whipped, sweetened with ¼ cup sugar

Chill berries about ½ hour.

Pears on Almond Crusts with Caramel Sauce

Yield: 4 servings

4 pears
Lemon
2 cups water
1¼ cups sugar
¼ teaspoon vanilla extract
1 stick of cinnamon

almond crusts
1 egg
2 egg whites
⅔ cup sugar
⅔ cup grated almonds
3½ tablespoons melted butter
¼ cup flour

caramel sauce
⅓ cup cream
⅓ cup sugar
1 tablespoon syrup
1 teaspoon cocoa
¼ teaspoon vanilla extract

Peel the pears. Rub them with lemon.

Meanwhile, brush baking sheet with melted butter.

Separate each biscuit into 2 thinner biscuits by pulling them apart between layers. Lightly brush both sides of each biscuit with butter. Dip both sides into the sugar-cinnamon mixture. Place the biscuits on a baking sheet. Leave about 1 inch between biscuits. Sprinkle pecans over biscuits and press them into the dough. Bake in a preheated 400°F oven 10 to 12 minutes or until done.

Line a large serving bowl with about 15 biscuits. Spoon ½ of the strawberries over the biscuits. Spoon whipped cream over the berries. Spoon remaining strawberries over cream; top with rest of biscuits. Serve immediately.

Strawberry Snow

Yield: 6 servings

2 cups fresh strawberries
Sugar to taste
4 egg whites
¾ cup whipping cream

Sprinkle the strawberries with sugar to taste, and crush the berries. Reserve 6 whole berries for decoration.

Flaming Fruit

Meringue Twist with Fresh Berries

Beat the egg whites until stiff.

Beat the whipping cream until stiff.

Gently mix together the berries, whipped cream, and stiff egg whites. Spoon this into dessert bowls. Put 1 whole berry on top of each serving.

Flaming Fruit

Yield: 6 to 8 servings

1 can peach halves, about 14 ounces
1 can apricot halves, about 14 ounces
1 can pitted cherries, about 14 ounces
1 can sliced kiwi, about 10½ ounces
¾ cup red currant jelly
⅔ cup brandy

Drain the fruits well, using a sieve. Save the juices for making a fruit soup or something similar. Divide the peach and apricot halves in half.

Melt the jelly in a frying pan over low heat. Do not let it boil. Add all the fruit. Cover and heat until the fruit is piping hot.

Place the fruit over a lit chafing dish on the table.

Carefully heat the brandy and pour it over the fruit. Ignite, and stir gently. Have a pan near by to squelch the flame should it become too high. Serve the flambéed fruit immediately.

Meringue Twist with Fresh Berries

Yield: 12 servings

1¼ cups whipped cream
Approximately 12 small meringues (bought or
   homemade)
Blueberries
Raspberries

Whip the cream. Alternate the whipped cream,
meringues, and berries in a dish. Serve immediately.

Minted Fruit Cup

Yield: 6 servings, ½ cup each

1 cup banana slices
1 tablespoon lemon juice
1 cup fresh strawberries, halved
½ cup seedless grapes, whole
¾ cup pineapple chunks, drained
½ cup mint syrup
Few sprigs of mint leaves

Coat banana slices with lemon juice.
Lightly mix fruits in a large bowl. Pour syrup over
fruits. Chill about 30 minutes. Garnish with mint
leaves and serve immediately.

Bread and Almond Pudding

Yield: 4 to 6 servings

¼ to ⅓ cup raisins
About ⅓ cup inexpensive white wine (preferably
   sweet)
¾ cup almonds
2 eggs
⅔ cup sugar
¾ cup milk
¾ cup heavy cream
About ¾ cup white bread, crust removed, cut into
   cubes
1½ teaspoons cinnamon
1 teaspoon nutmeg

Soak the raisins for about 30 minutes in the wine.
If the raisins are dry, warm the mixture slightly.
Strain away the wine (save this for another recipe).
Scald, peel, dry, and grind the almonds.
Beat the eggs and sugar together until white and
light. Add the milk, cream, and remaining ingredients. Blend well. Pour into a greased round dish or
into individual dishes. Stir with a fork so the raisins
do not sink to the bottom. Bake in a pan of water in a
350°F oven for about 25 minutes or until the
pudding has become firm and has a golden brown
crust on the top.
Serve hot or warm with chilled whipped cream,
grated orange peel, and a dash of orange liqueur.

Bread and Almond Pudding

Cloud Pudding

Yield: 4 to 6 servings

caramel
¾ cup sugar
2 tablespoons boiling water

"the cloud"
6 egg whites
⅔ cup sugar

decoration
2 cups red currants or other beries
¾ cup whipped cream

Prepare the caramel. Place the sugar in a clean,
dry frying pan and let it melt over low heat while
stirring. When the sugar has melted and is light
brown, add the water. Stir and pour the caramel
mixture into a 1½-quart ring-shaped mold. Twist
and scoop up the mixture with a spoon so the pan is
covered with caramel all the way up to the edge.
Preheat oven to 400°F. Place a roasting pan filled
with water on the bottom rack of the oven.
Prepare "The Cloud." Whip the egg whites and
sugar into a stiff foam in a clean bowl with a dry,
clean beater.

Fill the mold with the foam. Place it in the water-filled pan in the oven at 400°F for 10 minutes. Decrease the oven temperature to 200°F and let it bake for another 2 hours. Take out the mold. Loosen around the inner and outer edges with a knife. Turn over onto a plate. Pour the caramel sauce over the mold. Decorate with berries and whipped cream.

This can be served immediately or after it has cooled. It can be made in advance and kept on a plate until serving time.

Old-Fashioned Noodle Pudding

Yield: 7 servings

5 tablespoons butter
2½ cups peeled cooking apples cut into ½-inch slices
7 tablespoons sugar
⅓ cup packed dark brown sugar
1¾ teaspoons ground cinnamon, divided
2 tablespoons finely chopped walnuts
2½ cups drained, cooked broad noodles
½ cup sour cream
1¼ cups creamed cottage cheese, sieved
½ teaspoon salt
2 eggs, well beaten

Melt 3 tablespoons butter in a heavy skillet. Add sliced apples. Sprinkle with 3 tablespoons sugar. Stir until apples are completely coated with butter. Cover and cook over low heat about 8 minutes.

Mix brown sugar, ¼ teaspoon cinnamon, and nuts well. Spread the mixture evenly over the bottom of a well-greased 8 × 8 × 2-inch pan.

Add 2 tablespoons butter to the noodles and toss until well-coated. Add sour cream, cottage cheese, salt, eggs, cooked apples and their liquid, and 2 tablespoons sugar which has been mixed with 1 teaspoon cinnamon. Blend well. Put the noodle mixture over brown sugar layer in the pan. Bake in a moderate 325°F oven for 50 minutes or until done. Immediately sprinkle a mixture of 2 tablespoons sugar and ½ teaspoon cinnamon over top. Serve at once.

Cloud Pudding

Chocolate Candies

Plum Pudding

Yield: 4 puddings

1½ cups dried currants
2 cups seedless raisins
2 cups white raisins
¾ cup finely chopped candied mixed fruit peel
¾ cup finely chopped candied cherries
1 cup blanched slivered almonds
1 medium-size tart cooking apple, peeled, quartered, cored, and coarsely chopped
1 small carrot, scraped, and coarsely chopped
2 tablespoons finely grated orange peel
2 teaspoons finely grated lemon peel
½ pound finely chopped beef suet
2 cups all-purpose flour
4 cups fresh soft crumbs, made from homemade-type white bread, pulverized in a blender or shredded with a fork
1 cup dark brown sugar
1 teaspoon ground allspice
1 teaspoon salt
6 eggs
1 cup brandy
⅓ cup fresh orange juice
¼ cup fresh lemon juice
½ cup brandy, for flaming (optional)

In a large, deep bowl combine the currants, seedless raisins, white raisins, candied fruit peel, cherries, almonds, apple, carrot, orange and lemon peel, and beef suet, tossing them about with a spoon or your hands until well mixed. Stir in the flour, bread crumbs, brown sugar, allspice, and salt.

In a separate bowl beat the eggs until frothy. Stir in 1 cup brandy, and orange and lemon juice. Pour this mixture over the fruit mixture. Knead vigorously with both hands, then beat with a wooden spoon until all ingredients are blended. Drape a dampened kitchen towel over the bowl and refrigerate for at least 12 hours.

Spoon the mixture into 4 1-quart plain molds, filling them to within 2 inches of their tops. Cover each mold with a strip of buttered foil, turning the edges down and pressing the foil tightly around the sides to secure it. Drape a dampened kitchen towel over each mold and tie it in place around the sides with a long piece of kitchen cord. Bring 2 opposite corners of the towel up to the top and knot them in the center of the mold, then bring up the remaining 2 corners and knot them similarly. Place the molds in a large pot and pour in enough boiling water to come about three-quarters of the way up their

Raspberry Cream Cookie Bowls

sides. Bring the water to a boil over high heat, and cover the pot tightly. Reduce the heat to its lowest point and steam the puddings for 8 hours. As the water in the steamer boils away, replenish it with additional boiling water.

When the puddings are done, remove them from the water and let them cool to room temperature. Then remove the towels and foil and re-cover the molds tightly with fresh foil. Refrigerate the puddings for at least 3 weeks before serving. Plum puddings can be kept up to a year in the refrigerator or other cool place.

To serve, place the mold in a pot and pour in enough boiling water to come about three-quarters of the way up the sides of the mold. Bring to a boil over high heat. Cover the pot. Reduce the heat to low and steam for 2 hours. Run a knife around the inside edges of the mold and place an inverted serving plate over it. Grasping the mold and plate firmly together, turn them over. The pudding should slide out easily.

If you would like to set the pudding aflame before you serve it, warm ½ cup of brandy in a small saucepan over low heat. Ignite it with a match, and pour it flaming over the pudding.

Chocolate Candies

Yield: 30 large or 50 small candies

1¾ cups confectioners' sugar
1⅓ cups cocoa
5¼ tablespoons butter
⅓ cup heavy cream
1½ tablespoons brandy
7 to 9 ounces dark cooking chocolate

Sift the confectioners' sugar and cocoa together into a bowl. Crumble the soft butter into the mixture as much as possible. Add the cream and brandy. Mix well, using an electric beater. In the beginning the mixture will seem impossibly dry, but after awhile it will turn into a smooth dough. Refrigerate for several hours. Roll the chocolate into balls and refrigerate again.

Melt the cooking chocolate over a barely simmering double-boiler. Roll the balls in the chocolate, using 2 forks. Place the balls on waxed paper and let the chocolate harden. This process has even better results if the balls are placed in a net while the chocolate is hardening.

Those who wish to skip the cooking chocolate can roll the balls in cocoa. This is a classic way of making truffle candy.

Note: It is best to make these candies a week in advance. The proportions given in the recipe are important, so it is best not to double the recipe. Instead, make one batch at a time.

Pasha

Raspberry-Cream Cookie Bowls

Yield: About 10 cookies

1 egg
¼ cup sugar
¼ cup flour
1 tablespoon melted butter or margarine

filling
Whipped cream
Raspberries

Beat together the egg and sugar. Stir in the flour and butter. Onto a well-greased baking sheet spread the batter into thin, round cookies with ample space between them. Bake in a 400°F oven for about 5 minutes. Loosen them immediately from the baking sheet. Shape them into bowls, using a cup or a glass; or form them into cones by rolling them up: The cookies harden quickly, so do not make too many at a time. If the cookies become hard before you have shaped them, just place them back into the oven for a few minutes.

Whip the cream and stir in a small amount of raspberries. Fill the bowls. Garnish with a raspberry. Serve immediately.

Unfilled cookies can be stored in a dry place.

Baked Custard

Yield: 6 servings

3 cups milk
4 eggs
⅓ cup sugar
¼ teaspoon salt
1 teaspoon vanilla
Nutmeg or cinnamon (optional)

Heat milk until hot but not boiling.

Beat eggs in a large bowl. Add sugar and salt. Add milk slowly, stirring all the time. Mix in vanilla. Pour into a baking pan. Sprinkle with nutmeg or cinnamon. Bake at 300°F about 1 hour, until a knife stuck in the center comes out clean.

Baked Caramel Custard

Yield: 6 servings

¾ cup sugar
2 large eggs or 4 yolks
⅓ cup sugar
¼ teaspoon salt
½ teaspoon vanilla
2 cups milk, scalded

Butterscotch Ice Cream with Black-Raspberry Liqueur

Melt ¾ cup sugar in a small skillet, stirring constantly until pale brown. Divide the caramelized sugar among 6 custard cups. Turn the cups so the caramel will coat the sides. Let the sugar harden.

Meanwhile, mix eggs, ⅓ cup sugar, salt, and vanilla. Add milk gradually. Strain into the prepared custard cups. Place the cups in a pan of hot water.

Bake in a 350°F oven 30 to 35 minutes or until a silver knife comes out clean. Remove from hot water immediately. Serve chilled and unmolded.

Little Chocolate Pots

Yield: 6 servings

1½ cups milk
2 cups chocolate chips
2 eggs
¼ cup sugar
Pinch of salt

Pour the milk into a heavy saucepan and heat to boiling.

Combine remaining ingredients in a blender or food-processor container. Pour in the hot milk and blend at low speed 1 minute or until smooth. Pour into 6 custard cups. Chill at least 2 hours before serving. Garnish, if desired, with piped whipped cream, dusted with chopped nuts.

Butterscotch Ice Cream with Black-Raspberry Liqueur

Yield: 5 servings

¼ cup sugar
⅓ cup hot water
⅔ cup heavy cream
2 cups vanilla ice cream
Black-raspberry liqueur

Melt the sugar in a dry, clean frying pan. Remove the pan from the heat when the sugar has melted. Add the hot water. Beat and stir over heat until the sugar melts again. Then boil into a rich, thick sauce. Cool.

Beat the cream. Stir the cooled butterscotch sauce into the cream. Refrigerate the cream while cutting the ice cream into cubes. This can be done in the ice-cream package so as not to make too much of a mess.

Quickly, partially mix the ice cream and cream together. Place it in a ring form or in individual glasses. Freeze for at least ½ hour or more.

Dip the form into hot water before turning the ice cream out onto a serving plate. Serve with black-raspberry liqueur.

Coupe Tropicana

Elderberry Parfait

Pasha

Yield: 12 to 15 servings

2 pounds cottage cheese
1 cup plus 1½ tablespoons sweet butter, room
    temperature
1¼ cups confectioners' sugar
3 egg yolks, beaten lightly
¾ cup crème fraîche or sour cream
⅓ cup raisins or currants
⅓ cup red and green candied peel
¼ cup preserved orange peels
¼ cup coarsely chopped walnuts or almonds

Mix the cottage cheese with the butter in a food processor, or strain it several times through a fine strainer, until the mixture becomes very smooth. Mix this with the sugar, egg yolks, and crème fraîche. Add the raisins, candied and preserved peels, and the nuts. The mixture should now be of a consistency so that it drains drop by drop into a dish.

You can use a new 6-inch clay flower pot, a strainer, or a large drip-coffee funnel. Cover the inside of the form with a thin, damp cloth and fill it with the mixture. You can continue to add more of the mixture as it drains off. Fold the cloth over the mixture and place a saucer upside down on top. Place a weight on the saucer. Place the form over a draining bowl that can collect the liquid that drains off.

Refrigerate the pasha for at least 24 hours, preferably longer. Turn it upside down, decorate it, and serve it as dessert.

Coupe Tropicana

Yield: 1 serving

8 to 10 strawberries
1½ teaspoons sugar
1 peeled mango, cut in half
Butter for frying
Several drops of brandy (or several drops of lemon
    juice)
2 to 3 tablespoons vanilla ice cream

Mix well the strawberries and sugar in a blender, or press through a sieve.

Fry the mango slowly over low heat in a little butter in a frying pan. Sprinkle with a little brandy and ignite. Place the blazed mango fruit in a tall glass. Put vanilla ice cream on top and pour the strawberry sauce over all.

Elderberry Parfait

Yield: 8 servings

2⅓ cups whipping cream
4 egg yolks
⅓ cup sugar
⅓ cup elderberry juice

Whip the cream until it is very thick.

Beat the egg yolks and sugar together until light and airy. Add to the cream. Fold in the elderberry juice. Pour the mixture into a pretty dish and place in the freezer for at least 3 to 4 hours. Serve with whipped cream.

Melon à la Mode

Yield: 4 servings

2 canteloupes
8 tablespoons nougat ice-cream
4 tablespoons good brandy

Wash the melons, cut them in half and remove the seeds. Put the melon halves on serving plates. Just before serving, place 2 spoonfuls of the ice cream in each melon half and pour a tablespoon of brandy on top.

Georgia Peach Ice Cream

Yield: About 1¼ quarts

1 envelope unflavored gelatin
1 cup cold water
1 can sweetened condensed milk
2 cups half-and-half
2 teaspoons vanilla
1 cup mashed peaches

In a small saucepan soften gelatin in ¼ cup water. Heat and stir until dissolved. Stir in remaining water. Add condensed milk, half-and-half, vanilla, and peaches. Refrigerate at least 3 hours.

Pour into freezer container and freeze according to manufacturer's directions. Allow to ripen about 2 hours before serving.

Note: To freeze in a regular refrigerator or free-standing freezer, combine softened gelatin and other ingredients. Blend well and turn into a 13 × 9-inch baking pan. Freeze to firm mush, about 1 hour. Break into pieces and turn into chilled mixer bowl. Beat until smooth. Return to pan. Cover with foil and freeze until firm.

Melon à la Mode

Rum Raisin Ice Cream

Yield: 16 servings (2 quarts)

1 cup milk
3 cups heavy cream, divided
6 egg yolks
1 cup granulated sugar
1 teaspoon vanilla
1 teaspoon cornstarch
½ cup raisins
¾ cup water
¼ cup rum
2 cups heavy cream
2 tablespoons granulated sugar

Pour the milk and 1 cup of cream into the top of a double boiler.

Beat together the egg yolks, sugar, vanilla, and cornstarch. Add to the double boiler and cook over simmering water, stirring constantly, until the mixture thickens. Remove from heat and cool.

Heat raisins and water to boiling. Remove from heat, cool, and drain. Discard water. Add raisins and rum to cooled custard. Chill for several hours.

Whip 2 cups heavy cream until soft peaks form. Beat in 2 tablespoons sugar. Fold whipped cream into custard and place mixture in a tightly covered freezer container. Place in the freezer for 2 hours.

Remove ice cream from freezer container and stir thoroughly to break up frozen pieces and redistribute raisins. Return mixture to container and freeze until firm.

To prepare ice cream in a mechanical ice cream maker, place custard and 2 cups of heavy cream in ice-cream container and proceed as above.

Ice Cream and Peaches with Almond Sauce

Yield: 4 servings

ice cream
1⅓ cups whipping cream
2 egg yolks
1¼ cups confectioners' sugar
Small amount of orange liqueur (optional)
Peeled fresh or canned peaches, whole or sliced in half

almond sauce
⅔ cup extra finely ground almonds
Slightly more than ½ tablespoon grated orange peel
2 egg yolks
⅔ cup heavy cream
⅓ cup confectioners' sugar

Ice Cream and Peaches with Almond Sauce

Beat the whipping cream for the ice cream into stiff peaks.

Whip the egg yolks and sugar together until white and fluffy. Carefully fold the whipped cream into the egg and sugar mixture. Flavor with orange liqueur, if desired. Freeze the mixture overnight. Stir the mixture once during the beginning of the freezing process.

Blend the almonds with the orange peel.

Mix the egg yolks with the cream and sugar, preferably in a stainless-steel pot. Add the almond mixture. Bring the sauce to a slow boil, stirring constantly. Watch the pot carefully until the sauce thickens. Cool sauce until warm. Serve warm with the ice cream and peaches.

Strawberry Frappé with Almond Crisps

Yield: 8 servings

1 package strawberry ice cream
2 quarts fresh strawberries
⅓ cup milk
1 package vanilla ice cream
2 kiwi fruits
8 strawberries as garnish

almond crisps
½ cup sliced almonds
4 tablespoons flour
½ cup sugar
9 tablespoons melted butter
2 tablespoons heavy cream

Prepare immediately before serving.

Remove strawberry ice cream from the freezer and divide in into pieces.

Mix the strawberries in several batches in a blender or food processor together with the strawberry ice cream and a little milk. Pour into large coupe glasses or into small bowls. Place a dab or ball of vanilla ice cream in the middle of the glass. Place a slice of kiwi on top of the ice-cream ball. Top with a strawberry. Serve with almond crisps.

To make almond crisps, mix all the listed ingredients together. Drop the batter onto a greased baking sheet, using a dessert spoon. Allow for ample space between the dabs. Bake the cookies in a preheated 400°F oven for about 10 minutes, until they have become a pretty golden brown. Let them cool somewhat before carefully removing them from the baking sheet with a thin spatula. Place on a flat surface until cold.

Royal Dessert

Strawberry Frappe

Coffee Ice

Yield: 6 servings

2 cups water
1 cup sugar
4 cups espresso coffee (fresh or made from instant according to package directions)
½ cup whipping cream
½ teaspoon vanilla
2 tablespoons sugar
Chopped pistachio nuts (optional)

Combine the water and sugar in a small heavy saucepan. Bring to a boil over moderate heat, stirring until the sugar is dissolved. Reduce heat to low. Cook, stirring occasionally, 3 to 4 minutes, until the mixture is syrupy. Combine with espresso, mixing well, then cool. Place in freezer trays. Freeze for 3 hours. Stir several times the first hour, until firm ice is formed.

Whip the cream, vanilla, and sugar until stiff.

Empty the coffee ice into a blender or food processor; whirl briefly to break up ice crystals. Serve in chilled sherbet glasses, top with whipped cream. Sprinkle with chopped pistachio nuts.

Wine or Champagne Sherbet

Yield: 6 servings

1 small bottle of white wine, or champagne, sparkling or non-fizzy
⅓ cup sugar
2 egg whites

Mix the wine and sugar until the sugar has dissolved. Pour the mixture into a wide bowl. Place it in the freezer. Stir occasionally until it has become an icy slush.

Beat the egg whites until stiff. Fold them into the "slush." Freeze again.

Thirty to 60 minutes before serving, beat the sherbet with an electric beater. Return to the freezer. Serve in sherbet glasses.

Royal Dessert

Yield: 4 servings

8 medium meringues
8 balls vanilla ice cream
¾ cup chocolate sauce
¾ cup whipped cream
Grated cooking chocolate

Mint Sherbet

Alternate the meringues and ice cream in a tall glass. Pour the chocolate sauce over them. Top with a dab of whipped cream and the grated cooking chocolate. Serve with bananas or fresh berries, if desired.

Peach Sherbet

Yield: About 12 servings

1½ cups sieved canned peaches
½ cup lemon juice
1½ cups sugar
2 teaspoons plain gelatin
¼ cup cold water
½ cup boiling water
2 cups whipped cream
2 egg yolks, beaten
2 egg whites, beaten

Mix together the peaches, lemon juice, and sugar.

Dissolve the gelatin in cold water and let stand for 5 minutes. Stir in the boiling water. When dissolved, add to the first mixture and freeze to mush. Remove from freezer and beat. Add 2 cups whipped cream, egg yolks, and egg whites. Mix thoroughly and return to freezing tray. Freeze firm.

Lemon Sherbet

Yield: 4 servings

3 lemons
¾ cup confectioners' sugar
1 cup water
2 egg whites
Strawberries for garnish

Peel the lemons with a knife. Remove even the white part of the peel. Halve the lemons and remove the seeds. Mix the lemons in a blender or food processor until they become a smooth mass. Add the confectioners' sugar and water. Freeze the sherbet halfway. Beat the mixture several times while it is freezing.

Beat the egg whites into dry, stiff peaks. Mix them into the half-frozen sherbet. Continue to freeze.

When it is time to serve the sherbet, beat it until smooth, then spoon it into glasses or a bowl. Garnish with strawberries. Eat immediately with small cookies.

Mint Sherbet

Yield: 2 servings

¾ cup water
2 tablespoons sugar
The juice of ½ lemon
2 tablespoons white wine
2 to 3 tablespoons mint liqueur
1 egg white
¼ cup confectioners' sugar

Combine the water, sugar, lemon juice, wine, and the liqueur in a stainless steel bowl. Stir well, until the sugar is dissolved. Freeze the sherbet 2 to 3 hours, or until half frozen.

Beat the egg white until stiff. Add the confectioners' sugar and beat until the meringue is stiff and shiny. Stir into the half-frozen sherbet and return to the freezer 2 to 3 hours.

Spoon the sherbet into tall glasses and serve immediately.

Apple-Filled Crêpes

Yield: 4 servings

4 sour apples
½ lemon
1 package frozen sliced strawberries in sugar
¼ cup water
8 crêpes, newly made or warmed up in the oven
¼ to ⅓ cup skinned, thinly sliced, roasted almonds

sauce
¼ cup concentrated apple juice
¼ cup water

Crêpes with Fresh Berries

Lemon Sherbet

½ tablespoon potato flour
1 to 2 tablespoons crème fraîche or sour cream

If desired, peel the apples. Core them. Divide each apple into 8 to 10 wedges.

Peel the lemon with a potato peeler so that just the yellow is removed.

Place the apples in a pan. Squeeze the lemon juice over them. Add the strawberries. Simmer the fruit over low heat for about 5 minutes, until the apples feel soft.

Finely chop the lemon peel. Add it to the fruit mixture.

Prepare the sauce. Beat together the juice, water, and potato flour. Simmer the mixture until it becomes a clear, thick sauce. Stir in the crème fraîche.

Fill the crêpes with the fruit mixture and roll them up.

Serve the crêpes from a serving dish, garnished with the sauce and sprinkled with the roasted almonds.

This dish can be prepared in advance and then warmed up in the oven. The crêpes, however, become slightly soggy.

Fried Custard

Yield: 6 servings

2 tablespoons cornstarch
¼ cup all-purpose flour
½ cup sugar
2 cups milk
4 egg yolks, beaten
Dash of nutmeg
Dash of salt
1 teaspoon vanilla extract
Fine cracker crumbs
1 egg, beaten
Confectioners' sugar

Combine the cornstarch, flour, and sugar in the top of a double boiler. Gradually add milk, stirring constantly. Cook over boiling water until thickened, then cook 5 minutes longer, stirring constantly. Gradually stir part of the hot mixture into the egg yolks. Stir the egg yolks into the hot mixture. Add the nutmeg and salt and cook about 1 minute. Remove from heat. Stir in vanilla. Pour into an oiled 8-inch-square pan and let stand in the refrigerator 4 to 5 hours or overnight.

Cut firm custard into rounds, using a biscuit cutter. Dredge in cracker crumbs. Dip in egg, then dredge in crumbs again. Fry in deep hot (380°F) fat until golden brown. Sprinkle with sugar and serve while hot.

Strained orange juice can be poured over each serving, if desired. Hot custard can be poured into an oiled 8×4-inch loaf pan and, after chilling, cut into 6 strips for frying, if desired.

Crêpes with Fresh Berries

Yield: About 40 crêpes

3 eggs
¾ to 1 cup flour
2 cups milk (can be mixed with a small amount of cream)
½ teaspoon salt
3 tablespoons melted butter or margarine
Oil
Fresh berries

Beat the eggs, flour, and a little of the milk together into a smooth batter. Add the rest of the milk, the salt, and melted butter.

Pour several drops of oil in a small (5 to 6 inches) frying pan or crêpe pan; heat it so that it almost

Apple-Filled Crêpes with Red-Raspberry Sauce

Soufflé-Filled Crêpes

starts to smoke. Remove the pan from the heat and dry it with paper. Pour in the batter so that it just covers the bottom of the pan. Cook the crêpes until light brown on both sides. If you make the crêpes in advance, store them in aluminum foil.

Serve them hot or cold with berries or jam.

Almond Soufflé with Cognac Sauce

Yield: 4 servings

3 tablespoons butter
2 tablespoons flour
¾ cup milk
⅛ teaspoon salt
⅔ cup sugar
1 teaspoon almond extract
1 drop bitter almond oil (optional)
4 egg yolks
⅔ cup scalded, skinned, and finely chopped almonds, roasted
6 egg whites
12 whole almonds, scalded and skinned

cognac sauce
4 egg yolks
4 teaspoons sugar

4 tablespoons cognac
4 tablespoons heavy cream, warmed

Heat the butter and flour together in a pot. Dilute, beating constantly, with the milk, a few drops at a time. Add the salt, sugar, almond essence, and bitter almond oil. Remove from the heat. Let cool a few minutes, while beating. Add the egg yolks, one at a time. Beat constantly. Blend in the roasted chopped almonds.

Grease well a large, high soufflé dish or 4 large individual dishes.

Beat the egg whites until very dry and very stiff. Fold them carefully into the almond mixture. Pour the batter into the dish or dishes until slightly more than half full. Divide the whole almonds on top. Bake in a 350°F oven on the lowest rack for 30 to 35 minutes or until the soufflé has set and the surface has become slightly brown. Serve immediately with the cognac sauce served in a separate bowl.

Make the cognac sauce by beating the egg yolks and sugar together. Then beat over boiling water until the mixture thickens. Beat in the cognac and warmed cream. Just before the sauce is to be served, beat for several more minutes over heat.

Almond Soufflé with Cognac Sauce

juice out of the oranges. Strain and carefully simmer the juice over low heat until it becomes a thick juice. Stir occasionally, going all the way down to the bottom of the pot.

Simmer the cream in a pot over low heat, while stirring until it is almost creamy. Remove from the heat. Immediately stir in the sugar. Let the cream mixture cool. Stir in the yolks, one at a time, then add the thickened orange juice and grated orange peels.

Grease 4 small soufflé dishes. Each dish should hold about 1⅔ cups. Use your fingertips to grease. Go all the way up over the edge. Be generous with the amount of butter used. Sugar the butter.

Whip the egg whites until they are as dry as possible, then beat for another few minutes. Mix ¼ of the whipped egg whites with the orange-juice mixture until well blended. Fold in the rest of the egg whites with great care, as delicately as possible.

Divide the batter among the soufflé dishes. Place them in a preheated 350°F oven on the bottom rack for about 25 minutes. During the final minutes, the soufflé should stop rising. Remove from the oven. Serve immediately, preferably with a superior sweet Madeira wine.

Frozen Chocolate Soufflé

Fruit in Cream

Yield: 6 servings

2 apples
2 oranges
2 bananas
½ cup sugar
1 cup whipping cream
¼ cup chopped almonds

Peel all the fruits and cut them in slices or pieces. Sprinkle the sugar over the fruit. Let it stand for 10 minutes.

Whip the cream until stiff and fold it into the fruit. Sprinkle the chopped nuts over the top, and serve.

Orange Soufflé

Yield: 4 servings

3 large oranges
About 1¼ cups heavy cream
⅓ cup sugar
4 large eggs, separated

Grate the peels off the oranges. Save the peels in an airtight container or plastic wrap. Squeeze the

Apricot Soufflé

Soufflé-Filled Crêpes with Red-Raspberry Sauce

Yield: 12 crêpes

crêpe batter
¾ cup flour
1 cup milk
2 eggs
1 tablespoon sugar
¼ teaspoon salt

soufflé batter
4 egg yolks
⅓ cup sugar
2 tablespoons flour
1 cup milk
⅓ cup Grand Marnier
4 egg whites
Confectioners' sugar

red-raspberry sauce
1 package frozen red raspberries
1 package frozen black raspberries
Confectioners' sugar

Mix together the crêpe batter ingredients. Pour several drops of oil in a small frying pan. Heat it so that it almost starts to smoke. Remove the pan from the heat and dry it with paper. Pour in the batter so that it just covers the bottom of the pan. It should be like a very thin pancake. Fry the crêpes until light brown. Twelve crêpes can be made with this batter. If you make the crêpes in advance, store them in aluminum foil.

To make the soufflé batter, beat the egg yolks and sugar together for about a minute. Stir in the flour.

Heat up the milk—it should not be allowed to boil—and pour it slowly into the egg mixture, beating constantly. Bring to a boil, decrease the heat, and simmer for about 2 minutes. Beat constantly to avoid lumping. Remove the pot from the heat and add the liqueur.

Beat the egg whites until stiff. If you have any extra egg whites, add them also.

When the egg-yolk mixture has cooled, fold in the egg whites very carefully.

Place the crêpes on a greased cookie sheet or large ovenproof plate. Place 3 to 4 tablespoons of the soufflé batter on half of the crêpes. Fold the other half loosely over the batter. Place in a preheated 425°F oven for about 7 to 10 minutes, until the crêpes have risen and have become nicely browned. Sprinkle the confectioners' sugar over the crêpes, using a sieve. Serve immediately.

To make the sauce, mash the red raspberries in a blender until they become a smooth sauce. Pass through a sieve. Add sugar if necessary. Cover half

Liqueur Soufflé

the plate with the sauce. Decorate with the black raspberries.

If you prepare the soufflé batter in advance, warming it up slightly before adding the egg whites, it will take less time to put this arrangement together. Sweet sherry, Port wine, or dessert wine taste good with this dessert.

Frozen Chocolate Soufflé

Yield: 4 servings

½ vanilla bean*
⅓ cup confectioners' sugar
3 egg yolks
3 to 4 ounces cooking chocolate
2 teaspoons instant coffee
¼ cup cocoa liqueur
1¼ cups whipping cream

Cut the ½ stick of vanilla lengthwise into 4 pieces. Scrape out the black marrow and place in a non-aluminum double-boiler top. Also add the rest of the stick and the sugar and egg yolks. Place the pan over simmering water. Beat vigorously until the mixture becomes creamy but is still light and fluffy. Remove the pan from the double boiler. Beat until the mixture is completely cold.

Melt the chocolate. Add it to the egg mixture, together with the instant coffee and liqueur. Chill the mixture thoroughly.

Beat the cream until stiff. Stir the chocolate mixture and cream together.

Tape pieces of heavy paper onto individual soufflé dishes so that they stick up an inch over the edges. Fill the dishes with the chocolate mixture to the top of the paper edges. Place in the freezer, but do not allow the dessert to freeze completely. The inner part should still be unfrozen, which gives the dessert the character of a soufflé. It takes about 3 to 4 hours for small dishes, and longer if you use a large soufflé dish.

Just before serving, remove the paper edging. Decorate with small rolls of chocolate, or sift a little cocoa on top.

*If vanilla bean is not available, substitute 1 teaspoon vanilla extract and add it to the egg mixture.

Apricot Soufflé

Yield: 4 servings

1 package dried apricots
½ cup scalded almonds (Pistachio almonds should preferably be used but they are very

difficult to find.)
¾ to 1¼ cups sugar
4 egg whites
Butter for greasing the pan

Thoroughly rinse the apricots. Place them to soak for awhile in water. Then boil the apricots in water until they become soft.

Finely chop the almonds. Strain the apricots. Mix them with the sugar and almonds.

Beat the egg whites into as stiff peaks as possible. Fold half of the whites into the apricot purée. Fold in the rest of the egg whites with a few large, deep turns of a spoon. Pour the batter into a generously greased soufflé form, and bake in a 400°F oven for about 30 minutes.

Remove the soufflé from the oven. Garnish it with a few extra chopped almonds. Serve immediately, preferably with softly whipped cream that has been flavored with brandy.

If you pour the batter into individual soufflé dishes, baking time should be decreased to about 20 minutes.

Yogurt Mousse with Berry Sauce

Yield: 4 servings

2 envelopes unflavored gelatin
½ cup water
2 cups light yogurt
1 container (¾ cup) crème fraîche or sour cream
2 egg yolks
2 to 3 tablespoons sugar
2 teaspoons vanilla sugar
2 egg whites
Strained raspberries or whole fresh berries (strawberries, blueberries, currants, or raspberries) for garnish

Put gelatin granules in water for about 5 minutes.

Beat together the yogurt, crème fraîche, and egg yolks. Sweeten with the sugar and vanilla sugar.

Melt the gelatin over low heat, then pour in a thin stream into the yogurt mixture. Stir.

Beat the egg whites into stiff peaks. Fold into the yogurt mixture. Pour into a round mold or a round cake pan. Place the mousse in the refrigerator for about 3 hours.

When the mousse is to be served, dip the pan in hot water, then turn it upside down. Pour strained raspberries over the mousse, or garnish it with fresh berries.

Orange Soufflé

Liqueur Soufflé

Yield: 6 servings

3 tablespoons flour
¾ cup milk
1 tablespoon butter
2 tablespoons sugar
⅓ cup orange liqueur (curaçao orange)
3 egg yolks
About ⅓ cup crumbled yellow cake
10 egg whites
2 teaspoons cornstarch
Butter and sugar for a 2 quart ovenproof dish with straight sides (soufflé dish)
Confectioners' sugar to sprinkle over the soufflé

Prepare the batter as follows: Measure the flour into a nonaluminum pan. Add the milk a little at a time, whisking constantly so that the batter does not become lumpy. Let the batter come to a boil, continuing to beat constantly. Let the batter boil for 2 to 3 minutes. Beat vigorously the entire time. Add the butter, sugar, and half of the liqueur. Mix well. Remove the pan from the heat. Place it on a damp cloth so that it stands in place. Add the egg yolks one at a time while the batter is still hot. Beat vigorously the entire time.

Let the cake crumbs swell in the remaining liqueur.

Beat the egg whites into very dry, stiff peaks. Mix in the cornstarch.

Grease the soufflé dish generously. Sprinkle it with sugar.

Lighten the batter by mixing in ¼ of the egg whites. Carefully fold in the rest of the egg whites and the cake crumbs. Mix well with a wooden spoon, but do not stir unnecessarily or the whites will sink together. Fill the dish and place it on the lowest oven rack. Bake in a preheated 425°F oven for 25 minutes without opening the oven door. Sprinkle confectioners' sugar over the soufflé, using a sieve. Serve immediately.

Frozen Chocolate Mousse with Orange Cream

Yield: 8 servings

1⅔ cups whipped cream
1 can frozen orange juice
1 package ladyfingers

chocolate mousse
½ pound semisweet chocolate
6 egg yolks
6 egg whites

Frozen Chocolate Mousse with Orange Cream

Prepare the mousse first. Slowly melt the semisweet chocolate over low heat or over a double boiler. Stir the egg yolks, one at a time, into the warm, liquidy chocolate. Let the mixture totally cool before folding in the egg whites, which have been beaten into stiff peaks.

Whip the cream into firm peaks. Beat in the thawed orange juice.

Place the ladyfingers standing up, tightly together, around a round, high pan. Alternate spooning in the chocolate mousse and the orange cream in layers. Start with the chocolate mousse. Place the pan in the freezer for at least 12 hours. Turn out the mousse upside down onto a plate. Decorate with orange slices or wedges, which can be dipped into melted chocolate for added effect.

Pies

Apple Pie with Creamy Filling

Yield: 1 12-inch pie

crust

1⅔ cups flour
14 tablespoons butter or margarine
2 tablespoons sugar
2 tablespoons water

filling

1 quart frozen apple slices or 4 to 6 fresh apples, peeled and sliced
2 tablespoons sugar
½ teaspoon cinnamon, or 2 to 3 tablespoons Cointreau or Grand Marnier
1¼ cups heavy cream
2 tablespoons sugar
3 egg yolks

Work together the flour, butter, and sugar. Add the water and knead quickly together into a pastry. Refrigerate for ½ hour. Grease a 12-inch round pie pan with about 1 tablespoon margarine. Divide the pastry into 2 parts. Roll out each part between 2 sheets of plastic wrap into half moons, as large as half the pan. Pull off the plastic from one of the sides. Turn the pastry upside-down into the pan and pull off the plastic from the other side. Place the other half of the pastry so that it overlaps in the middle; with your hand, flatten the pastry up over the sides of the pan. Refrigerate for 15 minutes.

Preheat oven to 425°F. Cover the edge of the pan with aluminum foil so that the pastry edge does not slip down while baking. Prick the pie shell with a fork. Bake for 10 minutes.

Fill the pie shell with the apple slices. Sprinkle with the sugar and cinnamon. Leave out the cinnamon if liqueur is to be used instead in the egg mixture.

Lightly whip the cream. Sweeten it with sugar and mix it with the egg yolks and perhaps 2 to 3 tablespoons liqueur. Pour the mixture over the apples and bake in the middle of the oven for 25 minutes.

Almond Pie

Scald and peel the almonds; then cut them in half. Beat the egg whites into dry, stiff peaks. Fold the marzipan into the egg whites, and spread the marzipan batter into the pie crust. Cover with the almond halves.

Bake the pie in the middle of the oven for another 20 minutes. Remove from the oven and allow to cool before carefully removing the detachable sides of the pan. Place the pie on a serving plate.

Apple Pie

Yield: 1 9-inch pie

crust
1 to 1¼ cups butter or margarine
1¾ cups flour
⅓ cup water
1 egg, beaten

filling
2 pounds sour apples
⅓ to ⅔ cup sugar
2 to 3 teaspoons cinnamon

Crumble the butter into the flour. Add the water. Quickly work into a dough. Refrigerate

Roll out the dough into a thin crust. Cover an iron pot (or an ovenproof dish with high edges) with the dough. Save some of the dough for the top crust.

Peel and cut the apples into thin wedges. Alternate them in the pot with the sugar and cinnamon. Cover with an upper pie crust. Pinch the edges well together. Brush with the beaten egg. Prick small air holes in the dough. Bake on the bottom of the oven (not on a rack) at 350°F for about 1 hour.

Serve the pie warm with cream or ice cream.

Crisp Nut Apple Pie

Yield: 6 servings

4 to 5 apples
A little sugar on the apples if they are sour (optional)
½ package nut cake or gingerbread mix
3½ to 5¼ tablespoons cold butter

Peel and cut the apples into thin wedges. Place in a greased, ovenproof dish. Sprinkle a little sugar on top, if desired. Sprinkle the cake mix (that is, dry, without adding any water or eggs) over the dish. Cover the dish with thin slices of butter. Use cold butter and, preferably, a cheese cutter.

Bake at 425°F until the pie is golden brown, 20 to 25 minutes. Serve the pie warm with cream or ice cream.

Apple Pie

Almond Pie

Yield: 1 10-inch pie

crust
7 tablespoons butter, at room temperature
¼ pound marzipan, grated
¾ cup flour
1 teaspoon salt
1 egg

filling
½ pound marzipan, grated
Juice of 1 lemon
¼ pound almonds
4 egg whites

Chop the butter, marzipan, flour, and salt together. Mix in the egg so that the mixture becomes a workable dough. Refrigerate for about an hour.

Mix the marzipan for the filling with the lemon juice; place to one side for the time being.

Preheat the oven to 350°F. Roll out the dough, using a little flour, and cover the bottom and sides of a springform pie pan. The pan should have a diameter of about 10 inches. Prick the pie crust with a fork and bake it in the middle of the oven for about 10 minutes.

Angel Pie

Yield: 1 8- or 9-inch pie

3 egg whites
⅛ teaspoon cream of tartar
1 cup sugar
25 crackers, crushed
½ to 1 cup pecans or walnuts, chopped
1 4-ounce package German sweet chocolate
3 tablespoons hot water
1 teaspoon vanilla
1 cup heavy cream, whipped
Chocolate curls for garnish, if desired

With an electric mixer, beat the egg whites and cream of tartar until soft peaks form. Beating on high speed, add sugar gradually until the meringue forms stiff peaks. Fold in the crushed crackers and nuts.

Turn into a lightly greased 8- or 9-inch pie pan. With a spatula, push the meringue up the sides of the pan, forming a pie shell shape. Bake at 325°F about 40 minutes, until lightly browned. Remove and cool on a wire rack.

Meanwhile, melt the chocolate in the top of a double boiler. Add the water to the chocolate and blend; cool until thickened. Stir in vanilla. Fold the chocolate into whipped cream until the color is solid. Spoon into the cooled meringue shell and chill 2 hours before serving. Garnish with chocolate curls, if desired.

Puff Pastry Tartlets with Apples

Yield: Varies

Frozen puff pastry patties
Sour apples
1 egg yolk
1 lemon
Apricot sauce (apricot jam stirred with a little water)

Line small pastry tins with rolled-out puff pastry dough, and place them in the freezer.

Peel the apples, remove the cores, and cut them into thin slices. Arrange the slices in the tins. Drip a little lemon juice on top. Brush the edges with the egg, mixed with a little water. Bake in a 425°F oven for 15 to 20 minutes.

Heat the apricot jam with a little water, and brush the apple slices to give an attractive surface. Serve warm with whipped cream.

Apple Pie with Creamy Filling

French Apple Pie

Yield: 1 10-inch pie

crust
2⅓ cups flour
17½ tablespoons margarine
4 tablespoons cream

filling
3½ ounces marzipan
1 egg
3 apples
3 tablespoons sugar

glaze
3 to 4 tablespoons apricot or pineapple purée (can of baby food)
2 tablespoons raisins

Cut the crust ingredients together with a pastry blender or food processor. Form into a ball without kneading. Cover and refrigerate for about 40 minutes. Roll the pastry out on a baking sheet into a thin square, 10x10 inches. Trim the edges evenly and roll them into a ½-inch rim. Mix the marzipan with the egg so that it becomes a smooth batter and spread this over the pastry. Bake at 425°F for 10 minutes.

Peel and core the apples and cut them into thin slices. Place the slices, overlapping, on the baked pastry square. Sprinkle with a little sugar. Bake for another 15 minutes at 400°F.

Warm the raisins in a little water; drain. Take the pie out of the oven. Brush with the apricot purée and sprinkle with the raisins.

Banana Cream Pie

Yield: 1 9-inch pie

Pastry for 1-crust pie, baked
½ cup sugar
¼ teaspoon salt
⅓ cup flour
1⅓ cups milk
¾ cup water
3 egg yolks, beaten
1 cup bananas, thinly sliced

meringue
3 egg whites
⅓ cup sugar
½ teaspoon baking powder

Combine the sugar, salt, flour, milk, and water over low heat. When hot, add a small amount to the egg yolks; mix. Pour the egg yolks back into the custard; cook 3 to 4 minutes. Add the bananas. Pour into a pie shell.

Make the meringue: Beat egg whites until almost stiff. Add sugar gradually, beating continuously. Add baking powder; beat until glossy. Top the pie with the meringue.

Fresh Apricot Pie

Yield: 1 9-inch pie

Pastry for 2-crust pie
⅔ cup sugar
1 cup pineapple juice
1½ dozen fresh apricots, pitted and halved
2 teaspoons cornstarch
½ teaspoon salt
2 tablespoons margarine
½ teaspoon vanilla

Line a 9-inch pie plate with ½ the pastry. Combine the sugar and pineapple juice and boil 1 minute. Simmer the apricots, a few at a time in the syrup, until just tender. Lift the apricots carefully from their juice and arrange in a pie shell.

Mix cornstarch with a little cold water; add to the juice and cook until thickened. Add salt, margarine, and vanilla and pour over the apricots. Cover with a lattice top. Bake in a 450°F oven 10 minutes; reduce heat to 350°F and bake about 20 minutes.

Blueberry Custard Cream Pie

Yield: 1 10-inch pie

crust
7 tablespoons butter or margarine
3 tablespoons confectioners' sugar
1 cup flour

filling
1 package vanilla pudding (instant)
⅓ cup heavy cream, whipped
2 envelopes unflavored gelatin
1¼ cups blueberries
¾ cup currant juice or blueberry juice

Mix all the ingredients for the crust together and let stand in a cool place. Line a lightly buttered cake pan with detachable bottom with the crust. Fasten a strip of aluminum foil around the edge so that the crust does not slide down during baking. Bake at 400°F for about 20 minutes.

Make the vanilla pudding according to directions on the package. Soak 1 tablespoon of the gelatin in a little water, then stir them into the warm pudding and mix so that it melts. When the pudding has cooled, add the whipped cream.

Take the pie shell out of the pan and fill it with the pudding. Place blueberries on top. Dissolve the remaining gelatin and blend with the juice. Pour the jelly over the berries when it starts to harden.

Serve with a dab of whipped cream.

Blackberry Pie

Yield: 1 8-inch pie

Pastry for 2-crust pie
3 cups blackberries
1 cup sugar
2 tablespoons orange juice
2 tablespoons flour
Pinch nutmeg
1 tablespoon butter

Line an 8-inch pie pan with pastry and chill.

Cook the berries and sugar over low heat, stirring; bring to a slow boil, then simmer 3 minutes. Cool. Add the orange juice.

Sprinkle a little flour over the bottom of the crust; pour in the berries, sprinkle with flour and nutmeg, and dot with butter. Put on the top crust, seal the edges with a little milk, and crimp them. Cut air holes in the center of the crust. Bake at 450°F 10 minutes. Lower the heat to 350°F and bake ½ hour, or until the crust is lightly browned. Serve with cream.

Crisp Nut Apple Pie

Bourbon Pie

Yield: 1 10-inch pie

brownie crust
4 tablespoons butter
2 1-ounce squares unsweetened chocolate
2 eggs
¼ teaspoon salt
1 cup sugar
½ teaspoon vanilla
¾ cup flour
½ cup pecans or walnuts, chopped

filling and topping
5 egg yolks
1 cup sugar
1 ¼-ounce envelope unflavored gelatin
¼ cup cold water
½ cup bourbon
3 cups whipping cream
Chocolate curls or shavings

To make the brownie crust, melt the butter and chocolate in the top of a double boiler over hot water. Cool the mixture. In a bowl, beat the eggs and salt until light and foamy. Add sugar and vanilla gradually and continue beating until well creamed. Stir the cooled chocolate mixture into the egg mixture and then fold in the flour. Gently stir in the nuts. Turn the batter into an ungreased 10-inch pie plate, lining the bottom. Bake in a 350°F oven 25 minutes or until a cake tester inserted in the center comes out clean. Cool.

To make the filling, beat the egg yolks until thick and lemon-colored. Slowly beat in ¾ cup of sugar. Soften the gelatin in cold water and add to it ⅓ of the bourbon. Heat the gelatin mixture in a double boiler over boiling water until the gelatin dissolves. Pour into the yolk mixture and stir briskly. Stir in the remaining bourbon. Whip 1 cup of the cream and fold into the yolk mixture. Pour the filling over the cooled brownie and refrigerate at least 4 hours.

To make the topping, whip the remaining cream, gradually adding the remaining ¼ cup sugar. Top the pie with whipped cream and garnish with chocolate curls or shavings.

Pennsylvania Cheese Pie

Yield: 1 9-inch pie

Pastry for 1-crust pie
2 teaspoons cornstarch
⅔ cup sugar
1 cup cottage cheese, riced or sieved
2 eggs, separated
2 tablespoons milk
⅛ teaspoon salt
1 tablespoon lemon rind, grated

Mix the cornstarch and sugar; add cottage cheese, egg yolks, milk, salt, and lemon rind and blend well. Fold in stiffly beaten egg whites and pour into the unbaked pie shell.

Bake in a 450°F oven 10 minutes. Reduce the temperature to 325°F and continue baking 25 to 30 minutes.

Super Chocolate Pie

Yield: 1 9-inch pie

pie shell
3 egg whites
Salt
¼ teaspoon cream of tartar
⅔ cup sugar, sifted
½ teaspoon vanilla extract
⅓ cup walnuts or pecans, finely chopped

chocolate cream filling
5 ounces semisweet chocolate
1 cup heavy cream
¼ cup hot milk
1 teaspoon vanilla extract
Salt

cream topping
¾ cup heavy cream

2 tablespoons confectioner's sugar
Chocolate curls

For the pie shell, beat together the egg whites, salt, and cream of tartar until soft peaks form. Beat in sugar, a little at a time, until a very stiff meringue is formed. Then beat in the vanilla.

Butter the bottom and sides of a 9-inch glass pie plate. Spread meringue over the bottom and sides as high as possible. Sprinkle nuts over the bottom. Bake in a preheated 275°F oven for 1 hour. If after 10 minutes the sides start to sag, gently push them back into place. Turn off the oven and allow the shell to cool in the oven for 30 minutes. Remove the shell from the oven and let cool completely.

For the filling, melt the chocolate in the top of a double boiler over hot water. Add milk, vanilla, and salt. Stir until smooth. Cool.

Whip the cream until stiff and fold into the cooled chocolate. Spread the filling in the cooled pie shell. Refrigerate for 4 hours.

No more than 1½ hours before serving, whip the cream for topping with confectioners' sugar; spread over the pie. Decorate the whipped cream with chocolate curls. Refrigerate pie until serving time.

Puff Pastry Patties can be filled with apples (below left) or other fruits.

Cherry Pie

Yield: 1 9-inch pie

crust
1 cup flour
2 to 3 tablespoons sugar (optional)
10½ tablespoons butter or margarine
2 tablespoons water or cream

filling
½ to ¾ quart pitted cherries
¼ to ⅓ cup sugar

Mix the flour and sugar together and place in a pile on a baking board. Slice the butter, and place on top. Chop the butter and flour together using a long knife until the mixture becomes crumb-like. Pour the water or cream on the top and quickly work into a dough. Refrigerate for ½ hour. Roll out ⅔ of the dough, and cover a 9-inch pie plate on both the bottom and sides. Alternate the cherries and sugar in the pie crust.

Make strips from the dough, and make a lattice pattern on top of the cherries. Bake at 425°F for about 30 minutes, until the surface has become golden brown.

Serve warm or cold, with whipped cream, if desired.

Chocolate Pecan Pie

Yield: 1 9-inch pie

Pastry for 1-crust pie
2 tablespoons margarine
2 ounces unsweetened chocolate
2 eggs
1 cup corn syrup
1 cup sugar
1 teaspoon vanilla
⅛ teaspoon salt
1 cup pecans

In a small saucepan over low heat, melt the margarine and chocolate; cool. In a small bowl, beat the eggs slightly with an electric mixer. Mix in the corn syrup, sugar, margarine, chocolate, vanilla, and salt. Stir in the pecans. Pour the filling into the unbaked pastry shell.

Bake in a 400°F oven 15 minutes; reduce heat to 350°F and bake 30 to 35 minutes longer (filling should be slightly less set in the center than around edge). Cool. Serve with whipped cream topping, if desired.

Blueberry Custard Cream Pie

Fruit Shell

Yield: 1 9-inch pie

7 tablespoons butter or margarine
¼ cup sugar
1 egg
⅓ cup whole-wheat flour
1 cup all-purpose flour

filling
¾ cup crème fraîche or sour cream
1½ tablespoons confectioners' sugar
½ to 1 tablespoon vanilla
About 3 peeled and sliced kiwi, or other fruit

Beat the butter and sugar together until smooth. Add the egg and the flours. Refrigerate the dough for at least 1 hour.

Roll or flatten out the dough and line a greased 9-inch pie tin with the dough. Prick well. Bake at 350°F for about 20 minutes.

Blend the crème fraîche and the confectioners' sugar together and flavor with the vanilla extract. Spread a thin layer of the filling over the bottom of the cooled pastry shell, and place sliced kiwi fruit on top. Serve the rest of the filling sauce next to the pie.

Rainbow Ice Cream Pie

Yield: 1 9-inch pie

sauce
½ cup mixed candied fruits, chopped
¼ cup pecans, chopped
½ cup light corn syrup
¼ cup sugar
¼ cup orange juice
½ teaspoon rum flavoring

crumb crust
⅔ cup fine brown-edge or vanilla wafer cookie
   crumbs
3 tablespoons butter, melted
11 to 12 brown-edge or vanilla wafer cookies

filling
1 pint chocolate ice cream
1 pint vanilla ice cream
1 pint strawberry ice cream

Combine the fruits, pecans, corn syrup, sugar, and orange juice in a saucepan. Bring to a boil and simmer 1 minute. Remove from the heat and stir in rum flavoring. Set aside and chill.

Combine the cookie crumbs and butter; mix well. Press the mixture evenly over the bottom of a buttered 9-inch pie plate. Stand whole cookies upright around the edge. Chill.

Spoon chocolate ice cream into the cookie crust and drizzle with ¼ of the sauce. Repeat, using a

Fruit Shell

layer of vanilla ice cream, then sauce, then a layer of strawberry ice cream and more sauce. Freeze until serving time. Pass the remaining sauce.

Lemon Chiffon Pie

Yield: 1 8-inch pie

Pastry for 1-crust pie, baked
1 envelope unflavored gelatin
¼ cup cold water
1 cup sugar
½ cup lemon juice
½ teaspoon salt
4 egg yolks, beaten
1 teaspoon lemon rind, grated
4 egg whites
½ cup heavy cream, whipped

Soften the gelatin in cold water. Add ½ cup of the sugar, lemon juice, and salt to the beaten egg yolks in the top of a double boiler; cook over boiling water until thick. Add the lemon rind and softened gelatin. Stir until the gelatin is dissolved. Cool.

Beat the egg whites until stiff. Gradually beat in the sugar until the mixture is smooth and glossy. Fold the egg whites into the gelatin mixture. Pour into the baked pie shell. Chill until firm. Just before serving, garnish with whipped cream.

Kiwi Pastries

Yield: 10 to 12 servings

rich shortcrust pastry
1¾ to 2 cups flour
Almost ⅓ cup sugar
½ teaspoon salt
1 egg
⅛ teaspoon vanilla extract
10½ tablespoons butter, at room temperature
1 tablespoon grated almonds (optional)

filling
4 eggs
1 cup whipping cream
⅓ pound sugar
1 tablespoon Kirschwasser
10 kiwi fruits

Mix the flour, sugar, and salt together. Form an indentation in the middle; place the egg, vanilla, and the butter in the hole. Mix the dough together with your fingertips until it becomes smooth. Refrigerate, preferably in a plastic bag.

Line pastry tins with the shortcrust dough. Prick the dough. Prebake the crust for about 10 minutes at 400°F. Beat together the eggs, cream, sugar, and liqueur in a bowl.

Peel the kiwi fruits and cut them into slices. Divide them between the pastries. Pour in the egg batter and bake at 350°F for 20 minutes. Sprinkle a little extra sugar on the top, and place under the broiler so that they become slightly browned without the pastry becoming burned.

You can use almost any kind of fruit or berry in this recipe: plums, cherries, pineapples, peaches, and wild strawberries.

Cranberry Pie

Yield: 1 9-inch pie

Pastry for 1-crust pie
2 cups cranberries
1 cup sugar
½ cup water
1 tablespoon cornstarch
1 teaspoon butter, softened

Wash and pick over the cranberries. Cook the sugar and water for 2 minutes; add the cranberries and cook for 5 minutes.

Mix the cornstarch and the softened butter and add enough of the hot cranberry liquid to make a smooth paste. Stir this mixture into the simmering cranberries. Cook 3 minutes, stirring constantly.

Pour the cranberry mixture into the unbaked pie shell. Cross with a lattice top. Bake 10 to 15 minutes in a preheated 450°F oven. Reduce the heat to 350°F and bake 25 to 30 minutes longer.

Easy Coconut Cream Pie

Yield: 1 9-inch pie

Pastry for 1-crust pie, baked
1 5-ounce package vanilla pudding and pie filling
3¼ cups milk
3 tablespoons sugar
1 egg, slightly beaten
2 tablespoons butter
1⅓ cup coconut, flaked
Whipped cream

Combine the pie filling mix, milk, sugar, and egg in a saucepan. Blend well. Cook and stir over medium heat until the mixture comes to a full boil. Remove from the heat. Stir in butter and 1 cup of the coconut. Cool about 5 minutes, stirring once or twice.

Pour into the pie shell. Cover the surface with wax paper; chill at least 3 hours. Remove the paper and garnish with whipped cream. Sprinkle with the remaining coconut.

Mango or Apricot Pie

Yield: 1 9-inch pie

8 digestive biscuits (available in gourmet shops)
8¾ tablespoons butter, melted
2 tablespoons brown sugar
4 teaspoons ginger
⅔ cup cream
¾ cup crème fraîche or sour cream
2 tablespoons sugar
1 drop mint oil or ⅓ cup chopped mint (optional)
3 fresh mangos or 1 large can apricots (1 pound, 13 ounces)
Juice and grated peel of 1 lemon
2 envelopes unflavored gelatin
Kiwi fruit, for garnish

Crush the biscuits and mix them with melted butter, brown sugar, and ginger. Cover a 9-inch pie plate with detachable bottom with the mixture. Push down with a spoon to cover the plate. Refrigerate.

Whip the cream and mix it with crème fraîche and sugar. (Flavor with mint oil or chopped mint, if you wish.) Place in pie plate.

Strain or purée the mangos or apricots, and mix with the lemon juice and peel. Place the gelatin in water, then dissolve it over low heat in its own liquid. Add the gelatin to the fruit mixture. Cool, stirring frequently.

Cover the cream mixture with the fruit mixture when it has thickened somewhat and garnish with kiwi fruit.

Cherry Pie

Mango or Apricot Pie

Spoon into the pastry shell; chill until firm. Spread with additional whipped cream; sprinkle additional grated lime peel around the edge of the pie.

Old-Time Lemon Pie

Yield: 1 8-inch pie

Pastry for 1-crust pie, baked
1 cup sugar
1¼ cups water
1 tablespoon butter
¼ cup cornstarch
3 tablespoons cold water
3 eggs, separated
2 tablespoons milk
6 tablespoons lemon juice
1 teaspoon lemon peel, grated
6 tablespoons sugar
1 teaspoon lemon juice

Combine the sugar, water, and butter in a saucepan; heat until the sugar dissolves. Blend the cornstarch with cold water, add to the hot mixture and cook slowly until clear, about 8 minutes.

In a bowl, beat the egg yolks with milk, slowly stir into the cornstarch mixture. Cook 2 minutes, stirring constantly. Remove from the heat. Add 6 tablespoons lemon juice and the lemon peel and let the mixture cool. Pour into a cooled, baked shell.

Beat the egg whites until stiff but not dry, adding the 6 tablespoons of sugar gradually; add 1 teaspoon of lemon juice toward the end of the beating. Spread the meringue over the cooled filling, sealing to the edges of the pastry to avoid shrinking. Brown in a 350°F oven for 12 to 15 minutes.

Maple Syrup Pie

Yield: 1 9-inch pie

Pastry for 1-crust pie, baked
1 cup plus 1 tablespoon maple syrup
1 cup hot water
1 teaspoon butter
2 tablespoons cornstarch
⅛ teaspoon salt
2 eggs, separated

Combine 1 cup of syrup, hot water, and butter. Bring to a full boil. Mix the cornstarch, salt, and enough cold water to make a thin paste. Add the egg yolks to the paste and beat well.

Add the hot syrup mixture gradually and return to the heat. Cook until thickened, stirring constantly. Cool slightly.

Pour the mixture into a baked pie shell. Beat the egg whites until stiff, slowly adding a tablespoon of syrup. Pile on the pie and brown until golden in a 400°F oven. Add chopped nuts if desired.

Key Lime Pie

Yield: 1 9-inch pie

Pastry for 1-crust pie, baked
1 tablespoon unflavored gelatin
1 cup sugar
¼ teaspoon salt
4 eggs, separated
½ cup lime juice
¼ cup water
1 teaspoon lime peel, grated
Green food coloring
1 cup whipping cream, whipped

Mix the gelatin, ½ cup sugar, and salt in a saucepan.

Beat the egg yolks, lime juice, and water together; stir into the gelatin mixture. Cook over medium heat, stirring constantly, until the mixture just comes to a boil. Remove from the heat; stir in the grated peel. Add enough coloring for a pale-green color. Chill, stirring occasionally, until thickened.

Beat the egg whites until soft peaks form. Add the remaining sugar gradually; beat until stiff peaks form. Fold the gelatin mixture into the egg whites; fold in the whipped cream.

Mincemeat Pecan Pies

Yield: 1 9-inch pie

Pastry for 1-crust pie
1 9-ounce package condensed mincemeat, broken
  up
½ cup corn syrup
¼ cup margarine
3 eggs, slightly beaten
½ cup pecans, coarsely chopped
1 tablespoon orange rind, grated
¼ cup sherry

In a medium saucepan, stir the mincemeat, corn syrup, and margarine together. Stirring constantly, bring to a boil over medium heat. Remove from the heat. Gradually mix in the eggs. Add pecans and rind. Pour into the unbaked pastry shell.

Bake in a 350°F oven 40 to 50 minutes or until a knife inserted near the center comes out clean. Pour sherry over the filling. Cool.

Montgomery Pie

Yield: 2 8-inch pies

Pastry for 2 1-crust pies
Juice and grated rind of 1 lemon
1 egg, lightly beaten
1 cup sugar
1 cup water
½ cup molasses
2 cups milk
2½ cups flour
2 teaspoons baking powder

Mix the lemon juice and rind, egg, sugar, water, and molasses together. Pour into the pie shells.

Mix the milk, flour, and baking powder together. Spoon this mixture over the lemon-molasses mixture in the pie shells. Do not stir. Bake 30 minutes in a 375°F oven.

Lemon Meringue Pie

Yield: 1 9-inch pie

Pastry for 1-crust pie, baked
7 tablespoons cornstarch
1⅓ cups sugar
¼ teaspoon salt
1½ cups hot water
3 egg yolks, beaten
½ cup lemon juice
1 teaspoon lemon rind, grated
2 tablespoons butter or margarine

meringue
3 egg whites
1 tablespoon lemon juice
6 tablespoons sugar

Mix the cornstarch, sugar, and salt in a saucepan. Stir in hot water gradually and bring to a boil over direct heat. Cook for 8 to 10 minutes over medium heat, stirring constantly until thick and clear. Remove from the heat. Stir several spoonfuls of this hot mixture into the beaten egg yolks. Mix well. Pour egg yolks back into the saucepan. Bring to a boil, then reduce heat and cook slowly for 4 to 5 minutes, stirring constantly. Remove from the heat and gradually add lemon juice, rind, and butter. Cool thoroughly, then pour into the cooled baked pie shell.

Top with meringue; put the egg whites (at room temperature) in a deep, medium-sized bowl. Add lemon juice. Beat until the whites stand in soft peaks. Add 6 tablespoons of sugar gradually, beating well after each addition. Beat until the egg whites stand in firm, glossy peaks. Spread over the cooled filling, starting at the edges and working toward the center of the pie, attaching the meringue securely to the edges of the crust. Bake at 350°F for 15 to 20 minutes. Cool but do not refrigerate before serving.

Oatmeal Pie with Nectar Mousse

Oatmeal Pie with Nectar Mousse

Yield: 1 10-inch pie

crust
1¼ cups oatmeal
⅔ cup flour
¼ cup sugar
10½ tablespoons margarine

filling
2 envelopes gelatin
¼ cup concentrated nectar or juice
⅔ cup cold water
¾ cup heavy cream
About ½ teaspoon vanilla
1 pint fresh or frozen blueberries

Cut and knead the crust ingredients together. Press out the dough onto the bottom and sides of a pan with a detachable bottom. Bake the pie pastry for 20 minutes at 350°F on the oven's lowest rack.

Dissolve the gelatin in a little water, then melt the gelatin in the nectar or juice over low heat. Add the cold water. Stir occasionally until the mixture starts to thicken. Whip the cream and add it to the gelatin mixture, which has thickened. Sweeten with vanilla; pour the mousse into the cooled pie shell.

Put a mound of berries on the top.

Spicy Deep-Dish Peach Pie

Yield: 1 8-inch pie

Pastry for 1-crust pie, with ¼ teaspoon nutmeg, cinnamon, and allspice added to the flour
1 1-pound, 13-ounce can cling peach slices, or 4 cups fresh or frozen peach slices
½ cup sugar (¾ cup for fresh peaches)
¼ teaspoon nutmeg
2 tablespoons cornstarch
¼ teaspoon salt
1 teaspoon orange rind, grated
1 tablespoon lemon juice
2 tablespoons butter or margarine

Grease an 8-inch round baking dish. Arrange the peaches and syrup in the dish. Blend the sugar, nutmeg, cornstarch, salt, and orange rind together. Sprinkle over the peaches. Sprinkle the lemon juice over the pie. Dot with bits of butter or margarine.

Roll out the pastry ½ inch larger than the baking dish. Cut slits to let the steam escape and place over the peaches. Press the overhanging pastry firmly against the edge of the dish. Flute the edges. Bake 25 to 30 minutes in a preheated 425°F oven.

Cranberry Glazed Pear Pie

Yield: 1 9-inch pie

crust
10½ tablespoons butter
1¼ cups flour
2 tablespoons water

filling
⅔ cup marzipan, coarsely grated
2 to 3 ripe, but not overly ripe, pears
1½ teaspoons lemon juice

glaze
1½ 6-ounce jars cranberry jelly

garnish
¾ to 1¼ cups stirred crème fraîche or whipped cream, flavored with a little vanilla

Mix together the crust ingredients in a bowl. Let stand in a cool place for about ½ hour. Flatten out the dough in a 9-inch pie plate with a detachable bottom. Make sure that the dough has an even thickness across the bottom of the pan and that it also covers the sides of the dish. Prick the bottom with a fork.

Preheat the oven to 425°F and bake the pie crust for 10 minutes. Divide the marzipan over the pie crust. Core and cut the pears into thin slices and place them in the pie crust in an attractive design. Moisten the pear slices with the lemon juice.

Cranberry Glazed Pear Pie

Place the pie on a rack in the middle of the oven and bake for 10 to 12 minutes. Melt the jelly and pour it over the pie after it has been baked and still is warm.

When the pie has cooled, place it on a board or a plate. Serve it with the stirred crème fraîche. Whipped cream or soft ice cream also do well as toppings.

Crunchy Pear Pie

Yield: 1 9-inch pie

Pastry for 1-crust pie
¼ cup sugar
2 tablespoons cornstarch
⅛ teaspoon salt
½ teaspoon ginger
1½ cups juice drained from canned pears
1 teaspoon lemon rind, grated
1 tablespoon lemon juice
2 cups pear halves, drained
1 cup flour, sifted
½ cup brown sugar, firmly packed
½ cup butter or margarine
½ cup nuts, chopped

Combine the sugar, cornstarch, salt, and ¼ teaspoon of ginger in a saucepan. Blend in the pear juice. Cook over medium heat, stirring constantly, until the mixture thickens and comes to a boil. Remove from the heat. Add lemon rind and lemon juice. Cut the pear halves in half lengthwise; arrange in the unbaked pastry shell. Pour thickened syrup over top of the pears.

Blend the flour, brown sugar, butter, and remaining sugar with a pastry blender until the mixture looks like coarse crumbs. Stir in nuts. Sprinkle over top of the pears. Bake in a 425°F oven 20 to 25 minutes.

Pecan Pie

Yield: 1 9-inch pie

Pastry for 1-crust pie
5 eggs
¾ cup sugar
1½ cups dark syrup
1½ cups pecans, chopped or halved
¾ teaspoon salt
2 teaspoons vanilla
Whipped cream

Beat the eggs slightly in a large bowl. Add sugar, syrup, nuts, salt, and vanilla; mix until nicely blended. Pour into the unbaked pie shell. Bake at 325°F 50 minutes. When cool, garnish with whipped cream; serve at once.

Strawberry Pie with Vanilla Cream Custard

Yield: 1 9-inch pie

Pastry for 1-crust pie
Strawberries
1 package instant vanilla pudding
Apricot jam
Chopped pistachio nuts

Line a pie tin with the pastry, then cover the pastry with waxed paper; pour in a layer of dried beans or peas on the bottom so that the pastry does not slide down the sides.

Bake the crust at 400°F until golden brown, about 10 minutes. Cover the bottom with vanilla pudding, made according to package directions, and place sliced strawberries on top. Brush with the apricot jam, which has been mixed with a little water, and sprinkle with chopped pistachio nuts.

This recipe may be made using all different kinds of berries: blackberries, raspberries, and wild strawberries. Serve warm with ice cream or whipped cream.

Pie with Pineapple Mousse

Rhubarb Pie

Yield: 1 9-inch pie

Pastry for 2-crust pie
4 cups unpeeled young rhubarb stalks, diced
¼ cup flour
1¼ to 2 cups sugar
1 teaspoon orange rind, grated
1 tablespoon butter

Line a 9-inch pie pan with the pastry.

Combine the remaining ingredients in a bowl; toss well. Turn into the shell. Dot with 1 to 2 tablespoons of butter. Cover the pie with a well-pricked top or a lattice.

Bake in a 450°F oven 10 minutes. Reduce the heat to 350°F; bake 35 to 40 minutes, until golden brown.

Pennsylvania Dutch Shoo Fly Pie

Yield: 1 9-inch pie

Pastry for 1-crust pie

crumb mixture
½ cup butter
1½ cups flour
1 cup light brown sugar

liquid mixture
1 cup molasses
1 egg, beaten
¾ cup boiling water
¾ teaspoon baking soda

Mix the crumb mixture together with your hands.

Mix the liquid mixture together. Pour it into an unbaked pie shell. Sprinkle the crumb mixture on top of the liquid mixture.

Bake at 400°F for 15 minutes. Reduce the heat to 350°F. Bake approximately 30 minutes more, or until the mixture is set.

Pie with Pineapple Mousse

Yield: 1 9-inch pie

crust
1¼ cups flour
¼ cup sugar
7 tablespoons margarine or butter
⅓ cup cottage cheese

mousse
1 18-ounce can pineapple slices in their own juices
2 envelopes gelatin
3 eggs, separated
¼ cup sugar
¾ cup whipping cream
3½ ounces cooking chocolate

Measure the flour and sugar into a bowl. Crumble the margarine into the mixture. Add the cottage cheese, and make into a workable dough. (You can also place all the ingredients in a food processor and mix into a dough.) Refrigerate 1 hour.

Pour the juice from the pineapple can (about ¾ cup) into a pot. Add the gelatin and let them soak in the juice for about 5 minutes, until soft. Then melt the gelatin in the juice over low heat.

Separate the egg yolks and whites. Beat the yolks together with the sugar. Beat the egg whites into stiff peaks. Whip the cream. Cut the pineapple slices into pieces; save 3 to 4 slices for decoration.

Mix the egg yolk mixture, whipped cream, and pieces of pineapple together. Add the juice in an even, little trickle while stirring constantly. Mix well. Fold in the egg whites. Refrigerate the mousse for about 1 hour so that it becomes partially firm.

Preheat the oven to 400°F. Press the dough into a pie plate or ovenproof dish. Prick well. Bake the pie crust for about 20 minutes in the oven. Meanwhile, melt about 3 ounces of the cooking chocolate over very low heat.

Remove the pie crust from the oven. Spread the chocolate in the crust. Allow the crust to become cold.

When the mousse has become partially firm, spread it over the chocolate in the pie crust. Place the dessert back in the refrigerator to become totally firm.

Decorate with slices of pineapple and chopped chocolate.

Summer Pie

Yield: 1 8½-inch pie

⅔ cup flour
¾ cup oatmeal
⅓ cup sugar
1 teaspoon baking powder
7 tablespoons butter or margarine

filling
Fresh berries: for example, blueberries and raspberries

Mix all the dry ingredients together in a bowl. Work in the butter until the mixture is crumbly. Place half of the dough in a greased and floured, 8½-inch round pan with detachable sides. Flatten the crumbs slightly and press them up toward the sides.

Sprinkle a layer of berries over the crumbs and then cover with the rest of the crumbs. Bake at 400°F for 20 to 25 minutes.

Serve the pie warm with partially thawed vanilla ice cream or lightly whipped cream.

Strawberry Heart

Strawberry Heart

Yield: 4 to 6 servings

pastry
1½ cups flour
2 tablespoons sugar
10½ tablespoons margarine

almond paste
⅓ pound marzipan
1 egg yolk
1½ tablespoons water

meringue
1 egg white
⅓ cup sugar
½ to 1 quart strawberries
A little jellied juice or wine (optional)

Cut and knead the pastry ingredients together into a dough. Roll it out directly onto baking paper with a flour-sprinkled rolling pin. Cut out a plate-sized circle, a large heart, or an oval, whatever suits your pie plate. Remove any excess dough.

Grate and mix the marzipan with the egg yolk and ½ tablespoon of the water. Put it into a pastry bag and pipe a border along the outer edge of the crust.

Press out the rest of the almond paste into a cup and stir in 1 tablespoon of water so that the paste becomes thinner in consistency. Spread this out inside the paste border.

Whip the egg white until stiff, first without and then with the sugar. Use the pastry bag again—it doesn't have to be washed between use—and press out a row of little peaks right next to the marzipan line.

Bake the pie at 350°F for 20 minutes on the lowest rack of the oven.

Fill the cooled pie with whole or divided strawberries, which can also be made glossy with a little jellied juice or wine (estimate 1 tablespoon gelatin per ¼ cup liquid).

Cookie Crumb Crust

Yield: Crust for 1 8-inch pie shell

2 cups cookie crumbs
6 tablespoons unblanched almonds, ground
5 tablespoons thin cream
⅝ cup butter, melted
⅓ teaspoon cinnamon

Crush the crumbs by hand or in a food processor. Mix the crumbs well with the butter. Press firmly into the bottom and sides of a pie pan. Chill.

Pastry for 1-Crust Pie

Yield: Crust for 1 9-inch pie shell

1 cup flour, sifted
½ teaspoon salt
⅓ cup plus 1 tablespoon shortening or ⅓ cup lard
2 to 2½ tablespoons cold water

Place the flour and salt in a mixing bowl. Cut in the shortening with a pastry blender or 2 knifes until the mixture is the consistency of coarse cornmeal. Sprinkle on the cold water, a little bit at a time, tossing the mixture lightly and stirring with a fork. The dough should not be sticky and should be just moist enough to hold together when pressed gently with a fork.

Shape 1 smooth ball of dough; roll out a little larger than a 9-inch pie pan. For a baked shell, prick the bottom and sides with a fork. Bake at 450°F for about 10 minutes.

Yogurt Pastry for 1-Crust Pie

Yield: Crust for 1 9-inch pie shell

1¼ cups flour, sifted
½ teaspoon salt
½ cup hydrogenated shortening
3 to 4 tablespoons yogurt

Stir the flour and salt together. Cut in the shortening until the pieces are the size of very coarse cornmeal. Sprinkle yogurt over this mixture and stir lightly with a fork until the dough can be formed into a ball. Let rest about 10 minutes.

Roll out on a piece of floured waxed paper until the crust is 1½ inches larger than the inverted pie pan. Ease the dough into the pan without stretching. Trim the crust ½ inch beyond the edge of the pan and fold under to make a double thickness of dough around the rim. Flute the edge.

For a baked pie shell, prick the bottom and sides with a fork. Bake at 450°F on top shelf of oven for about 10 minutes.

Graham Cracker Crust

Yield: Crust for 1 9-inch pie

1⅓ cups graham cracker crumbs (16 to 18 crackers)
¼ cup sugar
¼ cup butter or margarine, softened
¼ teaspoon ground nutmeg or cinnamon (optional)

Combine the graham cracker crumbs, sugar, butter, and nutmeg; blend until crumbly. Leave out ⅓ cup of crumbs to sprinkle on the top of the pie, if desired. Press the remaining crumbs evenly on the bottom and sides of a 9-inch pie pan, making a small rim.

Bake in a 375°F oven 8 minutes, or until the edges are lightly browned. Cool, then fill as the pie recipe directs.

For an unbaked graham cracker crust, use the same ingredients as for the baked crust; do not make a rim on the pie shell. Chill for about 1 hour, or until set, before filling.

Sweet Pastry

Yield: Crust for 1 9-inch pie shell

1 cup flour, sifted
½ cup sugar
¼ cup butter and lard, mixed
1 egg

Combine all the ingredients. Form into a ball and chill. Roll out lightly on a floured board. Line a 9-inch pie pan with the pastry and chill again.

For pies with strips on top, reserve ⅓ of the dough and add to it 1 teaspoon of baking powder and 2 tablespoons of milk. Mix again and roll out. Cut in strips and place on top of the pie, all in one direction. These strips may not be crossed because they puff up. Use for fruit and berry pies.

Pastry for 2-Crust Pie

Yield: Crust for 1 9-inch pie

2 cups flour, sifted
1 teaspoon salt
¾ cup shortening or ⅔ cup lard
4 to 5 tablespoons cold water

Place the flour and salt in a mixing bowl. Cut in the shortening with a pastry blender or 2 knifes until the mixture is the consistency of coarse cornmeal.

Sprinkle on the cold water, 1 tablespoon at a time, tossing the mixture lightly and stirring with a fork. Add water each time to the driest part of the mixture. The dough should not be sticky and should be just moist enough to hold together when pressed gently with a fork.

Shape the dough into a smooth ball with your hands; roll it to be a little larger than a 9-inch pie pan.

Meringue Pie Crust

Yield: Crust for 1 9-inch pie shell

3 egg whites (room temperature)
¼ teaspoon cream of tartar
⅛ teaspoon salt
¾ cup sugar

Mix the egg whites, cream of tartar, and salt together. Beat until frothy. (Do not underbeat.) Gradually add the sugar and beat until stiff peaks form. The meringue should be shiny and moist, with all the sugar dissolved.

Spread over the bottom and sides of a well-greased 9-inch pie pan. Bake in a 275°F oven 1½ hours. Turn off the oven; leave the crust in the oven with a closed door for 1 hour. Finish cooling the crust in the pan away from the drafts. Spoon in the filling and chill.

Baked meringue pie shells almost always crack and fall in the center.

Summer Pie

Cakes and Cookies

Almond Mousse Layers

Yield: 6 to 8 servings

cake
½ to ⅔ cup almonds
⅓ cup sugar
3 egg whites

mocha-cream icing
5 ounces bittersweet chocolate
¾ cup heavy cream
2 tablespoons confectioners' sugar
2 tablespoons strong coffee, or 3 or 4 drops pep-
    permint oil, or 2 tablespoons rum
2 egg yolks

garnish
Chocolate or roasted slivered almonds

Grind the unskinned almonds. Mix them with the sugar.

Beat the egg whites until stiff. Carefully fold in the almonds and sugar. Spread the batter into 2 round "cookies," about 8 inches in diameter, on a cookie sheet that has been covered with baking paper. Bake in the center of a preheated 350°F oven until they feel dry and are light brown in color, about 15 minutes. Let them cool somewhat. Loosen them from the paper with a sharp knife.

Break the chocolate into pieces. Place in a bowl. Cover with foil. Place the bowl over a pan of boiling water. Remove the pan from the heat and let the chocolate melt slowly.

Whip the cream, but not too stiffly. Add the sugar, flavoring, egg yolks, and 2 tablespoons of the cream to the chocolate. Beat vigorously. Let cool. Mix in the rest of the cream.

Put the layers together with slightly more than half of the icing between the layers. Spread the rest of the icing on top. Refrigerate the cake for at least a couple of hours before serving.

Garnish with chocolate almonds or chocolate curls.

Almond Mousse Layers

Forgotten Meringue Cake

Saffron Advent Cake

Yield: 10 servings

2 cups flour
3 teaspoons baking powder
¾ cup sugar
7 tablespoons butter or margarine
⅔ cup milk
1 egg
⅛ to ¼ teaspoon saffron, ground
Butter and bread crumbs or flour for preparing the pan
3 or 4 apples, thinly sliced
A little sugar and several dabs of butter

Blend the flour, baking powder, and sugar. Crumble the butter into the mixture until it is grainy.

Beat together the milk, egg, and saffron. Pour into the flour mixture. Quickly work together into a dough. Place the dough in a greased baking pan preferably with a detachable edge (springform) which has been dusted with bread crumbs or flour. Stick thin slices of apples close together into the dough. Sprinkle with a little sugar. Place several dabs of butter on top. Bake in a 425°F oven for 25 to 30 minutes.

Alexander Cake

Yield: 8 to 10 servings

cake
¼ cup almonds
5 egg whites
¾ cup sugar

custard cream
5 egg yolks
1¼ cups heavy cream
¾ cup sugar
1 teaspoon cornstarch
2 teaspoons rum

garnish
Toasted sliced almonds

Grind the almonds.

Beat the egg whites into stiff peaks. Fold in the almonds and sugar. Spread the batter into 2 heart-shaped layers on a greased cookie sheet or on baking-sheet paper. Bake in a 350°F oven for about 15 minutes.

Mix the egg yolks, cream, sugar, and cornstarch together in a thick-bottomed pan or in a double boiler. Let the custard cream simmer slowly, stirring constantly, for 10 to 15 minutes, until it be-

Saffron Advent Cake and Orange-Nut Ring

comes thick. Stir in the rum. Cool. Spread part of the custard cream over one of the cake layers. Place the second layer on top. Spread the rest of the custard cream over the second layer. Garnish with almonds.

Angel Food Cake

Yield: 12 servings

½ cup flour
½ cup plus 1 tablespoon sugar
⅝ cup egg whites
Pinch salt
½ teaspoon cream of tartar
½ teaspoon vanilla extract

Use a 6-inch cake pan or a tube pan, not greased. Sift the flour and sugar separately 3 times, then sift the flour with ¼ of the sugar.

Put the egg whites and salt in a large, clean, dry bowl and beat until frothy. Sprinkle on the cream of tartar and continue beating until the white stands up in peaks. Avoid overbeating, or the white will lose its glossiness. Lightly beat in the remaining sugar and flavoring; then, using a tablespoon, fold in the sifted flour-sugar mixture carefully and gradually.

Pour into a tube pan and gently cut through the mixture with a knife to release air bubbles. Bake for 40-45 minutes in a 290°F oven increasing the heat to 335°F for the last 10-15 minutes. Allow the cake to stand in the inverted pan for 30 minutes, then turn out onto a cooling rack.

Almond Apple Cake

Yield: 4 servings

About 1 pound 10 ounces apples (6 medium)
⅓ cup almonds
½ to ⅔ cup margarine or butter
⅓ cup sugar
2 eggs
¾ cup bread crumbs

Grease an ovenproof dish.
Coarsely grate the apples, with peels, and place the gratings in the bottom of the dish.
Grind the almonds.
Beat the margarine and sugar until light. Add the eggs, almonds, and bread crumbs. Make into a batter. Spread the batter over the apples. Bake in a preheated 400°F oven for about 30 minutes.
Serve with custard sauce or cream.

Alexander Cake

Almond Shortcrust Cake

Yield: 8 to 12 servings

shortcrust pastry
1 egg
⅔ cup butter or margarine
⅓ cup sugar
1¼ cups flour

filling
¾ to 1 cup almonds
7 tablespoons butter or margarine
⅔ cup sugar
2 eggs
⅛ teaspoon vanilla extract
¼ teaspoon ground cardamom
¼ teaspoon baking powder

Make the pastry. Beat the egg. Save a tablespoon for brushing the pastry. Work all the ingredients of the pastry together into a dough. Refrigerate for about an hour.

Roll out about ⅔ of the dough. Line a greased pan with detachable edge, about 8½ to 9 inches in diameter, with the dough. The dough should go 1 inch up the side of the pan. To make the filling,

grind the almonds. (The skins do not need to be removed.)

Beat the butter and sugar together until light. Add the eggs, one at a time. Beat vigorously.

Mix the almonds with the vanilla, cardamom, and baking powder. Add to the egg mixture. Spread the batter out in the pan. Bake in a 350°F oven for about 20 minutes.

Roll out the rest of the dough. Cut out strips and place them crisscross over one another on the partially baked cake. Finally place a border of dough around the edge of the cake. Brush with egg. Bake for 25 minutes. Let the cake cool before removing the detachable edge.

Apple Cake

Yield: 10 servings

1 tablespoon margarine and 1½ tablespoons bread crumbs or flour for preparing the cake pan
1⅔ cups flour
¾ cup sugar
2 teaspoons baking powder
3½ tablespoons margarine

Almond Shortcrust Cake

Almond Apple Cake

Apple Cake

¾ cup milk
About 2 cups frozen apple slices (2 or 3 apples)
1 teaspoon cinnamon and 1 to 2 tablespoons sugar,
  mixed together

Grease a 9½-inch round cake pan. Dust it with bread crumbs or flour.

Mix together the flour, sugar, and baking powder.

Finely chop the margarine into the flour mxture. Crumble it with your fingertips. For those with a food processor, use the metal knife attachment. Add the milk. Quickly mix together into a batter. Pour the batter into the greased pan. Press the frozen apple slices down into the cake (they do not need to defrost). Make a decorative sun-ray pattern. Sprinkle the cinnamon and sugar mixture over the cake. Bake in a preheated 350°F oven for 40 to 45 minutes.

Turn the cake out of the pan and tip it right side up again onto the plate from which it is to be served.

French Apple Cake

Yield: About 10 servings

7 tablespoons butter
⅔ cup sugar
About 6 ounces ground almonds
Juice and grated peel of ½ lemon
2 egg yolks
3 egg whites, beaten until stiff
Apple compote made from 6 to 8 apples, or 2 cups
  applesauce
1¼ cups whipped cream, flavored with sugar and
  vanilla or sherry

Allow the butter to soften and then beat it with the sugar until it becomes airy and light in color. Add the ground almonds, grated lemon peel, and lemon juice. Add the egg yolks, one at a time, and finally fold in the beaten egg whites.

Pour not-too-juicy apple compote or applesauce into a greased pan. Cover with the batter. Bake at 400°F for 20 minutes. (This may be prepared a day in advance. Cover with aluminum foil and warm when it is time to serve the cake. It tastes best when served warm.) Serve with cream that has been lightly whipped.

Quick Apple Cake

Sprinkle with a small amount of sugar. Place several dabs of butter here and there on the cake. Bake in a 425° to 450°F oven for about 20 minutes. Cut the cake into pieces when serving.

Quick Puff-Pastry Apple Cake

Yield: 4 servings

1 sheet puff pastry, frozen
1 apple
¼ cup marzipan
1½ tablespoons sugar
1 tablespoon cinnamon
1 egg

Thaw the puff pastry. Roll it out on a floured board. Make it round or rectangular, depending on your serving plate. Place the pastry on a baking sheet.

Grate the apple and marzipan. Sprinkle them over the pastry. Sprinkle with the sugar and cinnamon.

Beat the egg. Brush it around the pastry edges. Bake in a 425°F oven for about 20 minutes.

Serve with ice cream, or with whipped cream sweetened with a little vanilla and sugar.

Quick Apple Cake

Yield: 6 to 8 servings

2⅓ cups flour
3 teaspoons baking powder
1¼ cups sugar
⅔ cup butter or margarine
1¼ cups coffe cream
About 6 apples
Grated peel from 1 orange and 1 lemon
A little squeezed juice (optional)
Sugar
Dabs of butter

Mix the flour, baking powder, and sugar together in a bowl. Crumble the butter into the mixture so that the dough becomes small pebbles. Add the cream and work quickly into a dough. Spread the dough into a baking pan that has been covered with greased baking paper. The dough should be about 9½ × 13½ inches.

Remove the cores from the apples. Cut the apples into thin wedges. Place the wedges close together on top of the dough. Sprinkle with the peel from the orange and lemon. Squeeze several drops of orange or lemon juice over the top of the cake.

Quick Puff Pastry Apple Cake

Berry Roll

Yield: About 8 servings

3 eggs
⅔ cup sugar
¾ cup flour
1 teaspoon baking powder

filling
⅔ to ¾ cup jam or fresh berries

Beat the eggs and sugar together until light and airy. Carefully fold in the flour, which has first been blended with the baking powder. Spread the batter in a 12 × 15½-inch baking pan that has been lined with baking paper. Bake in a 425°F to 450°F oven for about 5 minutes. Turn the cake out onto sugared waxed paper. Peel away the baking paper on which the cake baked. (Brush the paper with cold water if it does not loosen easily.) Spread the filling on the warm cake. Roll it up from the long side.

Variation: Place ice cream on a cake slice and top with berries.

French Apple Cake

Blueberry Cake

Yield: 8 to 10 servings

1½ cups flour, sifted
1 cup sugar
Dash salt
½ cup butter, softened
4 cups blueberries
1 tablespoon lemon juice
3 tablespoons quick-cooking tapioca
¼ teaspoon salt
⅛ teaspoon cinnamon

Combine the flour, ½ cup of sugar, dash salt, and butter. Mix with a pastry blender or fork until the crumbs are formed. Measure ¾ cup and set aside.

Press the remaining crumbs over the bottom and about ¾ inch up the sides of a 9-inch springform pan.

Combine the blueberries, lemon juice, remaining ½ cup of sugar, tapioca, salt, and cinnamon. Let stand 15 minutes. Spoon the blueberry mixture into the crumb-lined pan. Bake at 425°F for 20 minutes. Then sprinkle with the ¾ cup of reserved crumbs. Bake 20 to 25 minutes longer, or until the crumbs are golden brown. Serve warm or cold with whipped cream.

Berry Roll

Let the cake cool. Serve it chilled. The cake can be stored in the refrigerator for several days as long as it is covered well. It can also be frozen.

Serve well chilled. If desired, decorate with berries, fruit, or jam.

Crisp Cheesecake

Yield: 10 servings

⅔ cup butter
1½ cups flour
6 tablespoons grated Parmesan cheese
4 tablespoons heavy cream

garnish
¼ to ⅓ cup scalded, peeled almonds, cut in half
1 egg

filling
5 egg yolks
¾ cup heavy cream
⅔ cup butter
½ to ⅔ cup finely grated aged cheese
1/16 teaspoon cayenne pepper

garnish
Green and purple grapes

Chop together the butter, flour, and the Parmesan cheese, either by hand with a chopping knife or in a food processor, using the metal knife attachment. Add the cream. Make a dough. Divide dough into 2 parts. Make each part into a round, thick cake. Cover them with plastic wrap and refrigerate for an hour or more.

Scald the almonds. Peel, and cut them in half.

Separate the egg yolks from the whites for the filling. (The egg whites are not needed in this recipe but can be saved for several weeks in the refrigerator in a container with a tightly fitting lid, or they can be frozen.) Place the egg yolks in a saucepan. Beat them together with the cream. Let thicken over a double boiler. Stir occasionally with a wooden fork. The yolks should not be allowed to boil. Remove from the heat and stir in the butter in dabs. Let each dab of butter totally mix with the egg yolks before adding the next dab of butter. Finally add the cheese and cayenne pepper. Let cool.

Remove the dough from the refrigerator. Roll out the dough into plate-size round layers. Roll out between pieces of plastic wrap. Pull away the plastic wrap from the top. Place a plate over the dough and even off the edges. Turn the dough upside down onto baking paper. Remove the other piece of plastic wrap. Brush the layers with a beaten egg. Garnish one of the crusts with almonds. Bake in a preheated 400°F oven for 10 minutes. Let cool on the paper.

American Cheesecake

Yield: About 8 servings

½ pound plain crackers
1 teaspoon cinnamon
7 tablespoons melted butter

filling
17½ ounces cream cheese
¾ cup sugar
3 eggs
½ teaspoon vanilla extract

top layer
1¼ to 1⅔ cups crème fraîche or sour cream

Finely crush the crackers. Mix them with the cinnamon and butter. Press the crumb mixture onto the bottom and partially up the sides of a pan with a detachable bottom. The pan should be at least 9½ inches in diameter, preferably even larger. Bake in a preheated 350°F oven for 5 minutes.

Beat the cream cheese until creamy. Add the eggs, sugar, and vanilla sugar. Pour the batter into the pan and bake for 45 minutes.

Stir the crème fraîche until it is somewhat thinner. Spread it over the cake. Place in the oven for 5 minutes.

Place the crust without the almonds on a serving plate. It can be moved with the help of the bottom part of a round pan with detachable bottom. Spread the cheese filling over the crust. Place the almond crust on top.

The cake should be made several hours in advance. Garnish it with the grapes.

The layers can be frozen separately. If the cake is put together before it is frozen, it will become soft when thawing and will lose its crispness.

Mint Chocolate Cake

Yield: About 8 servings

2½ ounces cooking chocolate
5¼ tablespoons butter or margarine
¾ cup sugar
¼ teaspoon vanilla extract
2 eggs
1 cup flour
1 teaspoon baking powder
⅓ cup cream

mint filling

⅓ cup sugar
⅓ cup strong coffee
3 egg yolks
⅔ cup unsalted butter, room temperature
1¾ ounces melted light cooking chocolate
2 to 3 drops peppermint oil

Break the cooking chocolate into smaller pieces. Melt it in a double boiler.

Mix the butter, sugar, and vanilla until airy. Add the eggs, one at a time. Beat the mixture until smooth. Blend in the chocolate.

Mix together the flour and baking powder. Add this and the cream to the batter. Pour the batter into a well-greased and floured 1½-quart pan. Bake in a 350°F oven about 50 minutes. Test with a toothpick.

To make the mint filling, boil the sugar and coffee together until syrupy.

Beat the egg yolks lightly. Add the sugar and coffee mixture in a thin trickle, stirring constantly and vigorously. Let cool. Add the butter in dabs, continuing to beat vigorously. Flavor with the melted chocolate and peppermint oil.

Divide the cake into 3 layers. Spread the mint filling between the layers.

Serve the cake with cold whipped cream.

American Cheesecake

Walnut Cheesecake

Yield: About 8 servings

½ cup walnuts
1 cup blue cheese
¾ cup butter
½ to ⅔ cup firm whipped cheese or block cheese
⅔ cup heavy cream

garnish
Green and purple grapes
Chives

Remove several of the more decorative walnuts for the garnish. Finely chop or grind the rest of the walnuts. Add them to the blue cheese and 7 tablespoons of the butter. Make into a soft mixture.

Warm the whipped cheese in the cream and mix in the rest of the butter. Remove from the heat as soon as the cheese has melted. Spread half of the cheese mixture, about ½ inch thick, over the bottom of a small springform pan. (Place cut greased baking paper on the bottom of this form.) Cover with the soft blue-cheese mixture. Cover this with the rest of the whipped-cheese mixture. Even the top with a small, warmed spatula. Decorate with the reserved walnuts. Refrigerate for at least 24 hours.

Remove the edge and bottom of the pan when the cake is cold. Take the cake out of the refrigerator and serve it at room temperature. Garnish with grapes. Make division lines on the cake with chives.

This cake tastes best when it is two days old and not served too cold.

Sticky Chocolate Cake

Yield: 8 to 12 servings

1¼ cups sugar
¼ teaspoon salt
4 tablespoons cocoa
⅔ cup flour
2 eggs
7 tablespoons melted, cooled butter
½ teaspoon vanilla extract
Butter and bread crumbs or flour for preparing the pan
½ to 1 package sliced almonds

Mix all the dry ingredients together. Mix in the eggs, butter, and vanilla.

Grease a 9½-inch round cake pan, preferably a springform. Sprinkle it with bread crumbs or flour. Spread the batter in the pan. Sprinkle with the sliced almonds. Bake in the bottom of a preheated 325° oven for about 35 minutes. The cake should be sticky on the inside.

Serve with whipped cream and berries or fruit.

Crisp Cheesecake

Chocolate Cake

Yield: About 10 servings

2 eggs
1¼ cups sugar
4 tablespoons cocoa
⅔ cup flour
7 tablespoons melted butter or margarine
¼ teaspoon salt

mocha cream filling
3½ tablespoons butter
⅓ cup confectioners' sugar
2 tablespoons strong coffee

topping
¾ cup whipping cream
Slivered cooking chocolate
Tiny candies (optional)

Mix the eggs and sugar together, but do not beat. Add the cocoa, flour, butter, and salt. Stir until the batter is no longer lumpy. Pour into a greased springform cake pan that has been sprinkled with bread crumbs. Bake in a 350°F oven for about 25 minutes. The cake should not be entirely dry.

To make the cream filling, stir the butter, confectioners' sugar, and coffee into a smooth cream. It should have a strong coffee flavor.

Spread the cream filling over the cold cake, which has not been removed from the bottom of the cake pan. Spread the whipped cream on top and sprinkle with the slivered cooking chocolate. Garnish with tiny candies. Serve the cake cold.

Minute Chocolate Cake

Yield: 8 to 10 servings

½ package chocolate pudding mix
Heavy cream
1 teaspoon instant coffee
1 to 2 tablespoons cocoa
1 meringue cake layer (not too thin)
⅔ cup whipped cream
Cocoa
Chocolate thins

Mix the chocolate-pudding powder according to the package directions, but substitute half the milk with heavy cream. Add the instant coffee and cocoa to create a fuller taste. Adjust the flavoring. Immediately spread the pudding icing over the meringue cake. Spread a layer of whipped cream on top of this. Sift over with the cocoa. Press the chocolate thins into the whipped cream. Refrigerate the cake before serving.

Chewy Cake Sections

Yield: 10 to 12 servings

¾ to 1 cup butter or margarine
4 eggs
2⅓ cups sugar
2⅓ cups flour
¼ teaspoon vanilla extract
Grated peel of 2 well-rinsed lemons
1 bag almond slivers

Melt the butter. Let it cool.

Quickly mix the egg, sugar, flour, vanilla, and lemon peel with the butter. Stir just until the ingredients are mixed together, but no longer. Spread out the batter in a baking pan 12 × 16 inches that has been covered with a greased sheet of baking paper. Sprinkle with the almonds. Bake in a 400°F oven for about 25 minutes. Cut the cake into bite-size pieces.

Walnut Cheesecake

Chewy Cake Sections, Marzipan Cake with Chocolate, Coconut Squares, and Apple Squares

French Chocolate Cake

Yield: About 10 servings

7 ounces bittersweet chocolate
14 tablespoons butter or margarine
4 eggs
¾ cup sugar
1 cup flour
⅓ cup hazel nuts, coarsely chopped
1 teaspoon baking powder

Grease a springform pan with detachable bottom that has a diameter of about 9½ inches. Preheat the oven to 425°F.

Melt the cooking chocolate and butter in a thick-bottomed pot over low heat. Beat the eggs and sugar until light and airy. Carefully stir the somewhat cooled chocolate mixture into the egg mixture.

Blend the flour, nuts, and baking powder together, and fold carefully into the batter. It's important to fold it in gently.

Pour the batter into the pan and bake in the oven for about 15 minutes. The cake should not become firm. The "unbaked" batter tastes like a delicious filling.

You may garnish the cooled cake with a little bit of grated chocolate and a ring of whipped cream.

Cinnamon Cake

Yield: About 8 servings

7 tablespoons butter or margarine
¾ cup sugar
3 large eggs
1⅔ cups flour
2 teaspoons baking powder
½ teaspoon vanilla extract
¾ cups sour cream
Butter
Bread crumbs or flour

filling

Almost ¼ cup sugar
1 teaspoon cinnamon

Beat the butter and sugar together until light and fluffy. Add the eggs, one at a time, beating constantly.

Blend the flour and baking powder.

Stir the vanilla into the sour cream. Alternate adding the flour mixture and the sour cream to the

Chocolate Cake

French Chocolate Cake

batter. Pour half of the batter into a 1½-quart greased baking pan that has been dusted with bread crumbs or flour. Sprinkle with about half of the sugar and cinnamon mixed together. Spread the rest of the batter on top. Sprinkle with the rest of the sugar and cinnamon. Bake the cake in a 350°F oven for about 1 hour. Cover the cake with aluminum foil if it should start to get too dark while baking.

Old-Fashioned Honeycake

Yield: 8 servings

⅔ cup butter
1½ cups honey
3 eggs
3 cups flour, sifted
3 teaspoons baking powder
1 teaspoon cinnamon
1 teaspoon powdered cloves
½ teaspoon salt
2 cups raisins, chopped
½ cup milk

Cream the butter; add honey. Beat the eggs and add, mixing well. Sift the flour, baking powder, cinnamon, cloves, and salt together. Add the chopped raisins. Add the flour alternately with the milk to the creamed mixture. Pour into a tube or loaf pan and bake in a 350° oven for 1½ hours.

Hazelnut Cake

Yield: 8 servings

¾ cup hazelnut meats
5 bitter almonds
⅔ cup flour
1 teaspoon baking powder
7 tablespoons butter or margarine
⅔ cup coffee cream
2 eggs
¾ cup sugar
Butter and bread crumbs or flour for preparing the
    pan

Grind the hazelnut meats with the bitter almonds. Mix with the flour and the baking powder.

Melt the margarine in a pan. Pour in the cream.

Beat the eggs and sugar together until fluffy and light. Add the flour and butter-cream mixtures. Pour the batter into a well-greased 1½-quart baking pan that has also been dusted with bread crumbs or flour. Bake in a 350°F oven for about 55 minutes. Test with a toothpick.

When served as dessert, add a dab of ice cream or whipped cream on top.

Mint Chocolate Cake

Old-Fashioned Gingerbread Cake

Yield: 12 to 14 servings

⅔ cup butter or margarine
3 eggs
1¼ cups sugar
1 tablespoon ginger
1 tablespoon cinnamon
1 tablespoon ground cloves
⅔ cup ligonberry or cranberry jam, firm variety
⅔ cup sour cream
About 2 cups flour
1 teaspoon baking soda
Butter and bread crumbs or flour for preparing the pan

Melt the butter.

Beat the eggs and sugar together until light and airy. Stir in the cooled butter, spices, jam, sour cream, and the flour that first has been blended with the baking soda. Pour the batter into a 2-quart greased oblong pan that has been dusted with bread crumbs or flour. Bake in a 350°F oven for about 1 hour or until the cake feels dry.

Minute Chocolate Cake

Apricot Cream of Wheat Cake

Yield: 4 servings

1 cup (or 7 ounces) dried apricots
1¼ cups water
¼ cup sugar
1 tablespoon potato flour

cake layers
2 eggs
¼ cup sugar
⅓ cup cream of wheat
1 tablespoon butter or margarine

topping
Confectioners' sugar

Place the rinsed fruit in a saucepan with 1 cup of water. Let stand for 30 minutes.

Simmer the apricots over low heat for about 10 minutes. Add the sugar. Simmer for a few more minutes or until the apricots feel soft.

Prepare the cake layers. Mix the potato flour with ¼ cup water. Add to the fruit, stirring constantly. Bring to a boil.

Beat the eggs and sugar together. Stir in the cream of wheat. "Bake" ⅓ of the cake batter in a greased frying pan, about 4 minutes on each side.

Repeat with the remaining batter, so that you have 3 cake layers. When the layers have cooled, make them into a cake with the warm, stewed apricots in between the layers. Sprinkle confectioners' sugar over the cake, using a sieve, just before serving the cake.

Marzipan Cake with Chocolate

Yield: About 8 servings

1⅓ cups marzipan
7 tablespoons butter or margarine
3 eggs
⅔ cup flour
½ teaspoon baking powder
3½ ounces bittersweet chocolate, melted
Skinned almonds

Finely grate the marzipan on a grater. Mix it with the butter. Beat until light. Add the eggs, one at a time. Mix in the flour, which has been blended with the baking powder. Spread the batter into a small baking pan, about 8 × 12 inches, which has been lined with a greased sheet of baking paper. Bake in a 400°F oven for 8 to 10 minutes. Cool on rack. Spread melted chocolate over the cake. Garnish with skinned almonds, whole or chopped. Cut the cake into pieces before the chocolate has totally hardened.

Variation: Cover the entire surface with thin apple slices and bake as above. Exclude the chocolate.

Forgotten Meringue Cake

Yield: 8 to 10 servings

5 egg whites
1¼ cups sugar
½ teaspoon baking powder

garnish
Ice cream
Strawberries

Beat the egg whites until stiff. Add the sugar and baking powder, beating continuously. Pour the batter into a greased ring pan. Smooth the top slightly. Heat the oven to 450°F. When the oven has reached the desired temperature, turn it off. Then place the meringue in the oven. Let it stay there for about 9 hours or overnight.

Garnish with ice cream and strawberries in the middle. You can use other kinds of berries, fresh or frozen, depending on the season.

Apricot Cream of Wheat Cake

Ice-Cream Cake

Yield: 8 to 10 servings

1 nut cake layer (bought, or made from ½ nut-cake mix)

Butter and bread crumbs or flour for preparing the pan

1 meringue layer (bought, or made from 2 egg whites and 4 tablespoons sugar)

filling

2 cups vanilla ice cream

decoration

¾ cup whipped cream

Roasted hazelnuts

Make the nut cake layer according to the package directions. Bake it in a round, well-greased cake pan that has been dusted with bread crumbs or flour.

To make the meringue layer, beat the egg whites into stiff, firm peaks. Fold in the sugar. Bake on a well-greased, floured baking sheet in a 250°F oven until the layer feels dry and light.

Cut the ice cream into slices. Cover the nut-cake layer. Place the meringue layer on top.

Whip the cream. Spread it over the meringue. Sprinkle roasted nuts on top. Freeze the cake for about 1 hour. It can also be served immediately.

Ice-Cream Cake with Chocolate Icing

Yield: About 6 servings

1 quart vanilla ice cream

½ to ⅔ cup chopped walnuts

2 to 3 tablespoons white rum (optional)

4¼ ounces bittersweet chocolate

garnish

Roasted almonds or pistachio nuts

Candied violets or silver balls (optional)

Stir the ice cream until soft. Add the walnuts. Add the rum.

Quickly pour the mixture into a form with a detachable edge. Place in the freezer to harden.

Melt the cooking chocolate over a double boiler.

When the ice cream has hardened, release the spring on the edge and remove the side of the form. Brush the sides and the top with a carelessly applied first layer of chocolate. Place the ice cream back in the freezer without the form edge. Let it freeze again for ½ to 1 hour. Take out of the freezer. Brush again with the chocolate. None of the ice cream should show through after this brushing. If it does, patch up the spots with more of the chocolate. Spread out the rest of the chocolate with a spatula. Sprinkle with the garnish before the chocolate hardens. Place again in the freezer.

Ice-Cream Cake

Remove the ice cream from the freezer shortly before it is to be served, but do not detach it from the bottom of the dish.

Variations: The ice cream is also tasty when about ½ tablespoon instant coffee is added. The ice cream cake shown in the picture has been made from doubling the recipe.

Jam- and Custard-Filled Cake

Yield: About 10 servings

3 cake layers

topping

1 cup marzipan

2 small egg whites

About 1½ pints fresh berries; for example, strawberries, raspberries, etc.

Jelly (strawberry, raspberry, etc.)

filling

1 package instant vanilla pudding (for a special touch, stir a little whipped cream into the cold custard.)

About ¾ cup jam; for example, strawberry, raspberry, etc.

Make the topping first. Grate the marzipan. Mix it into a smooth batter together with the egg whites. Press the mixture through a pastry bag into a crisscross decoration, with a round edge around the crisscross, onto one of the cake layers. Bake in a 350°F oven for about 10 minutes or until the marzipan is golden brown. Let stand until cold.

Place the other two cake layers together with a layer of jam between them. Spread a layer of custard on the second layer. Place the cake layer with the marzipan on top.

Decorate the cake by placing fresh berries in the marzipan squares. Pour a little melted jelly over the berries.

Refrigerate the cake so that the cake layers soak up the juices of the fruit.

Variation: Instead of using jam, mash fresh berries and mix them with a little sugar.

Mocha Cream Cake

Yield: About 8 servings

yellow cake layers
2 eggs
⅔ cup sugar
⅓ cup flour
¼ cup potato flour
1 teaspoon baking powder
2 tablespoons warm water
Butter and bread crumbs or flour for preparing the pan

meringue layer
2 small egg whites
⅓ cup sugar

mocha-cream filling
¾ cup instant vanilla pudding
1⅓ cups butter
2 tablespoons confectioners' sugar
1 small egg
2 to 3 tablespoons very strong instant coffee

nougat
⅔ cup sugar

To make the yellow cake layers, beat the eggs and sugar together until very light.

Mix the flour, potato flour, and baking powder together. Sift them into the batter. Carefully stir in the warm water. Pour the batter into a well-greased 1½-quart round cake pan that has been dusted with bread crumbs or flour. Bake in a 300 to 350°F oven for about 25 to 30 minutes.

To make the meringue layer, beat the egg whites into firm, stiff peaks. Fold in the sugar. On a greased and floured baking sheet spread out the batter into

Hazelnut Cake

a round cake with a slightly smaller diameter than the yellow cake. Bake in a 250°F oven for about 15 minutes. Lower the temperature to 200°F. Bake until the cake feels dry and light.

To make the mocha-cream filling, make the vanilla pudding according to the package directions. Let it become cold.

Stir the butter until soft. Beat in the vanilla pudding, sugar, and egg. (If you use an electric beater, you can add all the ingredients at the same time.) Flavor with the strong coffee. Beat vigorously.

To make the nougat, melt the sugar in a frying pan. Stir until it becomes a smooth, light-brown mass. Pour out onto a baking sheet that has been greased with cooking oil. When the nougat is cold, crush it into pieces, using a mortar.

Divide the yellow cake into 2 layers. Put the 2 yellow cake layers and the meringue layer together with the mocha cream filling in between. Spread the cream filling around the top and sides of the cake. Sprinkle nougat over the cake. Decorate with the rest of the mocha cream filling and the nougat.

Macaroon Cake

Yield: 6 servings

2 cups marzipan
2 eggs

chocolate-cream filling
1⅔ cups whipping cream
3 tablespoons confectioners' sugar
3 tablespoons cocoa
3 tablespoons strong, cold coffee

decoration
Roasted sliced almonds
Tiny, candied pearls (optional)

Finely grate the marzipan with a grater. Mix it with the eggs. Stir into a smooth batter. Spread it out into 4 thin, round "cookie" layers, about 7 inches in diameter, on well-greased baking paper that has been sprinkled with flour. Bake in a 400°F oven for 8 to 10 minutes or until the layers have become golden brown. Let them become cold on a flat surface.

To make the filling, whip the cream. Stir in the confectioners' sugar, cocoa, and coffee, which both have first been sifted. Adjust the flavoring.

Jam- and Custard-Filled Cake

Place the cake layers together with the filling in between and on top. Sprinkle with the almonds and candied pearls.

Refrigerate the cake overnight or for several hours before it is to be served.

Miami Birthday Cake

Yield: 10 to 12 servings

7 tablespoons butter or margarine
4 or 5 plain crackers, finely chopped
¼ pound milk chocolate
5¼ cups flour
4 cups sugar
1 teaspoon baking soda
1¼ cups sour milk
4 eggs
⅓ cup candied orange peel
½ cup coarsely chopped walnuts
¼ pound milk chocolate, chopped
Icing sugar
1 orange, thinly chopped

Melt the butter in a saucepan. Add the crumbled crackers. Allow to cool.

Melt the chocolate with 2 tablespoons water in a saucepan. Stir until smooth.

In a large bowl mix the flour, sugar, baking soda, sour milk, melted chocolate, eggs, and candied peel. Mix until smooth and creamy. Add the walnuts and the chopped chocolate to the biscuit mixture. Pour the cake batter into a round, large, well-greased cake pan. Pour the cracker mixture over it. It sinks to the bottom through the batter. Bake in a preheated 350°F oven for 45 to 55 minutes. Garnish with the icing sugar and thinly sliced oranges.

Mocha Parfait Cake

Yield: 6 to 8 servings

1⅔ cups heavy cream
4 egg yolks
⅔ cup sifted confectioners' sugar
1 teaspoon vanilla extract
4 tablespoons instant coffee

garnish
3½ ounces bittersweet chocolate
1 tablespoon ground instant coffee

Whip and refrigerate the cream.

Beat the egg yolks with the confectioners' sugar and vanilla in a round-bottomed bowl over a double boiler. The water in the double boiler should not be allowed to boil. Beat until airy and white. Remove from the heat. Place in a pan of cold water. Add the instant coffee. Beat until the batter becomes cold. Fold the batter into the whipped

Ice-Cream Cake with Chocolate Icing

cream. Pour into a dish or pan that holds at least 1 quart. Freeze for at least 4 hours. Remove the parfait from the freezer 1 hour before it is to be served.

Melt the cooking chocolate over a double boiler. Add the ground instant coffee. Spread the chocolate in a thin layer on aluminum foil (the shiny side). Let it cool. It can be refrigerated.

Wrinkle up the foil so that the chocolate breaks into small pieces. Remove the pieces. Sprinkle them over or around the parfait cake.

Mocha Cake

Yield: 8 to 10 servings

cake
About 1⅔ cups marzipan
2 egg whites from large eggs, lightly beaten

coffee-cream filling
About 1⅔ cups heavy cream
Instant coffee, dissolved in a very small amount of warm water

garnish
Peeled, thinly slivered almonds
1 tablespoon instant coffee, dissolved in ½ tablespoon warm water

½ cup marzipan
A little whipped cream
Coffee jelly beans/chocolate jelly beans

Finely grate the marzipan, using a grater. Beat it into a smooth batter with the egg whites. Spread the batter out into 3 thin, round "cookies," about 8 inches in diameter, on greased and floured baking-sheet paper. Bake in a 400°F oven for about 10 minutes. Let them cool so that they remain flat.

Whip the cream into peaks. Add the instant coffee that has been dissolved in a little warm water. It should be very concentrated.

Place the cakes together with the mocha whipped cream between the layers, on top, and on the sides. Fasten almonds around the edge.

Mix the coffee with the marzipan. Roll it out on baking-sheet paper into a thin round "cookie" the same size as the cake layers. Place it on top of the cake and garnish with a little mocha cream and the coffee/chocolate jelly beans around the edge.

The cake will stay fresh for 2 days, protected by the marzipan. It tastes best when it has been refrigerated several hours or overnight before serving.

Macaroon Cake

pan, which has been sprinkled with bread crumbs. Bake in a preheated 350°F oven for about 40 minutes or until the cake feels dry. Let the cake cool before removing it from the pan.

To make the icing, beat together in a saucepan the egg yolks, sugar, cream and potato flour. Let it come to a boil and become a custard. Remove from the heat. Beat until cool.

Beat the butter until soft and smooth. Beat it into the custard a little at a time.

To make the nougat, melt the sugar in a frying pan. Stir in the almonds. Pour the mixture onto an oiled baking sheet. Let it cool. Finely chop the nougat.

Divide the cake into 2 layers. Spread the icing between the layers and around the entire cake. Sprinkle the nougat over the entire cake and press into the icing so that it does not fall off. Refrigerate cake several hours before serving.

Variation: Moisten the cake with a little arrack or rum and water before applying the icing. The icing can also be flavored with arrack or rum.

Miami Birthday Cake

Nougat Ring

Yield: About 8 servings

cake
2 eggs
¾ cup sugar
¼ cup warm water
¾ cup flour
1 teaspoon baking powder
Bread crumbs

egg-custard icing
2 egg yolks
⅓ cup sugar
⅔ cup coffee cream
1 teaspoon potato flour
1 cup butter

nougat
¾ cup sugar
⅓ cup chopped almonds

Beat the eggs and sugar together until very light. Add the warm water. Sift in the flour, which has been mixed with the baking powder. Pour the batter into a well-greased 1½-quart ring-shaped

Orange and Chocolate Mousse Cake

Yield: 12 to 14 servings

cake layers
butter and bread crumbs or flour
4 eggs
⅔ cup sugar
⅓ cup flour
⅓ cup potato flour
2 teaspoons baking powder

orange-chocolate filling
1⅔ cups whipped cream
1 can frozen orange juice (7 ounces)
5 eggs, separated
7 ounces baking chocolate
2 envelopes gelatin

decorations
¼ pound (4 squares) baking chocolate
1 orange
¼ cup slivered almonds

Grease a 1¾ to 2-quart cake pan. Sprinkle it with bread crumbs or dust with flour. An 8½-inch frying pan can be used.

Beat the eggs and sugar together until light and fluffy.

Blend the other ingredients together. Add them to the egg and sugar mixture. Stir until the batter is well mixed. Pour the batter into the prepared cake pan. Bake in a preheated 400°F oven on the lowest rack for 30 to 35 minutes. Test with a toothpick to make sure the cake is done. If the toothpick comes out dry, remove the cake from the oven. Let the cake stand for a few minutes before turning it out onto a rack to cool. Let it cool under the cake pan. Cut the cold yellow cake into three layers.

To make the filling, beat the cream until it starts to stand in peaks. Add the thawed orange juice. Beat for a few minutes so that the juice and the whipped cream become well-blended. Refrigerate.

Separate the egg yolks and the whites.

Melt the chocolate over a double boiler. Add the egg yolks, one at a time, stirring constantly. Place the gelatin in cold water. Let it soak.

Beat the egg whites into stiff, dry peaks. Squeeze out the gelatin. Stir it into the warm chocolate batter. Carefully fold the chocolate into the egg whites. Blend well.

Put the cake together in the following order: cake, orange cream, cake, chocolate cream, and cake. Finish with a pretty layer of orange cream around and on top of the cake. To prepare the decorations, melt the chocolate over a double boiler. Peel the orange. Cut the orange into thin slices. Dip half of each orange slice in the chocolate. Let it harden on a piece of waxed paper.

Roast the almonds in the oven or in a frying pan.

Mocha Cake

Press them onto the sides of the cake. Place the orange slices on top of the cake.

This cake can be prepared a day ahead and kept refrigerated. It is best not to freeze it.

Orange-Nut Ring

Yield: 10 servings

¾ cup soft butter or margarine
3 eggs
1 cup sugar
Grated peel of 1 large or 2 smaller oranges
¼ to ⅓ cup chopped nuts
1 cup flour
Bread crumbs

Beat the butter. Beat the eggs and sugar together until light and airy. Beat the mixture into the butter. Carefully stir in the orange peel, nuts, and flour. Pour the batter into a greased ring cake pan that has been sprinkled with bread crumbs. Bake in a 350°F oven until the cake feels dry, 30 to 40 minutes.

The flavor of this cake is enhanced if it is moistened with a sugar syrup (confectioners' sugar flavored with squeezed orange juice and even a little orange liqueur or brandy). Prick the cake all over and spoon the liquid over the cake.

Serve the cake with berries and lightly whipped cream.

Mocha Cream Cake

Meanwhile, make the filling. Keep the metal knife attachment on the food processor. Divide the butter or margarine into 4 to 6 pieces. Place them and the other filling ingredients in the food processor. Start the machine and quickly mix together the ingredients to a smooth icing. Spread the butter cream filling on the cake. Roll it into a roll cake.

Orange Cake

Yield: About 12 servings

cake
Butter
Bread crumbs or flour
4 eggs
¾ cup sugar
⅔ cup flour
⅔ cup potato flour
1 teaspoon baking powder
Juice and peel from 1 orange

orange curd
3 oranges
1 cup sugar
7 tablespoons butter
2 eggs, beaten

garnish
1 bag slivered almonds
3 oranges

filling
Orange curd
1¼ cups heavy cream, whipped

jelly
2 envelopes gelatin
¾ cup freshly squeezed strained orange juice
2 tablespoons sugar

Grease a 9-inch round cake pan with detachable edges. Sprinkle with bread crumbs.

Beat the eggs and sugar until white and airy.

Sift the flours with the baking powder. Add to the egg and sugar mixture. Add the juice and peel. Pour the batter into the cake pan and bake in a preheated 350°F oven for about 30 minutes. It is important not to take the cake out too early, as it will easily fall. Take it out of the cake pan. Let it cool.

To make the orange curd, grate the peel of three oranges. Press the juice out of two. Place the peels, juice, sugar, and butter in a bowl over boiling water. Heat until the butter has melted. Mix in the eggs. Beat until the mixture is thick and airy. It is best to make the orange curd a day before the cake is to be made.

Roast the almonds. Peel the oranges so that even the outer membrane is removed. Slice the oranges.

Mix the orange curd with the whipped heavy cream.

Nut-Roll Cake

Yield: About 8 servings

⅔ cup hazelnut meats
⅓ cup potato flour
¾ cup sugar
2 teaspoons baking powder
3 eggs

butter-cream filling
7 tablespoons butter or margarine
⅔ cup confectioners' sugar
1 egg
½ teaspoon vanilla extract

Attach the metal knife to your food processor. Finely chop the nut meats in the machine. Add the potato flour, sugar, baking powder, and eggs. Quickly mix the batter 20 to 30 seconds. Spread it out on a baking sheet or in a 12 × 16-inch baking pan that has been covered with baking paper. Bake in the center of a preheated 450° oven for about 5 minutes. Sprinkle a little sugar over the cake. Turn it over onto a baking-paper sheet or a sheet of aluminum foil. Pull off the paper on which the cake was baked. Let the cake cool, covered with a baking cloth.

Divide the cake into three layers. Spread the orange curd between the layers, on top, and around the sides of the cake. Press the almonds around the sides of the cake. Cover the top of the cake with the sliced oranges. Cover with plastic wrap. Refrigerate.

Moisten the gelatin in ¼ cup cold water for 5 minutes.

Heat ¼ cup orange juice. Melt it in the hot juice, stirring constantly. Mix in the sugar. Remove from the heat. Beat the mixture into the remaining ice-cold juice. Refrigerate the mixture.

Lightly grease the same cake pan used in making the cake layers. Cut out a piece of baking-sheet paper the same size as the bottom of the cake pan. Press it into the greased pan. Place the cake pan in the freezer for 5 minutes so that it becomes really cold. Pour the liquid gelatin onto the paper in the cake pan. Freeze immediately. After 15 minutes the gelatin should be hard and frozen. Take it out of the cake pan. Place it with the baking-paper side up on top of the cake's orange slices. Pull the paper carefully away from the gelatin. Keep the cake refrigerated until it is to be served.

Plum Cake

Yield: 8 servings

¾ cup granulated sugar
¼ cup shortening
2 eggs
¼ cup milk
½ cup all-purpose flour
½ cup whole-wheat flour
1 teaspoon baking powder
Dash salt
1 teaspoon vanilla
1½ cups fresh purple plum halves
½ cup pecans, chopped
¼ cup brown sugar
½ teaspoon cinnamon

Cream the granulated sugar and shortening until smooth. Add the eggs; beat until blended. Add the milk alternately with the combined flours, baking powder, and salt; blend. Stir in the vanilla. Pour the dough into a greased and floured, 9-inch square cake pan. Top the dough with plum halves.

Combine the pecans, brown sugar, and cinnamon. Sprinkle over the plum halves. Bake in a 350°F oven 30 minutes or until done.

Nougat Ring

Sand Cake

Yield: About 8 servings

¾ to 1 cup butter or margarine
1⅔ cups potato flour
1 teaspoon baking powder
3 eggs
¾ cup sugar
2 tablespoons brandy
Butter and bread crumbs or flour for preparing the
   pan

Beat the butter, potato flour, and baking powder
together until very light and fluffy.

In another bowl, beat the eggs and sugar together
until light and airy. Add the egg mixture to the
butter mixture. Add only a little at a time, and beat
constantly. Add the brandy, one tablespoon at a
time. Pour the batter into a well-greased 1½-quart
baking pan that has been dusted with bread crumbs
or flour. Bake in a 350°F oven for about 40 minutes.

Sour Cream Pound Cake

Yield: 12 to 16 servings

1½ cups butter, at room temperature
3 cups sugar
6 large eggs, at room temperature
1 cup sour cream
3 cups flour
½ teaspoon baking soda
⅛ teaspoon salt
1 teaspoon flavoring (either vanilla, lemon or half
   vanilla/half almond)
2 tablespoons brandy (optional)
Confectioners' sugar

Cream the butter by hand or with an electric
mixer until it reaches the consistency of whipped
cream. Slowly dribble in the sugar a tablespoon at a
time; beat well. Add the eggs one at a time, beating
well after each addition. Stir in the sour cream.

Put the measured flour into a sifter with the
baking soda and salt and sift 3 times. Add the flour
½ cup at a time to the creamed mixture, blending
well with the mixer set at lowest speed. Add flavoring and brandy, if desired. Beat again to combine
thoroughly.

Pour the batter into a greased 10-inch bundt or
tube pan and bake in a 325°F oven for 1¼ to 1½
hours, until the cake tests done. Cool 15 minutes in
the pan on a cake rack before turning out on a rack
to cool completely. Sprinkle with confectioners'
sugar. This cake may be served with fresh, hulled
strawberries and whipped cream.

Mocha Parfait Cake

Easy Sacher Cake

Yield: 8 to 10 servings

5 ounces baking chocolate
⅔ cup butter
¾ cup sugar
4 eggs, separated
¼ cup flour
½ teaspoon baking powder
Butter and bread crumbs or flour for preparing the
   pan

garnish

⅓ cup apricot marmalade
3½ ounces baking chocolate
2 tablespoons butter
Desired amount of whipped cream

Melt the chocolate in the top of a double boiler.

Beat the butter and sugar until light. Add the egg
yolks. Stir in the chocolate and the flour that has
been mixed with the baking powder.

Beat the egg whites until stiff. Fold them into the
batter. Pour the batter into a greased pan that has
also been dusted with bread crumbs or flour. Bake
for about 30 minutes in a 350°F oven. Let the cake
cool.

Spread the marmalade over the entire cake.

Melt the chocolate. Add the butter. Spread the mixture over the cake.

Serve cold with plenty of whipped cream.

Slightly Frozen Cake

Yield: 6 to 8 servings

2 meringue cake layers, bought or homemade
¾ to 1¼ cups whipped cream
½ package orange sherbet

meringue layers
3 or 4 egg whites (⅓ cup)
⅔ cup sugar

chocolate sauce
¼ cup heavy cream
1½ ounces baking chocolate, broken into pieces

To make the meringue layers, beat the egg whites in a clean bowl with a dry, clean beater until they form stiff, dry peaks. Continue to beat for a few more minutes. Sprinkle with the sugar. Fold the sugar into the egg whites with a couple of deep strokes with a spoon.

Draw 2 circles on a piece of baking paper. Spread the meringue on the paper within these circles. Bake in a 300°F oven for about 45 minutes. The meringue is done when it separates from the paper.

Make the chocolate sauce by placing the heavy cream and the chocolate into a saucepan. Heat and stir until the chocolate melts and the sauce is smooth.

To put the cake together, alternate meringue cake layers, chocolate sauce, whipped cream, and sherbet. Grate the sherbet over the whipped cream, using the coarse side of a grater. Repeat with the next layer. Place the cake in the freezer for an hour or until time to serve it. If it is in the freezer longer than an hour, thaw it some before serving.

If you wish to decorate the cake, make decorations with soft sherbet and a pastry bag.

Swedish Coffee-Cake Ring

Yield: 2 rings

2 cakes compressed yeast
7 tablespoons butter
¾ cup milk
⅓ cup sugar
½ teaspoon cardamom
¼ teaspoon salt
2¾ to 3⅓ cups flour

filling
5¼ tablespoons butter
¼ cup sugar

garnish
1 egg, beaten
Whole almonds

Crumble the yeast into a large mixing bowl.

Melt the butter in a saucepan. Add the milk. Warm to finger temperature (98.6°F). Pour over the yeast so that the yeast dissolves. Add the sugar, cardamom, salt, and flour. Work the dough until it becomes smooth and shiny. Cover, and let rise for about 30 minutes.

Knead the dough. Divide it in half. Roll out each half into a rectangle.

Make the filling by mixing the butter and sugar until mixture is soft and smooth. Spread the filling over the dough, but not all the way to the edges. Roll up the dough. Pinch the edges tightly together. Form into a ring. Place on a greased baking sheet with the rolled edge facing down.

Brush the ends with a beaten egg. Fasten them together well. Let the bread rise under a baking cloth until it is very airy, 30 to 40 minutes.

Brush with egg. Place the almonds on top. Bake in a 400°F oven for about 20 minutes.

Nut-Roll Cake

Spice Cake

Yield: 16 servings

1 14-ounce package seedless raisins
2 cups sugar
½ cup shortening
3 cups water
½ teaspoon salt
5 cups flour, sifted
1 teaspoon soda
3 teaspoons cinnamon
1 teaspoon cloves
1 teaspoon allspice

Place the raisins, sugar, shortening, water, and salt in a saucepan and cook about 5 minutes, stirring. Cool. Add the flour, soda, and spices and mix well.

Bake in 2 small or 1 large greased and floured loaf cake pan in a 350°F oven for 45-60 minutes.

Spring Candy Cake

Yield: 8 to 12 servings

1 cup marzipan
3 tablespoons cherry liqueur or juice
3 egg yolks
1 tablespoon potato flour
½ teaspoon baking powder
Butter and bread crumbs or flour for preparing the pan
3 egg whites

filling
7 tablespoons soft butter
4 to 5 tablespoons confectioners' sugar
2 egg yolks
1½ tablespoons cherry liqueur or juice
1 small can pears

garnish
8½ to 9 ounces baking chocolate
Small yellow candies or small marzipan candies

Coarsely grate the marzipan on a grater. Mix it well with the liqueur or juice. Beat in the egg yolks, one at a time. Mix in the flour, which has first been blended with the baking powder.

Grease a 9½-inch round cake pan with detachable bottom. Sprinkle it with bread crumbs.

Beat the egg whites into stiff, dry peaks. Carefully fold them into the batter. Pour the batter into the cake pan. Bake in a preheated 350°F oven for 30 to 40 minutes. Test the cake with a toothpick to make sure it is done. Let the cake cool before removing the edge of the cake pan. Carefully separate the bottom of the pan from the cake.

Beat the butter and confectioners' sugar together until light and airy. Add the egg yolks, one at a time. Add the juice, a little at a time.

When the cake has cooled, divide it into 2 layers. Spread the filling over 1 of the layers. Cover it with a layer of ¼-inch thick pear slices. Place the other cake layer on top.

Ice the cake with melted chocolate. Save a little chocolate for grating on top. It is easiest to spread the chocolate with a lollipop or a baking brush. Decorate the cake with candies as desired.

Summer Marzipan Cake with Strawberries

Yield: 8 to 10 servings

1⅓ cups marzipan
3 eggs
Grated peel of 1 orange
Butter and bread crumbs or flour for preparing the pan

garnish
Vanilla cream custard or whipped cream
Sliced and whole strawberries

Coarsely grate the marzipan on a grater. Mix it with the eggs and orange peel. Beat it into a smooth batter. Pour the batter into a well-greased 1½-quart cake pan that has been coated with bread crumbs. Bake in a 350°F oven for 35 to 40 minutes. Let cool.

Place a layer of sliced strawberries on the cold cake, then a layer of custard or whipped cream. Press the strawberries close together into the custard or whipped cream. Decorate the plate with strawberries for an extra special touch.

Sugar Cake

Yield: About 8 servings

1¼ cups flour
¾ cups sugar
½ teaspoon vanilla extract
1 teaspoon baking powder
2 eggs
¼ cup water
⅔ cup margarine or butter
Butter and bread crumbs or flour for preparing the pan

Fasten the metal knife attachment onto your food processor.

Measure all cake ingredients into the food processor. Divide the margarine into 6 to 8 pieces before adding. Mix for 20 to 30 seconds. Pour the batter into 1½-quart round cake pan that has been greased and sprinkled with bread crumbs. Bake in the lower half of a preheated 350°F oven for about 40 minutes. Let the cake cool before taking it out of the pan.

Orange Cake

Strawberry Meringue Cake

Yield: 6 to 8 servings

3 egg whites
¾ cup sugar
Butter and bread crumbs or flour for preparing the
    pan

filling and topping
1⅔ cups whipping cream, whipped
1 to 1½ quarts strawberries
Roasted sliced almonds

Beat the egg whites into firm, stiff peaks. Carefully fold in the sugar. Spread the batter out onto lightly greased baking paper that has been sprinkled with flour. Spread it into 2 6½ to 7 inches round layers. Bake in a 300°F oven for 20 minutes. Lower the oven temperature to 200°F. Continue baking until the meringue feels dry and light, about 40 to 50 minutes. Put the meringue together with whipped cream and sliced strawberries in between. Spread the whipped cream over the cake. Press large strawberries close together into the whipped cream. Sprinkle almonds on top.

The meringue layers can be made in advance, but do not put the cake together until just before it is to be served.

Temptation Cake

Yield: 10 servings

nut cake-cookies
½ cup chopped hazel nuts
½ cup sugar
7 tablespoons butter
1 tablespoon flour
2 tablespoons cream

filling
About 1 quart vanilla ice cream

garnish
¾ cup heavy cream, whipped into peaks
2 cups fresh berries, preferably red currants or
    raspberries

Mix all the cake-cookie ingredients together in a saucepan. Let the mixture melt, stirring constantly and vigorously. It must not boil. Make 2 "cookies" by spreading out the nut mixture on baking paper on 2 cookie sheets. Use a third of the mixture for each "cookie." Spoon out the last third of the mixture in small dabs on a third cookie sheet, also covered with baking paper. Bake the "cookies" in a preheated 350°F oven for 15 to 20 minutes. The

Orange and Chocolate Mousse Cake

Easy Sacher Cake

cookie sheets can all be in the oven at the same time, with the small "cookies" on the bottom. Change positions several times during baking. Let the "cookies" cool. Remove them carefully from the cookie sheets, using a spatula. Keep them in a dry place until just before serving.

Place one large "cookie" on a cake plate. Place ice cream balls close together, or lay ½-inch ice-cream slices on the "cookie." Place the second "cookie" on top of the ice cream.

Garnish with the piped whipped cream and plenty of fresh red currants, raspberries, or strawberries, depending on the season. The little cookies can be used as extra decoration.

Tutti-Frutti Cake

Yield: About 8 servings

shortcrust pastry
1 cup flour
¼ cup sugar
7 tablespoons butter or margarine
½ egg

lemon filling
7 tablespoons butter or margarine
⅓ cup sugar

1½ eggs
1 tablespoon flour
1 tablespoon grated lemon peel

topping
About ¾ cup whipped cream
Mixed berries and fruits; for example, raspberries, bananas, and red currants or blueberries

Work together the flour, sugar, butter, and ½ egg into a smooth dough, using your fingertips.* Refrigerate the dough for 20-30 minutes. Roll out the dough. Line a lightly greased 9-inch pie pan with the dough. Mix all the filling ingredients together in a saucepan. Heat carefully, stirring constantly, until the butter has melted. Pour the filling into the dough-covered pie pan. Bake in a 350°F oven for 15 to 20 minutes. Cool completely.

Dab the whipped cream onto the cold cake or press it through a pastry bag into an attractive decoration. Garnish generously with berries.

The cake can be made in advance and stored in the freezer. Do not add the whipped cream and berries until time to serve the cake.

*To measure ½ egg, blend the yolk and white of a whole egg, measure in a cup, and divide in half.

Three Christmas Cakes—Sand Cake, Old-Fashioned Ginger-bread Cake, and Cinnamon Cake

Twelfth Day of Christmas Cake

Yield: About 10 servings

7 tablespoons butter or margarine
½ cup sugar
½ to ⅔ cup coarsely chopped almonds

icing
7 tablespoons butter
⅓ cup confectioners' sugar
1 tablespoon finely ground instant coffee
1 egg yolk
3 ounces bittersweet chocolate
1¼ cups heavy cream for whipping
Cocoa

Beat the butter and sugar together until light. Add the almonds. Spoon half of the batter into a lightly greased frying pan. Bake in a 350°F oven for about 15 to 20 minutes. Let the cake cool before removing it from the pan. Place it on a flat surface. Bake the other layer.

To make the icing, beat the butter with the confectioners' sugar until smooth. Add the instant coffee and the egg yolk.

Melt the cooking chocolate over a double boiler. Let it cool before beating it into the butter mixture. Spread the icing over one cake layer.

Whip the cream. Spread about half of the cream over this layer. Place the second layer on top. Garnish with the rest of the cream. Sprinkle the cocoa on top, using a sieve. Refrigerate the cake until serving time.

Success Cake

Yield: About 15 servings

4 cake layers
8 egg whites, cold
1⅔ cups sugar
¾ cup marzipan, cold

chocolate-mousse filling
1 pound bittersweet chocolate, or half bittersweet and half milk chocolate, melted
2⅓ cups whipping cream, whipped
4 tablespoons confectioners' or regular sugar
4 egg yolks

garnish
Sliced white or brown chocolate, or small thin chocolate pieces in different shapes

Cake layers. Draw 4 9½-inch circles on 4 sheets of baking paper. Grease the insides of the circles.

Pour the egg whites into a large bowl. Beat the

Slightly Frozen Cake

Spring Candy Cake

whites vigorously for 10 minutes, using an electric beater. They should be whipped into very stiff peaks. Add ⅓ cup sugar at a time. Beat vigorously until all the sugar has been added and the mixture has become stiff and satiny, glossy smooth.

Grate the marzipan on a grater. Mix slightly less than half the meringue batter with the marzipan, and stir. Mix in the rest of the meringue. Divide the batter among the 4 circles on the greased baking-sheet paper. Spread into even layers. Bake one layer at a time on the lowest rack in a preheated 300°F oven for 25 to 30 minutes. Each layer is done when it feels dry and has become slightly browned. Let cool on a rack. Carefully remove the baking-sheet paper when the layers have cooled.

It is easiest to make the chocolate mousse in 2 large bowls. Break the chocolate into pieces. Melt it slowly in a large pan over a double boiler, carefully stirring occasionally. Let the chocolate cool.

Whip 1¼ cups whipping cream in each bowl.

Whip half the chocolate into one bowl and half the chocolate into the other, using an electric beater. Add 2 tablespoons sugar and 2 egg yolks to each bowl. Beat vigorously into a fluffy mousse. Refrigerate the mousse for about half an hour.

Spread the mousse on the layers. Spread slightly more mousse on the top layer. Put the layers together. Chill the cake for a couple of hours.

Garnish as desired. Keep the cake chilled until serving time.

Basic Yellow Cake

Yield: 12 servings

¾ cup butter or margarine, softened
1⅔ cups sugar
2 eggs
2 teaspoons vanilla
3 cups cake flour, sifted
2½ teaspoons baking powder
½ teaspoon salt
1⅓ cups milk

Beat the butter, sugar, eggs, and vanilla in a large bowl. Sift the dry ingredients together; add alternately with milk to the butter mixture. Beat until smooth after each addition. Pour into 2 greased and floured, 9-inch layer cake pans.

Bake in a preheated 350°F oven 30 minutes, or until the cake tests done. Cool in pans on wire racks 10 minutes. Turn out onto racks; cool completely. Fill and frost as desired.

Strawberry Meringue Cake

Carrot Cake Frosting

Yield: Frosting for 1 cake

8 ounces cream cheese
1 stick butter, softened
2 teaspoons vanilla
¾ pound confectioners' sugar
¾ cup pecans, finely chopped
1½ cups coconut

Cream the cheese and butter, then slowly add powdered sugar, beating until light. Add the vanilla and beat until absorbed. Add the pecans and coconut. Mix until well distributed.

Basic White Cake

Yield: 12 servings

2⅔ cups cake flour, sifted
1½ cups sugar
4 teaspoons baking powder
1 teaspoon salt
⅔ cup vegetable shortening
1¼ cups milk
1 teaspoon vanilla
4 egg whites, beaten

Grease the bottoms of 2 9-inch round layer cake

pans. Line the pans with waxed paper; grease and flour the paper.

Combine the flour, sugar, baking powder, salt, shortening, ¾ cup of milk, and vanilla in a large bowl; beat until well blended. Add the remaining milk and egg whites; beat well. Pour into the prepared pans.

Bake in a preheated 350°F oven 30 minutes or until the cake tests done. Cool in the pans on wire racks 10 minutes. Turn out onto the racks. Remove the paper; cool completely. Fill and frost as desired.

Tropical Frosting

Yield: Frosting for 1 cake

2 cups sugar
1 cup water
⅛ teaspoon salt
1 teaspoon white vinegar
3 egg whites
½ teaspoon vanilla

Combine the sugar, water, salt, and white vinegar in a heavy saucepan. Cook over medium heat, stirring constantly until clear. Without stirring, cook until the mixture forms a thin thread when dropped

Summer Marzipan Cake

Success Cake

from a spoon (242°F on a candy thermometer).

Beat the egg whites until stiff. Add the hot syrup, beating constantly. Continue beating until the frosting holds its shape. Add the vanilla and blend well.

Advent Stars

Yield: About 40 cookies

¾ to 1 cup butter or margarine
1 cup sugar
Grated peel of 1 lemon
2 eggs
2¾ cups flour
1 teaspoon baking powder
1 egg, beaten
Chopped almonds
Pearl sugar

Beat the butter and sugar together until light and fluffy. Add the lemon peel; the eggs, one at a time; and finally, the flour, which has first been mixed with the baking powder. Thinly roll out the dough. Cut out cookies, using a large, star-shaped cookie cutter. Brush with beaten egg. Dip in almonds and pearl sugar. Place the cookies on a greased cookie sheet. Bake in a 400°F oven until the cookies are pale light-yellow color.

Apple Squares

Yield: About 50 squares

1¾ to 2 cups flour
3 teaspoons baking powder
¾ cup sugar
7 tablespoons butter or margarine
⅔ cup milk
1 egg
4 or 5 apples
A little sugar
Several dabs of butter

Mix the flour, baking powder, and sugar.

Finely chop the butter into the mixture until it becomes granular.

Beat the milk and egg together. Add to the flour mixture. Quickly make into a batter. Pour into a baking pan 10x14 inches that has been covered with greased baking paper. Press wedges of apple close together into the batter. Sprinkle with sugar. Place dabs of butter on top. Bake in a 425°F oven for 15 to 20 minutes. Cut the cake into pieces when it has cooled some.

Variation: Add ¾ teaspoon cinnamon and ¾ teaspoon ginger to the flour mixture.

Almond Butter-Cream Squares

Yield: About 30 squares

¾ to 1 cup almonds
1 cup sugar
6 egg whites
1 bag sliced almonds

butter cream
3 egg yolks
⅓ cup milk
⅓ cup sugar
7 tablespoons butter, soft

Grind the almonds. Mix them with the sugar.

Beat the egg whites until stiff peaks form. Carefully fold them into the almond-sugar mixture. Spread the batter onto a well-greased baking paper that has been sprinkled with flour. Spread it into a rectangle of about 9½ × 14 inches. Sprinkle with the sliced almonds. Bake in a 350°F oven for about 20 minutes. Immediately remove the cake from the paper. Let it cool on a rack.

To make the butter cream, mix the egg yolks, milk, and sugar in a saucepan. Simmer, beating vigorously, until the cream thickens. Add the butter. Let it melt in the warm cream custard. Stir well. Let

Swedish Coffee Cake Ring

Sugar Cake

the custard become cold and thick.

Divide the almond cake into 2 parts. Put the 2 parts together with the cream icing between the layers. Refrigerate. Cut into small squares.

The squares are excellent to freeze. They taste best when served cold.

Variation: Bake the almond batter as a round cake and ice the top with the butter cream.

Oatmeal Nut Cookies

Yield: About 40 cookies

8¾ tablespoons butter or margarine
¼ to ⅓ cup ground hazelnut meats
1¼ cups oatmeal
⅓ cup sugar
Almost 1 teaspoon baking powder
⅔ cup flour

decoration
Hazelnuts

Work all the cookie ingredients together into a smooth dough. Rub the oatmeal grains between your hands if they are large. Roll the dough into small balls. Place them on a greased cookie sheet. Press a nut into the center of each cookie. Bake in a 350° to 400°F oven for 10 to 12 minutes.

Butternuts

Yield: 125 cookies

1 cup hazelnuts
¾ to 1 cup butter
⅔ cup sugar
About 1⅔ cups flour
¼ teaspoon baking powder
⅛ teaspoon salt

Roast the nuts in the oven. Rub them between the palms of your hands to remove the skins. Chop the nuts into large pieces or divide them in half.

Work the ingredients together on a baking board. Refrigerate the dough, if desired. Roll out the dough into a cake, about ½ inch thick. Place it onto a lightly floured cutting board. Put it into the refrigerator.

Cut the cold dough into small cubes 1 × 1 inch or slightly smaller. Place the cubes onto a greased baking sheet. They can be placed fairly close together. Bake in a 400°F oven for 10-12 minutes.

Vanilla Sticks

Yield: 60 to 70 cookies

¼ cup marzipan
¾ to 1 cup butter or margarine
Almost ⅓ cup sugar
1 egg
1 teaspoon vanilla extract
¼ teaspoon baking powder
About 2 cups flour

for brushing and decorating
1 egg white
Chopped almonds
Pearl sugar

Finely grate the marzipan. Mix all ingredients together. Roll out the dough into finger-thick lengths. Cut these into ½-inch-long pieces.

Brush with egg white. Dip in chopped almonds and pearl sugar.

Bake the cookies on a greased baking sheet in a 350°F oven for about 10 minutes.

Tutti-Frutti Cake

Chocolate Meringue Squares

Yield: 20 to 25 squares

chocolate batter
7 tablespoons margarine or butter
⅓ cup sugar
3 egg yolks
⅔ cup flour
3 tablespoons cocoa
2 teaspoons baking powder
¼ cup milk

meringue batter
3 egg whites
¾ cup sugar
½ cup chopped hazelnuts

Cover a baking pan with baking paper. Grease it with margarine.

Beat the margarine and sugar together until airy. Add the egg yolks, one at a time.

Mix together the flour, cocoa, and baking powder. Alternate adding this mixture and the milk to the egg-yolk mixture. Spread the batter into the baking pan, using a rubber spatula.

Whip the egg whites into dry peaks. Whip in the sugar. Spread the meringue batter over the chocolate batter. Sprinkle with the nuts. Bake in the center of a preheated 350°F oven for 20-25 minutes. Let the cake cool. Cut it into squares with a sharp knife.

Brandy Wreaths

Yield: 50 to 60 cookies

¾ to 1 cup soft butter or margarine
⅔ cup confectioners' sugar, sifted
2 cups flour
1½ tablespoons brandy

Mix all the ingredients together into a workable dough. Refrigerate. Roll the dough out into very thin rolls that are slightly smaller than the diameter of a pencil. Twist the rolls around each other, 2 by 2. Cut the twisted roll into pieces about 4½ inches long. Shape the pieces into wreaths on a greased baking sheet. Bake in a 350°F oven for about 10 minutes.

Ginger Cookies

Yield: About 40 cookies

¾ cup butter or margarine
2 cups oatmeal
⅓ cup sugar
¼ cup corn syrup
2 teaspoons ginger
⅛ teaspoon salt

Melt the butter. Stir in the remaining ingredients.

Temptation Cake

Mix the batter well. Spread the batter onto a piece of greased baking-sheet paper on a 9½ × 13½-inch baking sheet. Even the surface with a spatula. Bake in a 350°F oven for 8 to 10 minutes. Cut the cake into pieces when it has cooled some. Loosen from the baking sheet.

Cinnamon Squares

Yield: 48 squares

½ pound butter
1 cup sugar
1 egg, separated
2 cups flour
1½ tablespoons cinnamon
1 teaspoon salt
1½ cups nuts, chopped

Cream the butter and sugar; add the egg yolk. Add flour, cinnamon, and salt. Press the batter into a generously greased 8 × 14-inch pan or 2 8-inch square pans.

Beat the egg white until foamy; spread on top of the batter. (You will not need the egg white for this.) Press the chopped nuts on top. Bake at 325°F 30 minutes. Allow to cool slightly; cut into squares.

Coconut Squares

Yield: About 50 squares

5 eggs
1⅔ cups sugar
1⅔ cups flour
3 teaspoons baking powder
2 tablespoons cocoa
¾ cup water
1¾ to 2 cups butter or margarine

coconut icing
7 tablespoons butter or margarine
1⅔ cups coconut
¾ cup sugar
2 tablespoons strong coffee
2 eggs

Beat the eggs and sugar together until very light.
Blend the flour with the baking powder and cocoa. Sift it into the batter. Boil the water and butter until the butter melts. Add to the batter. Pour the batter into a large baking pan, about 12 × 16 inches, which has been covered with greased baking paper. Bake in a 400°F oven until the cake is almost done, about 20 minutes.

Make the icing while the cake is baking. Beat together all the icing ingredients in a pan. Bring to a boil, stirring constantly. Spread the icing over the partially baked cake. Bake it for 10 minutes in a 425°F oven until the icing has a nice color.

Chocolate Breads

Yield: About 100 cookies

¾ to 1 cup butter or margarine
¾ cup sugar
2 cups flour
1 egg
4 teaspoons cocoa
½ teaspoon vanilla extract

for brushing and decorating
1 egg
Pearl sugar
Chopped almonds

Mix all the ingredients together into a workable dough. Refrigerate. Roll out into a thin dough. Cut out cookies with a cookie cutter.

Brush with a beaten egg. Dip the cookies in pearl sugar and chopped almonds.

Place the cookies on a greased baking sheet. Bake in a 400°F oven for about 8 minutes.

Twelfth Day of Christmas Cake

Almond Butter-Cream Squares

of almond down into the middle of each dab. Bake in a 350° to 400°F oven for about 8 to 10 minutes. Carefully remove the cookies from the cookie sheet while they are still warm. Let them become cold on a rack under a baking cloth.

Christmas Ginger Cookies

Yield: About 200 cookies

⅔ cup butter or margarine
1 cup sugar
¼ cup molasses or corn syrup
⅓ cup water
½ tablespoon ginger
1 tablespoon cinnamon
½ tablespoon cloves
1 teaspoon finely ground cardamom
½ tablespoon baking soda
3 cups flour

Stir the butter, sugar, and molasses or syrup until smooth. Add the water, spices, and baking soda. Work in the flour. Make the dough into a workable batter on a baking board. Let stand overnight.

Roll out into a thin dough. Cut out cookies with a cookie cutter. Bake the cookies in the middle of a 425°F oven for about 5 minutes. Let them become cold on the cookie sheet.

Large, Soft Christmas Cookies

Yield: About 50 cookies

¾ cup brown or white sugar
¾ cup molasses or corn syrup
2 tablespoons boiled and finely chopped bitter orange peel
1½ teaspoons cinnamon
1 teaspoon cloves
1 teaspoon ginger
5¼ tablespoons butter or margarine
2 eggs, beaten
⅓ cup sour cream
1 tablespoon baking soda
3 to 3½ cups flour

decoration
Almonds, chopped into pieces

Bring the sugar, molasses or syrup, and spices to a boil in a saucepan. Add the butter. Stir until butter melts. Let cool. Add the eggs, sour cream, baking soda, and flour. Dab the dough onto a greased cookie sheet. Dab about 1 tablespoon of dough, with plenty of space between the dabs. Stick a piece

Easy Orange Cookies

Yield: 14 servings

⅔ cup margarine
2 eggs
⅓ cup sugar
A little vanilla extract
⅔ cup flour

garnish
3 tablespoons confectioners' sugar
3 to 4 teaspoons orange juice
Chopped candied orange peels

Melt the margarine. Let it cool. Beat in the eggs, sugar, vanilla, and flour. Spoon the batter onto a greased pancake iron. Bake for about 10 minutes in a 400°F oven. Let the cookies cool some. Curl them around a greased, paper-covered, thin cylindrical-shaped object.

Mix the confectioners' sugar with the orange juice. Brush over the cookies when they have stiffened. Sprinkle with the orange peels.

Cookie Bows

Yield: About 100 cookies

⅔ cup butter or margarine
½ cup sugar
1 egg
1¼ to 1⅓ cups flour

for brushing and decorating
1 egg white
Pearl sugar
Chopped almonds

Stir the butter until soft. Mix in the sugar and egg. Add the flour. Save a small amount of flour for rolling out the dough. Make into a workable dough and refrigerate.

Roll out the dough thinly (half the dough at a time). Cut out cookie bows with a cookie cutter.

Brush with the egg white. Dip in pearl sugar and almonds. Bake the cookies on a greased baking sheet in a 350°F oven for about 10 minutes.

Butter Cookies

Yield: 60 cookies

⅔ cup butter
1¼ cups sugar
2 eggs
3 cups flour
1½ teaspoons salt
2 teaspoons baking powder
1 teaspoon vanilla

Cream the butter, sugar, and eggs together until light and foamy. Sift the flour, salt, and baking powder together; add to the first mixture. Add vanilla. Mix until smooth. Chill.

Roll to ¼-inch thickness on a slightly floured board. Cut with a cookie cutter. Sprinkle with sugar; bake in a 350°F oven 12 to 15 minutes.

Brown Breads

Yield: About 45 cookies

½ beaten egg (see starred note on page 355)
½ teaspoon cinnamon
½ teaspoon ground cardamom

From the left: Ginger Cookies, Granny's Bows, Oatmeal Nut Cookies, Vanilla Sticks, Chocolate Breads, Brandy Wreaths, Brown Breads

Chocolate Meringue Squares

⅔ cup melted butter or margarine, cooled
⅓ cup chopped almonds
3 ground bitter almonds
½ cup brown sugar
About 1⅓ cups flour
1 teaspoon baking powder
Pearl sugar in which to dip the cookies

Mix the egg with the spices. Stir in the butter, almonds, and brown sugar. Add the flour, which has been blended with the baking powder. Roll into small round balls. Lightly press pearl sugar into the balls. Place on a greased cookie sheet. Bake in a 350° to 400°F oven for 10 to 12 minutes.

Gingerbread Christmas Cookies

Yield: 175 to 200 cookies

1¼ cups sugar
⅔ cup molasses or corn syrup
¾ to 1 cup butter or margarine
⅔ cup heavy cream
1¾ tablespoons ginger
1 tablespoon baking soda
1⅔ pounds flour

Heat the sugar, molasses or syrup, and butter. Stir so that the butter melts. Let the mixture cool. Stir in the cream, ginger, baking soda, and most of the flour. Let the dough stand overnight.

Thinly roll out the dough. Cut out cookies with a cookie cutter. Bake them on a greased cookie sheet in a 400° to 425°F oven for 5 to 7 minutes.

Slice-and-Bake Christmas Cookies

Yield: About 100 cookies

1¾ to 2 cups butter or margarine
½ cup corn syrup
⅓ cup sugar
2 teaspoons cinnamon
2 teaspoons ground cloves
1 tablespoon bitter orange peel
2 teaspoons baking soda
½ cup almonds, chopped
2¾ cups flour

Heat the butter, syrup, and sugar in a saucepan. Let cool. Add the spices, baking soda, almonds, and flour. Work together into a dough. Shape the dough into rolls 1½ inch in diameter. Refrigerate them until firm.

Cut the rolls into thin slices. Bake on a greased cookie sheet in a 400°F oven for about 7 minutes.

Chocolate Cookies with Black Walnuts

Yield: 12 cookies

1 cup sugar
2 eggs, well beaten
2 squares unsweetened chocolate
½ cup butter or margarine
1 cup flour, sifted
1 teaspoon baking powder
¼ teaspoon salt
1 cup black walnuts, finely chopped
1 teaspoon vanilla
Sifted confectioners' sugar

Gradually add the sugar to the eggs. Melt the chocolate with butter, then stir into the eggs. Sift the flour, baking powder, and salt together. Add the flour mixture to the chocolate mixture; add nuts and vanilla.

Bake in a greased 15½ × 10½ × 1-inch jelly roll pan in a 350°F oven 12 to 15 minutes. Cool slightly in the pan; dust with confectioners' sugar. Cool completely in the pan on a rack; cut in 1¾-inch bars.

Gingerbread Christmas Cookies

Gingerbread Heart Village

Dough For Large Figures

Yield: Depends on size of figures made

⅔ cup butter or margarine
¾ cup molasses or corn syrup
¾ cup water
1 tablespoon cinnamon
1 tablespoon ginger
1 tablespoon cloves
1 tablespoon baking soda
6 to 7 cups flour

lemon icing
1 egg white
1⅔ cups confectioners' sugar
1 teaspoon lemon juice

Stir the butter, sugar, and molasses or corn syrup together until smooth. Add the water, spices, baking soda, and flour. Use the larger amount of flour suggested when making a gingerbread house. Make into a workable dough on a baking board. Refrigerate well covered overnight.

Work the dough. It should be rather firm if it is to be rolled out into different figures. Large figures and large parts of the house should be cut out on the cookie sheet. They easily lose their shape when moved from baking board to cookie sheet. Bake in a 350° to 400°F oven. Let the figures become cold on the cookie sheet.

To make the icing, mix the egg white, confectioners' sugar, and lemon juice together. Stir until the icing becomes thick and is firm enough to keep its shape. The consistency can be varied, using more egg white or confectioners' sugar. Decorate large figures with icing.

Gingerbread-Hearts Village: To make this village, place 3 hearts together with their tips up. The sizes of the huts can be varied from tiny to extra large, depending on the size of the hearts used.

The recipe given for larger figures is ideal if the huts are to be of the larger variety. But if you are only going to make small huts, use the recipe for Christmas Ginger Cookies (see above), as this dough is also easy to roll out.

After the cookies are baked, decorate the hearts with icing, making doors and windows.

Glue the sides of the hearts together by dipping the cookie edges into sugar that has been melted in a frying pan. The sugar becomes hard very quickly, so put the hearts together as soon as you have dipped them in the sugar. The points of the hearts meet at the top of the "huts." Candy is suitable for the chimneys. Press the icing through a pastry bag and go over all the edges. Place the "huts" on a bed of cotton. Add some Santas and some greens. Sprinkle confectioners' sugar over the huts.

Butternuts

Brownies

Yield: About 35 brownies

4 eggs
1⅔ cups sugar
7 ounces bittersweet chocolate
1¾ to 2 cups butter or margarine, melted
1¼ to 1⅔ cups chopped nuts (walnuts or almonds)
1⅔ cups flour
2 teaspoons baking powder

icing
About 7 ounces baking chocolate

Beat the eggs and sugar together until light.
Break up the chocolate. Melt it over low heat. Stir occasionally.
Stir the butter into the egg mixture. Add the chocolate and nuts. Add the flour, which has been well mixed with the baking powder. Bake in a small baking pan in a 400°F oven for about 20 minutes. Cut the cake into 1½ to 2-inch squares. Let cool.
Ice the cake with melted, cooled cooking chocolate.

Beverages and Jellies

Homemade Apple Juice

Yield: Varies

Apples
¼ to ½ teaspoon ascorbic acid

Rinse the apples; remove the stems; Cut them into large wedges. The cores and peels should not be removed. Work the apples through a blender or food processor. The result is a thick, somewhat cloudy juice. Strain through a straining-cloth. Add ascorbic acid, as this will help the juice keep better.

Pour the finished raw juice into suitable freezing containers and freeze. Keep in mind that it will take some time to thaw when you are ready to use it.

A Brown, A Red, and A White

Yield: 2 large glasses

the brown
¼ pound bittersweet chocolate
1 cup boiling milk, preferably skim milk
2 tablespoons sugar
⅓ teaspoon vanilla extract
4 to 5 leaves fresh peppermint or
¼ teaspoon peppermint oil
¾ cup crushed ice

the red
¼ cup light rum (optional)
2 egg whites
½ quart fresh berries, preferably red currants
⅔ cup water
¾ cup crushed ice
6 tablespoons sugar

the white
1¼ cups milk
⅔ cup crushed ice

Fruity Wine Punch

1 tablespoon whisky or brandy
¼ teaspoon nutmeg

A tall drink, with or without alcohol, really hits the spot on a mild summer evening. Choose between a brown, a red, or a white.

To make the brown: Break the chocolate into pieces; beat it and the hot milk in the mixer. Add the rest of the ingredients and beat until everything is well blended and the ice has disappeared. Serve immediately.

To make the red: Mix all ingredients in a mixer and beat until the ice has melted and the berries have blended evenly. Pour immediately into cold glasses. Substitute water instead of rum, if desired.

To make the white: Pour the milk, ice, and whisky or brandy into a mixer. Beat until the ice has melted and the milk becomes foamy. Pour into cold glasses. Sprinkle with the nutmeg. Serve immediately.

Egg Nog

Yield: 8 servings

6 eggs, separated
1 cup sugar
2 cups heavy cream
2 cups milk
1 cup blended whiskey
½ cup rum
Nutmeg

Beat the egg yolks until pale yellow, then gradually beat in ½ cup of sugar. Beat the egg whites until stiff, not dry, and add the remaining ½ cup of sugar. Combine both mixtures. Stir in the cream, milk, whiskey, and rum. Mix well and serve cold with a sprinkling of nutmeg. Omit liquors for non alcoholic egg nog.

Homemade Apple Juice

Boiled Berry Juice Concentrate

Yield: About 8 servings

2 quarts berries, well ripened, without any bad spots
1¼ to 1⅔ cups water
2⅓ cups sugar per quart drained juice
¼ teaspoon sodium benzoate per quart juice

Boil the water and the cleaned berries (currants do not need to be cleaned, just rinsed, and the pits do not need to be removed from cherries) until they become runny, about 10 minutes. Crush the berries against the side of the pot while boiling. Strain the mixture through a straining-cloth. Do not let it drain for more than 30 minutes.

Measure the juice and pour it back into the pot. Bring to a boil, add the sugar, and bring to a boil again. Skim the surface whenever necessary.

Add the sodium benzoate, which first has been stirred into a small amount of juice, and then fill warm, well-cleaned bottles up to the brims. Seal immediately.

It is a good idea to cover the bottle corks with paraffin. Do this by dipping them into melted paraf-

fin. The bottles will then seal more tightly. Store the juice in a cold and dark place.

Dilute the concentrate with water when serving.

Currant Juice Concentrate: Use more water than with other juices when making juice from currants. Allow 2¾ cups water per 2 quarts well-ripened black currants, and 1⅔ cups to 2 cups water for red currants. Dilute with water when serving.

Fruity Wine Punch

Yield: 8 servings

2 oranges
1 well-ripened mango
2 kiwi fruits
1 bottle cold white wine, for example a German country wine
1¼ cups dry white vermouth
2 bottles clear tonic water, chilled
¾ cup orange juice (preferably frozen)
Plenty of pieces of ice

Peel one of the oranges, removing as much of the white membrane as possible. Wash the other

Boiled Berry Juice Concentrate

A Brown, a Red, and a White

orange and the kiwi fruits, and cut these into thin slices. Peel the mango and cut it into small pieces. If you cannot find mango or kiwi fruits, use other fruits, such as several well-ripened pears, or cut grapes from which the seeds have been removed.

Place all the fruit, with the exception of the unpeeled orange, in a bowl or pitcher that holds at least 2¼ quarts. Pour in the wine and the vermouth, cover, and refrigerate for several hours so that the fruit draws in the flavor of the wine.

Right before serving, pour in the well-chilled tonic water and orange juice, and add the sliced, unpeeled orange, plus pieces of ice. Serve with a punch spoon in the glasses so the guests may taste the wine-soaked pieces of fruit.

Hot Buttered Rum

Yield: 1 serving

2 ounces light rum
Juice of 1 small lemon
1 small strip lemon peel
1½ teaspoons brown sugar
1½ tablespoons butter

Place a long spoon in a tall glass. Pour the rum into the glass. Add the lemon juice and peel. Pour enough boiling water into the glass over the handle of the spoon to fill the glass. Stir in the brown sugar. Add the butter; stir until melted.

Garnish with a slice of lemon and additional lemon peel.

Mulled Wine

Yield: 6 servings

½ cup sugar
¼ cup water
2 orange slices
6 cloves
2 cinnamon sticks
½ cup orange juice
1 bottle red Bordeaux wine

Boil the sugar, water, orange slices, cloves, and cinnamon 5 minutes. Remove from heat. Add the juice and wine. Keep hot but do not boil. Serve with cinnamon sticks or orange slices.

Cider can be substituted for wine. Sweeten to taste.

Summer Freshness

Yield: 1 serving

1 to 2 slices kiwi fruit
1 to 2 sliced strawberries
Dab orange sherbet
About 1 cup chilled bubbly cider or champagne

Cover the bottom of a glass with the kiwi slices and strawberries. Add a dab of sherbet, fill the glass with cider or champagne.

Green Tomato Jam

Yield: About 4 8-ounce glasses

2¼ pounds small green tomatoes
Water

juice
¾ cup distilled white vinegar
1¼ cups water
1⅔ cups sugar
1 piece cinnamon
8 cloves

Summer Freshness

Cherry Jam

Prick the skins of the tomatoes, and boil them in water until almost soft. Drain off the water. Bring the juice to a boil (the spices should be placed in a little cheesecloth bag), and skim well. Add the tomatoes to the juice and simmer over low heat until they become soft.

Place the tomatoes in earthenware or glass jars with a slotted spoon. Let the juice boil until lightly syrupy. Remove the spices (save them), and pour the juice over the tomatoes. Seal the jars.

Pour off the juice after a couple of days and cook it together with the spices. Skim the surface of the juice and pour once again over the tomatoes. The tomatoes should be well covered by the juice. Seal the jars tightly and store in a cool place.

Green Tomato Jam

Green Tomato Marmalade

Yield: 3 to 4 8-ounce glasses

2¼ pounds green tomatoes
Water
Grated peel of 2 well-washed lemons
4 to 5 pieces whole ginger
1⅓ pounds sugar

Rinse the tomatoes, cut them into pieces, grind them in a meat grinder, and place them into a stew pot. Add a tiny amount of water, the lemon peel, and ginger. Boil the tomatoes until soft in the covered pot. They should be well mashed. Stir occasionally.

Add the sugar and boil, uncovered, until the mixture becomes the consistency of marmalade, 25 to 30 minutes. Shake the pot several times while boiling. Remove the ginger pieces and skim well.

Pour into warm, well-cleaned jars. Cover with paraffin and seal tightly. Store in a cool place.

Mixed Berry Boiled Jam

Red and Green Tomato Marmalades

Cherry Jam

Yield: About 2 pints

2¼ pounds sour cherries
2⅓ to 3¼ cups sugar

Clean, rinse, and remove the pits from the cherries. Place them in a jam pot and slowly bring to a boil over low heat. Boil for 5 minutes. Add the sugar. Boil the jam slowly without stirring for about 15 minutes. Shake the pot occasionally. Skim the surface whenever necessary.

Pour the jam into warm, clean jars. Put paraffin on the top of the jam when it has cooled somewhat, and seal the jars well. Store in a dark, cool place.

Cherry jam will have a special taste if almonds are added. It will also taste delicious if you stir several tablespoons of brandy into the jam when it is done.

Red Tomato Marmalade

Yield: 3 to 4 8-ounce glasses

2¼ pounds ripe tomatoes
2 lemons
1⅓ pounds sugar

Dip the tomatoes into boiling water and peel away the skins. Cut the tomatoes into pieces. Brush the lemons well, peel them, and cut the peel into thin shreds. Squeeze the juice out of the lemons.

Mix the tomatoes, lemon peel, and juice from the lemons together and place in a stew pot. Boil, uncovered, for about 30 minutes. Stir in the sugar and boil for another 25 to 30 minutes, uncovered, until the mixture begins to have the consistency of marmalade. Shake the pot several times while cooking. Skim well.

Pour into warm, well-cleaned jars. Top with paraffin and seal tightly. Store in a cool place.

Black Current Jelly

Carrhub

Plum Jam

Yield: About 4 8-ounce jars

2¼ pounds plums
About ¼ cup water
A little over 1 pound sugar

Rinse the plums and remove the pits. Place them in a stew pot and cover with the water. Simmer the plums over low heat until they start to break up into pieces. Remove any peels that float to the top with a wooden, slotted spoon.

Add the sugar and simmer for 15 to 20 minutes. Shake the pot occasionally while it is simmering.

Skim the jam well and pour it into warm, well-cleaned jars. Cover the jam with paraffin and close the jars tightly with the lids. Store in a cool place.

Note: You can also boil the plums without having first removed the pits. When the plums start breaking up, the pits will rise to the surface and may be removed with a spoon. Then add the sugar.

Carrhub

Yield: About 4 pints

2¼ pounds carrots
2¼ pounds rhubarb
2¼ pounds sugar

Mount a metal knife onto the food processor. Peel the carrots and cut them into small pieces. Mince them in the food processor. Do not fill the processor more than half full each time. Pour the carrot mixture into a 5-quart pot.

Peel and chop the rhubarb mixture and mince this the same way as the carrots.

Boil the carrot and rhubarb mixture together with the sugar until the mash becomes the desired consistency, about 60 minutes. Stir occasionally. Stir in the preservative, if desired.

Pour the mixture into clean, warm jars and let it cool. Store in a cool place and eat promptly, or else freeze it. If it is to be stored in the freezer, let cool; pour the jam into freezing containers. Seal tightly.

Plum Jam

Mixed Berry Boiled Jam

Yield: About 2 pints

2 quarts berries
2⅓ to 3⅔ cups sugar
½ teaspoon citric acid

Boiled jam may be made using one kind of berry or several kinds of berries. A favorite jam is one made from both raspberries and blueberries. Other tasty mixed jams are: strawberries and gooseberries; strawberries and rhubarb; red and black currants and raspberries; black currants and blueberries; currants and sour cherries.

Clean the berries well (just rinse if that is all that is required). Alternate berries and sugar in a stew pot and allow the mixture to stand and draw for several hours.

Place the pot over low heat and warm up the mixture. Shake the pot occasionally, but avoid stirring the jam. Bring to a boil and let simmer, uncovered, for 15 to 20 minutes, or until the berries seem filled of their own syrup and sink to the bottom of the pot. Skim the top of the jam whenever necessary.

Remove the pot from the heat and stir in the citric acid, which has first been mixed up with a small amount of the jam. Pour into warm jars which have been well cleaned. Seal the tops of the jars with paraffin when the jam has cooled somewhat and tightly put on the lids. Store the jam in a cool, dark place.

Black Currant Jelly

Yield: 2 to 3 pints

2¼ pounds black currants
1¼ cups water
3⅔ cups sugar per quart of drained juice

Bring the berries and water to a boil over low heat (do not add the sugar). Shake the pot occasionally, but avoid stirring. Bring to a boil and let simmer, uncovered, for 15 to 20 minutes or until the berries sink to the bottom of the pot. Skim the top if necessary.

Pour the sour juice into a cooking pot and allow it to boil for 5 minutes. Stir in the sugar a little at a time and then boil the juice, without stirring, until it passes the jelly test. (**Jelly Test**: Pour a little jelly on a plate and pull a spoon right through it — if the jelly does not flow back together, it is done.)

Let the jelly mass stand for a few minutes before skimming it well. Pour it into small clean, warm glasses, and let cool. Pour paraffin on top, and put on the lid. Store in a cool, dark place.

Red Currant Jelly: Use ¾ cup water for every 2¼ pounds berries. Boil in the same way as black currant jelly.

Note: If the jelly does not become firm, you can add pure pectin. Use 1 teaspoon pure pectin per quart juice (jelly), 1 teaspoon citric acid, and 2 teaspoons sugar. Stir this mixture into a small amount of the hot juice. Then mix this into the rest of the jelly and allow to boil for 1 minute.

Squash or Pumpkin Jam

Yield: About 8 pints

About 8½ to 9 pounds squash or pumpkin
Water
Salt (1 tablespoon per quart/water)

juice
1⅔ cups distilled white vinegar
2⅓ cups water
3¼ cups sugar

3 to 4 pieces mace
3 pieces ginger
1 teaspoon white peppercorns
2 teaspoons yellow mustard seed

Peel and divide the squash or the pumpkin lengthwise. Remove the seeds from the halves, and cut them into pieces. Boil the pieces in lightly salted water until just soft.

Bring the juice ingredients to a boil. It is a good idea to place the spices in a cheesecloth bag. Boil several pieces at a time until they are soft and clear. Remove them when done with a slotted, wooden spoon, and place them in well-cleaned jars.

Let the juice boil together somewhat, skim the surface when necessary, and allow it to become cold. Remove the spice bag and pour the juice over the pieces of squash or pumpkin. They should be well covered by the juice. Place a tightly fitting lid on the jars and store in a cool place.

Squash or Pumpkin Jam

Index